The Bootleggers

KENNETH ALLSOP

The Bootleggers

THE STORY OF CHICAGO'S PROHIBITION ERA

ARLINGTON HOUSE   New Rochelle, N.Y.

Contents

Illustrations

Unless otherwise acknowledged above all the photographs are reproduced by permission of United Press International (U.K.).

Acknowledgements

Over a long period of preparation innumerable books, newspaper files and cuttings, old magazines, crime reports and sociological studies contributed to the accumulation of material. The books which were of especial value are listed in the Bibliography.

I am indebted to the Chicago Crime Commission for allowing me access to their surveys and records; to the Chicago Historical Society; to the University of Chicago and the Univesity of Chicago Press; to Mr. Henry F. Greenberg, Mr. Malvin Wald and Miss Lee Langley, of Allied Artists Pictures Corporation; to Mr. P. J. Madigan, Warden of Alcatraz Penitentiary; to Mr. R. N. York, of the American Photocopy Equipment Company, of Evanston, for so generously photostating material; to the National Book League, London; to the United States Information Service, London; and to my wife for her invaluable help with the research and the preparation of the manuscript.

I am also grateful to Mr. Paul Oliver for his help with filling in the background of the blues and the blues-singers of Prohibition Chicago; to the editors of the Chicago *Tribune*, the Chicago *Daily News* and the St. Louis *Post-Dispatch* for permission to quote from their columns; to The Cresset Press and Random House for permission to quote from John O'Hara's *Butterfield 8*; and to The Bodley Head and Scribners for permission to quote from F. Scott Fitzgerald's *The Great Gatsby*.

I also wish to express my personal gratitude for their hospitality, help and guidance during my stay in Chicago to Mr. Nelson Algren; Miss Margaret Cross and Miss Molly Imlach, of the British Information Services; Mr. Walter T. Fischer; Colonel Jacob Arvey; Mr. Saul Alinsky, of the Industrial Areas Foundation; Dr. Stanley Pargellis, of the Newberry Library; Dr. Philip M. Hauser, Dean Alan Simpson and Dr. Bessie Pierce, of the University of Chicago; Mr. and Mrs. A. C. Spectorsky; Mr. Joseph D. Lohman, State Treasurer for Illinois; Mr. Adrian Gale; Miss Janet Kaye; Mr. Virgil W. Peterson, Operating Director of the Chicago Commission; Miss Virginia Lee and Mr. Mike Meredith, of the Chicago

American; Mr. Don Maxwell, editor, Mr. Stanley Armstrong and Mr. James Doherty, of the Chicago *Tribune*; Mr. and Mrs. Bertrand Goldberg; Mr. Studs Terkel, of WMFT Broadcasting System; Mr. and Mrs. William R. Rivkin; Judge U. S. Schwarz, of the Apellate Court; Mr. Paul Angle and Miss Baughman, of the Chicago Historical Society; Miss Barbara Ina Siegel; Mr. Nelam Hill; and Mr. Paul Carroll, editor of *Big Table*.

Introduction to New Edition

'The old familiar figures have mostly gone; the landscape remains much the same . . . it is improbable that the grasp that the old Capone system has on the life and the living of Chicago will slip; it is embedded, deep and matted as an oak's roots, and has had forty years of near immunity in which to take hold.'

For the first page of this new edition of *The Bootleggers* I lift from its last pages those words which I wrote eight years ago. They were, I fear, accurate. Since I finished *The Bootleggers* I have been back to Chicago only twice, and briefly, yet it seemed to me then that the old place hadn't changed much: no profound repentance, no audible mass chorus when I was there, of the Psalm:

> *Make me a clean heart, O God: and renew a right spirit within me . . .*
> *Then I shall teach thy ways unto the wicked: and sinners shall be*
> *converted unto thee.*
> *Deliver me from blood-guiltiness, O God.*

That is not to say that no efforts have been made to attain redemption from a blood-guiltiness more deeply stained than in any other city in Christendom. In 1960, after yet another police scandal (eight uniformed men had been engaging in extramural duties for a North Side burglar and had used patrol wagons to ship away the loot), Mayor Richard J. Daley appointed Professor Orlando Winfield Wilson to salvage a decrepit, corrupt and slovenly force.

Professor Wilson as a student had put himself through college by working as a cop; had been police chief of Wichita, Kansas; during world war two had served as a colonel in the Military government of Italy and Germany, and run the de-Nazification of the U.S. zone; and as Dean of the School of Criminology at the University of California had directed reorganizational surveys for a dozen police forces.

So he brought to his Chicago appointment a mind versed in practical, academic and executive experience. He tackled the job of cleaning up the biggest and muckiest Aegean Stable in the world with energy and imagination. His methods have been schematic and technological. He re-diagrammed the function and the method of law-enforcement in Chicago. He reduced the number of police districts from thirty-eight to twenty-one, thus dismembering the baronry pattern under which the districts had more or less coincided with the boundaries of Chicago wards, so that each station was a cosy social club for politicians presided over by the local alderman. He initiated an 'aggressive preventive patrol' policy which has eliminated the old flatfoot-on-the-beat and mounted him in a distinctively marked blue-and-white car, 1,800 of which unpredictably circulate the main thoroughfares and the back alleys. He gave his 10,000 staff salary increases and sent 6,500 of them back to school to brush up on their trade. He built a £1 million radio-communications centre equipped with computers and electronic consoles giving instantaneous link-up between incoming emergency calls and squad cars. He also summoned his force to a mass meeting at which he told them that anyone accepting a gift would be fired: 'Even a ten-cent cup of coffee.' It may be a measure of Professor Wilson's vigour and demand for high performance that during the first two years of his regime 600 officers left, some for routine retirement, most just one jump ahead of being investigated.

Professor Wilson and his 'Operation Crime-Stop' have received much coverage, as they say, in the media. 'America's cop-intellectual', 'the crime-busting professor', 'a town-tamer', the press have fondly called him. He has been host to many a deputation from overseas, including British C.I.D. and Home Office observers and Mr. Roy Jenkins, when Home Secretary, eager to learn new and tested tactics for the fight against crime.

It would, therefore, be pleasant to be able to complete this inspiring homily of Chicago's change of heart with a parade of righteous statistics showing honesty triumphant and the villains all locked away. Indeed, it is maintained that in spite of a rise in the United States national crime rate of 18 per cent during the past two years, Chicago's has dropped 15 per cent – although the cynics and Wilson's personal critics point out that the only source for this salutary figure is the police department itself. Wilson's reply to these hints that the figures 'have been funnied up' is to say that their truth is reflected in a sharp decrease in insurance costs in the Chicago area.

Yet all is relative. The latest figures available as I write reveal that in 1966 for every 100,000 persons of Chicago's 3.5 million population, 14.6 were murdered: three every two days, one every sixteen hours, or 510 in all, a 30 per cent rise over the previous year.

For the first six months of 1967, 275 people were murdered, a 40 per cent rise over the corresponding period in the year before, and in July Chicago broke its own record (not easily done) with seventy-two murders in that month, the highest in its history. Still Chicago has at least managed to divest itself of its traditional title of murder city. Now it comes only a modest fourth in the national Top Ten, with Atlanta, Washington and Dallas holding the first three positions in the chart. But Wilson himself concedes that little progress has been made in the prosecution of the controllers of the organized crime, and a recent report observed 'The mob, as the crime syndicate is often called, seems still to be interwoven with Chicago's social fabric'.

The extent to which it is has now been detailed not by a speculating newsman but by the city's own citizen body, the Chicago Crime Commission, founded in 1919 as an independent investigative watchdog committee to act in the public interest. The Commission last winter published a unique booklet, a sort of local classified directory of crime-backed business, with little *Which*-style reports attached providing useful data for customers and consumers. The booklet states that 'in the past thirty months a significant number of these hoodlums have been successfully prosecuted', and proceeds to tick off the more satisfactory deliveries to the cooler, including a group of friends who received ten to twenty years for interstate commerce in stolen goods, including Ernest Infelice, Anthony Legato, Frank Gallo, Emil Crovedi and John Varelli. (It is to be hoped one will not be thought racially biased when one remarks upon the predominance of Italian/Sicilian names throughout these pages: merely that it demonstrates that the fine old family and clan traditions of Cosa Nostra, or Mafia, business are little diminished.) The Commission then prints an index – described as a *Hood's Who* by one American magazine – of names and addresses (and ages) of 227 men whom it identifies as some of the local Syndicate bosses, lieutenants and fellow travellers. The list glitters with such celebrated and familiar names from 'the upper echelon' as Paul the Waiter Ricca, Gus Alex, Tony Accardo, Jack Cerone and Sam Battaglia. Moreover the system of mandated territories hammered out by Capone (in May 1929, three months after the bloodbath of the St. Valentine's Day Massacre, when nine years of gang warfare were brought to a climax and when it was borne upon the rival leaders that this internecine killing was needlessly detracting from the quiet dedicated money-making that would be the fruit of peaceful co-existence) is still the paradigm. Allowing for 'a continual shifting of boundaries and overlapping of areas of interest', the Commission tabulates these as 'the major geographical areas of influence', with their viceroys: The Loop – Gus Alex; Near North Side – Joseph DiVarco, Joseph Arnold; Far North and Northwest Suburbs – Leonard Patrick, Ross Prio; Far West and West Suburbs – Sam Battaglia, William Daddano, Sam Giancana; South Side – Ralph Pierce; South and Southwest Suburbs – Frank LaPorte, Fiore Buccieri.

The booklet further extends its consumer service by describing the areas of apparently respectable commerce which the syndicate has penetrated and incidentally shows that the diversification begun by Capone has been energetically advanced by his heirs. The Commission directs the reader's attention to 'the many advantages to be gained from undisclosed ownership of a business' – tax evasion – which has 'resulted in the concealment of the organized crime element names from most of the businesses they own or control. This concealment through the use of the "respectable" front as the owner is a device that results in the unaware public pouring more and more money into the coffers of the mob'. It details the fields in which 'powerful underworld leaders' are operating, including food manufacturing distribution and sales business, automobile sales, the steel industry, oil wells, dairy business, breweries, liquor sales and distribution, stock brokerage houses, banks, savings and loan associations, restaurants, night clubs, real estate, coin machine business, garbage collection, trucking, insurance, travel agencies, parking lots, shopping centres, television and radio manufacturing. In fact, 'there are few types of businesses or industries that have not been touched at one time or another by organized crime investments and there have been instances where crime syndicates have controlled substantial segments of the economy. In numerous instances the leaders of organized crime have controlled labour unions. And in whatever activity organized crime engages, legitimate or illicit, its method of operation is the same – the maintenance of a monopoly through extortion and violence or imposing the fear of violence'.

The booklet then sets down alphabetically some of the businesses owned by, or manipulated by, the Chicago crime syndicate, beginning with the Apex Amusement Corporation, 7730 North Milwaukee Avenue, Niles, Illinois, and ending with the Zenith Vending Corporation, 2634–38 West Fullerton Avenue, Chicago. The documentation of each Company is fascinating reading. For example, the Alhara Management Corporation, which builds and manages hotels and motels, has as its president Harry Boshes, who 'has been identified with former North Clark Street strip tease joints. . . .

In 1950 he was charged with beating two conventioneers who protested paying 28 dollars for eight drinks'. The battery was alleged to have been done with a baseball bat; B–G Builders has as its president Sander Caravello, 'arrested numerous times' and involved in a 1963 juice (usurious loans made at interest rates of from 50 to 100 per cent, the collateral being life itself) trial at which victims of kidnapping, assault and intimidation 'testified that they were taken to the offices of B–G Builders where the demands for juice payments were made'; Milano Incorporated, a restaurant directed by Anthony Armadeo, Ruth Armadeo and Louise Greico, and 'frequented by such Chicago crime syndicate members as Dominic Di-Bella, Dominic Brancat, Albert Frabotta, Charles English, James Allegretti and Marshall Caifano, the latter two presently receiving their culinary appointments under the United States Bureau of Prisons chefs'; and the Spa Motel, 'another of the hotels-motels owned by the Trans-American Construction Company Inc. and controlled by the Alhara Management Corporation. . . . The lounge in the Spa Motel was known to authorities as a hangout for Arthur Boodie Cowan who was recently found murdered, the body being in the trunk of his auto'.

This indispensible little publication (certainly indispensible if you are thinking of having any building done in Chicago, or even just staying there in a motel for a night or two) demonstrates that Professor Wilson's blue-and-white prowl cars and his electronic Operation Crime-Stop has not –not yet, at any rate – noticeably intruded upon this plateau of successful big-time racketeering. The reason is, quite simply, that the scale of the national ramifications of the syndicates, with their infrastructure of defence built into the civic administration and economy, is beyond the reach of any local crusader. In fact, organized crime has now been placed as America's biggest business, with a turnover of some 50 billion dollars a year, a figure more than the entire United States military budget, more than the combined profits of all the car-making giants, more than the annual value of all shares traded on the New York Stock Exchange. The Mafia syndicates across the nation mesh into a net which gathers in nine billion dollars annually from illegal gambling, 1.5 billion from narcotics, and the rest from the 'juice' squeeze from money-lending, prostitution and quasi-legitimate business. It is estimated that half the syndicate's gambling profit is paid out in police bribes – 'the best cops money can buy' as has been said. As that 4.5 billion dollars exceeds the total official wages to all the United States police, it would seem that Professor Wilson's battle is a somewhat solitary one.

The truth is that, although the 14 unbridled years of Prohibition (and in particular the inordinant violence with which they were lived in Chicago) remain an unexampled little paragraph of social-history, they have been long superseded by the steady, relentless, annual climb in domestic felony throughout the republic. More American citizens are dying as victims of homicide at home than are dying as soldiers in Vietnam, a situation which President Johnson has described as 'monstrous' (he meant crime not the Vietnam war). To particularize, 10,000 murders were committed in America last year; a new record, as almost every year proves to be. (In England and Wales there were 494.) To attempt to bring these astronomical abstractions of the overall crime statistics down to reality, in America someone is murdered every hour, someone is raped and burglary is committed (not necessarily together) every half-hour, and a car is stolen every minute. During the first six months of last year violent crimes in America jumped by 18 per cent. 'Serious crime' (as it is categorized) has, according to Herbert Hoover, Director of the Federal Bureau of Investigation, increased by 62 per cent since 1960 – seven times faster than the population.

Only one-quarter of these crimes were solved. Despite that, there are 217,000 people at this moment confined in prisons and reformatories and another 1,083,000 Americans under 'correctional jurisdiction' – on parole or probation. Mathematically, 40 per cent of all male children now living in the U.S. will in their lifetime be arrested for some offence other than a traffic violation.

Needless to say, all this is merely 'visible crime'. By definition, most successful crime is invisible and undiscovered. But the President's Crime Commission recently admitted that, murder apart, the actual rate of 'serious crime' is several times that reported to the police – and it was estimated that there are twice as many personal injuries and three times as many rapes and burglaries as laid bare in the figures. Also, as one American journal remarked in a survey of what it denounced as 'a national disgrace, a situation so ominous and dreadful that it seems virtually impossible, so bleak that it threatens the very foundations of the Great Society', no figures 'can account for the ordinary consumer or the bilked businessman who does not know that he has been cheated'. Embezzlement, price-rigging, tax evasion, bribery, graft are all far more prevalent than the number of cases prosecuted suggest.

In this book the diagnosis of the Prohibition Era gangster I put forward is that of the immigrant's child, slum-born and ghetto-bound, denied, by inadequate education and by deviation from the archetypal American norm, access to the life-goals advertised so dinningly in the culture of the big prizes, those codified by Max Lerner as 'the success system' and its components: success, prestige, money, power and security. 'Dislocated from their old culture but having not absorbed anything of the new culture except its cruder aspects they reached for quick affluence by breaking the windows of the mansion of American success rather than by entering at the door.' The point about the American criminal, says, Lerner, is not that he scorns property but that he values it enough to be ruthless in seeking short cuts for making it his own.

In other words, the criminal is, by his own lights, responding dynamically to the quintessential stimuli within American society. The principles which fuel the American culture with its energy are those of freedom and acquisition, and the criminal fuses the two into freedom of acquisition. 'The gangster of the Prohibition Era was almost invariably second-generation American; he was almost invariably a Sicilian, an Irishman or a Jew,' I say in the following pages. The rich, reticent, shadowy overlords of today's syndicates are the slum delinquents of yesterday. (It is noticeable that few of those in the Chicago Crime Commission's roll-call referred to earlier are under 40; most are in their 50s and 60s, and there are several over 70, including one venerable hood of 78.)

At street-level, where crime and violence are at high volume and density, the European immigrant has been supplanted by the Negro who, though native-born and of native-born parentage, is belatedly at that degree of under-class deprivation and consequent tension for the most part passed through by the white poor, and not surprisingly Negroes contribute disproportionately to the crime ledger. In cities where they amount to 11 per cent of the population they account for about 35 per cent of arrests for 'serious crime' and for 60 per cent for murder and crimes of violence. (It was recently pointed out to me by a Democrat politician that 'the city' has become, in these racially hair-triggered times, a euphemism for the Negro – when public men speak of 'the crisis of the cities' they mean black riots and black power.)

Yet, black or white, honest or crooked, there is a shared inheritance of attitudes toward competitiveness and aggression, the ethic of being in for grabs. The gangster, like the Western bandit and the frontier bank and train robber, is pushing just a desperate degree further those qualities which are the force of the American purpose: daring, enterprise, determination and ruthlessness. He is crushing the opposition – only he does it with bullets.

We still rooted in Europe tend to forget that the Americans were originally those who took the dauntingly huge step of getting out of Europe – the adventurous, the rebellious, the misfits, the anarchic, the outcasts, the restless, the brave; and that authority – law – symbolized most often in their experience the tyrants and the persecutors they were either fleeing or refusing to knuckle under to. We tend to forget how close America of the 1960s – despite its neon-lit landscape, like a strip-cartoon of pop-art colours, despite the multi-lane highways and automated factory plants – is to its wilderness past. The frontier has not been closed all that long. Oklahoma wasn't embraced by the Union until 1906 – it was, only fifty-odd years ago, unconstituted territory, Indian country. We tend to forget that almost up to the turn of the century those who were carving out America in the West had very little law to make recourse to: they handled personal and community conflicts arbitrarily. Respect for the desk-squatting legislators of Washington was not very dominant in the minds of the early settlers and the pioneers; contempt for subservience and obedience was stronger.

On the other hand, there was one other strain strong in the early Americans. That was the Puritanism that sustained them through the early struggle and hardships, the uprightness and discipline of Judaeo-Christian teaching that held the families and small rural communities together through suffering and solitude. It was this experience that made the essential American soul, in D. H. Lawrence's words, 'hard, isolate, stoic, and a killer'. Elsewhere Lawrence wrote about the black side of the pioneer experience: 'The grimness of it, the savage fight and the savage failure which broke the back of the country but also broke something in the human soul. The spirit and the will survived: but something in the soul perished: the softness, the floweriness, the natural tenderness.'

So the tough guy, the uncompromising individualist, the bad man, the killer – the man who was often only marginally more extreme in his conduct of life than the man who was performing the blessed undertaking of opening the new country – has always occupied a glamorous and romantic role in what one might call irregular American history, history at the stratum of vernacular folk-lore and regional myth. Our folk heroes in Britain may well have been less altruistic than they are presented, less imbued with the Arthurian virtues of 'chyvalrye, curtoyse, humanyte, frendlynesse, hardyness, love', and King Arthur may well have been our ur-Capone, and Camelot his Chicago. But at least in the myth the

Robin Hoods and the Dick Turpins are always sort of early rogue Fabians, on the side of the humble against the oppressors.

Not always so in America. America's folk-heroes most frequently *are* the oppressors and the killers, at least the challengers of the encroaching *lex loci*, like the James-Younger gang and Pretty Boy Floyd and Billy the Kid and Baby Face Nelson and John Dillinger and Clyde Barrow – and Al Capone. In this book I describe the ambivalence I found in Chicago toward its most notorious son of Belial, a mixture of formal disapprobation and sneaking idolization. Evidently this has not altered in substance, for a recent despatch from Chicago to *The Economist* referred to the 'perverse vicarious thrill of pride' Chicagoans found in such flamboyant outrages as the St. Valentine's Day massacre, and continued: 'Even today there are those who search a dark night club for the thrill of identifying members of the mob.' [On this point, in an article in *Life* (February 1968) David Snell recalls when he was 13 and living in Minden, Louisiana, 15 miles from where Bonnie and Clyde were ambushed. On that hot May day in 1934 the roads around were jammed with sightseers' cars. Queues of thousands shuffled past the bullet-riddled car hauled into town and through the makeshift funeral parlour in a furniture store to inspect the equally bullet-riddled corpses arrayed side-by-side. Bonnie, the future inspirer of fashion, was wearing no pants under her dress. Snell relates how the fast-footed souvenir hunters had snapped up the empty cartridge cases in the undergrowth from where the possemen had fired, but with his Scout knife he dug from a tree a bullet that had probably passed through the flesh of Bonnie or Clyde. Again, after Dillinger was dropped in a Chicago alleyway, crowds dipped handkerchiefs, pieces of paper and even the hems of dresses into the pool of his blood. Early in 1968 George Patty, a Vancouver food company executive, acquired by top bid the garage wall which was the backdrop for the St. Valentine's Day Massacre. Mr. Patty stated that he intended to reassemble the wall, complete with bullet scars – whether for his private bar or as an icon, or sacred relic of crime, was not reported.]

The criteria survive. Professor Wilson in an interview with a British journalist this year said: 'To disarm any American police force is unthinkable. Just as it is traditional for the American cop, and indeed the American citizen, to bear arms, so it is traditional for the American criminal.' It is therefore not incongruous among the national statistics I quoted earlier to discover this one: 'Last year there were 43,500 assaults in which a gun was fired and 89,000 robberies in which a weapon of some kind was used.' In America the gun is familiar, an item of equipment rationally to be resorted to, in a way we cannot in Britain easily comprehend. Bullets kill 17,000 Americans every year. Since 1900 the death roll from this homely genocide has been 750,000 people – more than the total in all the U.S.A.'s foreign wars, which of course omits unrecorded multitudes just winged, the mere walking wounded casualties of the incessant jungle guerilla warfare in suburb and town.

The U.S. Constitution upholds that a citizen's right to keep and bear arms shall not be infringed by Congress, a law enacted to create 'a well-regulated militia'. The idea was that a pistol-packing citizenry, supporting an armed constabulary, would guarantee law and order. That was when British Redcoats and indigenous Redskins were the threat. Now that both have been put in their respective reservations, the concession, and the carnage, continue. In only seven states is a permit needed to buy a gun. The National Rifle Association reckons that 30 million Americans own and can use firearms – and that is the figure of a respectable body which has in mind hunters and competition marksmen. It does not cover the uncountable numbers of psychopath sharpshooters, Ku Klux Klanners, hold-up thugs, teenage tearaways and even ordinary householders with a loaded revolver in desk or car pocket. President Kennedy was shot with a mail-order carbine, but when I was last there, four years after the assassination, I bought a copy of *Sports Afield*, a magazine for game shots, which has a 'Bargain Counter' small ads column through which I could have obtained quite legally, 7 mm. Mauser rifles and surplus Army carbines for about £6 each.

As the sentimentalized drama of *West Side Story* showed to a wide and comfortably safe audience, today the Puerto Ricans, the latest intake to the urban theatre of war, continue the long tradition of each wave of new Americans fighting the environment for their personal cut. But although the crime problem in America worsens and compounds, and although according to *The Violent Gang* (a study by Lewis Yablonsky of the breed of young metropolitan Neanderthals whom Hubert Selby Jr. wrote about so frighteningly well in *Last Exit to Brooklyn*) the elevation of 'the hoodlum as hero' may partially be accounted for by 'a traditional American worship of aggressive, adventuresome, sociopathic heroes who "go it alone", unencumbered by social restraints or conscience', there has been a significant change.

Crime today is either institutionalized, a consortium at the commanding heights such as the Chicago Crime Commission inveighs against – identifiable but seemingly almost inviolable – or is rampant and random within the great labyrinthine cities. What has vanished is the individualist outlaw, the knight errant gone wrong, the violent loner who was the trans-Atlantic version of Camus's Stranger, the alienated man who could still, like Huckleberry Finn, 'light out for the territories', for the lost Eden in the American idyll. That may be the immeasurable element in the American regard for the outlaw, the melancholy sense of having forfeited the option to be a free man beyond the reach of authority and orthodoxy. He is now seldom other than fiction: the focal figure in so much American literature in which violence equates with vitality in the hero, in which he repeatedly proves himself, not in civilized relations with other human beings, but in pitting himself against a harsh and hostile universe – he can be more violent (stronger) than it.

I wouldn't wish to claim – or to be held responsible for – touching off with *The Bootleggers* the rekindled interest, cult even, of the pre-war period and its more lurid lead players. The time was probably ripe for the cyclic fascination with a period still just within the memory of many yet distant enough to be legendary. Yet I confess that I have watched the emanation of this one, of its more preposterous aspects, with mild surprise: the proliferation of speak-easy type clubs in Soho and Chelsea; the sprouting in the boutique windows, among the synthetic fibre space-suits of the late 1960s, of the wide-shouldered, double-breasted chalk-striped Legs Diamond suits and floral kipper ties such as worn by gangsters of forty years past; the art-nouveauish posters of mobsters with antique tommy-guns and in white fedoras of Cavalier breadth sold in trendy gear junkshops; the Marcel waves and red cupid bows of girls suddenly transferred from mini-skirts to calf-length tents and monkey jackets. And there came the new wave of pastiche period gangster films of which *Bonnie and Clyde* was the most poignant and disturbing specimen.*

Philip French in a brilliant analysis in *Sight and Sound* (Winter Issue, 1967–8) delineates Hollywood's shifts of moral attitude in the genre since the first major gangster film, Von Sternberg's *Underworld* (1927), sidestepped the hitherto prevailing ethic of the film as a pulpit view of human misconduct. (Ben Hecht, the screenwriter of

---

* As I write, the current issue of *Nova*, which has a pervasive Thirtyish atmosphere of berets and brass-trimmed tourers, carries three coloured ads in which the models are cuddling sub-machine-guns. Concurrently Harrods is offering for sale (for 20 gns) an amusing gewgaw in calf named "The Bootlegger": a black leather violin case, such as gangsters used for the transportation of a tommygun, which in fact holds three bottles, two beakers, a corkscrew and bottle-opener, two packs of playing cards and a set of dice.

Underworld, has told how the idea came to him: '. . . to skip the heroes and heroines, to write a movie containing only villains and bawds. I would not have to tell any lies then.')

French points out that it was the coming of talkies that, literally, triggered the first gangster cycle, for these productions would have been unthinkable 'without a soundtrack to capture the screech of tyres, the chatter of machine guns and the rasping dialogue. . . . Reflecting the mood of their times, these movies were harsh, cynical, angry and above all ambivalent in their attitudes towards their protagonists'. This was the span of *Little Caesar* (1930), *Public Enemy* and *Quick Millions* (1931), *Scarface* and *The Last Mile* (1932). The endlessly radiating, successive ripples of image and reality, of life's imitation – or caricature – of art, is evocatively caught by French: 'And sitting in the audience when these movies appeared was another group of criminals or potential criminals from different backgrounds, their names soon to become household words as nearly as familiar as Capone's: John Dillinger, Lester Gillis (alias George "Baby Face" Nelson), the Barker family, Charles "Pretty Boy" Floyd, Alvin Karpis, George "Machine Gun" Kelly, Bonnie Parker and the Barrow brothers. Whereas the urban gangsters were members of immigrant minorities, grotesquely parodying the Horatio Alger myth and consciously in search of social status, this latter group were fourth or fifth generation WASPs from rural communities of the Mid-West and South-West. All of them had minor criminal records, had served the inevitable periods in state reform schools. Then suddenly they took off on the most extraordinary and widely publicized crime-wave in American history in the years 1933–35. They robbed filling stations and banks, and staged kidnappings in colourful, reckless ways. They loved guns, were enthralled with images of violence, were compulsive exhibitionists. . . . In effect, these pathetic psychopaths were more like the cinematic image of the big-time gangsters than the real gangsters that inspired the films.'

Yet it would be unfair, over-simple, to hold Hollywood responsible for Frankensteining these mediocre monsters. Much as Hell's Angels – those Californian roughneck motorcycle corps, with their permanent LSD-and-pills highs, their rape and sodomy badges on their grease-caked denim jackets, and their Harley-Davidsons emblazoned with swastikas – had their persona crystallized for them, an existing phenomenon, by Marlon Brando's *The Wild One* (itself based on the real-life incident when in 1947 a troupe named the Black Rebels roared into and terrorized Hollister, California), so were the life-roles and the play itself suddenly made apparent to these drop-outs and delinquents by the Great Casting Director of the period, Hollywood. This was the cauldron from which all the magic then came, and which in those Depression years was playing fast and loose with its own Production Code by turning out ever sexier, ever more brutal dramas (or brash, brassy and peptimistic, that morale-boosting word of the time combining peppy and optimistic, musicals) to draw a hard-up population through the ticket office.

The film industry got the customers but it also got censorship, at both official and citizen-vigilante levels. To beat the ban while continuing to exploit the formula, the producers speciously responded to the public disfavour by swinging the heroic focus from gangster to law enforcement agent. Hence the cycle, of a savagery indistinguishable from their predecessors, in which Federal Bureau of Investigation officers, campaigning newspaper editors, Treasury Department detectives, social workers, sheriffs and district attorneys entered the halo of klieg lights, and FBI, Fed, G-man, T-man and DA became syncopes as colloquial as hood and tommy-gun.

Thus, under the thin disguise of piety and righteousness, the guns went on barking and the bodies toppling in *G-Men*, *Jesse James* and their like, until wholesome small-town soap-opera, screwball comedy and then anti-Nazi war films took over. It was in the late Fifties that the crime film returned, dealing now with the outlaw not as a contemporary scourge (although, as we've seen, he was much as ever that despite his external modulations) but as part fable, part demigod. So there came, in 1957 *Baby Face Nelson*, in 1958 *Machine Gun Kelly* and *The Bonnie Parker Story*, in 1959 *The Scarface Mob* (stemming from *The Untouchables* television series), *Al Capone*, *The Rise and Fall of Legs Diamond*, and *The Big Bankroll*. In 1961 came *Portrait of a Mobster* (Dutch Schultz, hitherto neglected, got his posthumous stardom in this), and after that, reciprocally influenced by Godard and Truffaut who had transmuted the Hollywood second-helping into the French New Wave cinema, came Roger Corman's *The St. Valentine's Day Massacre* and Arthur Penn's *Bonnie and Clyde* – so, says Philip French, 'has the energy, the economy and the exigency of the traditional gangster film re-entered the American cinema via *Breathless*, *Shoot the Pianist* and *Pierrot le Fou*.'

What is significant about both *The St. Valentine's Day Massacre* and *Bonnie and Clyde* is that in this era of freedom from injunction to graft on value judgements and moral gesticulations, both achieve, in their different sophisticated manner, such evident anthropological truthfulness about their chosen subjects in their own habitats. The first was laconic, detached, quasi-documentary, urban in feeling as hard city pavements. The other was wry, tender, romantic with an exquisite shimmer of sadness upon the mindless viciousness, the mood set (as French shrewdly notes) by those faded sepia credit snapshots recalling Walker Evans's photographs for James Agee's *Let Us Now Praise Famous Men*. Whether or not there was much factual resemblance to the originals, what was so marvellously alchemized was the essence of that disjointed couple and their 'strange, timeless, drifting existence, shifting between dream and nightmare', doomed wanderers through a ruined rural idyll, the nihilistic children of that annihilated region.

The advertisement copy for *Bonnie and Clyde*, under the photograph of the five smiling chums cuddling their artillery in front of a get-away car, ran:

'Clyde was the leader. Bonnie wrote poetry. C. W. was a Myrna Loy fan who had a bluebird tattooed on his chest. Buck told corny jokes and carried a Kodak. Blanche was a preacher's daughter who kept her fingers in her ears during the gunfights. They played checkers and photographed each other incessantly. On Sunday nights they listened to Eddie Cantor on the radio. All in all, they killed eighteen people. They were the strangest damned gang you ever heard of.'

Of course the complaints have been loud against the film as an incitement to violence. Personally I found it difficult to see any corrupting allure in their aimless, jittery, fugitive zigzagging from seedy motor-court to seedy motor-court through that derelict landscape, the ring of guns always closing tighter in on them, and the illusion of the big-time – as filtered through to them from Hollywood's mirage world on small-town movie theatre screens – never to be found on the horizon of eroded fields and ghost towns. Philip French finally quotes an American writer of low-budget thrillers to whom he mentioned that one of his scripts had been turned into a peculiarly inflammatory movie, 'an incitement to violence'. The writer agreed: 'That's the way it turned out. And I wrote it as an incitement *against* violence.'

Whatever the pristine motives, and however perversely the commercial outcome might run counter to the creative intention, there seems little doubt that the excellence of both *The St. Valentine's Day Massacre* and *Bonnie and Clyde*, and the box-office bounty they brought, has begun a third-phase explosion of gangster films – which, I'm willing to bet, as I write are furiously fomenting behind many a studio door. It remains to be seen whether attention now moves away from the costume killers of American legend and on to the new species, either upon the *Wall Street Journal* reader variety which so exercises the Chicago Crime Commission, or upon the gutter-level handiwork of the tenement slum, now black, now the burning centre of America's greatest and most ominously appalling domestic problem – the adolescent personalities studied in Lewis Yablonsky's *The Violent Gang*. This generation may, as Yablonsky found, again follow the prescription of idolizing 'the hoodlum as hero', and 'this pattern of pathology may be partially accounted for by a traditional American worship of aggressive, adventuresome, sociopathic heroes who "go it alone", unencumbered by social restraints or conscience'. But their drives are compounded by deeper racial and social divisions than the earlier types ever knew; their emotional needs are far more complicated than Al Capone's and Clyde Barrow's relatively limited garbling of inspirational Algerism into their own methods of obtaining money and status.

Even so, if the film-makers decide that the time is ripe for message films about the underside of society now, and that 1920–40 is a temporarily worked-out part of the jungle, it is still unlikely that we have heard or seen the last of Capone and Barrow and their genus, for they stand as monuments, historical markers; they are proto-types not to be separated from the tenure of their time or expunged from its annals. Of course Capone and Clyde Barrow were infinitely far apart in style of life: one the ghetto wop who became a paranoiac czar; the other a poor-white Texan, a punk, whose foursome – it was more a family party on an outing than a gang – killed eighteen people on their foray through the South and Mid-West, but who never became more than a punk. Yet both Capone and Barrow were of the stuff of which Americans make their heroes, both men of their moment, on the public's side in a distorted sense.

Capone kept the dry times wet: he provided a thirsty town popula-tion with booze they wanted and were forbidden to have by an edict imposed upon them by agrarian, temperance America. Barrow provided a Depression-stricken rural America with vicarious revenge against the banks, the Them who foreclosed on sharecropper holdings or tractored them out or went bankrupt with their savings, and he shot his way into minor mythology by being the common man who became a man of action in a region stagnant with despair and apathy, who, not content to sink under with the mass of the workless and the drifters, fought his way through – to the inevitable grave. But at least when the clock struck he had a bill-roll in his pocket and food in his belly, the standard by which success and manhood are gauged.

This book is not concerned with the nomadic bandit of the earlier frontier cast, but with the city gang of that age whose peculiar conditions produced a particular species. Yet all of them, the dictator of the internal corporate state and the free-lance robber gunman, were products of society as it then was and were also the end of a long line of sports of the free enterprise system in its most dynamic and savage phase.

It was in 1934 that Capone was transferred from the relative ease of Atlanta Penitentiary to Alcatraz, America's Devil's Island, his appeal dismissed, the Eighteenth Amendment repealed and Prohibition – the source of all his riches – finished, and his power finally shattered; that Dillinger was gunned down by F.B.I. men as he left the Biograph Cinema in Chicago; and that Bonnie Parker and Clyde Barrow were trapped in ambush and fell under eighty-seven bullets from six automatic weapons which delivered a shattering broadside into their stolen Ford V-8.

Bonnie and Clyde were killed (she with a half-eaten sandwich in her hand and a pistol with three notches in her lap) on a gravelled road cutting through a pine-wooded hill outside a town named Arcadia: perhaps the place they had, without quite knowing it, all the time been looking for. The landscape is cleared of their sort now. It could be for that reason that we now look back to then, to what seems, for all its brutal wickedness, to have had style and a tainted lyricism: the last fling of the self-sufficient brigand.

K. A.

1968

Chicago, Chicago
You toddlin' town.
Chicago, Chicago,
I'll show you around.
　　Chicago, Hit song of 1922

Chicago . . . it's a joint where the bulls and the foxes live
well and the lambs wind up head-down from the hook.
　　　　　　　　　　NELSON ALGREN,
　　　　　　　　Chicago: City on the Make

Any bootlegger sure is a pal of mine . . .
　　　　BESSIE SMITH, *Me And My Gin*

Bootlegger. *Dealer or distributor of contraband liquor. Most*
likely derives from boot-leg, *the upper part of a high boot*
(1634), in which flat bottles could be smuggled. The origin of
the present use has been placed as far back as early Colonial
days, but A Dictionary of American English on Historical
Principles *(Craigie and Hulbert) finds the first example in*
1889, and H. L. Mencken in his The American Language
suggests that the term "is not as old as most Americans are apt
to assume", and he considers that it originated in what is now
Oklahoma before the region was opened to white settlement.
Sale of liquor to the Indians was prohibited, thereby providing
a market for illicit traffickers, or bootleggers.

'Chicago always has to have the best –
Even if it's the worst'

'Chicago is unique. It is the only completely corrupt city in America.'
ALDERMAN ROBERT MERRIAM

'Doggone my black soul, I'm sweet Chicago bound.'
COW COW DAVENPORT, *Jim Crow Blues*

AT 816 on Chicago's North Rush Street, a bedizened strip of night-clubs, burlesques, jazz rooms and beatnik bars, is the Gaslight. This is a key club. To assist the atmosphere of exclusiveness and stimulating furtiveness a member is given a latchkey and with this he admits himself, through a door anonymous and eccentrically blank of neon. Within, the lights are bright and brassy. There is a vast, Ninetyish bar, waitresses spiderlegging about in truncated skirts and fishnet stockings, a pianist wearing a Derby, and the tables are supplied with wooden hammers for beating time. The walls are hung with romantic gold-framed paintings of beefy pink nude girls, acquired from the renowned Everleigh Sisters' Dearborn Street brothel of the 1900s, which was furnished with gold spittoons, perfume-machines to drench the cloistered air, and fifty-dollar strumpets of singular gentility.

No similar entertainment is provided at the Gaslight, but for the initiate there is a further concealed attraction to enhance his sense of belonging to a knowing privileged inner-circle. In the farthermost shadowy corner of the L-shaped bar is a wooden telephone booth. There is a telephone inside, but it does not work. The purpose of entering and closing the door behind you is to knock three times at the side that adjoins the wall. A small panel slides back and a mascaraed eye scans you. If you pass scrutiny there is a click and the side of the booth swings inward, and you step into a different, cramped, smoky, noisy and nostalgia-saturated world.

At the end of the small low-ceilinged room, dimly lit by bulbs in

13

orange silk shades, is a Dixieland band. The clarinettist, banjo-player, pianist and drummer wear striped waistcoats and high stiff collars. *The Jelly Roll Morton Folio* stands on the music rack, but they play mostly tunes like 'I Wish I Could Shimmy Like My Sister Kate' and 'That's My Weakness Now', and the girls in short straight fringed dresses and looping ropes of beads intermittently cease serving at the tables to perform the Black Bottom and the Charleston. Above the piano is the notice WE PLAY REQUESTS and a washing line on which are pegged dollar bill gratuities from pleased patrons. The flowered wallpaper is spotted with satin-doll silhouettes, framed photographs of such dignitaries as Al Smith and Rudolph Valentino, and also the date 17 January 1920 – the day upon which the Volstead Act, the Eighteenth Amendment to the United States Constitution, which prohibited intoxicating liquors, became law – edged with black. Beyond the tiny bottle-clogged bar is a big square window which gives convenient sight of all that is happening in the outer bar but which from that side appears to be an ordinary mirror. The room is congested with wooden tables covered with red-check cloths, and which have upon them bowls of popcorn and photostat copies of *The Chicago Evening Post* for Saturday, 21 May 1927, which carries the exultant black headlines: FLYING FOOL HITS 150-MILE PACE: LINDBERGH OVER FRANCE.

The elaborate point of this seedy little masque is that your drink is delivered to your table in a china tea-cup, but at least now you stand an excellent chance that it is Scotch of reputable brand and not a brew that will peel the enamel off your teeth. For this is a meticulously constructed, but probably considerably glamorized, replica of a Prohibition speakeasy, an illicit drinking den of the kind that served Chicago and all American towns so efficiently during that long, dry epoch when alcohol was outlawed throughout the United States, when most of the population put Federal law in contempt and became, without remorse, statutory criminals, when the community suffered a breakdown in standards of conduct that still flaws public and private life in America.

In Chicago today there is an endemic schizophrenia about this recent period of garish history, those fourteen years when civic authority was poisoned and emasculated by corruption, when gunmen ran the city with the ostentatious arrogance of feudal barons and battled with each other to protect or extend their fiefs. That is not an over-colourful analogue. A Chicago professor said to me flatly: 'We nearly had feudalism,' and when he was lecturing in history at Yale on the twelfth-century English barons and their internecine warfare for territory with their private armies he used the case of the Chicago gangs as a parallel. Or, rather, the attitude to this time is less a split condition than a mercurial mixture of shame and pride. 'It was disgraceful, an ineradicable stain upon our fine record', is the generic way the admission is expressed with fitting disapproval – to be followed, with a ribald nudge and wink, 'but, boy, that was a hell of a period.' The existence today of the Gaslight and its thriving night-time trade, is a small but significant indication of the reluctance of Chicago to let that gaudy time entirely lapse: it was a juicy fruit still not sucked dry of excitement. And, when the proper censure has been dispensed with, the Chicagoan feels free to expound upon the more interesting aspect of that infamous period within the perspective of the city's rough, free-booting, frontier tradition. This, however, is not the first reaction when the subject is raised. There is, and very understandably when the questioner is a foreigner, an Englishman probing inquisitively at this sensitive spot, a preliminary aggressive resentment. The view that most Chicagoans have of Al Capone, the world's most famous criminal, and who, although not a son of Chicago, is for ever and inextricably a part of the city's mythology, is interestingly complex, and not one in which condemnation looms large, as will later be seen. But because of Capone and the events of his lifetime, the Chicagoan bears a burden of guilt that often he carries on his shoulder in the shape of a chip. 'Damn it,' a banker said to me, 'I was on a vacation in the Middle East, and right out in the desert outside Cairo, and I was asked where I came from, and I said "Chicago", and these Arabs' faces lit up and they stuck out their fingers and went "rat-a-tat-tat" and yelled "Hah, Alcaponee!" ' So that I fairly quickly got to recognize the vibration of the antennae when, after introductions, the reason for my presence in Chicago was broached. When the Chicagoan became reassured that I was concerned not with rehashing yet again a kind of city Wild West thriller from the mouldering bones of the St. Valentine's Day massacre victims, but with the social and political context in which these grotesque events became possible, with the kind of people the gangsters were and the circumstances that produced them, he became frank and endlessly helpful. The same banker who could not escape his origins even in Egypt, said a little later: 'Well, in Chicago we always have to have the best – even if it's the worst.' But there remained the hard-core patriots still loyal to the exhortation of Big Bill Thompson – William Hale Thompson, the three-term mayor whose wide-open town policy gave the gangs the condonation and conditions they desired – 'Be a Booster! Don't be a Knocker! Throw away your hammer and get a horn.' The question that usually came swiftly and truculently back at me from the booster-citizen was: 'Why pick on Chicago? We weren't the only place with bootleggers. It was just as bad in any American city then.'

There are several reasons why I picked on Chicago. First, in examining the unique phenomena bred by the Prohibition Era in America, there seemed more chance of achieving clarity and perspective with this curiously amorphous piece of legislation (for its origins and its effects metastasized far beyond its purpose and its legal life) if I kept within territorial limits. Second, Chicago is a good town to take because, emblematically, this is the one that everyone associates with the régime of the gangsters, a strange real-life era of gun-law allied to unscrupulous commerce and power politics that has been shifted into the realm of legend by its popularization the world over by films, newspapers, books and now television, and so bestowed with an established familiarity which makes understandable much of its complex history. Third – and it is here that possible affront enters – the booster-citizen is wrong when he claims that all other American cities were as bad. They were not. Chicago had more of everything, of blood and bullets, of graft and corruption, of violence and immorality that soaked through into every area of the administration and business life.

This is not my opinion alone. 'Chicago is the most loved and most hated city in the United States and perhaps in the world.' 'In some respects Chicago is a national symptom; a sermon on what's wrong with urban America.' 'A sick city.' 'The city that took such a childish pride in its gangsters and so little in its artists.' 'Hustlertown.' 'Chicagoans have always taken a secret pride in the wickedness of their city – but a pride which is strangely offended when outsiders make any reference to its bad reputation.' 'You may say the old gags about gunmen in Chicago are exaggerated, but there have been seven hundred unsolved murders *since* the days of Prohibition and Al Capone. Perhaps the crimes of violence have diminished, but only because the Syndicate has murdered its way to monopoly. Here in Chicago segments of both political parties are in cahoots with this monopoly of murder. Chicago is unique. It is the only completely corrupt city in America.' All the foregoing are the words of Chicagoans.[1]

[1] Alson J. Smith, Fred D. Pasley, Chicago *Sun Times* headline, Herman Kogan and Lloyd Wendt, Nelson Algren, Virgil Peterson and Alderman Robert Merriam.

There are many sets of wildly varying figures, but during the fourteen Prohibition years there was in Chicago an official total of 703 gang murders arising from the drink traffic. This total did not include miscellaneous homicide, alcoholic poisoning and the tipplers sniped by keen Prohibition agents. Many of those 703 were committed in public places, in metropolitan streets and buildings – a winning score with ease when set against any other city's statistics. During the 'twenties Chicago was effectively a city without a police force, for it operated partially as a private army for the gangs (in 1923 sixty per cent of the police were officially estimated to be engaged in the liquor business, 'not in connivance, but actually'). And, furthermore, Chicago was the chosen field of one of the most formidably clever organizing brains of his time, Alphonse Capone, a slum-bred Italian delinquent who, as no criminal had done before or has done since – not even today, in the new, refined phase of quasi-respectable rackets that pervade urban America – made over a modern city for his own use and lived off it as blatantly and richly as a caesar of Rome.

Why was this so? Why did Chicago *rightly* acquire its reputation as the most lawless and vicious city in the world, a rugged, granite reputation which the frothy waves of propaganda by Chambers of Commerce, citizens' councils and public relations officers about clean-ups, industrial growth and the steady growth of responsibility and respectability, have done little to erode? The reasons are many and intricately interlocking – geographical, racial, economic and historical. It is this unique combination of circumstances that fascinated me for many years before I had my first opportunity of seeing the chimerical city – Carl Sandburg's 'Hog-Butcher for the world . . . City of the Big Shoulders', Nelson Algren's 'joint where the bulls and the foxes live well and the lambs wind up head-down from the hook' – for myself.

Yet it would be to dissemble to leave the impression that from the start it was the moral and civic aberrations that first and alone attracted my interest. Of course it was the melodrama.

I was introduced to Al Capone – at least, to the legend – at an early age. In January 1934 I was taken to Bertram Mills's Christmas circus at Olympia by my mother. After the performance, I cajoled her into a lengthy tour of the sideshows, the distorting mirrors, pinball machines and shooting galleries installed in that concrete-and-girder cavern, with its curiously squalid, bleak ambience. I came to a stop before a huge and ugly car, a saloon constructed like a tank:

which is precisely what it was. It was a 40 h.p. V8 Cadillac, custom-built in 1928, at a cost of £6,000, for Mr. Capone. It weighed three and a half tons, this being contributed to by armour-plated bodywork, a steel-visored petrol-tank, and windscreen and side windows of bullet-proof glass one and a half inches thick; it was also equipped with a movable back window (the rear-gunner's position), a police siren and a secret gun-locker behind a back-seat panel.

There was a placard on the dais, upon which the juggernaut bulked like a mezozoic creature of the dinosaur breed, announcing: THE CAR OF SCARFACE AL CAPONE, KING OF THE GANGSTERS. Along-side was a gallery of photographs of the king himself and his courtiers, many of them flashlit in uncomfortable postures, damp with their own blood in gutters and on the bullet-ripped upholstery of less fortress-like cars. Presiding over the exhibit which had, I later learned, been bought by a British speculator after Capone's enforced retirement from gang-rule in 1931, was a young man in chalk-stripe flannels, a sports coat with pleated pockets, and a bow tie. Business was slackish, and while pattering away with the spiel about the car's lurid history, he lifted me into the driving seat (which seemed a fantastic distance from the ground), and said: 'Imagine, kid, that you're driving through Chicago with a rival gang after you going rat-a-tat-a-tat-a-tat-a-tat.'

I did. This strange and grubbily sinister car lingered in my memory. I know the exact date that I saw it because a Charles Letts's *School-Boy's Diary* of the year has somehow stayed among my belongings, and there is a pencilled entry for Tuesday, 2 January, which reads: 'Whoopee! Setting off for the circus in 2 hours,' and, later: 'Boy, the circus was fine, but we had to pay 6/- each to get in. There were seals (they were the best turn), lions, horses (about 75), tigers, acrobats and clowns. Went to see Al Capone's armour plated car, with glass 1½ inches thick.' Then came the awed footnote: 'I actually handled a real Thomson [sic] sub-machine-gun.'

It was soon after this that my interest in the recent weird events in that distant American city, where life seemed totally unlike anything that had impinged upon me in London and its suburbs – a sort of pirate adventure transplanted into modern times and landscape – was increased by the discovery of a fly-blown little cache of information. This was at Ealing, where I went to visit an aunt. It was an open-fronted shop which was a midden of magazines. Scores of thousands of them were piled up in dusty alleyways. I went in, the first time, to rummage for back copies of *The Gem*, *The Magnet* and the *Nelson Lee Library*. Then I discovered that among the heaps of imported American pulp magazines – *True Confessions*, *Popular Mechanics*, dozens of Hollywood fan-magazines, and another rather mysteriously incomprehensible kind with cover-pictures of girls in black stockings and cami-knickers hanging upside-down off divans to talk on the telephone – were some with titles like *Real Detective* and *True Crime* which documented in excited, punchy prose splattered with smudgy photographs of corpses, police line-ups (impossible to distinguish detectives from mobsters in those groups of glowering men with blue chins and silver trilbies), and gangsters' molls (girls with little hard cupid's bows and frizzy hair combed slantwise across their foreheads), the saga of Chicago of the Prohibition Era.

I began, somewhat furtively, to buy these. Parental opposition apart, even to me they *looked* rancidly morbid – but none the less fascinating. Most were at least a year old. They cost threepence each, and could be sold back for a penny. Reading them I began to get some inkling of what the Chicago gangsters had been about, that they did not put each other on the spot and bump each other off out of sport, but as necessary measures of their business operations. I began to gather what Prohibition was, and to understand such exotic terms as bootlegger, hijacker, speakeasy and gat. I suppose such boyhood preoccupations might be defined by social-workers, school-teachers and child psychologists as rich humus for delinquency to root in, and I would not argue against that. Yet I don't think this diet of crime, guns and blood aberrated my personality; certainly I never consciously wished to experiment personally with such techniques, and I can state that I have never been convicted of an illegality of greater gravity than exceeding thirty miles an hour in a built-up area.

I suppose it was the strange amalgam of reality and fantasy that intrigued me. These were adventures as bizarrely desperate as any undertaken by King Arthur's knights, by Captain Kidd and his sea-rovers, by the outlaws and gun-slingers of the Wild West, but the difference was that they were a part of the world I was living in, or at least the world of just a few years ago: the fact that I had then been too young to read the headlines and had been four thousand miles beyond ear-shot of the automatics did not essentially affect the fact that this was contemporary and actual drama.

There were other factors. I was beginning to be addicted to jazz, musicians and singers like Louis Armstrong, Billie Holiday, the Mound City Blue-Blowers and Billy Banks, of whom nobody I knew had ever heard, but whose occasional records, encountered accidentally on B.B.C. programmes, excited and obsessed me, and I was learning that jazz was thickly intertwined with the Chicago gangs and their night-clubs and drinking dens. Also, I was becoming increasingly fascinated by America as a whole. The picture that I was gaining was one of patchy sensationalism, derived from American films like *Forty-Second Street*, *Scarface*, and *Street Scene*, from the big pastel-coloured Buicks and Hudson Terraplanes that a few monied show-biz types drove about London, from the appearance at the Palladium of such entertainers as Sophie Tucker and Cab Calloway, from partially assimilated newspaper stories about the Depression, bread-lines and the New Deal, from pop-songs like 'Brother, Can You Spare A Dime?' and 'Happy Days Are Here Again', from my first Steinbeck and Hemingway novels, and from the crime and movie magazines I continued to gollop up. It was a picture which both repelled and enchanted me: a *collage* of tough, gum-chewing chorines, slang of the 'Oh, yeah?' and 'Sez you' vogue, skyscrapers and Brooklyn tenements, police sirens and Gershwin quasi-jazz, Tombstone and Las Vegas, hobos and lynch-law, G-men and the ubiquitous gangster – a neon-blinking, metropolitan prospect of violence, neurosis and stridency, yet containing an hypnotic and meretricious kind of dynamism. It is exactly the picture that the average American unhappily suspects that the European has of his country. While understanding his regret about this, having since been to the United States three times I fear that it is an accurate one – in its most superficial aspect. As has been said, America infallibly puts her worst face forward. And, by the perverse rules of life, this raffish and tainted visage has its intrinsic attraction.

Although I did not visit Chicago for the first time until 1958, my interest in the city and its history, and especially in those fourteen turbulent years when the bootleggers and gunmen were masters, had meanwhile broadened and deepened beyond the blood-and-thunder stage into a curiosity about the political and social context in which those extraordinary events became possible, about the origins and personality of the gangster, and about the reciprocal effects that he as a success-symbol had upon society and public morality.

I give this explanation to anticipate the hostile question that could justifiably be asked by an American, particularly a Chicagoan, and even by a Briton, why I, an Englishman, should have taken it upon myself to attempt to tell in perspective and with as full a documentation as can be gathered (and it was like trying to reconstruct the swirl and sway of battles for a war-history without regimental records, without generals' memoirs and without any field-commanders to interview) the story of that period. Additionally I suppose, this book is an explanation to myself.

PART ONE

Blind Pigs and Ice-cream Parlours

She became one of the world's heaviest drinkers between 1927 and 1930, when the world saw some pretty heavy drinking. The Dizzy Club, the Hotsy-Totsy, Tommy Guinan's Chez Florence, the Type and Print Club, the Basque's, Michel's, Tony's, East Fifty-third Street, Tony's West Forty-ninth Street, Forty-two West Forty-nine, the Aquarium, Mario's, the Clamhouse, the Bandbox, the West Forty-fourth Street Club, McDermott's, the Sligo Slasher's, the Newswriters', Billy Duffy's, Jack Delaney's, Sam Schwartz's, the Richmond, Frank and Jack's, Felix's, Louis', Phyllis's, Twenty-one West Forty-third, Marlborough House – these were the places where she was known by name and sight, where she awed the bartenders by the amount she drank . . . It was understood and agreed that the big thing in life was liquor.

JOHN O'HARA, *Butterfield 8*

'*I was T.T. until Prohibition.*'

GROUCHO MARX

The Mud-Hole of the Prairies

'A new nation will be born.'
THE ANTI-SALOON LEAGUE

*I got a barrelhouse flat in Chicago, it's fifteen storeys
high . . .*

*Those babies like my good whisky, and they drink my
sherry wine . . .*
*If you want good time, come and try this barrelhouse flat o'
mine.*
MARY JOHNSON: Barrel House Flat Blues

CHICAGO's malodorous reputation is no novice guise. From the start, from the days in the 1830s when it was 'the Mud-hole of the Prairies', an Indian trading post doing a spanking business in pelts, guns, blankets, girls and whisky, it was a brawling, swaggering, brash, tough and hell-raising town, although it was ten years before it had its first official hanging. At the portal of the new frontier, a-boil with plainsmen and cattle-dealers, merchants and whores, canal boatmen and covered wagoners, pioneers and property investors, it was also a magnetic field for gamblers, con-men and chisellers of all hue and stripe. The condition became chronic.

In 1840 it was said to be rife with 'rowdies, blacklegs and all species of loafers'. In 1855 there was an attempt (which ended in riot and mayhem) to close the 'low-class dives' by imposing a local prohibition law. In 1857 it had a district of brothels, grog-shops, bare-fist prize-fighting booths and clip-joints denounced as 'the vilest and most dangerous place in Chicago'. In 1860 the Chicago *Journal* cried: 'We are beset on every side by a gang of desperate villains.' In 1872 a citizens' committee was formed to fight crime and promote legal reform, because 'one jostles the elbow of a murderer at every angle of the street, and yet' – and how reiterative this complaint was to become – 'the law seems powerless to bring the evil-doers to justice.' In 1876 the *Times* denounced a bagnio and wine-house owned by the superintendent of police as 'an epitome of hell and an infernal hell-hole', and the same year said: 'Big thieves are boldly traversing our streets by day, planning their rackets' (using the later highly familiar word at this early date). In 1893 W. T. Stead, the English journalist, published his book *If Christ Came To Chicago*, which disclosed respected citizens living off red-light rents, politicians swinging elections on whisky payola, policemen collecting dues from brothels and saloon-keepers, and gambling syndicates protected by City Hall. In one six-month period of 1906 there was a burglary every three hours, a hold-up every six hours, and a murder every day, and the Chicago *Tribune* declared: 'A reign of terror is upon the city. No city in time of peace ever held so high a place in the category of crime-ridden, terrorized, murder-breeding cities as is now held by Chicago.'

It was even beginning to produce fruity best-sellers: *Twenty Years a Detective in the Wickedest City In The World*, was the unequivocal title of an autobiography by a Clifton Rodman Wooldridge published in 1908. During the first twenty years of the present century, gangsters, Black Handers, gunmen, racketeers, political grafters and pimps were so energetically and successfully active that there seemed ample justification for the title of ex-Detective Wooldridge's book.

So it may be seen that when Prohibition entered in 1920, Chicago was not unrehearsed or inexperienced in the techniques of countering and turning to advantage such a situation. Vice, lawlessness and corruption were not born of that ban on alcohol. Yet the following fourteen years were a distinct and special phase, for what the new law did was to present in a barrel undreamed of opportunities for the artisans and artists of crime.

Prohibition did not suddenly pounce upon the unsuspecting American public on 17 January 1920. It had been for a long time, menacingly and noisily, lumbering in for the kill.

Yet it is true, as F. L. Allen wrote, that 'the country accepted it not only willingly, but almost absentmindedly'. The causes of that improbable addition to the statute book, the Eighteenth Amendment to the American Constitution, that became the contentious and blood-stained Volstead Act, were involved. Perhaps the two fundamental causes – and which may in fact be the halves of the one characteristic – were the old tradition of hard, wild drinking of the pioneer days and the deep-rooted Puritanism in the psychology of the Americans, which continues, in this present age of lavish good-living, to make them so vulnerable to guilty misgivings and unease. It is those which create the strange ambivalence apparent in contemporary America, the confused love-hate so many feel towards their industrial-technological cornucopia disgorging such a profligacy of goods into their laps.

It is generally believed that 'the era of clear thinking and clean living', as Prohibition was exultantly hailed by the Anti-Saloon League at the dawn of that January day in 1920, was the most alcoholic period in American history. Actually, although the new law converted millions of citizens hitherto fairly disinterested in hard liquor into rebellious tipplers, home-brewers and hipflask-swiggers, there had been a more excessively intemperate time. For about a hundred years up to the end of the eighteenth century liquor – 'the good creature of God' as it was gratefully ennobled in early colonial ordinances – was as accepted a factor in the routine of life as bread or money. Indeed, it functioned as money, for rum was the principal article of barter in the slave trade (in the beginning a muscular young Negro could be bought for twenty gallons), and whisky was found to be a sensible means of marketing grain. Spirits were an integral part of colonial economy and prosperity. They were drunk by everyone, of both sexes and all ages and their intake was indiscriminately routine. Rum in particular was prescribed by physicians, sipped in all households throughout the day, and crying babies were almost unknown, for they lolled in their cradles permanently squiffy on dosages of mixed opium and rum. In the South a mint-julep was the waking beverage as orange-juice is now: it was considered reviving and health-preserving. As in France, where despite the brief milk campaign of Mendès-France, the theory survived that the extract of grape or cereal is safer than water, alcoholism was of such a general and diluted nature that it beatifically permeated the national character. Even the Puritans, who thundered against all fleshly pleasures it was practicable to forbid, disregarded this staple food, although they formally condemned intoxication. Anyway, they themselves drank as consistently and enthusiastically as anyone else, and the fact that they were the first rum-distillers in America may have been an economically relevant factor. Gin and applejack, or Jersey lightning, fondly known as blue ruin or strip-and-go-naked, were the popular hooch of slaves and servants. The cocktail-mixer was then emerging as a working professional, devising imaginative mixtures like blackstrap (rum and molasses), kill-devil (gin and beer), rum flip (rum, beer and sugar), and sillabub (port or madeira and milk and sugar).

It was a carousing century. The Puritans' censure of drunkenness did not profoundly influence the majority opinion that, its anti-toxin properties apart, drink was there to be enjoyed simply for its euphoric powers. The jug of rum stood on every sideboard and was constantly referred to; workers of all kind expected, and got, their daily dispensation from employers; there was the customary inter-mission in all business offices for the purpose of stoking up a little in the morning, which was known as the 'leven o'clock bitters and which has since been debilitated into the coffee-break. In addition to those routine rations, the general principle existed that feast-days, high-days and holidays were proper occasions for ritualistic tipsiness. The 1830 edition of *The Old American Encyclopedia* says with pursed lips: 'Sots were common in both sexes, of various ages, and of every condition.' And the truth is that taverns of that time, the tippling-houses, dramshops, and gin-mills, were dirty, degraded rough dives, and as the profit-motive grew more powerful and the liquor business more organized, endemic drunkenness began to amount to a social problem.

Not astonishingly a reaction to this state of affairs set in, and about 1840 this formulated into a religious movement, with the Methodist Church as the propulsive force, despite – or perhaps because of – the fact that Methodism was encumbered with a huge number of dipsomaniac ministers. A temperance campaigner of the 1880s, the Rev. Daniel Dorchester, totted up forty preachers of his acquaintance who were 'either drunkards or so far addicted to drinking that their reputation and usefulness were greatly impaired, if not utterly ruined', and who further wrote that 'a great many deacons in New England died drunkards'. He had even undertaken the painful task of composing a list of 'intemperate deacons in Massachusetts, forty-three of whom became sots'. Yet not all the churches were sold on the ideal of a liquorless nation, and in the 1850s some Kentucky congregations impatiently cast out zealot members who had joined temperance societies.

Nevertheless, the anti-drink crusade had begun – the crusade which eighty years later was to find its victory turning, with melan-choly irony, into the source of prodigious vice, fantastic wealth for gangsters, and abundant death by sub-machine-gun and poisonous counterfeit liquor. The intervening years swirled with a blizzard of propaganda. In a pamphlet entitled *The Curse of Chicago* Professor George E. Foster intoned: 'Drink is powerful enough in itself to draw men to seek it. Alone it is more than a match for the prudence of thousands. Why should it be supplemented by the additional lures of exhibitions and singing women? How many are led into the places where drink is sold and so lured to destruction?' In another broadsheet, *Can Chicago Live Without Saloon Revenue?* the author, Frank S. Regan, thundered Yes. 'The city that built the first skyscraper on earth,' he wrote, 'that went to London and built her underground railway,[1] will build herself a better revenue system than that which is based upon the degradation of her citizens and the robbery of her poor.'

January 17, 1920, was the slamming of a door that had been pushed to, inch by inch, for decades. It proved to be a flimsily vulnerable barricade, but legally the bolts were shot. Nevertheless the speakeasy, the wildcat still and the bootlegger were not products of the 'twenties, although it was then that they suddenly assumed national importance and status. When 'the noble experiment' (Hoover's emotional description) started, twenty-four states already had comprehensive prohibition laws instituted by local option, and there were many others in which counties or whole regions were dry. None the less under the leadership of such tough and tenacious reformers as Wayne B. Wheeler (of the Anti-Saloon League), Bishop James Cannon Jr., Clarence True Wilson (of the Methodist Board of Temperance, Prohibition and Public Morals), Representative Andrew J. Volstead of Minnesota (author of the Volstead Act), and Senator Morris Sheppard of Texas (author of the Eighteenth Amendment), the campaign made relentless progress, assisted in the most practical and physical manner by the terrifying Carry Nation, who for ten years tramped through Kansas saloons carrying beneath her robes a hatchet with which she split open beer kegs, smashed bottles and wrecked bars. To purify their source, the Prohibitionists cleaned-up the Bible. Dr. Charles Foster Kent, Professor of Biblical History at Yale, was assigned to bowdlerizing the Scriptures of all references to alcohol. For example, he changed: 'And the vine said unto them, Should I leave my wine, which cheereth God and man?' in Judges ix, 13 to: 'Shall I leave my juice that gladdens gods and men', and the professor censored II Samuel vi, 19: 'And he dealt among all the people, even among the whole multitude of Israel, as well to the women as men, to every one a cake of bread, and a good piece of flesh and a flagon of wine', so that it read: 'And he distributed to the whole assembled multitude a roll of bread, a portion of meat and a cake of raisins.'

---

[1] The extent of Chicago's contribution to providing London with an underground railway was that Charles T. Yerkes, the city's traction millionaire was one of the early investors in the original Metropolitan District Railway.

The first state to succumb and raise the teetotal banner was Georgia in 1907, to be followed rapidly by others with large rural and chapel populations, North Carolina, Tennessee, Mississippi, West Virginia and Oklahoma. The first sobering jolt to the happy-go-lucky drinkers, who had hitherto regarded the prohibition movement as the comic eccentricity of inept crackpots, was when the constitutional amendment was thrust before the House of Representatives in 1914 – and got a vote of 197 to 190 in favour. A two-thirds majority was needed to carry it through, but the result of this pilot-run came as an ominous surprise to sophisticated America. At that time the Anti-Saloon League and the Women's Christian Temperance Union marched to a stirring battle-hymn entitled 'A Saloonless Nation in 1920', borrowed from the Christian Endeavour's slogan 'A saloonless nation in 1920, the three hundredth anniversary of the landing of the Pilgrims'.

This was unerringly prophetic, yet, despite the fact that the Anti-Saloon League had become the most powerful lobby ever to operate in Washington (the headquarters was immediately across the street from the Capitol, from where legislators, sensitively aware of the League's increasing command of votes, came scurrying at the summons of Clarence True Wilson) and despite the generous donations from rich industrialists persuaded that drinking workmen were a drag upon mass production speed-up, only two years before it had seemed an ambition preposterously remote from fulfilment. It was America's entry into the war that brought about the dramatic change and made it a looming possibility.

The pro-drink forces were already held in low esteem by the average non-partisan moderate drinker, for they were so blatantly vested in interest, being composed almost solely of the liquor trade which was often in league with prostitution and gambling. The sort of saloon scene and skid-row atmosphere portrayed, for instance, by Eugene O'Neill in *The Iceman Cometh*, were entirely typical of the early 1900s. It was declaration of war in April 1917 that created a new emotional climate. The arguments of the dry campaigners that sober soldiers and factory-hands were better soldiers and factory-hands, that in this time of food-conservance, grain was more necessary for bread than for whisky, that this was the hour for discipline and not indulgence, seemed irrefutable. Also, there was a sweep of jingoistic revulsion against all things German, and, to the good fortune of the prohibitionists, the owners of many of the breweries and distilleries were of German-extraction and name. Finally there was temporary faith in the concept that out of the conflict would come everlasting peace and utopia for man upon earth. This, plainly, was no time for wallowing in the old degeneracy of drink. Not missing a trick, the dry-brigade exploited the new situation like the seasoned tacticians they were.

When the Eighteenth Amendment again came before the Senate in 1917 it was passed after only thirteen hours of debate. A few months later it was ratified by the House of Representatives after only one day's discussion. With reluctance the state legislatures confirmed the decision, and by January 1919, two months after the Armistice, the necessary thirty-six states had expressed their approval. The Constitution was longer by one Amendment, and Senator Volstead's act for its enforcement hurtled through – despite the unexpected veto of Woodrow Wilson, the President, due, apparently to eleventh-hour misgivings as to its intrinsic wisdom. There were a few squalls of indignation. The American Federation of Labour briefly clamoured for the retention of enough flexibility still to permit the worker his glass of beer and there were mass demonstrations in New York and Baltimore. It was too late. On the eve of 17 January 1920 the Anti-Saloon League trumpeted: 'It is here at last – dry America's first birthday. At one minute past twelve tomorrow morning a new nation will be born. Tonight John Barleycorn makes his last will and testament. Now for an era of clear thinking and clean living. The Anti-Saloon League wishes every man and woman and child a Happy Dry Year.' Henceforth 105 million re-born Americans would have bright eyes, sweet breath and peaceful livers. Or, at least, that was the theory. 'When we get Prohibition,' Billy Sunday, the ardent evangelist, promised, 'the problem of what to do with farm surplus will be solved in a jiffy. The children of drunkards will consume this surplus in the form of flap-jacks for breakfast.' Flap-jacks were not the only thing there was going to be more of.

2

A Trail of Graft and Slime

'An era of clear thinking and clean living.'
THE ANTI-SALOON LEAGUE

Keep away from bootleg hooch
When you're on the spree.
Take good care of yourself,
You belong to me.
'Button Up Your Overcoat',
hit song of 1928

All night the saxophones wailed the hopeless comment of
the Beale St. Blues while a hundred pairs of golden and
silver slippers shuffled the shining dust. At the gray tea hour
there were always rooms that throbbed incessantly with this
low, sweet fever, while fresh faces drifted here and there like
rose petals blown by the sad horns around the floor.
F. SCOTT FITZGERALD, *The Great Gatsby*

ON the morning of 16 January the thirty-two page issue of the Chicago *Tribune*, then under the control of that ferocious patriot Colonel Robert Rutherford McCormick, rippled off the presses emblazoned with the thick black headline:

NEW WAR LOOMS
BRITAIN FEARS DRIVE ON INDIA BY SOVIET
VICTORIES OF RUSSIAN REDS BRING CRISIS

Relatively unobtrusive beneath this early uprush of anti-Communism was a squashed one-column story headed: LIQUOR'S KNELL TO TOLL IN U.S. AT MIDNIGHT: LAST RITES JOYLESS THOUGH LAW NODS. It began: 'Federal prohibition arrives tonight at the stroke of twelve. Liquor, which had most of the robustness knocked out of it on the first of last July takes official leave of its life in the USA tonight. At least half of the one million gallons of "hard likker"

30

reported stored in Chicago on July 1 is still here. Major A. V. Dalrymple, district prohibition agent, said: "We have made final arrangements to take over the work of nailing down the lid." Trucks, limousines and baby buggies rumbled from saloon, store and hotel with private stocks. Fifty thousand gallons moved from public places to private homes last week.' Below was a short separate story headed U.S. TO BE DRY AS SAHARA, and also another item about the theft of a whisky-laden lorry on West Lake Street, which contained greater meaningfulness as a pointer of the hi-jacking (the abduction by gangsters of a consignment of liquor, usually being transported by a rival gang) to come. There was no editorial on the subject; the issue had a tepid atmosphere of fatalistic indifference. It is obvious that Colonel McCormick was more concerned with the upheavals in far-off Russia, for the most noticeable feature on the front page was a displayed photograph of a bearded man captioned: 'Nicolai Lenine: Leader of the Russian Bolsheviks whose power threatens the peace of the world.'

The Colonel's news-sense was indisputably accurate in his assessment of the relative importance of these two matters in their world context, but he badly misjudged the significance and the potential problems to his own town with which this new law was loaded. But why should he, or anyone else have had those forebodings, for John F. Kramer, the newly appointed Prohibition Commissioner, had stated sonorously: 'This law will be obeyed in cities, large and small, and in villages, and where it is not obeyed it will be enforced. The law says that liquor to be used as a beverage must not be manufactured. We shall see that it is not manufactured. Nor sold, nor given away, nor hauled in anything on the surface of the earth or under the earth or in the air.'

Seldom can any prophecy have been so extravagantly wrong. There were little fantasies enacted briefly in the press to try to prove Kramer correct. One British newspaper correspondent in those early days reported the manifestation on an ice-cream and soda-pop craze throughout the American nation. 'Banishment of the cocktail and the high-ball,' wrote this journalist, 'instead of driving Americans to dope or plunging them into political anarchy, has merely sent them into the candy stores and the ice-cream parlours. The saloon has been closed up or converted into an innocuous lunch room. In the place of the tens of thousands of these forlorn establishments there has sprung into existence a vast number of soft drink parlours, where men, women and children jostle one another from early morning till late at night in a scramble for weird ice mixtures. Men who never in their lives stooped to anything below the rank of whisky straight nowadays lean contentedly across the marble counter of a drug store where amazing concoctions called milk-shakes, pine-apple sundaes, cherry smash, marshmallow-flips and Coca-cola are dispensed. It is ice-cream and candy to which bone-dry America, in its emergency, has turned on an almost incredible scale.'

Had that British newspaperman looked closer at those amazing milk-shakes he might have formed a better appreciation of the contentment of the apparently reformed whisky-drinkers, for the soft drink parlour became one of the trusty fronts for the sale of the hard stuff, as did coffee shops, restaurants and drug stores. Blind pigs – establishments with anonymous blank façades, entered by a basement front door with a peep-hole, or hidden behind shops or in tenement buildings – began operating in their thousands in every big city. In New York, where there had been fifteen thousand legal saloons, thirty-two thousand speakeasies spangled the city like dandelions in spring; in Chicago hundreds of bars which were supposed to be padlocked simply stayed flagrantly open, but additional thousands of undercover saloons, beer flats, blind pigs and basement speaks opened. Yet this was only the more public side of the farce. Prohibition, says Asbury, 'became almost a national obsession; it overshadowed all other questions. The people talked of little else.' The most popular subject, and one which acquired the most subtle degrees of social status, was one's skill as a handyman distiller. Magazines and newspapers rushed out articles giving guidance on how to make your own beverages in conveniently available kitchen utensils, from kettles to wash boilers. There were even official publications issued by the Department of Agriculture – and which continued to be circulated long after the advent of the Eighteenth Amendment – which contained old Colonial wrinkles, such as how to manufacture liquor from 'pumpkins and parsnips and walnut-tree chips'. Shops opened specializing in hops, yeast, malt, corn meal, grains, copper tubing, charred kegs, bottle tops, crocks and kettles – the entire do-it-yourself kit for the home moon-shiner; within one week of the new law different sized portable stills, ranging from one- to five-gallon capacity, were on sale throughout the country despite official strictures against their illegality. The focal point of any party became the bathroom, where the gin was being prepared to wither the tongues and scorify the stomach-linings of guests at that night's whoopee party. 'Thousands of homes every-where in the United States', Asbury writes, 'were rapidly being transformed into miniature distilleries and breweries, and the pop of the home-brew bottle was heard in the land . . . At parties it soon became the custom for everyone to drink as much as he could hold as quickly as possible.'

The dedicated dries did their best to persuade themselves and everyone else that Prohibition was not only working practically but was the turbine generating a new spirituality throughout the nation. It was praised by Commissioner Roy A. Haynes in these words: 'The results are nothing short of remarkable. The Amendment is being enforced to an even greater extent than many devoted friends anticipated . . . People generally, both foreign and otherwise, have quietly acquiesced in the new law, and those now engaged in the illicit traffic constitute a negligible minority.' And he continued with some astonishing statistics, the source of which was not volunteered: 'It is estimated that there were twenty million drinkers in the United States before the country went dry.' If there were twenty million drinkers when liquor was accessible, and it is doubtful, and if there are 2,500,000 drinkers now, more doubtful, then 17,500,000 former drinkers have quit – a wonderful record. Only fifteen per cent of the former drinkers are drinking now, and these are drinking but five per cent of the quantity of liquor that was formerly consumed, while the drink bill of the nation has been decreased two billion dollars a year.'

Commissioner Haynes bounded on down the years looking persistently on the bright side. During the following eighteen months he declared in speeches and interviews that 'the home-brew fad is taking its final gasp', that 'bootleg patronage has fallen off more than fifty per cent', that 'moonshining in the cities is on the wane', that the bootleggers 'are in a desperate plight', and that 'the death rattle has begun'.

What Commissioner Haynes mistook for the death rattle of the illicit drink trade was probably the rustle of countless bank-notes that flowed into the tills of the nation's proliferating speakeasies. Statistics with more basis in fact than those Haynes produced show that in a single year of Prohibition the United States consumed 200 million gallons of hard liquor, 684 million gallons of malt liquor, and 118 million gallons of wine, and in that twelve months the income of professional bootleggers was assessed at 4,000 million dollars. It was America's biggest industry.

Americans drank oceans of bootleg alcohol, but they did not hold it in high regard, as the vast glossary of slang terms in use at the time implies. With a kind of affectionate revulsion it was called coffin varnish, craw rot, rot gut, panther piss, busthead, squirrel juice, horse liniment, razors, tarantula juice, junk, strike-me-dead, belch, sheep dip, and a hundred other horror-comic names. The tributaries of the eerily varied thirst-quenching liquids that they poured down their throats were as diverse.

In Chicago alone, in 1930, Federal officials estimated that ten thousand speakeasies were operating, each buying weekly six barrels of beer at fifty-five dollars each, this giving the gangs a weekly 3,500,000 dollars revenue. Also, each speakeasy bought an average of two cases of liquor a week at ninety dollars a case – a further 1,800,000 dollars a week for the gang. The beer cost about four dollars a barrel to manufacture, the liquor about twenty dollars a case. This Federal assessment of ten thousand speakeasies was considered by many to be just about half the actual number – for the tobacconists, drug stores and grocers which peddled gin and whisky on the side had not been taken into account. Many ingenious citizens procured prescriptions from their doctors stating that they needed alcohol for medicinal reasons, to keep them organically functioning, and found that most chemists were willing to take a prescription as a permit for unlimited supplies; some doctors did a labour-saving deal with druggists by selling their prescription books outright. As drink fever mounted, the age of initiation proportionately dropped; it became a mark of manliness in a teen-age boy to brag about getting plastered. To cater for this new market, speakeasies sprang up around schools and colleges – in Chicago more than a dozen in the neighbourhood of three high schools prospered on the custom of the pupils – and the gangs' travelling salesmen delivered to the schools stuff even more virulent than that they sold the children's parents. The composition of the various brews was hair-raising, and quite often hair-destroying. Breweries were still open making the legal near-beer ('Soap-suds', a newspaperman who stayed wet throughout described it to me) which was de-alcoholized by running it across heated plates, and it was no insuperable problem to charge up the debilitated product. Often this was done by supplying speakeasies with near-beer, and, secretly, with a consignment of wood alcohol. This was then either forced into the barrels with a compression pump, or spiked in the glass by the bartender, who gave each a squirt from a syringe as he served it – the legendary needled beer of the time which caused so much violent stomach disorder and drunken illness. Chicago also pioneered the production of wort, or green beer, the result of the manufacturing process being suspended before the addition of yeast. To hot this up to the mark, a cake of yeast was dropped into the barrel in the speakeasy, and it was allowed to ferment on the premises.

The liquids that went under the name of whisky, gin and brandy were as nightmarishly nefarious. An Italian, now head-waiter in a Loop restaurant who had his own speak on the North Side in the 'twenties and who was a customer of the Bugs Moran gang, told me: 'We used to sell mostly what we called whisky sours, old fashioneds and gin rickies. This was the start of the cocktail, because you had to kill the taste of the stuff. I'd cut the alcohol with distilled water and mineral oil to give it smoothness. Three gallons of whisky could be got from one gallon of alky, treated, and then I'd just slap the labels I'd bought on the bottles. I got the colouring in the drug store – burnt sugar or caramel or oil of rye for the whisky, juniper juice for the gin taste. There was an eighty per cent profit on everything I sold.' Some even less scrupulous cutters used a sulphuric acid compound. A Chicago city chemist, while analysing an impounded shipment of bootleg hooch, spilled a little on a sink in his laboratory: it ate away the enamel.

The Volstead Act permitted the manufacture of 'cereal beverages' with an alcohol content of not more than half of one per cent. Permits were granted, as Mrs. Mabel Walker Willibrandt (Assistant Attorney General in charge of Prohibition prosecutions) put it, to 'any person with a nice clean face and no gun sticking out of his pocket'. With little difficulty in obtaining the basic ingredients, Chicago became a gigantic brewery. The stench of malt, fermenting mash and alcoholic distillate hung in a permanent miasmic pall over whole neighbourhoods, and police estimated that there were a hundred stills running in every block in the West Madison Street area. In the early flush of exultation the Prohibitionists had believed victory for ever secure; a big section of the Chicago City House of Correction and the delirium tremens ward of Cook County Hospital were closed, as obviously they would no longer be needed for drunks, and it was proudly broadcast by the dries that doctors now lacked enough D.T. cases for clinical experiments and that a local alcoholics' home was going bankrupt because of lack of customers. They were unwarrantably sanguine. The first Federal raid on a Chicago speakeasy was on 1 February, two weeks after the law came in. At 1 a.m. the officers burst into a basement bar named The Red Lantern at Clark and Kinzie Streets and herded forty well-dressed men and women into the police station as prisoners – 'Nothing like this had happened before,' commented a newspaper. By June 1920 Chicago's courts were bottlenecked by five to six hundred Prohibition violation cases awaiting trial. In 1925 Chicago, with three million population, had sixteen thousand more arrests for drunkenness than un-Prohibited England and Wales with a population of forty millions. By 1927 drunken driving had risen in Chicago by 476 per cent and deaths from alcoholism by 600 per cent. By 1930, 550 thousand Americans had been arrested and 230 thousand of them had served an aggregate of 33 thousand years in Federal prisons for drink offences, and 3,500 million dollars had been lost in excise duties. And in that period 35 thousand people had been killed from poison liquor – apart from the countless thousands more left blinded or crippled by damaged nervous systems. In one of its hundreds of wet editorials, the *Tribune* said in October 1923: 'Mayor Dever's seven thousand policemen face a city which rejects the law they try to enforce. The city still eludes the enforcement. Half a million people in Chicago whose mother tongue was German nearly all have a profound conviction against the prohibition of beer. Not one per cent of the 166,500 whose mother tongue was Italian or Greek can believe that wine is morally bad or can be made bad by law.' By 1932 two thousand civilians – that is, mainly gangsters and allied beer-runners – and five hundred Prohibition agents had been killed in warfare; in Chicago twenty-three innocent, definitely non-gangster citizens were slain by agents. Indictments were returned in every case but not one 'Fed' was punished.

In fact, it was the severity with which the authorities, desperate and bewildered, tried to enforce the law that finally contributed importantly to its rejection by the nation. A Chicago *Tribune* reporter said to me: 'The paper – and that went for all of the staff – was against Prohibition because of the methods of enforcement.' By that he meant such cases as the life imprisonment given in 1928 to Fred Palm of Lansing, Michigan, for possessing a pint of gin; the 1931 jailing of a Lithuanian janitor who had made some home brew for an American Legion social; the 1929 killing of an Aurora house-wife and the clubbing of her husband by a deputy sherriff sniffing out liquor; the 1928 murder of an innocent insurance agent by Federal agents letting fly with dum-dum bullets during a raid in Chicago; and the sensational trial of Virgil Kirkland and four friends for raping and murdering Arlene Draves, an 18-year-old Gary high school girl, after a party at which wine laced with formaldehyde had been tippled. A month after the Volstead Act became law a New Yorker was sent to jail for carrying a hip-flask of whisky – but a few years later a Michigan mother of ten children received life imprisonment for possessing a pint of gin.

Law or no law, to most sane people this state of affairs seemed insane.

A doggerel verse that was much repeated in the early 'thirties sardonically expressed the cynical disgust that most people – including, by now, the less dogmatic dries – felt towards Prohibition. It ran:

> *Prohibition is an awful flop,*
>   *We like it.*
> *It can't stop what it's meant to stop.*
>   *We like it.*
> *It's filled our land with vice and crime,*
> *It's left a trail of graft and slime,*
> *It don't prohibit worth a dime,*
>   *Nevertheless we're for it.*

By 1933 the nation was unmistakably – even to the most cautiously lobby-conscious politicians – sickened by the results of this 'era of clear thinking and clean living', and even sicker in the stomach from fourteen years of rotgut. Herbert Hoover's praise for Prohibition – 'A great social and economic experiment,' he had written in a letter to Senator William E. Borah, 'noble in motive and far-reaching in purpose' – recoiled batteringly upon his head when he ran for re-election in 1932 on a platform that tried to ignore the wet-dry controversy, and he understood his misjudgement when he saw the support that flooded towards Franklin D. Roosevelt, whose Democratic programme advocated repeal of the Eighteenth Amendment – the slogan was 'A New Deal and a pot of beer for everyone'.

Nine days after his inauguration as President, Roosevelt asked Congress to amend the Volstead Act to permit the brewing and sale of 3·2 per cent alcohol. Resolutions to submit a repealing amendment followed in February 1933 and were passed in Congress. It was necessary for thirty-six States to ratify it. Utah, on 5 December, was the thirty-sixth, and Prohibition was formally dead, dishonoured and done with.

On the morning of 5 December the headline in the Chicago *Tribune* was: 14-YEAR DRY ERA ENDS TODAY: CHICAGO TO GIVE LEGAL LIQUOR A GOOD WELCOME. In readiness seven thousand taverns, hotels and restaurants were stocked up with 3·2 per cent beer, and prices had been drastically marked down. Bootleg Scotch had cost seventy-five cents a shot, Bourbon seventy-five cents and cocktails a dollar; now they would be fifty cents, twenty-five cents and fifty cents respectively. The lead story in the *Tribune* opened: 'Beginning at three o'clock Chicago is due to start drinking legal liquor again after a lapse of fourteen years five months and five days[1] of machine-gun murders, prohibition bribery and poison booze. There will be no shortage of Bourbon whisky, the standard drink of pre-Prohibition America. There are an estimated 200 thousand cases in the city now, brought in under medicinal liquor permits, most of which, however, is blended (the bootleggers call it cutting). Sixty thousand cases are held in bond at the Railway Terminal warehouse. For the information of hijackers, the warehouse is a good place to avoid – it is swarming with guards and armed Custom Inspectors.' The *Tribune*'s leader issued a friendly warning: 'It is probably unnecessary to remind participants in the celebration of the end of Volstead that intoxicating liquor contains its headache. The bootlegger saw to it that this information did not vanish completely from the country. It is still common knowledge that the facts of indiscretion in the use of potable alcohol are about as unpleasant as anything which happens inside the human frame.'

It was an apposite, but largely ignored, warning. It was a frenzied night throughout most of the United States, and certainly in Chicago. Every bar had a six-deep crush until the early hours. Women – who, since the opening of the speakeasy fourteen years earlier, were part of the new landscape in drinking premises – were photographed standing emancipatedly on bars and tables raising their glasses high in triumphant toasts. The police themselves were too busy getting their own share of lawful alcohol to bother the tipsy citizenry – at midnight only five men had been taken down to the South State police station, reception centre for prisoners in the Loop where most of the drinking was concentrated. It was a carnival but slightly unreal night, in which the odd sensation of being able to swig without fear of arrest or poisoning mingled with nostalgia for the old hazards of enjoyable danger and deceit: But such contrary qualifications did not inhibit that whingding night. In all of Chicago there were but a minority who did not fill up at least one celebratory glass: the thwarted purist dries – and that even stauncher group of supporters of the Volstead Act, Al Capone and his business colleagues who had kept the drink flowing and had become millionaires and powers in the land in the process. For them it was the sad and bitter close of a charmed time.

[1] The *Tribune's* calculation down to the last dry day is dated from 22 July 1919, when the National Prohibition Act, colloquially known as the Volstead Act, was passed by the House of Representatives.

PART TWO

The Booze War

I'm gonna take you for an easy ride,
Drop you off by the riverside.
PEETIE WHEAT'STRAW, *Gangster Blues*

'*A one-legged prohibition agent on a bicycle could stop the*
beer in the Loop in a day — if he were honest.'
PATRICK ROCHE,
State's Attorney's Chief Investigator, 1926

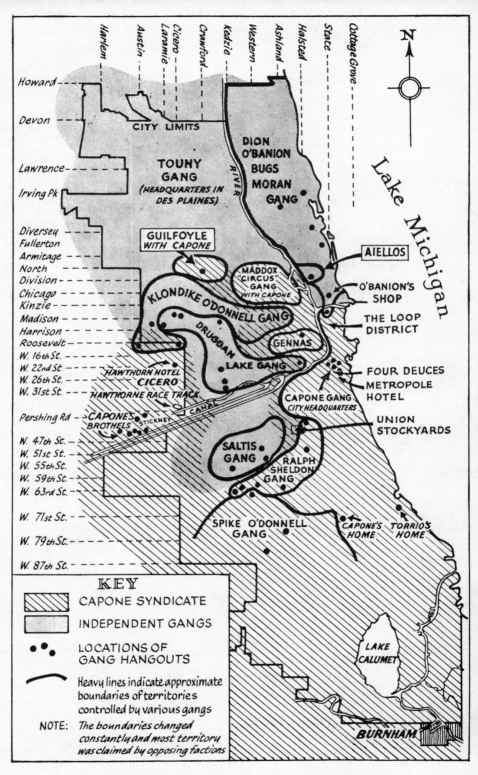

The temporary balance of power in Chicago
Gangland in the early 'twenties

3

Charlemagne and the Second-hand Furniture Dealer

'One long, unclouded honeymoon.'

MRS. JOHN TORRIO

I'm going down on State Street just to buy me a gallon of booze.

PINETOP SMITH, *Pinetop's Blues*

ON a tropically hot afternoon in July 1921 some children playing hopscotch on the corner of Halstead and Fourteenth Streets, near Chicago's Maxwell Street ghetto, paused in their game to watch with momentary curiosity a man being hustled by four others into a black touring car parked at the kerb. He looked agitated and frightened, in a numbed sort of way, and did not cry out. He was shoved into the car, which accelerated away into the traffic. Next day his cold body was found beside a country road near Libertyville, a small town twenty-five miles north of the city. He had been shot in the head. His name was Steve Wisiewski.

He was killed because he had hijacked a consignment of beer belonging to the West Side gang operated by Terry Druggan and Frankie Lake, who themselves had got started in the bootlegging business by hijacking beer lorries owned by Barney Grogan, a West Side saloon-keeper. Wisiewski was an obscure, small-time racketeer, a corner-boy nobody. His only importance to this record is that he is officially registered as the first of the 703 gangland fatalities of Chicago's fourteen years of Prohibition warfare. Upon him, also, fell the distinction of being the inaugural victim of a technique of murder that was to be busily employed. He was the first man to be taken for a one-way ride – that is, whisked off by car to a quiet place for dispatch at leisure and in safety, a term coined by Big Tim Murphy, pioneer labour racketeer, State representative and mail robber who was shot to death in June 1928.

A war historian, undertaking to reconstruct a modern military campaign in all its intricacy and gargantuan confusion of movement, has a straightforward task compared with that of describing the fighting between Chicago's booze barons during those fourteen years. At least, in a contest of arms between nations the theatre of war is discernible, the issues in contention are declared although they may become blurred and even repudiated by the passage of time, the opposing sides remain distinguishable, and there are regimental records and personal memoirs to be consulted; whereas the booze gangs issued no communiqués and preserved no battle-orders, the reasons for particular assaults and assassinations were often recondite personal feuds arising out of deeply internal quarrels and betrayals, the pattern of alliances was for ever in a stage of fluidity and flux, and, in place of a sustained clash of arms, the battles took the form of sporadic skirmishes, ambushes, sudden pounces upon individuals, jousts between moving cars similar to dog-fights between fighter aircraft, and the unpredictable, shifting collisions of guerilla warfare.

In those young days of Prohibition Chicago was a fragmentation of hostile criminal duchies. It was Johnny Torrio who performed the function of Charlemagne by bringing the warring factions together, laying down the first crude system of profit-sharing and allocation of territory, and maintaining a temporary, insecure peace by a relatively benevolent despotism and flexibility towards the aspirations of neighbouring overlords; it was Dion O'Banion whose insurrection burst asunder that first capricious federation; and it was Al Capone who became the modern dictator, ruthlessly crushing mutiny and finally, by blaze of gun-power and spilling of blood, forcing the surviving independent barons to accept the principle of central government.

The genesis of this eventual domination of a city by a criminal dictator – and whose authority extended through the State of Illinois and beyond – is to be found in the decade before Prohibition came into being. Between 1910 and 1920 Big Jim Colosimo was at the pinnacle of his success as boss of Chicago's underworld. He had arrived in America as the child of Italian immigrants, had industriously worked his way up from South Side newsvendor and shoe-shine boy to prosperous Black Hand terrorist, pickpocket and pimp, had worked briefly at street sweeping as refuge from imminent arrest, and had organized his fellow street-cleaners into a social club and union, the bloc voting of which he swung to Alderman Hinky Dink Kenna, chief of the First Ward Democratic machine, in return for political favours and remuneration. In 1902 he married the madame of a brothel and, with the experienced aid of his wife, rapidly expanded until he was director of a chain of levee bordellos, gambling houses and cafés, including the famous Colosimo's Café at 2126 on South Wabash Avenue, a gaudy night spot renowned from coast to coast, and the resort of society slumming parties out on the town. His income then was five hundred thousand dollars a year, a pittance compared with the sums later trawled in by his successors but enormous for that period. He acquired his name of Diamond Jim by arraying his huge check-suited body with diamonds, diamonds on fingers, clothes and accessories, and diamonds carried in leather bags in his pockets, through which he delved as he talked, like a child with a heap of coloured beads. Then the one-time Black Hander himself became the target of Black Hand extortionists, and it was to protect himself that he engaged a New York gunman as bodyguard. He was Johnny Torrio, leader of an East River waterfront mob of hoodlums called the James Street gang.

Torrio took up residence in Chicago in 1910. By 1920 he had risen from strong-arm man to be the practical head of Colosimo's vice industry, and was fermenting with ideas of modernization and development. The ideas remained frustrated, for Colosimo's ambition had lost its drive. He was middle-aged, rich and complacent and, additionally, his emotional zest was diverted upon the person of a café singer named Dale Winters, whom he married after divorcing his wife early in 1920. On 11 May, three weeks after his marriage, Colosimo ceased to be a hindrance to Torrio's career. On that day he went to his café to receive a truckload of bootleg whisky which Torrio had arranged to be delivered. Torrio had also arranged for Frankie Yale (or Uale), a New York mobster who was also national head of the Unione Siciliana, to be in attendance. No official charge was ever brought against anyone, but the Chicago police afterwards revealed that they had good reason to believe that Torrio had paid Yale ten thousand dollars to dispose of Colosimo, which he did by shooting him through the head.

Colosimo's was the first of the gangster funeral extravaganzas – and, at that time, the most candid exhibition of the intimate friendship between Chicago's politics and crime. The last ride of the pimp and pickpocket was attended by five thousand mourners, not only gunmen, white-slavers, dive-keepers and bootleggers, but prominent public officials. His honorary pallbearers included three judges, an Assistant State's Attorney, two Congressmen, a State Representative, eight Chicago aldermen, and leading members of the Chicago Opera Company. The Catholic archbishop refused to permit the use of church or cemetery because of his divorce, but at the

Colosimo home a Presbyterian clergyman presided and Alderman Bathhouse John Coughlin – Kenna's confederate in the First Ward – knelt at the coffin and recited the Hail Marys and the prayers. Hymns were sung by the Apollo Quartet. Colosimo was carried out to the hearse while a band played 'Nearer My God To Thee'. A cavalcade, including a thousand members of the First Ward Democratic Club, moved towards Oakwood Cemetery – 'as moved', observed the Chicago *Tribune* next day, 'behind the funeral car of Caesar, to pay homage to the memory of the man who for more than a decade has been recognized as the overlord of Chicago's underworld . . . Raised to the throne of the half world, he was a maker and breaker of political aspirations . . . It is a strange commentary upon our system of law and justice. In how far can power, derived from the life of the underworld, influence institutions of law and order ?'

This was not a question with which Torrio – piously present at the funeral – was bothering himself, for the answer was obvious to him. He proceeded to use the power at which Colosimo had merely fumbled, with dramatically effective results. He reorganized the gang and turned it into an instrument capable of seizing the opportunities presented by the new fact of life, Prohibition, that Colosimo had been too lazy and old-fashioned to perceive. In other circumstances, Torrio could have had a brilliant career as a business efficiency expert. Asbury considers Torrio to be probably 'the nearest thing to a real master mind that this country has yet produced'. He built the modern machine of outlawry; he was the first planner and administrator of crime in the context of Twentieth Century capitalism; for three years he controlled and extended Chicago's vice industry by a delicate balancing of compromise and strategy, eschewing violence except for the occasional execution necessary to maintain discipline. By later standards of syndicated crime, Torrio was a novice, a self-made success cleverly improvising in the period before illegal free enterprise was rationalized into interlocking cartels, but he was a trail-blazer and an original thinker. And by now he had working with him a young man whose enterprise and talent was to outclass and outpace his present master's. He was Al Capone, whom Torrio had in turn just brought in from New York as a new recruit for the team, and who was to show outstanding aptitude for exploiting the changing conditions in which crime would operate for the next fourteen years.

It may make the coming disputes clearer, and help the reader to sort his way through the maze of massacre and internecine slaughter, if the composition and territories of the gangs are here described.

They underwent many amalgamations and severances of alliances, and the boundary lines wavered and reformed more fluidly than those of post-war Europe, but this was their state in the earlier years of Prohibition, after the first Torrio peace plan had broken down. Under the Torrio-Capone banner were almost the entire South and South-West Sides of Chicago, reaching down beyond Calumet City to Burnham and west to Stickney and Cicero and also thrusting up through the city centre into the Near-North Side, with one isolated Torrio-Capone pocket deep in the district of North Avenue and Division Street. Within this area, control was deputed to eight co-partnership gangs, each with its own ratified territory, operating rather like the satellite states of a dictatorship. These were the Sheldon, McGeoghegan, De Coursey, Genna, Murray, Maddox Circus and Guilfoyle gangs.

These covered a sizeable and strongly defended portion of the city, but ranged against them was an unappetizingly muscular opposition. Deep in their territory was a bulge, which crossed the river and pushed down into the Union Stockyards district, occupied by the Polack Joe Saltis gang. On the North Side, almost surrounding the Genna brothers' territory were the zones run by the West Side O'Donnells – Myles and Klondyke, not related to another mob called the South Side O'Donnells – and the Druggan-Lake gang. Overhanging the Torrio–Capone–Guilfoyle redoubt was the Touhy gang's huge territory, controlled from the town of Des Plaines. Adjacent, with its long waterfront stretch, was the territory of the Dion O'Banion and Bugs Moran gang, which had a singularly deadly cohort of killers, including Vincent the Schemer Drucci, Nails Morton, Two-Gun Louis Alterie, Hymie Weiss, Dapper Dan McCarthy, Maxie Eisen and Frank Gusenberg.

It was not until the late summer of 1920, six months after the Volstead Act had become law, that Torrio turned his attention fully to liquor traffic. In the meantime he had renovated and consolidated Colosimo's vice empire and struck out into new territory. He had a strong army, a force of more than a hundred troops split into platoons commanded by Capone, Mike de Pike Heitler, Harry Guzik and Charlie Carr. Under his direction they established beach-heads in Cook County suburban towns. The strategy was one of politeness and persuasion. Having decided on a sound location for a road-house brothel and cabaret, the district was cased. House-holders in the neighbourhood of the proposed establishment were interviewed. If they showed willingness not to start protesting,

Torrio through his agents showed his willingness to settle any out-standing bills, pay off the mortgage, supply a new car or have the house redecorated and repaired. Similarly the local civic authorities and police were approached and satisfactory stipends agreed upon in return for non-interference. By these means, a chain of brothels and gambling-parlours were opened in a dozen country towns west and south-west of Chicago, including Chicago Heights, Stickney, Posen, Forest View, Burr Oaks, Blue Island and Steger.

Immediately, at the inception of this strange epoch of generally condoned social brigandry there is found the complicity of the 'good people' indicted by those who take the Nelson Algren view[1] of the causes of the corruption and flight of civic standards. It was the up-right citizens, the business men, who in the beginning, lured by the prospect of big money-making, eagerly co-operated with Torrio in his scheme. In the *Chicago Daily News*, on 17 November 1924, Charles Gregston described the partnership between Torrio and pre-Volstead brewers. 'John Torrio and a Chicago brewer are the twin kings of commercialized crime in Cook County today,' he charged. 'They are the men back of the O'Banions and Druggans, the guns and the gangs. They are the organizers, the directors, the fixers and the profit-takers. Torrio is absolute in the field of vice and gambling; the brewer is king of the beer racket. They work together and the others, with a few exceptions, work for them.

'A strange pair: Torrio is a native of Italy, a Tammany graduate, a post-graduate pupil of the late Big Jim Colosimo. His colleague is the youngest of four brothers who were rich brewers before Prohibi-tion. While Torrio was learning the tricks of ward politics in New York and the rewards of sin in the old Twenty-second Street district and later in Burnham, his twin king of crime was living pleasantly on what is called the Gold Coast, the son of a wealthy and established family. A common genius for organization brought them together soon after Prohibition had ushered in the new era of crime through which Chicago is passing.

'They have made organized crime pay tremendous dividends. The brewer's earnings, from the syndicated beer racket he works under political protection, have been reckoned at twelve million dollars a year since 1920. Nobody has ever risked a guess at the clearings of the many-sided Torrio.

'They are the joint rulers of the underworld today. No one can cut in on the gambling racket without Torrio's sanction. Immune from prosecution themselves, the two kings of crime can count on the law

[1] See page 242.

as well as their own gunmen when they want an intruder driven out. And they have the power to protect their henchmen from prosecution when murder becomes necessary, as it sometimes does. And the brewer is so completely above the law, so thoroughly protected from prosecution, that it is unsafe to mention his name, though the police and the prosecutors of crime know quite well who he is . . . His brothers are said to have been frowning on his ventures, but their warnings weren't heeded. Natural attraction brought the pair together and their dovetailing abilities put crime on its new basis. Gunmen were lured away from the risks of highway robbery and safe-blowing to get into the far more lucrative business of peddling beer and driving out competitors. Breweries were leased from their despairing owners and reopened. Cheating saloon-keepers, thousands of them, found it easy to sell beer profitably after paying the syndicate fifty dollars a barrel or more, and thirty-five dollars easily covered the cost of production and the expense of fixing the public officials, policemen and prohibition agents.

'The brewer knew the methods of modern business and applied them to syndicated beer running. Torrio knew the gangsters and recruited them. Thus Druggan and Lake were drawn away from the hoodlum activities of the Valley Gang into a racket that made both of them rich beyond all their dreams. Working breweries for the combine, they soon were riding in expensive cars, dressing like millionaires and living in fashionable neighbourhoods.'

Torrio's first step under the shield of his partner's influence was to acquire five breweries which were then being operated by Druggan and Lake, and with the close connivance of Morris Eller, trustee of the Chicago Sanitary District and political controller of the 'Bloody Twentieth' Ward. His first acquisition was the Puro Products Company, known also as the West Hammond Brewery. On 19 October 1923 the directors were brought to trial in the Federal Court in proceedings to close it for one year under injunction, and it was during this trial that evidence leaked out of Torrio's brewery-buying activities and of his backers. It was revealed that part owner of the concern was W. R. Strook, a former United States Deputy Marshal, and that holder of one share of the stock was Timothy J. Mullen, an attorney, who also had interest in the Bielfeldt Brewery at Thornton. The Puro Products Company had gone bankrupt in 1915. It was washed back into affluence by the tidal wave of Prohibition. The anonymous brewer bought it in October 1920. In October 1922 ownership was legally transferred to Torrio, who, before the injunction was due for hearing, turned the lease over to the Puro

Products Company. Surprisingly, Torrio and Strook did not evade the charge, pleaded guilty and were fined two thousand dollars and one thousand dollars respectively, and the company two thousand dollars.

This did not cause Torrio to pause in his acquisition of the basic source of his swelling income. He bought the Manhattan and Best Breweries; also he acted for Terry Druggan and Frankie Lake in the purchase of the George Hoffman, the Gambrinus, the Standard, the Pfeiffer and the Stege brewing companies. And with them on the deals was the omniverous beer chancellor.

Torrio, by means of complete ownership and stock-holding, had a monopoly in Woodland and all precincts south to the Indiana State line. Only in Englewood was his position insecure, for here Captain Allman, commander of the police, held obstinately free from graft, and enjoyed the support of Englewood business men who resisted Torrio's efforts to get Allman transferred. But in the Stockyards and the New City districts he operated under official consent, selling his beer at the standardized rate of fifty dollars a barrel,[1] including protection. The enterprise expanded. Torrio's role was as 'front man' – that is, he became the ostensible proprietor, the man who would accept responsibility if difficulties arose, for a group of five brewers who, while on paper leasing or selling their plants to Torrio, remained the secret owners.

It is doubtful if at that time anyone other than Torrio could have fulfilled this function. Whereas many of the brewers might, despite the strong urgings of their cupidity, have finally hung back from doing a deal with the average disreputable roughneck from the city's underworld, they were able to convince themselves that Torrio was a 'nice guy', a man you could do business with in a manifestly normal way. He had a benign face, a soft and courteous voice, and dressed in respectably quiet clothes. His new associates quite certainly were aware that he traded in women, issued murder orders, drew income from brothels and employed pimps, and systematically bribed officials and police, but there were other aspects of his life upon which they could fix their attention and thereby ease their consciences. He claimed – improbably – that he was never armed and he had never fired a gun in his life. He neither smoked nor drank, and was never heard to utter an obscene or profane word. His Kentucky-born wife later indignantly refuted malicious stories that her husband had lived an immoral life. He had been, she declared, 'the best and dearest of husbands'. He conducted his business within respectably regular office hours, returned in the early evening to his Michigan

[1] Once monopoly was established the price – as is commonly the case – was raised.

Al Capone in 1932

Al Capone with his lawyers, Michael Ahern and Albert Fink
Opposite *Johnny Torrio*

Above *Dion O'Banion* Below *Big Jim Colosimo*

Avenue apartment to sit in slippers listening to broadcast concerts or his huge collection of operatic and classical records, and, said Mrs. Torrio, her married life had been 'one long, unclouded honeymoon'. Such high standard of personal probity apparently helped brewers and other hitherto legitimate business men speedily to argue themselves out of any initial misgivings they might have felt in entering the beer racket.

Similarly, Torrio was able, by means of his calm air of prosperity and authority, to bring about his early consolidation of Chicago's petty gangsters. In the late summer of 1920 he conducted a series of parleys and persuaded the anarchic bank-robbers, footpads, burglars, horse-track crooks and hold-up men to divert their energies into booze under his leadership. During the next year there was a surface harmony while the formulating beer trust organized its manufacturing arrangements, supply lines, and retail trade, with only minor disturbances when it became necessary to discipline free-lance hijackers and independents attempting to encroach upon allotted territory.

It was in this early period of hammering the city into shape that a lay-about safe-blower and odd-job criminal accredited with three murders, named Joe Howard, decided to cut himself in on the beer profits. He had already unsuccessfully tried to rob the Old Rose Distillery warehouse on North Clark Street, but had been apprehended as the last of ten barrels was being loaded on to his truck. That case, after dragging on for months, was dismissed. He next tried hijacking, and got away with two consignments. They were Torrio's supplies. The next day Howard was standing at the cigar counter in Heinie Jacob's saloon on South Wabash Avenue, a few doors away from the Four Deuces headquarters of the Torrio gang, when two men came in. Howard said, 'Hi, Al,' and put out his hand. David Runelsbeck, a local carpenter who was drinking in the bar at the time, described what happened next. 'The man he spoke to stuck out his hand, but it held a revolver, and he fired six times. Joe keeled over dead, still grinning.'

Half an hour later all police stations in the city were alerted to arrest Capone. 'I am certain,' the detective in charge of the investigation told reporters, 'that it was Capone.'

A photograph of Capone appeared in the next morning's papers – the first time that flabby but oddly menacing face had been displayed to the public – with this unambiguous caption: 'Tony (Scarface) Capone, also known as Al Brown, who killed Joe Howard by firing six shots into his body in the saloon of Heinie Jacobs at 2300 South Wabash Avenue, in a renewal of the beer war.'

The inquest was held next day, and abruptly the witnesses were attacked by loss of memory. Jacobs was now sure that he had just gone into a back room to answer the telephone when the shooting occurred, and naturally he had seen and heard nothing. Runelsbeck was sure he would not be able to identify the killer. The third witness, George Bilton, a garage mechanic, had vanished. So had Capone.

He reappeared a month later, when he entered the Cottage Grove police station and said that he had heard a rumour that the police were looking for him. Why was that? Told that he was wanted for the killing of Howard, Capone said: 'Who, me? I'm a respectable business man, a second-hand furniture dealer. I'm no gangster. I don't know this fellow Torrio. I haven't anything to do with the Four Deuces. Anyway I was out of town the day Howard was bumped off.'

Capone made that statement to William H. McSwiggin, a young, new Assistant State's Attorney (later to be machine-gunned to death) who announced that he would bring an indictment. The inquest remained open for two and a half months and cost the taxpayers four thousand dollars, but dissolved in indecision. The jury's unrevelationary verdict was that Howard's death came about from 'bullets being fired from a revolver or revolvers in the hands of one or more unknown white male persons' and it was recommended 'that the unknown persons be apprehended and held to the grand jury upon a charge of murder'.

The 'unknown persons' were never apprehended. Capone was not troubled with the matter again. The significance of this isolated and relatively trivial killing is that it sharply crystallizes the repetitive pattern of the booze war murders: the immediacy of the death sentence for infringement of the rules, the cold daylight assault in public, the brazen indifference to the presence of witnesses, and the ease with which police action was frustrated.

But bigger and more violent issues than this peripheral destruction of an unimportant individual law-breaker were being fought out. The first clash of major interests had occurred soon after Torrio's co-partnership deal with ward gangs. Totally excluded from the carve-up were the four O'Donnell brothers Edward (known as Spike), Steve, Walter and Tommy, designated the South Side O'Donnells to distinguish them from Klondike and Myles O'Donnell who operated on the far West Side.

The South Side O'Donnells had not been included in the territory division because at that time they were of no great importance and because Spike was in prison at Joliet for complicity in the hold up of the Stockyards Trust and Savings Bank. Spike, a deeply religious man who was invariably at Sunday mass at St. Peter's Catholic Church, had twice been tried for murder and had been accused of half a dozen other killings. Upon the petition of six State Senators, five State Representatives and a judge of Cook County Criminal Court, the governor, moved presumably by such a demonstration of charity in high places, paroled Spike O'Donnell.

Until then the other three O'Donnell brothers had been hangers-on of the Torrio-Capone gang, lower-echelon courtiers of the Four Deuces assembly, grateful for any casual labour – the terrorizing of saloon keepers, the collecting of dues – tossed over to them. Spike's return to circulation dramatically changed the situation. Unprovided for in the Torrio territorial alignment, the freed leader set about muscling into the profits by force of personality.

This was 1923 and an unexpected development had gravely disrupted Torrio's plan. In one of its brief spasms of reformist fervour, Chicago had voted out Big Bill Thomson from the mayoralty and elected William E. Dever. The system of protection collapsed. Suddenly no one could tell to whom bribes could safely be paid – and, if they were paid, if they would stick. Who was 'in'? Who was 'out'? No one knew for sure. In the resulting confusion, many ambitious and hitherto disenfranchised criminals grabbed the chance of invading the beer business, and among them were the South Side O'Donnells. Spike, arrogantly cutting across the old concessions, forced his services upon South Side saloons and speakeasies in the Stockyards and New City districts which were administered by Joe Saltis and Frank McErlane. He imported a renowned ace gun-man from New York, Henry Hasmiller, engaged a dozen paroled convicts as truck-drivers, bodyguards and liquor-salesmen, and began ambushing and robbing Torrio's consignments. And he sold better, less diluted, beer than Torrio's. Torrio, still cautious about unleashing too much publicity-attracting thuggery, retaliated on a commercial level by cutting his price per barrel by ten dollars. The O'Donnells, less concerned with finesse of technique, answered this by wrecking saloons and beating-up proprietors who, hideously sandwiched between the two rams' heads, lied, switched, and bought from both. Not all submitted to the new contestants for their trade. Jacob Geis, who ran a speakeasy on 2154 West Fifty-first Street, was with his bar-tender, Nicholas Gorysko, serving half a dozen customers early in the evening of 7 September 1923 when Steve, Walter and Tommy O'Donnell, accompanied by George Bucher, George Meeghan and Jerry O'Connor entered. Geis, a stubborn tradesman said flatly that he was continuing to buy Torrio-Capone beer. He was dragged across the counter and beaten almost to death; Gorysko was knocked unconscious.

This was the night of the naked outbreak of the booze war. The O'Donnell gang were out on a determined sweep of all recalcitrant saloon-keepers. From Geis's bar they went on to raid five more which were still selling their rivals' supplies, and then rounded off the night at Joseph Klepka's speakeasy at 5358 South Lincoln Street, one of their neighbourhood encampments, where they joined Spike O' Donnell for beer and sandwiches. Also abroad that night was a squad of Torrio-Capone enforcers led by McErlane and Daniel McFall (who carried the useful credentials of deputy sheriff) who were patrolling the South Side in search of O'Donnell salesmen. For a while Torrio had allowed the O'Donnells' strong-arm methods to prevail, and, in Spike's own words, they had built up 'a nice little business'. It was not to flourish for long. Subtlety having failed, Torrio cannily incited Saltis and McErlane to hit back. They found their opportunity when they burst into the Klepka bar and surprised the O'Donnell group, relaxed and reminiscing about the evening's *blitzkrieg*. Six locals playing cards in a back room later described what happened then. McFall shouted: 'Stick up your hands or I'll blow you to hell' and discharged a warning bullet from his ·38 over Spike's head. That did not stop the O'Donnell men. They scattered. Guns roared. The lights went out. All escaped through side and rear doors except O'Connor, a young South Side tough and a paroled Joliet lifer. He was seized by McFall and pushed out into the street. As he stepped out of the doorway a fifth man 'short and stocky, wearing a grey raincoat and carrying a sawn-off double-barrelled shot-gun' – which fairly certainly identified him as McErlane – blew off the side of his head.

Torrio evidently did not consider that the lesson had been pointed enough. Ten days later Meeghan and Bucher were driving in a roadster south along Laflin Street and halted at the Garfield Boulevard junction to allow cross-traffic through. A green touring car slid alongside, and Meeghan and Bucher were blasted to death by a close-range discharge of revolvers and shot-guns.

Dever, angry and shocked by this barefaced street killing only six months after he had taken office to put a stop to the eye-winking leniency of the Thompson régime, acted. He suspended Captain Thomas Wolfe, of the New City police precinct in which the three murders had been committed, and who had freed McFall after arrest for questioning. He revoked the licences of two thousand soft drink parlours with speakeasies at the back. He extracted from the Republican State's Attorney Robert E. Crowe a promise of 'a relentless investigation of the beer war'. He summoned Chief of Police Morgan A. Collins and Chief Detective Hughes to inform them that he was assuming personal direction of the investigation. He issued this statement: 'Until the murderers of Jerry O'Connor and the murderers of these two men have been apprehended and punished, and the illegal traffic for control of which they battle has been suppressed, the dignity of the law and the average man's repect for it is imperilled, and every officer of the law and every enforcing agency should lay aside other duties and join in the common cause – a restoration of law and order. The police will follow this case to a finish as they do all others. This guerilla war between hijackers, rum runners and illicit beer pedlars can and will be crushed. I am just as sure that this miserable traffic with its toll of human life and morals can be stamped out as I am that I am mayor, and I am not going to flinch for a minute.'

That was a resounding, patently sincere declaration of intentions and principles. But neither Mayor Dever nor anyone else could at that point know how feebly ineffectual such principles were to prove and how often they were to flinch before what was coming – an unrestrained savagery of a kind never before visited upon a modern city, a civil war that was to be fought out in the sight of the public whose cynicism and demands were its warrant.

The law went into motion. Capone was questioned and paraded for identification before the O'Donnells, who maintained the understanding between the fraternity by shaking their heads in non-recognition. The only fresh information that the authorities derived was that Capone now had a permit to carry a gun, issued to him by a justice of the peace.

A call went out for Torrio, but he was not at hand. He had gone to attend a wake, explained his attorney, Michael L. Igoe, who, sponsored by George E. Brennan, Democratic party boss in Illinois and State Representative, was a commissioner of Chicago's South Parks Board and three years previously had run for the office of State's Attorney with the militant plea that 'crime must be voted out, criminals must be speedily prosecuted, and the home must be safe-guarded'. After a long discussion with the State's Attorney, Igoe produced his client, who was submitted to some intensive but inconclusive interrogation about bootlegging.

Dever persisted and finally, after much devious stalling, Daniel McFall was indicted for the O'Connor killing. McFall was sent for trial in January 1924. He was, with little delay, acquitted. He admitted that he had been present in Klepka's bar on the night of the gun-battle, but pointed out that he was at the time carrying a ·38 calibre gun, which could not have caused the damage to O'Connor. He and two of his colleagues were also indicted for the Meeghan-Bucher murders, but when the O'Connor case failed the charges were *nolle prossed* and the accused were released from custody without being tried.

4

The Old-Fashioned O'Donnells

"I can whip this bird Capone with bare fists."
SPIKE O'DONNELL

THESE tiresome legal formalities did not inhibit the pursuance of the main objective: the struggle for booze-territory and its revenue. The O'Donnells fought on. The Torrio-Capone gang struck and struck again. Quicker than Dever could issue more statements about stamping out the guerilla war, the bodies piled up in the gutters and ditches of Greater Chicago. Before McFall could be brought to trial, on the night of 1 December Morrie Keane and Shorty Egan, two more members of the O'Donnell gang, were dispatched to bring in a load of beer from Joliet. On a quiet stretch of highway near the Sag Canal the truck was intercepted by a car containing McErlane and a party of Torrio gunmen. The hijackers were hijacked. The lorry was turned over to the custody of some trusty police patrolmen who obligingly escorted the beer on its way into Chicago. Keane and Egan were placed in the McErlane car and taken for another of those rides which were becoming increasingly familiar to newspaper readers. Next morning they were discovered, hands lashed behind back and filled with shot-gun pellets, in a ditch; Keane was dead, Egan seriously wounded.

McErlane was arrested next day, held briefly by State's Attorney Crowe in the Sherman Hotel, and then turned loose. After some reluctant shuffling, Crowe (who recently had made that fiery oath to carry out 'relentless investigation of the beer war'), under pressure, laid the case before the grand jury, and an indictment was voted. Long inexplicable – or perhaps entirely explicable – delays followed. Months later an Assistant State's Attorney went into court and *nolle prossed* the case. McErlane took a holiday out of Chicago, without a smear upon his recorded character.

Once again, these events had not been occupying the absorbed attention of the opposed powers, nor interfering with the business of keeping the booze and blood flowing. Torrio now had the

O'Donnells back-tracked against the wall, out-gunned and out-smarted. He continued to strike at the exposed flanks of their crumbling army. Early in 1924 Phillip Corrigan, an O'Donnell driver, was bringing a beer truck into town and was slain in his seat by a shot-gun charge. Next, Walter O'Donnell and Hasmiller, the crack New York sharpshooter, were trapped in a roadhouse at Evergreen Park, a suburb south of Chicago, and shot to death.

In the meantime Torrio gunmen had made ten separate attacks upon Spike O'Donnell and wounded him. During one of his visits to the detective bureau for questioning about the warfare, Spike, bitterly unhappy at the clear prospect of imminent defeat, burst out: 'I can whip this bird Capone with bare fists any time he wants to step in the open and fight like a man.'

The time of knuckledusters and dance-hall brawls, in which the O'Donnells had been reared, had passed. Capone and his corps were fighting by the new formula, using the weight, power, accuracy and terrorization of weapons improved by the experience of the Great War, the methods of army strategy and the newly available mobility of the fast car. The O'Donnells were out of date and out of place, about to be evicted by the modern men who were in this for business and not for street-corner fanfaronade. During the autumn of 1923, following Mayor Dever's proclamation, there were nine gang-killings, and with seven of his men slaughtered, Spike O'Donnell threw in his claim to the South Side, abandoned his 'nice little business' and left Chicago. (He returned a year later, apparently reached an agreement with Capone, resumed bootlegging on a reduced scale and also crashed into the wholesale coal business, in which capacity, despite his long police record and his place on the Crime Commission's list of public enemies, he obtained through the offices of political friends a contract to supply coal to City departments.) During the remainder of Mayor Dever's term gang carnage flared more fiercely. In 1924 sixteen men were shot to death; in 1925, forty-six; in 1926, Dever's final year, seventy-six. Of this total of 138 gang killings only six men were to be brought to trial. Of those six all were to be acquitted except one – Sam Vinci, who pushed public settlement of quarrels a little too far. He drew a ·45 automatic during an inquest on his brother Mike and shot John Minatti dead, his explanation being that it had begun to look as if the jury were going to set Minatti free, and he did not wish this to happen. Vinci went to Joliet Penitentiary for twenty-five years.

The war between Torrio and the O'Donnells was only one aspect of the struggle for supremacy. Simultaneously guns were exploding in other parts of Chicago. Cicero had fallen to the insurgents. Torrio moved in there in the autumn of 1923 and shortly afterwards went off with his family on a European sightseeing trip, taking with him more than a million dollars' worth of negotiable securities and letters of credit, which he deposited in Continental banks as a nest-egg for any conceivable future emergency; and also taking his aging mother, whom he established in her native Italy, leaving her to spend her twilight years in a coastal estate with fifteen servants and a chauffeur-driven limousine, the richest grande dame in the province. During his six months' absence the settling and organization of Cicero was left in the hands of Capone, by now emerging as the cleverest, coolest and most ruthlessly ambitious of the Torrio eaglets. Capone had under his command an army of seven hundred troops, twenty per cent of whom were aliens and thirty per cent paroled convicts. (The Board of Pardons and Paroles freed 950 felons in less than three years.) Among these were a nucleus of the most lethally expert gunmen in the United States, including McErlane, McFall and Walter Stevens. Stevens was an exceptional man, if only that he survived to be able to retire at the age of fifty-seven in 1924. He came to prominence in the early years of the century as a colleague of Mossy Enright, a goon-squad leader who specialized in bombing and beating jobs on behalf of organizing labour in the industrial wars, when the unions fought back against the employers' private strike-breaking armies with the same methods. Enright himself had been shot down in February 1920 by Sunny Jim Cosmano, a Black Hand extortionist who tried to blackmail Big Jim Colosimo and who was consequently one of the original reasons why Colosimo brought Torrio to Chicago. During Stevens's service with Enright he was widely acknowledged as the trigger-man in half a dozen killings – including that of Peter Gentlemen, a policeman's son turned gunman. Stevens was at one unfortunate point imprisoned in Aurora, Illinois, for the murder of a policeman – but he was promptly pardoned by the infinitely munificent Governor Small in return for assistance during the Governor's trial for malfeasance. Stevens was of similar cast to Torrio, gracious, quiet, decorous. For twenty years he cared devotedly for an invalid wife, adopted three children and gave them good educations. He had severely ascetic standards. He would not permit his adopted daughters to use lipsick or wear short skirts, and bowdlerized the classics before admitting them to his house. He inveighed against the unwholesomeness of the theatre and against the laxity of morals of the Scott Fitzgerald youth. He did not drink and never smoked until he was fifty. His rate for a murder was fifty dollars and for roughing up a man twenty dollars.

With such a dependably solid and serious servant as Stevens to keep order elsewhere, Capone, under instructions from Torrio, consolidated the occupation of Cicero. The infiltration had been done, according to established Torrio stratagem. He had previously circumspectly avoided this suburb of fifty thousand population, Illinois's fifth largest town and one of the state's most prosperous manufacturing centres. This was because it was already tightly organized. Relatively speaking, it was a clean-living community. There were no brothels and there was no gambling – apart from, that is, the chain of slot-machines owned by a local politician named Eddie Vogel. As elsewhere, the saloons remained open and wet after Prohibition began, and the bootlegging was supervised by Klondike and Myles O'Donnell but, being more consistent Catholics than the Sicilians, they abhorred prostitution and would not dabble in brothel-keeping. Supported by the O'Donnells and by Eddie Tancl, a Bohemian saloon-owner who commanded the votes of the foreign-born, Vogel dominated the city government which was nominally headed by Mayor Joseph Z. Klenha.

This was a formidable fortress of shared spoils to break into, yet the temptation of so much ripe fruit going unplucked was too great to be resisted. Before taking his European holiday, Torrio leased a house on Roosevelt Road in Cicero, put in a stable of whores, and deliberately made no attempt to secure protection; the police arrested the women and closed it down. Torrio took another house at Ogden and Fifty-second Avenues. It was raided and closed. Torrio pulled the strings that linked him with loftier political power than the Cicero chieftains could reach, and two days later a posse of deputy sheriffs swept through Cicero collecting on their way every slot machine in town.

It was the kind of enacted allegory that pleased Torrio. The situation was made theatrically manifest: if he was stopped from installing prostitutes in Cicero, no one else was going to operate slot machines. An approach was made to him, and Torrio met and talked to Vogel and the O'Donnell brothers. A working arrangement was arrived at, and again Torrio showed the flexibility of his diplomacy by conceding to the O'Donnells' antipathy towards prostitution. He agreed not to open brothels – a promise he broke later when he was sufficiently powerful to do so – and the treaty provided for the return of Vogel's slot machines, for the O'Donnells' exclusive beer-selling rights in the Roosevelt Road and other zones, and for their continued unmolested possession of that section of Chicago's West Side they already held. Torrio's benefit under the deal was freedom to open gambling parlours and night clubs, and to sell his beer anywhere in the town outside the O'Donnells' territory.

It no doubt at the time seemed to Vogel and the O'Donnells the only hard-headed way of dealing with the importuning of these frightening Sicilians – to admit them and then hold them to their undertaking. But they sadly miscalculated both the rapacity and the ruthlessness of Torrio and Capone. The Cicero bosses were tough, experienced politicians and quasi-racketeers, but when they opened the door they were in the position of sheep entertaining dragons. For the first few months Capone worked quietly with only a minimum of gun-fire, getting the beer trade running smoothly – 161 bars were soon open day and night, without any silly pretence at concealment.

Then the fattest fruit of all fell into Capone's ready hands. It was delivered by Ed Konvalinka, the proprietor of a Cicero soda fountain who was also a small but ascending star in Republican politics. A goodwill-beaver, Konvalinka had already ingratiated himself with the state political machine by his local campaigning and friend-winning activities, and he had worked his way upward from precinct captain to ward-leader, most recently having been appointed by Governor Small as Republican committee man from Cicero. With Dever running a Democratic administration in Chicago, there was an obvious danger that Cicero might be caught up in the reformist wave and unseat the Republican faction who had for six years been in control of Cicero's politics and saloons. Konvalinka conceived the idea of organizing the Republican ticket for Cicero in the forthcoming April election with the assistance of the Capone mob. The candidates were to be Klenha for Mayor, Frank Houchek for Town Clerk, T. J. Buckley for Town Collector and Edward J. Carmody for Town Attorney. The proposition was to be that if Capone could clinch their election by using his power of persuasion he would in return receive guarantee of free action in Cicero; Konvalinka's reward would be enhanced stock with the state political bosses. Konvalinka talked this over with Vogel, who thought it a sound scheme; he made the first overtures to Louis La Cava, a Capone go-between; La Cava put the proposal to Capone, and arranged a meeting with Konvalinka. The deal was settled. Capone, seeing the size of the potential prize, made his plans to ensure that his side of the bargain was met. Preparations began for what was to be the most melodramatically rigged election in the by no means scanty annals of American political history, one which was so monstrously and flamboyantly crooked, for all the world to see, that, despite the unamusing force and fear that made it a day of infamy in Cicero and in the whole of the United States, it came to within a degree of being a sombre joke.

5

'When you smell Gunpowder you're in Cicero'

'I own the police.'　　　　　　　　JOHNNY TORRIO

THERE are difficulties here for the British reader attempting to do a mental transposition and imagining a borough council election in, say, Windsor or Wolverhampton or Wisbech, with smoking pistols around the polling booths, battles of bullets between police and carloads of plug-uglies, voters pummelled, intimidated and press-ganged. But this is exactly what happened in April 1924 in this respectable lower middle-class American suburb, where sixty-eight per cent of citizens owned their own homes, with its Rotary and Kiwani clubs, its Chamber of Commerce and its ministers' association. The Illinois Crime Survey recorded: 'Automobiles filled with gunmen paraded the streets slugging and kidnapping election workers. Polling places were raided by armed thugs and ballots taken at the point of the gun from the hands of voters waiting to drop them in the box. Voters and workers were kidnapped, taken to Chicago and held prisoners until the polls closed.' The previous night Torrio, just back from his overseas holiday tour, had summoned his lieutenants to plan their campaign. Al and his brother Frank were appointed to direct the electioneering. At dawn the Torrio army moved into the town, took up their positions and turned on the heat. Each voter was asked by men in slouch hats and with guns stuck in their belts how he was casting his vote. If it was unsuitable he was advised to change his mind and stood over while he placed his cross on the correct line. Those who argued or refused were roughed up and thrown out, or shoved in cars and driven off. By early afternoon, Cicero was in a state of mixed rage and panic. The Democrat committee – backed by outraged Republican voters – appealed to Chicago for help. County Judge Edmund K. Jarecki swore in seventy policemen as deputy sheriffs and they were rushed out to Cicero by car. They opened fire on Torrio cars, and the gangsters shot back. A police squad under Detective-Sergeant William Cusick swung round a corner at Cicero Avenue and Twenty-second Street, and saw Al and Frank Capone, Dave Hedlin and Charley Fischetti standing at the door of a polling station with drawn pistols in their hands, ushering voters inside. As the police jumped out and ran across the road, Frank Capone shot at Patrolman McGlynn and missed. McGlynn fired back and mortally wounded Frank. Hedlin fell wounded. Fischetti was pursued into a field and captured unhurt. Al fled down Cicero Avenue and almost into the arms of another band of policemen. He fought them off, a gun flaming in each hand, and escaped into the darkness. During the day a man was killed in Eddie Tancl's saloon, two others shot dead in Twenty-second Street, another man's throat cut, and a policeman blackjacked. Four dead and forty wounded; Klenha and his clique were re-elected with immense majorities.

There was, of course, the customary inquest. County Judge Jarecki was appointed to conduct 'an investigation of bloodshed and riots in the election', and the State's Attorney's office devoted much time into inquiring how Capone and his troops had acquired pistol permits. Most, it transpired, had been issued by suburban justices of the peace. Capone was never arrested for his part in this sinister fantasy. He was, in any case, occupied with grief. In commemoration of the late departed Frank Capone every saloon and gambling resort in Cicero was requested to close and draw down its blinds for two hours. Capone appeared at his brother's inquest, but stated that he had no information of value to impart. Frank was given a splendid funeral, his body cradled in a silk-lined silver-plated casket and heaped with twenty thousand dollars' worth of flowers.

The keening faded and the chiming of the cash registers swelled again in the Cicero streets. The election had left an aftermath of scores for settlement. Capone, with a civic administration committed to his welfare, was the dragon emperor of Cicero. The conciliatory smile vanished from his face and he blew fire through his nostrils. Tancl, owner of the Hawthorne Inn, who had been a power in the old liaison, was the first to feel the lash of the new tyranny. He was an ex-boxer with cauliflower ears and a spread-eagled nose, a man of notorious brutality and evil temper. From the start he had refused to knuckle under to the insurgents or to buy their beer. He was told either to co-operate or depart, and his answer was that he wasn't going to co-operate, he was going to stay, and if he left he would leave in a coffin. He did.

The impasse had been overcome by a visit from Myles O'Donnell – who with his brother had malleably accepted the changed situation – and a gunman named James J. Doherty. After picking a quarrel over a meal bill, they opened fire on Tancl in front of the Hawthorne

Inn, while shopping housewives and local tradesmen threw them-selved behind cars and into doorways in the horizontal position that was becoming an identifiable posture of Cicero citizens. Tancl stood square where he was, snatched a gun from his arm-pit holster and exchanged shot for shot. He slumped down riddled, but flung his emptied gun in O'Donnell's face and yelled at Leo Klimas, one of his waiters who was at his side: 'Kill that rat. He got me.' Klimas, already wounded, leaped at O'Donnell but Doherty put a bullet in his back.

O'Donnell and Doherty were arrested, indicted and acquitted. The Assistant State's Attorney who prosecuted the case – and failed to send them to their death – was young William H. McSwiggin who had interviewed Capone a year earlier about the Howard murder.

Capone, hating to see a good business stand idle, took over Tancl's Hawthorne Inn and made it his local garrison and headquarters. He had the entire upper floor equipped as suite and office for himself, with bullet-proof steel shutters fitted at the windows and doors. It became the favourite discreet rendezvous of Chicago and Cook County politicians, where they were entertained – and instructed – by Capone. The character of Cicero underwent swift change. It came to be said that if you wanted to know when you had crossed the parish boundary from Chicago into Cicero all you had to do was raise your nose into the wind and sniff. 'If you smell gunpowder, you're there.' The erstwhile pleasantly placid suburb became Gangsters' Town.

'The one-time peaceful streets of down-town Cicero', wrote Asbury, 'were filled with arrogant, roistering, swaggering gangsters, and crowded with saloons and gambling-houses.' The centre was transformed into a neon-flashing inland Barbary Coast. Immediately next to the elevated railway terminal station, convenient for sports running out from Chicago for an evening's whoopee, was The Ship, run by Toots Mondi on behalf of the Torrio-Capone combine, a dance-hall with cabaret performing from midnight until dawn, and upstairs gambling parlours offering craps, poker, stush and faro. Near by was Lauterback's, with a big saloon in front and roulette wheels upstairs, which was the casino with the biggest turnover in the country, as much as 100 thousand dollars on the table for one spin of the wheel. In the Hawthorne Smoke Shop was a betting counter managed by Frankie Pope where fifty thousand dollars a day was bet on horse races. Available, too, were the Hawthorne Kennel Club dog-tracks, a 500 thousand dollar enterprise, with a stable of four hundred greyhounds controlled by Capone, and the 160 wide-open night-and-day bars, now and then subjected to a formalistic raid by the Federal Prohibition Department. But, after a day's token closing, they were open again. A saloon-keeper explained: 'When the cops and the Prohibition agents come here after hours all the time to get drunk, why, of course, they go along with us. They always tip us off to the raids. An injunction means nothing. When the owner of a place is caught by one he opens up somewhere else under another name.'

Whisky was sold in Cicero for seventy-five cents a shot, beer for thirty-five cents a stein, wine for thirty cents a small glass. Installed in every establishment not wholly owned by the Capone-Torrio combine was one of their agents, whose wages had to be paid by the proprietor and whose duties were to see that the place was 'protected' and that the combine got its cut of the gross receipts, which varied from twenty-five to fifty per cent. Capone and Torrio were taking 100 thousand dollars a week each out of Cicero. Capone, enjoying his first taste of total power, ruled the town through his gunmen despotically. Mayor Klenha and his circle dispiritedly endured what they had brought upon themselves. Now, it was Capone's voice that was listened to: his orders transcended law. Police, city officials and local businessmen took instructions direct from the Hawthorne Inn. Once when Klenha had failed to carry out a command, Capone paid him a personal call, knocked him down the steps of the City Hall and kicked him repeatedly as he scrambled up. A policeman stood watching the assault, twirled his night-stick and strolled off. Again, when the town council rebelliously tried to put through a measure which Capone had vetoed, his strong-arm men shouldered into the chamber, broke up the meeting, dragged one of the trustees into the street and blackjacked him. Robert St. John, editor of the Cicero *Tribune*, who bravely continued to print anti-Capone editorials, and who interfered when a policeman was being dealt out a disciplinary beating, was coshed, kicked and had his face smashed in by a squad led by Ralph Capone. His brother, Archer St. John, editor of the neighbouring Berwyn *Tribune*, who wrote leaders protesting against the invasion of Torrio's prostitutes and gangsters, during the election was shot from a car, kidnapped and held prisoner until the polls closed.

The name of Capone was becoming famous and feared. Chicago coach companies began running sightseeing tours out to Cicero, with 'Capone Castle' – the Hawthorne Inn – on the itinerary.

Early in his career in Chicago, during the five years before

Prohibition began, Torrio had looked far beyond Colosimo's constricted horizons, bound by the First Ward boundaries, and seen the harvest in harlotry offered by the 932 square miles of Cook County. He surveyed the industrial towns of East and South Chicago Heights, Calumet City, Hammond, Gary, Whiting and Burnham, with their big working-men populations employed by the oil refineries and steel plants, and here he spread a chain of cheap cribs and dance-hall brothels. He also foresaw the profound social change that the automobile was to bring about, and at cross-roads on the bleak prairie highways he set up his first roadhouses with gambling, prostitutes and music for the Stutz-Bearcat crowd, the new species of four-wheeled reveller and girl-friend who liked the excitement and anonymity of driving out into the dark country to an oasis of bright lights. After the fall of Cicero, Torrio's daring increased and he inaugurated suburban brothels by adding to his Cook County chain of twenty-five a whole reservation of them in Stickney, adjoining Cicero, which, although strictly not infringing his promise to the O'Donnells, served as auxiliary recreational facilities to the Cicero gambling and drinking dens. The Stickney stockade was composed of a dozen houses containing five hundred whores, who, when police confiscated the ledgers in a 1926 raid, were revealed to be earning the combine five thousand dollars a week. The Barn, the Burnham Inn and the Arrowhead Inn, at Burnham, the first of Torrio's renowned 'Fifty Girl Houses', earned fifteen thousand dollars profit a month. These were just two of the districts.

The joint income of Torrio and Capone was soaring deliriously. Account books seized from Torrio's office on Michigan Avenue recorded profits of three million dollars a year from beer, whisky and wine, and this, again, was merely one aspect of the combine's liquor business. The police estimated that the gang's total annual profits from the manufacture and sale of liquor were at least thirty million dollars, and Edwin A. Alson, United States District Attorney, assessed that by the mid-'twenties Torrio and Capone were collecting gross profits of seventy million dollars a year.

Torrio had vice packaged and sealed under his name. As well as selling liquor, he was, in collaboration with his concealed business-men partners, operating distilleries and breweries, and supplementing their production with supplies brought in from Canada and the Atlantic seaboard by truck, car, aeroplane, and launch. His fleets of armed lorries thundered regular as buses through the city and county streets, distributing booze to at least three-quarters of the twenty thousand speakeasies. Except for the occasional hijacking –

and after the crushing of the South Side O'Donnells there were few free-lances willing to risk defying the Torrio-Capone gang – they went on their way untrammelled. Indeed, when a specially valuable cargo was coming in, uniformed police outriders were detailed as escort.

Such immunity was costly, but the syndicate could afford it. Thirty thousand dollars a week was distributed in hush-money, much of it being paid over the counter each Friday in a downtown office to the queue of policemen, civic officials and Prohibition agents. Other payments went more subtly, but as regularly, to judges, politicians and high administrators. There were also the huge contributions to political campaign funds. 'In circles close to Capone,' reported the Illinois Crime Survey, 'it was well known that he had contributed substantially to the Thompson campaign,' and the Commission's president, Frank J. Loesch, put the sum at 260 thousand dollars. Not all public officials were to be bought. Morgan Collins, police chief from 1923 to 1927, rejected an offer of a thousand dollars a day for ignoring Torrio's activities. William F. Waugh, United States District Attorney, was offered fifty thousand dollars to drop the prosecution of a group of Torrio men accused of violation of the Volstead Act. E. C. Yellowley, Federal Prohibition Administrator for Illinois, refused 250 thousand dollars in return for abandoning closing-down proceedings against a distillery. But such isolated examples of honesty were nullified by the alacrity at every lower level – and on higher levels. When Torrio said simply on one occasion: 'I own the police', he was speaking the practical truth. Despite irritating checks during Dever's term of office, during the three terms of William Hale Thompson, Capone and Torrio ran and directed the political, police and Federal enforcement agencies of Chicago and Cook County.

6

Votes in the Pistol-pocket

'To hell with them Sicilians.' DION O'BANION

AT this time, in the mid-'twenties, the whole of Greater Chicago
seemed to have fallen into the hands of brigands. It resembled
a Caribbean pirates' island of the 1700s. Apart from the
ramifications of the new merchant millionaire gangs, the criminal
lumpen proletariat exploited the widespread breakdown of police
morality and law-enforcement. Crime, petty and not so petty,
proliferated. As many as two hundred hold-ups were reported any
night. Bank robberies became monotonously common. Whole
sections of the city were burgled systematically. Rich families
employed their personal bodyguards. Cars were stolen in monthly
thousands. Recalls Asbury: 'Chicago seemed to be filled with gangsters – gangsters slaughtering one another; gangsters shooting up
saloons for amusement; gangsters throwing bombs; gangsters
speeding in big automobiles, ignoring traffic laws; gangsters strutting
in the Loop, holstered pistols scarcely concealed; gangsters giving
orders to the police, to judges, to prosecutors, all sworn to uphold the
law; gangsters dining in expensive restaurants; tuxedoed gangsters
at the opera and the theatre, their mink-coated, Paris-gowned wives
or sweethearts on their arms; gangsters giving parties at which the
guests playfully doused each other with champagne at twenty
dollars a bottle, popping a thousand corks in a single evening;
gangsters armed with shotguns, rifles and machine-guns convoying
beer trucks; gangsters everywhere – except in jail. "It's all newspaper talk", said Big Bill Thompson, Mayor of Chicago.'

His riches, his eminence, his security must have seemed to Torrio,
now sixty, the proper reward for his acumen and adroitness. But the
halcyon times were running out, and the agent of Torrio's coming
misfortune was a thirty-two year old swashbuckling Irishman named
Dion O'Banion. By ironical logical sequence, Torrio and Capone
had made the same error as that made by the Cicero junta in
allowing the gang to get toehold in the town's administration. As part
of the same arrangement, Torrio had, in the spirit of peace and

67

goodwill, and in exchange for armed support in the April election campaign, bestowed upon O'Banion a third share in the Hawthorne Smoke Shop proceeds and a cut in the Cicero beer trade. The coalition was to prove inadvisable.

O'Banion was a complex and frightening man, whose bright blue eyes stared with a kind of frozen candour into others'. He had a round, frank Irish face, creased in a jovial grin that stayed bleakly in place even when he was pumping bullets into someone's body. He carried three guns – one in the right trouser pocket, one under his left armpit, one in the left outside coat pocket – and was equally lethal with both hands. He killed accurately, freely and dispassionately. The police credited him with twenty-five murders but he was never brought to trial for one of them. Like a fair number of bootleggers he disliked alcohol. He was an expert florist, tenderly dextrous in the arrangement of bouquets and wreaths. He had no apparent comprehension of morality; he divided humanity into 'right guys' and 'wrong guys', and the wrong ones he was always willing to kill and trample under. He had what was described by a psychologist as a 'sunny brutality'. He walked with a heavy list to the right, as that leg was four inches shorter than the other, but the lurch did not reduce his feline quickness with his guns. Landesco thought him 'just a superior sort of plugugly' but he was, in fact, with his aggression and hostility, and nerveless indifference to risking or administering pain, a case-book psychopath. He was also at this time, although not so interwoven in high politics and the rackets as Torrio and Capone, the most powerful and most dangerous mob-leader in the Chicago underworld, the roughneck king.

O'Banion was born in poverty, the son of an immigrant Irish plasterer, in the North Side's Little Hell, close by the Sicilian quarter and Death Corner. He had been choir boy at the Holy Name Cathedral and also served as an acolyte to Father O'Brien. The influence of mass was less pervasive than that of the congested slum tenements among the bawdy houses, honkytonks and sawdust saloons of his birthplace; he ran wild with the child gangs of the neighbourhood, and went through the normal pressure-cooker course of thieving, police-dodging and house-breaking. At the age of ten, when he was working as a newsboy in the Loop, he was knocked down by a street car which resulted in his permanently shortened leg. Because of this he was known as Gimpy (but, as with Capone and his nickname of Scarface, never in his presence). In his 'teens O'Banion was enrolled in the vicious Market Street gang and he became a singing waiter in McGovern's Cafe, a notoriously low and rowdy dive in North Clark Street, where befuddled customers were methodically looted of their money by the singing waiters before being thrown out. He then got a job with the Chicago *Herald and Examiner* as a circulation slugger, a rough fighter employed to see that his paper's news-pitches were not trespassed upon by rival vendors. He was also at the same time gaining practical experience as a safe-breaker and highwayman, and learning how to shoot to kill from a Neanderthal convicted murderer named Gene Geary, later committed to Chester Asylum as a homicidal maniac, but whose eyes misted with tears when the young Dion sang a ballad about an Irish mother in his clear and syrupy tenor.

O'Banion's first conflict with the police came in 1909, at seventeen, when he was committed to Bridewell Prison for three months for burglary; two years later he served another three months for assault. These were his only interludes behind bars, although he collected four more charges on his police record in 1921 and 1922, three for burglary and one for robbery. But by now O'Banion's political pull was beginning to be effective. On the occasion of his 1922 indictment the ten thousand dollars bond was furnished by an alderman, and the charge was *nolle prossed*. On one of his 1921 ventures he was actually come upon by a Detective-Sergeant John J. Ryan down on his knees with a tool embedded in a labour office safe in the Postal Telegraph Building; the jury wanted better evidence than that and he was acquitted, at a cost of thirty thousand dollars in bribes, it was estimated. As promptly as Torrio, O'Banion jumped into bootlegging. He conducted it with less diplomacy and more spontaneous violence than the Sicilians, but he had his huge North Side portion to exploit and he made a great deal of money. Unlike the Sicilians, he additionally conducted hold-ups, robberies and safe-cracking expeditions, and refused to touch prostitution. He was also personally active in ward politics, and by 1924 O'Banion had acquired sufficient political might to be able to state: 'I always deliver my borough as per requirements.'

But whose requirements? Until 1924 O'Banion pistoleers and knuckleduster bullyboys had kept his North Side domain solidly Democrat. There was a question-and-answer gag that went around at that time: Q. 'Who'll carry Forty-second and Forty-third wards?' A. 'O'Banion, in his pistol pocket.' But as November 1924 drew close the Democrat hierarchy was sorely troubled by grapevine reports that O'Banion was being wooed by the opposition, and was meeting and conferring with important Republicans. To forestall any change

of allegiance, the Democrats hastily organized a testimonial banquet
for O'Banion, as public reward for his past services and as a reminder
of where his loyalties lay.

The reception was held in a private dining-room of the Webster
Hotel on Lincoln Park West. It was an interesting fraternization of
ex-convicts, jobbers, murderers, union racketeers, gerrymanders,
gangsters, ward heelers, sold-out officials and gunmen. The guest list
is in itself a little parable of the state of American civic life at this
time. It included the top O'Banion men, Gusenberg, Drucci,
Moran, Weiss, Eisen and Alterie, who was additionally president
of the Theatre and Building Janitors' Union; William Scott Stewart,
a former Assistant State's Attorney; Colonel Albert A. Sprague,
Harvard graduate, a rich and eminent Chicagoan who was commissioner of public works in the Dever administration and Democratic nominee for United States Senator against Charles S. Deneen;
County Clerk Robert M. Sweitzer, defeated candidate for mayor of
Chicago on the Democratic ticket in 1911, 1915 and 1919; Cornelius
P. Con Shea, ex-Sing Sing inmate for the attempted murder of a
woman, Teamsters' strike-leader when twenty-one men were killed
and 416 injured, acquitted of murdering Police Lieutenant Terence
Lyons, and secretary of the Theatre and Building Janitors' Union;
Chief of Detectives Michael Hughes; Police Lieutenant Charles
Egan; Jerry O'Connor, Loop gambling-house proprietor and vice-
president of the Theatre and Building Janitors' Union (not the South
Side O'Donnells's Jerry O'Connor); and many other police officials
and lower-echelon politicians. They all – bootleggers and theoretical
upholders of Prohibition – drank much whisky, wine and beer in that
room decorated with paper streamers in the national colours.

When Mayor Dever heard of the banquet he summoned Hughes
for an explanation of why he had been dishonouring the police
department by consorting with these felons and fixers. Hughes said
that he had understood the party was to be in honour of O'Connor.
'But when I arrived and recognized a number of notorious characters
I had thrown into the detective bureau basement half a dozen times,
I knew I had been framed, and withdrew almost at once.'

In fact, O'Connor was honoured during the ceremony with the
presentation of a 2,500 dollar diamond stick pin. There was a brief
interruption while Alterie jerked out both his guns and threatened to
shoot a waiter who was pestering him for a tip. Then, after perora-
tions by Colonel Sprague and County Clerk Sweitzer, O'Banion was
presented with a platinum watch set with rubies and diamonds.

This dinner was the start of a new blatancy in the relationship between the gangs and the politicians, which, prior to 1924, says Pasley, 'had been maintained with more or less stealth', but which henceforth was marked by these ostentatious gatherings, denounced by a clergyman as 'Belshazzar feasts', at which 'politicians fraternized cheek by jowl with gangsters, openly, in the big downtown hotels'. Pasley continued: 'They became an institution of the Chicago scene and marked the way to the moral and financial collapse of the municipal and county governments in 1928-9.'

However, this inaugural feast did its sponsors no good whatever. O'Banion accepted his platinum watch and tributes to his loyalty, and proceeded with the bigger and better Republican deal. On election day – 4 November – he energetically marshalled his force of bludgeon-men, bribers and experts in forging repeat votes. The result was a landslide for the Republican candidates. In the Forty-second Ward Colonel Sprague was beaten by United States Senator Charles S. Deneen with a majority of 5,938. In the Forty-third Ward State's Attorney Robert E. Crowe had a majority of 9,315 over Michael L. Igoe, Torrio's counsel in the O'Connor-Bucher-Meeghan murders.

This further demonstration of O'Banion's ballooning power did not please Torrio and Capone. In the past year there had been too many examples of his euphoric self-confidence and self-aggrandisement for their liking. He behaved publicly with a cocky, swaggering truculence that offended their vulpine Latin minds, and behaved towards them personally with an unimpressed insolence that enraged them beneath their blandness. They were disturbed by his idiotic bravado – as, when his bodyguard, Yankee Schwartz, complained that he had been snubbed by Dave Miller, a prize-fight referee, chieftain of a Jewish gang and one of four brothers of tough reputation, who were Hirschey, a gambler-politician in loose beer-running league with Torrio and O'Banion, Frank, a policeman, and Max, the youngest. To settle this slight, O'Banion went down to the La Salle Theatre in the Loop, where, he had learned, Dave Miller was attending the opening of a musical comedy. At the end of the performance, Dave and Max came out into the brilliantly lit foyer among a surge of gowned and tuxedoed first-nighters. O'Banion drew his guns and fired at Dave, severely wounding him in the stomach. A second bullet ricocheted off Max's belt buckle, leaving him unhurt but in some distress. O'Banion tucked away his gun and walked out of the theatre; he was neither prosecuted nor even arrested. That sort of braggadocio, for that sort of reason, in the view of Torrio and Capone, was a nonsense.

A further example of the incompatible difference in personalities was when two policemen held up a Torrio beer convoy on a West Side street and demanded three hundred dollars to let it through. One of the beer-runners telephoned O'Banion – on a line tapped by the detective bureau – and reported the situation. O'Banion's reaction was: 'Three hundred dollars! To them bums? Why, I can get them knocked off for half that much.' Upon which the detective bureau despatched rifle squads to prevent trouble if O'Banion should send his gunmen out to deal with the hijacking policemen. But in the meantime the beer-runner, unhappy with this solution, telephoned Torrio and returned to O'Banion with the message: 'Say, Dionie, I just been talking to Johnny, and he said to let them cops have the three hundred. He says he don't want no trouble.'

But Torrio and Capone had graver cause to hate and distrust the Irishman. For three years, since the liquor territorial conference, Torrio had, with his elastic patience, and because he knew that retaliation could cause only violent warfare and disaster to business, tolerated O'Banion's impudent double-crossing. They had suffered, in sulky silence, the sight of his sharp practice in Cicero.

When, as a diplomatic gesture of amity and in payment for the loan of gunmen in the April election, Torrio had given O'Banion a slice of Cicero, the profits from that district had been twenty thousand dollars a month. In six months O'Banion had boosted the profits to a hundred thousand dollars a month – mainly by bringing pressure to bear on fifty Chicago speakeasy proprietors to shift out to the suburb. These booze customers had until then been buying their supplies from the Sheldon, Saltis-McErlane and Druggan-Lake gangs, and now they were competing for trade with the Torrio-Capone saloons; once again O'Banion's brash recklessness had caused a proliferation of ill-will. The revenue from O'Banion's Cicero territory went up still higher, until the yield was more than the Torrio-Capone takings from the far bigger trade area of Chicago's South and West Sides. But he still showed no intention of sharing with the syndicate. At last, even the controlled Torrio was unable to hold still, and he tentatively suggested that O'Banion should take a percentage in the Stickney brothels in return for one from his Cicero beer concession. O'Banion's reply was a raucous laugh and a flat refusal.

Still more jealous bitterness was engendered by the O'Banion gang's seizure from a West Side marshalling yard of a freight car load of Canadian whisky worth 100 thousand dollars and by one of the biggest coups of the Prohibition era – the Sibley warehouse robbery, which became famous for the cool brazenness of the operation. Here was stored a million dollars' worth of bonded whisky. These 1,750 cases were carted off in a one-night operation by the O'Banion men, who left in their stead the same number of barrels filled with water. A Federal grand jury indicted O'Banion, and warehouse officials, and also Lieutenant Michael Grady, of the Detective Bureau, and four of his sergeants on charges of convoying the loads to the bootleggers' cache – but, quite consistently, no one was convicted and the policemen were reinstated after temporary suspension from duty. O'Banion used the profits from this haul to buy the Cragin distillery, the biggest alcohol plant in the Mid-West (it was this distillery Yellowley was arranging to close when he was offered the restraining bribe of 250 thousand dollars).

For all this period O'Banion contemptuously shrugged off the obvious hostility of the confederate gangs, but while Torrio was prepared to endure the presumption and bumptiousness of O'Banion for the sake of undisturbed business, and to restrain the subsidiary gangs' resentful envy of O'Banion's successes, he was not prepared to be played for a sucker, which was O'Banion's imprudent misjudgment. For more than a year beneath the surface efficiency of the liquor pact the passions had been rising to a condition of electric tension. The internecine mortalities had crept up – thirty-seven in 1922, fifty-seven in 1923 – but were held in check by Torrio, guided from above by Diamond Joe Esposito and Mike Merlo, two of the most powerful Italians in Illinois and, as high counsellors of the Unione Siciliana, the law-makers among their countrymen. They were adamant against unnecessary murder and fighting, and Torrio entirely agreed in principle. Yet his reasonableness snapped when he discovered the truth about the Sieben brewery raid, and what followed was chaos in gangland, the outbreak of an unprecedented rage of feuding, in which for the first time the machine-gun began clattering, for this was the efficient solution to the need for mass slaughter.

The Sieben Brewery, on the North Side, was one of the most important sources of Chicago's illicit beer during Prohibition years. It was owned jointly by Torrio, Capone and O'Banion, backed by that cloudy Big Brother presence of the brewing interests, Torrio's sleeping partner, but the workaday management was left to O'Banion. For three years the plant had been producing full blast with little pretence at concealment, and the daily procession of outgoing delivery lorries was watched over conscientiously by the precinct police force. The Federal Prohibition agency finally became meanly insistent that the Sieben flow should be curbed, and the local cops, hearing that a raid was being planned for the morning of 19 May, passed on a warning to O'Banion. Alone of the gang-leaders O'Banion had this information. He used it for a plot that turned out to be far too clever for his own good.

He went to see Torrio and Capone and confided that he was quitting the booze racket. He was, he said, nervous of the antagonism of some of the Sicilian groups in town. He intended to realize his assets and retire to the ranch at Glenwood Springs, Colorado, owned by his henchman, Louis Alterie. He wished to sell out his share in the Sieben Brewery to his two partners.

It was a delightful surprise to them, for life without O'Banion would be altogether more tranquil and manageable. The price agreed upon without argument was half-a-million dollars, and the property was thereupon transferred. Taking his scheme a subtle step further, as protection to himself and as a demonstration of his innocence, O'Banion offered to hand over and explain the details of shipment and protection on the spot – on 19 May.

When Chief of Police Morgan Collins and Captain Matthew Zimmer, with their armed squad of police, pounced on the Sieben Brewery on 19 May they found there, ready to move away, thirteen truckloads of beer and several cars of gangsters, present for the little handing-over ceremony, including Torrio, Weiss, Alterie and O'Banion. The beer was confiscated, the gangsters arrested. They were not taken to police headquarters, but delivered direct to the Federal authorities – 'because,' explained Collins, 'the United States District Attorney has promised prompt co-operation. The prosecution will be handled by the Government.' All the gangsters gave false names but all were recognized. Torrio obtained his freedom almost immediately after arriving at the Federal Building by peeling 7,500 dollars off his roll, and he handed in another five thousand for James Casey. He did not assist in the bailing out of O'Banion, Alterie, Weiss and their friends, who lacked sufficient cash and who had to await the arrival of William Skidmore and Ike Roderick, professional bondsmen kept in prosperous business by such incidents. It was, one way and another, a melodramatic occasion, with a rare handful of untouchables in the bag and with Chief Collins personally ripping the stars from the uniforms of two of his squad who should have been guarding the brewery and who had been conveniently absent.

When the plan was shaping in O'Banion's impulsive mind it must have seemed immensely humorous to mulct Torrio and Capone of half-a-million dollars and then compromise them with the police, for he knew that, while he would most likely be fined, Torrio as a second offender (he had been fined two thousand dollars the previous year for manufacturing alcohol) would receive a far heavier penalty. What he presumably did not calculate – otherwise it is doubtful if even one as audacious as he would have gone ahead – is that Torrio would instantly smell treachery. This he did the moment the police cars arrived. For the time being he was occupied in extricating himself from the trouble. An attempt was made to get Assistant United States District Attorney William F. Waugh to take fifty thousand dollars to stifle the case, but he refused and it proceeded. Torrio was one of eleven defendants who came before the judge. He was fined five thousand dollars and sentenced to nine months in jail, but remained free on bail for nearly a year. O'Banion was not standing beside him in the dock to receive his fine. He was dead by the time the case came into court.

Torrio's patience had run out. He hated O'Banion and intended to see him dead. Apart from O'Banion's blatant disdain for Torrio's authority and his unscrupulous freebooting within the combine's system of trade, the bad blood was more thickly curdled by strong emotional undercurrents: racial hostility. The common purpose that had brought them together as distrustful business associates did not ameliorate the mutual contempt and dislike that went back to when they were Irish and Italian slum-children in their segregated city ghettoes. A truculent remark of O'Banion's, when he had been advised by the cannier Weiss to treat Torrio and Capone in a more conciliatory spirit, had travelled fast around the underworld. 'To hell with them Sicilians,' O'Banion had said. The Sicilians heard and remembered.

7

A Nice Little Moonshine Business

"This is war."
THE CHICAGO HERALD AND EXAMINER
November 1924

A CLAN of Sicilians especially sensitive to this manner of insult
were the Genna Brothers. There were six of them. They
were known as the Terrible Gennas and between them and
O'Banion there was an implacable reciprocal loathing. The Gennas–
Sam, Jim, Pete, Angelo, Antonio and Mike – were close allies of
Torrio and Capone, tied tightly by race and by affiliations within the
Unione Siciliana in which they held important positions under the
fond patronage of Diamond Joe Esposito, and they ruled the Italian
immigrant community around Taylor Street as feudally as island
landowners.

They were brought over by their immigrant parents in 1910 from
Marsala, in Sicily, and settled in Diamond Joe Esposito's Nineteenth
Ward, the Little Italy across the river in the Maxwell Street police
district. Prohibition brought them to prominence. Pete and Jim
ran saloons, Sam was a Mafia agent specializing in Black Hand
extortion and a ward-organizer, and Mike and Angelo took care of
the shooting, and all made vast fortunes from bootlegging. O'Banion
was a wild and capricious man compared with the suave, sophisticated Torrio and the cool shrewd Capone. But beside the Gennas,
O'Banion was a creature of grace. They were of an alley-cat breed,
the inbred savagery, duplicity and insane pride of the Sicilian bandit
overlaid by their training in competitive brutality in an American
metropolitan slum. They carried in their pockets rosaries, crucifixes
and revolvers. The family exception was Antonio – known as The
Gentleman – who, although invariably present as counsellor at
family murder conferences, never himself actually killed; he lived a
life of superficially quiet sobriety in a downtown hotel, attended the
opera, and, as a self-taught architect, designed modern apartment
blocks for his poor compatriots. His brothers were not similarly
reflective. They were in constant trouble, and rode out in their bright

76

suits and bright cars in pursuit of it: not a quality that attracted either Torrio or Capone to them.

Their value to the combine was their huge tenement network of alcohol cookers, dispersed in such tiny units that it was safe from the inconvenience that could be caused by the closure – however rare and temporary – of a centralized distilling plant. The organization was superintended by the brainy Antonio. The Gennas obtained from the Government a permit for the manufacture of industrial alcohol, which served as thin but satisfactory formal cover for their production and distribution of bootleg liquor. In the kitchens of hundreds of tenement homes in the area of Taylor Street they installed portable copper stills. They even shipped over Sicilian families and set them up with a cooker each. For fifteen dollars a day – a big, golden American wage to the poor immigrant – all the family had to do was keep the still stoked and strain off the sugar corn liquid. The raw alcohol was collected each week, taken to the Gennas' three-storey warehouse at 1022 Taylor Street – just four blocks from the Maxwell Street police station – and cut, flavoured, coloured, bottled and labelled, and sold as whisky and gin. From this operation they were, at their peak, grossing 350 thousand dollars a month, on which 150 thousand was clear profit – a business valued at five million dollars.

As had the South Side O'Donnells a little earlier, the Gennas had 'a nice little business'. To ensure that it continued to thrive certain overheads were necessary, payment for police and political protection arranged by Torrio and Esposito. Eventually the Government turned their attention to the Gennas' affairs and extracted a twenty-five page confession from their former office manager. It is a document of interest in any examination of how Prohibition was systematically flouted in Chicago – and in this particular 'reformist' period when Mayor Dever was making real efforts to enforce the law.

'The warehouse was run night and day, with two twelve-hour shifts,' explained the ex-Genna executive. 'Heavy trucks, automobiles and lighter trucks were used in the distribution. The warehouse was run openly and in full view of everybody, unmolested by the State authorities other than an occasional raid. But notification of twenty-four hours was always given to the Gennas. Sometimes the very letters sent out by the police to raid were exhibited to this affiant, and there would be a clean-up, then a raid, then a reopening . . . During all the period that I worked in the said warehouse the entire Genna enterprise was done with the full knowledge, consent and approval of the police of Chicago in so far as the police were in touch with or in the neighbourhood or had business under their jurisdiction. The Gennas for said protection paid, monthly, large sums, which rose from a small amount in the beginning to about 6,500 dollars in April of 1925. Moreover, said police received in addition thereto much alcohol at a discount price to permit the Gennas publicly to operate said stills and system of distribution. Each month said warehouse was visited by four hundred uniformed police and by squads – sometimes four per month – out of the central bureau. It was visited, moreover, by representatives with stars but not in uniform, commonly known around the warehouse as representatives of the State's Attorney's office of Cook County. That police might not impose upon the Gennas by falsely representing themselves as assigned to the Maxwell Street station, each month there came by letter or messenger a list of all stars worn by officers and men at the Maxwell Street station. These were on short slips of paper and were taken by this affiant. The entire list of stars was run off on the adding machine and the papers sent from the station were destroyed. As each man came in for his pay his star was observed. If his star was upon the list sent in he was paid; his star number was inserted on a loose leaf ledger page, and the amount of the payment was put opposite his star number. I had nothing to do with paying the squads or higher ups, but was held accountable for the money paid to them . . . On occasions, when truckloads of alcohol would be going to different parts of the city and they would be intercepted by strange policemen, complaint was lodged by the Gennas. It was arranged then between the Gennas and the squads in the central detail as follows. When a long haul was to be made through strange territory, the Gennas on the preceding night would call certain numbers and say "Tomorrow at seven". On the next morning at seven a uniformed squad of police would remain in the offing until a truckload of alcohol would start from the Genna warehouse. This squad would convoy them through the zones of danger. This affiant himself has called them, according to the number which indicated that the police were to convoy the alcohol for the Gennas.'

The situation was put simply by Attorney Patrick H. O'Donnell, during the first trial of Scalise and Anselmi for the murder of Policeman Harold F. Olson: 'For six years the Genna brothers maintained a barter house for moonshine alcohol; maintained it openly and notoriously, as public as the greatest department store in State Street.' At this trial O'Donnell produced the Genna accounts book containing the names of the procured policemen. This caused temporary indignation, and 187 uniformed men were transferred from the Maxwell Street station. There were many written and oral promises of the publication of names, but after the trial the book was never again referred to and disappeared.

Until the beginning of 1925 the Gennas appeared as invincible as Attila and his Huns in Central Europe. They were invulnerable to law processes – even when murder was involved, for Angelo and Jim had been two of the positively identified killers in the 1921 John Powers–Anthony D'Andrea aldermanic campaign, when two houses were bombed and thirty men lost their lives, the names of the condemned being posted in advance, by old Sicilian custom, on Dead Man's Tree, a sickly poplar in Loomis Street in the heart of Little Italy. Under the protection of Esposito, and the Unione Siciliana – which had become virtually an alky-cooking guild – their political influence waxed spectacularly. In October 1924, about the same time as the O'Banion party, they held their own Belshazzar feast. The Italian Republican Club, of which they were directors, gave a banquet at the Morrison Hotel for political friends. Again, the guest-list deserves to be on the record. It included State's Attorney Robert E. Crowe; Thomas O. Wallace, Clerk of the Circuit Court; John K. Lawlor, Sanitary District Trustee; and Bernard W. Snow, Chief Bailiff of the Municipal Court and later titular head of the Cook City Republican Party and chairman of the central committee. United States Senator Charles S. Deneen's group was represented by James Kearns, Clerk of the Municipal Court, Joseph F. Haas, County Recorder, and William C. Scherwat, then candidate for County Clerk.

This social gathering moved the Chicago Better Government Association to send to the United States Senate a resolution declaring: 'Chicago politicians are in league with gangsters and the city is overrun with a combination of lawless politics and protected vice.'

Such moral outbursts bothered the Gennas little. Apart from their political machinations, their business hours were occupied with their relations with the O'Banion gang, which were rapidly boiling to a crisis. There had in the course of a few months been a number of charged incidents.

Since Torrio's and O'Banion's taking of Cicero, the Gennas had become more ambitious. They began venturing out of their own territory – and into O'Banion's, and they found there a market for their booze. It was near-poisonous corrected wood alcohol; but it was labelled whisky and it was cheaper. They sold theirs for three dollars a gallon. O'Banion, who charged six to nine dollars – but for a decidedly better brew – protested angrily to Torrio at this muscling-in. Torrio, soothingly, evasively, said he would remonstrate with the Gennas; but the poaching continued. O'Banion, partly in a spirit of hot-headed revenge, partly to show his contempt for Torrio, hijacked a thirty thousand dollar shipment of Genna whisky. The Gennas loaded their guns and prepared to strike back. By this time, Torrio, deadly angry at the Sieben brewery double-cross, was tired of turning the other cheek and was in heartfelt favour of letting the Gennas loose on O'Banion. But again the impending detonation was at the last moment averted. Mike Merlo, president of the Unione Siciliana, intervened. He had final control over his countrymen in Chicago and he decreed that for the sake of stable business, a further effort must be made to live at peace with O'Banion. Then, on 3 November 1924 O'Banion went to the Ship in Cicero for the weekly division of spoils. Present were Capone, Nitti, Frank Maritote, Weiss, Frankie Rio and Drucci. Capone announced that during the week Angelo Genna had lost thirty thousand dollars gambling at the Ship and he proposed that the IOUs should be cancelled. O'Banion, seeing a further opportunity of needling the Gennas, flatly refused to agree to this, and he telephoned Angelo himself and gave him a week to pay up. It was the last provocation in the protracted but inexorable move towards open conflict. For the next day Merlo died – almost uniquely, a natural death – and the restraint was off.

There opened what Pasley called 'the Bootleg Battle of the Marne', when the Chicago *Herald and Examiner* sombrely ended an editorial on the extraordinary events that shook the city with gunfire and fear (and some vicarious excitement): 'This is war'. It was a war which for four years and three months – until the St. Valentine's Day massacre produced a climax of shock and, with Capone's control enforced, brought about a diminishing of gang-killings – rampaged to and fro across the no man's land of Madison Street, the central intersection of the city, through a series of abortive co-existence agreements and the fresh flare-ups of gun-battles.

8

Roses from Al and Judges round the Coffin

'O'Banion's head got away from his hat.' AL CAPONE

THE battle-array was, in essence, a fight for complete ownership or control of bootlegging and allied commercialized vice in Greater Chicago, between Al Capone (very soon now to be succeeding Torrio) and his Italian-Sicilian satellites and the Irish-Jewish confederacy at that moment led by Dion O'Banion. Yet it should not be supposed that all was harmony and solidarity within each camp. Torrio and Capone had no personal reason to like or trust the Gennas, whom they regarded as ridiculously volatile hoodlums, and they came to have reason to see them as dangerous cheats. Upon Merlo's death Capone saw the chance of consolidating his zone of racial influence by controlling the Chicago Unione Siciliana. He could not himself – not being a Sicilian – take office so, authorized by Torrio to whom power of appointment was given by Frank Yale, head of the United States Unione Siciliana, he chose as nominee a close friend and accomplice, Antonio Lombardo, partner of Joseph Aiello, cheese merchants, commission brokers and racketeers. The proposal did not in the least suit the Gennas, to whom the presidency of the Unione was not merely, as it was to Capone, another business investment, but mystically endowed with prestige and honour, a tribal aureole. They acted swiftly and before Capone was aware of what was happening they had canvassed the membership and, aided by both the regard and the terror in which they were held, installed young Angelo in the office. Capone did not enjoy being thwarted, but, with the maturer judgement of Torrio to guide him, he saw that settlement of this matter with the Gennas could wait until they had served the more urgent purpose of dealing with O'Banion.

One of O'Banion's more bizarre business interests was selling flowers. He had, in the past two years, acquired a respectable façade. In 1922 he had bought a half share in William E. Schofield's florist shop at 738 North State Street, immediately opposite the cathedral where he had once sung in the choir. A year later he had married Anne Kaniff, a quiet fair-haired girl unlike the hard-boiled floozies whom the gangsters usually prinked in mink and diamonds. During shop opening hours he pottered among his blooms, limping about in an apron serving customers and arranging bouquets and the window display stands of terra-cotta vases. But, although he apparently had a genuine attachment to this improbable skill, it was also a prosperous trade to be in, for to O'Banion came many of the orders for the last rites of his underworld colleagues, and they were of legendary costliness. In fact, to him had come business for Merlo's funeral – a ten thousand dollar order from Torrio, an eight thousand dollar order from Capone. Merlo's was to be one of the most lavishly imposing burials seen in Chicago. Altogether 100 thousand dollars' worth of flowers arrived at his home, and flooded out from the house to obliterate the winter lawn. Among the tributes was a wax effigy of the Unione president, modelled by a local sculptor at a cost of five thousand dollars, which, garlanded with flowers, was the some-what macabre exhibit in the open touring car preceding the hearse. Jim Genna even came to O'Banion's shop in the company of Carmen Vacco, one of Merlo's political appointees, to buy a 750-dollar wreath – but, as it transpired, their main object was to familiarize themselves with the shop's interior for a future occasion. O'Banion and his partner, Schofield, spent all Sunday making wreaths and chaplets. Late that evening, after O'Banion had gone, a man ordered a wreath by telephone and said he would call for it next day.

At noon on Monday, 10 November, a blue sedan containing four men came from the north and drew into the kerb outside the O'Banion shop, and parked there with its engine running. One stayed at the wheel and the other three alighted. The three – one a tall, burly man in a brown overcoat and brown fedora hat, the others short and stocky – entered and stood in line. O'Banion was in the rear, behind a partition, clipping the stems of a bunch of chrysanthemums. With him was William Crutchfield, a young Negro porter. O'Banion was saying to Crutchfield: 'The floor's in a mess, Bill. Better brush all those leaves and petals up,' when he heard the door open and walked through to the front of the shop. Crutchfield was sweeping up the leaves in the back room and over a hanging wicker basket saw O'Banion step towards the men and extend his right hand in greeting; his other was holding the secateurs. As O'Banion said: 'Hello, boys. You from Mike Merlo's?' one of the men reached out and gripped O'Banion's hand, saying 'Yes.' Crutchfield then turned his back to them. The rest he heard. There were five rapid explosions, a pause and then a sixth. O'Banion normally, whenever talking to a stranger, kept one hand in a pistol pocket, but this time, jerked forward in the grasp of the middle man, he had no chance to reach for any one of his three guns. Two bullets struck him in the right breast, a third cut through the larynx, the next just to the right of it, and the fifth went into the right cheek. As he lay among his lilies, the grace shot – the customary gangster, and especially Sicilian, procedure – was fired. It entered his left cheek and the revolver was held so close that the skin was powder-burned.

The killers left the shop, climbed into the car which turned the corner into Superior Street and was lost in the traffic. The theoretical reconstruction of the murder by Captain William 'Old Shoes' Schoemaker of the Detective Bureau was this: 'O'Banion above all things knew he was marked for death. He knew it might come at any moment. Ordinarily, when talking to strangers, he stood with feet apart, the right hand on the hip, thumb to the rear and fingers down in front. The left was usually in his coat pocket. In this position he was ready for instant action with the automatics in the specially tailored pockets. But we have him advancing to meet these fellows without hesitation – his right hand extended. He felt safe. He knew them – at least by sight – and did not suspect them.'

Apart from Crutchfield there was one other witness, Gregory Summers, an eleven-year-old schoolboy on duty as a junior traffic officer a hundred yards away at North State Street and East Chicago Avenue. He heard the shots and saw the men run from the shop. He said: 'Two of them were dark and they looked like foreigners. The other man had a light complexion.' Crutchfield's close-up view of them led him to the opinion that: 'The tall man might have been a Jew or a Greek, but the other two were Italians.'

The police questioned Torrio, Capone and the Gennas. All said, No, they couldn't imagine who would kill Dion. Torrio knew nothing except that: 'The day before he was killed I gave him an order for ten thousand dollars worth of flowers. Our boys wanted to send some floral pieces to Mike Merlo's house and we all chipped in and gave the business to Dion.' Capone's threnody took this form: 'Dion was all right and he was getting along, to begin with, better than he had any right to expect. But, like everyone else, his head got away from his hat. Weiss figured in that. Johnny Torrio had taught O'Banion all he knew and then O'Banion grabbed some of the best guys we had and decided to be the boss of the booze racket in Chicago. What a chance! O'Banion had a swell route to make it tough for us and he did. His job had been to smooth the coppers and we gave him a lot of authority with the booze and beer buyers.

When he broke away, for a while it wasn't so good. He knew the ropes and got running us ragged. It was his funeral.'

It indisputably was, and was the most Hollywoodian yet. The obsequies were undertaken by John A. Sbarbaro, a popular gangsters' undertaker, of 708 North Wells Street. (Sbarbaro was also an Assistant State's Attorney, he and William H. McSwiggin being the representatives of the State's Attorney's office in most gang-murder inquiries.) A ten thousand dollar coffin, bought in Philadelphia, was expressed to Chicago in a private freight car. It had solid silver and bronze double airtight walls, a thick plate-glass top, heavily carved solid silver corner posts, and within a couch of white satin and tufted cushions for O'Banion's remains to rest upon. On one side a scroll read: 'Dion O'Banion, 1892–1924.'

It is indicative of the public attitude at this time towards the gangsters to read the accounts in the contemporary newspapers, to note their curious mixture of maudlin reverence and excitement. This was how one newspaper's sob-sister painted the scene in Sbarbaro's Funeral Parlour chapel, through which a procession of forty thousand people shuffled for three days and nights to see O'Banion 'lying in state', as the Chicago *Tribune* phrased it. 'Silver angels', wrote the reporter, 'stood at the head and feet with their heads bowed in the light of ten candles that burned in solid golden candlesticks they held in their hands. Beneath the casket, on the marble slab that supports its glory, is the inscription, "Suffer little children to come unto me". And over it all the perfume of flowers. Vying with the perfume was that of beautifully dressed women of gangland, wrapped in costly furs and supported slowly down the aisles by excellently tailored gentlemen with steel-blue jaws and a furtive glance very active.' Another woman feature-writer described the 'graceful hands which could finger an automatic so effectively'.

Upon the day of the funeral mounted police were out early to clear a passage for the cortège. More than twenty thousand people gathered in the streets outside the funeral parlour. Twenty-six lorry-loads of flowers, worth fifty thousand dollars, wound their way in a mile-long train to Mount Carmel Cemetery. They included an eight-feet-high heart made of American Beauty roses, an eiderdown of orchids and roses to cover the grave, and an enormous wreath from the Teamsters' Union. There was also a basket of roses, simply labelled: 'From Al'. Three bands and a police escort from Stickney (Chief Collins having forbidden the Chicago force to participate) led the procession. A special detachment of police mingled with the gangster mourners, pleading for peace for at least this day, and by official request from the city authorities those carrying guns put them in the care of friends during the ceremony.

It was a ceremony such as no American president and few monarchs have been accorded. The only omission was a church service. His friends and family applied for this on the ground that O'Banion had been a Catholic and had attended the Holy Name Cathedral as a boy, but to their dismay the Roman Catholic Archdiocese refused a service and a burial in consecrated ground, Cardinal Mundelein stating: 'A person who refuses the ministrations of the church in life need not expect such ministrations after death.' Yet O'Banion was not completely denied shrift. At the graveside, the Reverend Patrick Malloy, of St. Thomas of Canterbury Church, who had known O'Banion since he was a boy and thought he was essentially a merry and good-natured lad, stepped forward from the crowd, and, as the casket was lowered into the unconsecrated ground, recited a litany, a Hail Mary and the Lord's Prayer. Nor was O'Banion for ever deserted, unatoned; five months later his family bought a plot of consecrated ground and the body was disinterred and reburied. The Archdiocese did not interfere, but they did direct his widow to remove a huge stone obelisk and replace it with a moderately sized stone. Afterwards, Captain John Stege, an honest and consistently anti-gang policeman, remarked: 'O'Banion was a thief and a murderer, but look at him now – buried next door to a bishop.' Near to O'Banion's new grave was the mausoleum containing the bodies of Archbishops Feehan and Quigley and Bishop Porter.

Among the distinguished mourners were five judges of the Municipal Court, Alderman Dorsey Crowe and other aldermen and legislators – and Capone and Torrio. They could not have wished to go. They could not, however, by absenting themselves strengthen the suspicion that they had directed O'Banion's assassination. They saw it through, sitting opposite Moran, Weiss and Drucci in the mortuary chapel, riding with them to the cemetery, and facing them across the grave. Immediately after Torrio left for a restless vacation – to Hot Springs, to Arkansas, to New Orleans, to the Bahamas, to Cuba.

By his departure, Torrio missed a public announcement that he may anyway have preferred to miss. Louis Alterie, O'Banion's friend, issued a challenge to those responsible for O'Banion's death to shoot it out with him on a specified day on the corner of State and Madison Streets. Mayor Dever, whose feeble reformist campaign again had been sent reeling first by the shooting and then by the funeral – the orchidaceous sumptuousness of which was not only a display of individual gangsters' wealth but a pageant, for all Chicago to consider, of gangland's power and opulence – said he was 'staggered'. He asked: 'Are we living by the code of the Dark Ages or is Chicago part of an American Commonwealth? One day we have this O'Banion slain as a result of a perfectly executed plot of assassins. It is followed by this amazing demonstration. In the meanwhile his followers and their rivals openly boast of what they will do in retaliation. They seek to fight it out in the street. There is no thought of the law or of the people who support the law.'

O'Banion's murderers did not present themselves at the junction of State and Madison, but, although no arrest was ever made and the crime remains officially unsolved, there is no doubt who the killers were. The Cook County coroner finally drew a line under the record with the comment: 'Slayers not apprehended. John Scalise and Albert Anselmi and Frank Yale suspected, but never brought to trial.' The coroner was wrong about Yale – Torrio's old chief from the Five Points gang – but right about Anselmi and Scalise. As O'Banion's followers quickly determined, they had been paid ten thousand dollars in cash and a three thousand dollar diamond ring each. Scalise sent his ring to his fiancée in Sicily. It was they who had fired the shots. The man in the middle who grasped O'Banion's hand in such firm friendship was Mike Genna.

Scalise and Anselmi were a pair of particularly malevolent killers. Both strangely gorilla-like in appearance – thick, bulging, barrel bodies, dangling arms always flexed for the fast grab at a gun, short-legged and with heavy, scowling, rubbery faces, they were Sicilians with long prison records in Italy before they entered America illegally. They were not used for any of the miscellaneous duties of bootlegging: their specialized function was as torpedoes, that is full-time professional homicides with a dedicated self-pride in des-patching the removal of fellow humans to order. It was they who devised the small refinement of rubbing their bullets with garlic, a delicate technique which increased the likelihood of gangrene infection in the wounds of any of their victims who survived instant death. They were at this period directly affiliated with the Gennas, but were used for general murder assignments by Torrio and Capone; in fact, their allegiance was to anyone with a fee to offer for an assassination, as will be seen in their eventual relationship with Mike Genna.

9

'Weiss Guys' and 'Capone Guys'

'Mother is the best bet and don't let Satan draw you too fast.'
Death-bed words of DUTCH SCHULTZ,
New York gangster.

WITH O'Banion gone, Hymie Weiss succeeded to the leadership of the North Side mob. Weiss was a Pole, brought over to America as a child by his immigrant parents, whose real name was Earl Wajciechowski, shortened to Weiss, and known generally as Hymie the Polack, Little Hymie or plain Hymie. He was a sullen lowering young man with sharp Sinatra-like features and big, dark, ominous eyes. Until Prohibition he had been a burglar, a safe-blowing colleague of O'Banion and car-thief, and had rented out his services as both killer and terrorist in a non-partisan spirit to both labour unions and employers' strike-breaking regiments. He conformed to the traditional Catholic Italian-Irish gangster pattern in remaining, throughout his career of murder and indiscriminate dishonesty, devoutly religious – he wore a crucifix around his neck nearby his armpit holster and carried a rosary in his pocket – and, as his admirers often pointed out, was endlessly kind to his mother. (This prevalent mother-fixation is an interesting facet of the gunman-personality. Torrio set up his mother in luxury in Italy; Capone idolized Momma; O'Banion bought a fine house for his, and visited her every week with bundles of new gramophone records, once telling a newspaperman: 'Believe me, she don't deserve a worry in the world'; and Dutch Schultz, the New York bootlegger, declaimed on his death-bed: 'Mother is the best bet and don't let Satan draw you too fast.') Weiss was probably the basic reason for O'Banion's success as a beer-runner, for he was broodingly sharp and far more malleable in his business methods, postponing violence towards bar-proprietors and contentious rivals until all peaceable measures had failed. Unemotional and bleakly ferocious, he was said to be the only man Capone feared.

The death of O'Banion brought about a rumbling re-grouping of the alliances and allegiances in Chicago's gangland. The old combine forged by Torrio had already been fissured by O'Banion's severance of diplomatic and business relations, and now the racial undercurrent that gave meaning to many of the disputes became heightened and more clearly canalized. The West Side O'Donnells transferred to Weiss, as did the Saltis-McErlane gang and many of the smaller predominantly American-Irish-Jewish bailiwicks. The Gennas, Aiellos and other Sicilian-Italian satellites remained expediently – but with various qualifications – federated with Capone, as did Ralph Sheldon and Danny Stanton. Broadly, any gangster was either a 'Capone guy' or a 'Weiss guy'. Not much room was left in Chicago for rugged individualism; bootleg 'free enterprise' was reaching the monopoly stage of capitalism. But first came what Merlo and Torrio had always feared and strived to avoid: an anarchy of free-for-all scrapping. The old union, for so long hard-pressed and quavering under the seething internal pressures, dissolved; the ratified territorial boundaries splintered and disintegrated; chaotic hi-jacking and street-to-street fighting broke out; the crash of shot-guns and the stutter of machine-guns began to vibrate through Chicago's streets, and there was seldom an issue of a daily newspaper that lacked a front-page obituary story arising out of yet another gang clash. Chicago was beginning to enter the world's consciousness as the modern Sodom and Gomorrah, where the average citizen wore a bullet-proof vest when taking the dog for a walk and swigged bootleg hooch in the office, where every car had its scars of sub-machine-gun assault, where the whole population lived a daily Grand Guignol fantasy of menace and gore: more gun-shots shrilled and hummed through the international headlines than were ever heard in actuality in the Mid-West capital.

Yet stylized and dramatized though the situation was, it had a greater and more garish reality than Chicago today cares to admit. As soon as O'Banion's satin-wrapped body was plushly entombed, Weiss opened his war of vengeance. The mind of Weiss was Sicilian in its subtlety. He not only attacked the obvious targets, but injured them indirectly. He knew that Capone had an affection for Tony the Greek, who ran a gourmet restaurant above Frankie Pope's Cicero establishment, and Tony the Greek was a Capone fan; he idealized Al. He told the story of how a ragged newsboy came into the restaurant on a November night of ice-laden rain. 'How many you got left, kid?' Capone asked. 'About fifty, I guess,' said the boy. 'Throw them on the floor and run along home to your mother,' said Capone handing him a twenty-dollar bill.

Tony's adoration cost him his life, for on a later night, when

Capone and he sat in a booth talking, the bell rang and Tony went forward to greet his customers. He did not reappear, and, it was reported with compassion, Capone sat sobbing in his booth when he realized that Tony had been grabbed and taken for a ride – when he realized that his enemies were striking at him through his friendships. It was reported in the next day's papers that the body of Tony Anton, restaurateur, had been found in quicklime; no arrests.

Weiss also hit direct at the men he knew had killed his friend. On 12 January 1925 Capone was out on a tour of inspection of his properties and had drawn up at a restaurant at State and Fifty-fifth streets. He missed death by seconds. He had just left the car and entered the building when a touring car with drawn curtains drove slowly by, and, at a range of three feet, out of the front and rear seats poured a barrage of bullets from automatic pistols and from a sub-machine-gun, the gangster's increasingly favoured weapon and the brutal clatter of which was becoming jocularly known as ukelele music in a ukelele-crazy time. Capone's chauffeur, Sylvester Barton, was wounded in the back; two bodyguards sitting in the back seat threw themselves to the floor and escaped injury. The car was riddled from nose to tail, left with hood flapping raggedly and engine wrecked. 'They let it have everything but the kitchen stove,' remarked a bureau squad sergeant. It was this unpleasant incident that moved Capone to order his custom-built four-wheeled fortress from the Cadillac company, seven tons of it, with armoured body, shell-proof glass and a tail-gun position.

Twelve days later, the afternoon after Torrio had returned from his harassed scurry around the hemisphere, the Weiss emissaries who had been on his track for thousands of miles caught up with him at his Clyde Avenue apartment block in the Jackson Park Section of the South Side. It was four-thirty in the afternoon and dusk was falling, and he and his wife had arrived back from a shopping outing in the Loop. Mrs. Torrio, with an armful of parcels, descended from the car and walked up the path. Torrio was still inside the car gathering up the rest of the packages, when two men leaped out of a grey saloon parked out of sight around the corner in Seventieth Street. One, flourishing an automatic pistol, ran to the front of Torrio's car, the other, carrying a sawn-off shot-gun got round to the rear, and they both opened fire simultaneously. The windshield was shattered and the chauffeur, Robert Barton – brother of Capone's driver, Sylvester – was hit in the right knee. Torrio was not touched. He dropped the parcels and ran, crouching, towards the house. Before he had gone half a dozen steps he was caught in the cross-fire.

A ·45 bullet from the automatic smashed his left arm. He wheeled, still running, and trying to pull out his own gun, and a charge of buckshot hit him squarely in front, breaking his jaw and entering lungs and abdomen. He collapsed on to the flags. The automatic-wielder ran over to administer the obligatory bullet in the brain but he pulled the trigger on a .blank chamber, for he had emptied the gun in the first fusillade. He hesitated, fumbling with a new cartridge clip, and the shot-gunner was also reloading, when there was a peremptory blast from the horn of the waiting car. It was presumably a pre-arranged signal, for both lingered no longer, hastened to the car and were driven off.

Torrio was taken to Jackson Park Hospital. He would say nothing to the police but 'I know who they are and it's my business'. Capone was at his bedside within the hour. He posted a bodyguard of four men – in addition to the two policemen – and had him moved to an inside room. He recovered astonishingly quickly. Sixteen days later he left the hospital, by way of the fire escape. Later that month he appeared, heavily bandaged, in the United States Court to receive sentence for his part in the Sieben Brewery case. He paid his fine and went to Lake County Jail, at Waukegan, for nine months. There the sheriff fitted his windows with bullet-proof steel-mesh blinds, posted two deputy sheriffs to patrol the corridor, and supplied the cell with rugs, chairs and a more comfortable bed. In March Torrio sent for Capone and his lawyers, and formally transferred all control of his affairs to the man he had brought in as a brothel chucker-out five years previously. When Torrio was released in the autumn of 1925, three cars filled with gunmen were awaiting him at the gates to escort him through Chicago to Gary, Indiana, where he caught the New York train. From there he went on a liner to Italy. After convalescence, Torrio returned to the United States, and was soon employing his undoubted talents in association with Lucky Luciano and other racket chiefs in New York.

Capone was left the most powerful man in Chicago, but one with a perilous problem on his hands.

10

Capone as King

'Take that, you dirty son-of-a-bitch.'
MIKE GENNA'S dying words, as he
kicked a stretcher-bearer in the face.

THE police had gone through the weary motions of investigating the attempt upon Torrio's life. In accordance with the underworld ethic, Barton, the chauffeur, and Capone, like Torrio, refused to impart any information or theories about the assailants. But untypically, on this occasion there was a witness who was prepared to speak up. He was Peter Veesaert, the seventeen-year-old son of the janitor of a near-by apartment block. He had seen the whole of the attack. He was shown a press photograph of O'Banion's funeral and picked out a pall-bearer as one of Torrio's attackers, this being Bugs Moran. He repeated his identification thrice more, at three separate identification parades, Moran, he stated decisively, was the man who had shot Torrio with the automatic. At the detective bureau he faced Moran and said: 'You're the man', and he described in detail how Moran had been the first to leap from the parked car and open fire.

Police headquarters requested that Moran 'be detained pending the uncovering of more evidence'. Judge William J. Lindsay seventy-two hours later released him on bonds of five thousand dollars. Moran was never brought to trial nor even indicted.

During the remainder of 1925 the holocaust of gang killings included three of the Genna brothers. In the beginning the Weiss mob were on the offensive, swinging in blow after blow. Capone, bereft of Torrio's experience, weakened by the secession of so many allies and by the confusion into which beer distribution had been thrown, was temporarily occupied with fending off the batterings while he recouped. But he did not mourn the loss of the three intractable Gennas, allies though they were, because his authority over the Sicilian community, and therefore the alky-cooking syndicate, was thus strengthened.

On a vivacious spring morning of that year, on 26 May, Angelo

Genna left his bride of four months in their suite at fashionable Belmont Hotel, immediately opposite Big Bill Thompson's house on Sheridan Road, climbed into his new six-thousand-dollar roadster, and drove away to the office. Eight blocks farther on, at the junction of Ogden Avenue and Hudson, the familiar, almost emblematic touring car, black hood raised and stolen number plates screwed on, slid up behind him. It contained Weiss, Moran and Drucci. It drew level and the muzzles of three sawn-off shot-guns were poked across the doors, and Angelo diéd in a pall of gunpowder smoke. He had thirty thousand dollars in notes in his hip pocket at the time.

This was a multiple grief for the Genna family. A brother was lost and their dictatorship of the Unione Siciliana, in the presidency of which they had established Angelo, was abruptly capsized. Also their social pretensions, in such a burgeoning state, were severely set back. For in the January they had pulled off a trickily ambitious deal. They had married off Angelo to Lucille, younger sister of an important member of the Sicilian community. The marriage was a happy consummation of this business bond, the fusion of money and blood in the manner which the Sicilians valued.

So the Gennas saw that the wedding was attended by a magnificence proper to the jubilation and satisfaction they felt as such a social and commercial conquest. Three thousand guests responded to Angelo's invitation advertised in the newspapers: 'Come one, come all.' They gathered in Carmen's Hall of the Ashland Auditorium on the West Side, and they included, as was to be expected, many prominent professional and political figures. The wedding was effusively reported in the newspapers, Angelo being described as 'the young importer'. One woman reporter employed 142 words in describing the wonder of the twelve-feet-high cake ('the most elaborately decorated cake ever baked in Chicago') made by 'the artist and sculptor', S. Ferrara. Iced upon it was the simple, but soon to be soured, sentiment 'Home Sweet Home'.

Angelo's funeral was equally splendid. His solid silver coffin cost 12,500 dollars and his name was embossed upon it in gold. It was, of course, heaped under by wreaths, and the mobile flower garden was followed to the cemetery by three hundred motor-cars, thirty of them stuffed with flowers valued at forty thousand dollars. Twenty thousand Chicago Italians formed the procession. The eight pallbearers were all prominent Unione Siciliana officers. There was also the traditional attendance from official circles: State Senator John T. Joyce, Alderman John Powers, State Representatives William V. Pacelli and Charles Coia, Carmen Vacco, the City Sealer (whose duty was to seal the doors of premises where bootleg hooch was on sale, an appointment indirectly endorsed by the bootleg gangs), Diamond Joe Esposito, Mike Carozzo and Al Capone. The church refused a service, but Father Bifoletti, of the Holy Guardian Church, officiated at the cemetery. Fifty policemen were detailed to keep the streets clear, but had to be helped by hastily summoned auxiliaries when the crowd swarmed too thickly. There was an apposite prelude to the funeral. Just before the ceremonials began, Mr. Frank Baran, City Custodian, watched by a gathering of press and public, dumped into Lake Michigan eight hundred pistols, shot-guns and rifles recently seized by the police from Chicago's 'murderers, burglars, armed robbers and other crooks'.

Capone could not have been anything but gladdened at Angelo's demise, and probably for the first time felt a small surge of benevolence towards Weiss and his friends, but there were still a number of obstacles between him and domination of the Unione. For the vacant chair was instantly seized by Sam Samoots Amatuna, manager of Citro's Restaurant, a political rendezvous, and the Gennas' chief police fixer. He and two of his own business associates, Eddie Zion, roadhouse owner, and Bummy Goldstein, also known as Pete the Pedlar, the keeper of a wildcat distillery, walked into the Unione's headquarters and, while they all idly toyed with guns, Amatuna declared himself president. Then Capone had another gratuitous flash of luck. On 13 November, while Amatuna was relaxed in a barber's chair receiving a shave and a manicure, two men approached him from behind and blew his head all over the towel. They were Schemer Drucci and Jim Doherty, the West Side O'Donnell gang killer, on an errand from Weiss who was ignorant that he was doing Capone a second favour and merely ardently intent upon thinning the Sicilian ranks. Four days later, with lugubrious appositeness, Zion was shot on his way back from Amatuna's funeral; thirteen days later still, Goldstein was killed in a drug store by two assailants who, with pert initiative, used a shot-gun stolen from a detective bureau squad car parked nearby.

This time Capone had his way. His stooge Lombardo was placed in the Unione presidency, but was to occupy it until only 1928, when he was cut down by dumdums in a rush-hour crowd at the corner of Madison and Dearborn streets, perhaps the busiest spot in Chicago. As shall be seen, this was one more complication in the bootleg and Mafia labyrinth.

But earlier in 1925, before the death of Amatuna, there had been a major clash between the two sides, again involving a Genna. For a fortnight after the murder of Angelo, his brothers had been riding around the North Side with guns in their hot hands looking for any member of the Weiss gang. Their bitterness and homicidal intent was known to the police and there was a degree of tension to be sensed. On the morning of 13 June a police patrol found Moran's car badly holed by bullets but empty except for some random splashes of blood. In fact it had recently contained Moran and Drucci who had been involved in a brief running battle with a car manned by Mike Genna, Anselmi, Scalise and a driver on their mission of retribution. In the exchange of shots Drucci was grazed. They got away and dumped the car. By the time the police traced Moran and reported to him the condition of his car, he was at home in his slippers and righteously indignant; all he knew, he declared, was that his car had been stolen earlier, and now look at it.

While he was being interviewed the Genna car was scouting frenziedly about for the lost quarry. As they came furiously down Western Avenue towards the North Side they skidded on the wet surface, nearly collided with another vehicle and roared on. This traffic offence was observed by a police patrol car cruising in the opposite direction in which were Detectives Michael J. Conway, Harold F. Olson, Charles B. Walsh and William Sweeney of Squad No. 8 assigned to the Chicago Lawn Station. Conway, who was in charge, recognized Mike Genna. 'Hoodlums – let's get after them,' he said. Olson, the driver, swung round and they set off in pursuit with gong clanging.

The gang car increased speed and the patrolmen did too. They reached seventy-three miles an hour on a hazardously slippery surface. The chase continued for a mile and a half down the city's longest thoroughfare. At Fifty-ninth Street the gang car was still in the lead when a lorry turned across their path. The Genna driver jammed on the brakes and they twisted into a wild skid, spun twice, jumped the kerb and felled a lamp-post. Olson used his emergency brake and the police car slithered broadside to a halt a few feet distant.

The gangster driver dodged away. Genna, Scalise and Anselmi scrambled out and stood on the further side of the car with only their heads visible. None of the police had drawn his gun. Conway strode across, saying: 'What's the idea? Why all the speed when we were giving you the gong?' The answer was a bombardment of slugs from repeating shotguns. Olson and Walsh fell torn in a dozen places; on top of them tumbled Conway with his jaw blown away. Sweeney, crouched behind the car, emptied his revolver at the gangsters, who turned and fled. As the hundreds of eye-witnesses – shoppers, office-workers and the mechanics at the garage at 5940 South Western Avenue – thronged forward, Sweeney snatched two guns dropped by his brother officers and chased the Genna men across a vacant lot and into an alley half-way along the block between Western and Artesian Avenues.

Firing as he ran, Sweeney saw Scalise and Anselmi duck into a passage between two houses. Genna was last. At the entrance he whirled round and levelled his shot-gun point-blank at Sweeney. The trigger clicked on a spent shell. Sweeney's next shot hit Genna in the leg.

Stumbling onward, Genna saw a basement window, smashed the pane with the butt of his gun and dived in head first. Sweeney had been joined by Policeman Albert Richert, of Brighton Park Station, who had seen the tussle and jumped off a street-car, and George Oakey, a retired policeman of West Sixtieth Street, whose wife had called him. Together Sweeney, Richert and Oakey shouldered open the locked basement door. Genna was sprawled on the floor, blood gushing from a severed artery in his leg. He fired at them once with his .38-calibre revolver as they rushed him. He was overcome and hauled out.

When the ambulance from the Bridewell Hospital arrived he was dying – but not too languished to kick a stretcher-bearer in the face, with the valediction: 'Take that, you dirty son-of-a-bitch', whereupon he fell back and died.

Anselmi and Scalise had pounded on, watched by scores of householders from apartment blocks as they crossed vacant lots. They got to Fifty-ninth Street, burst into a dry-goods store and tried to buy caps as disguise but were turned out by the suspicious proprietor, and boarded a northbound street-car on Western Avenue. A patrol car from West Englewood Station picked up the tip, overtook the street-car and arrested them. No, they said in indignant amazement, they knew nothing about any shooting – they were just a couple of boys looking for work.

In the turmoil Olson, Walsh and Conway had lain where they had fallen; then local people brought up a car and carried them to the German Deaconess Hospital. Olson and Walsh died without regaining consciousness. They were the fourth and fifth policemen murdered in Chicago in that June week of 1925. Conway, in the St. Bernard's Hospital, lay desperately ill for days before gradually recovering. He and Sweeney were promoted to detective sergeants.

There could hardly seem to be a case of greater clarity than that against Scalise and Anselmi, nor one which would arouse a greater pitch of outraged sympathy from the public. Yet, after two years of legal equivocation and an anguished reluctance on the part of the authorities to press the charge, and during which time Sweeney, the key witness, received threatening telephone calls and letters stamped with skulls and Black Hands, and had the front of his house blown off by a bomb, Scalise and Anselmi walked free from the courtroom.

It was later suggested that, unbeknown to Mike Genna, he was in any case on his way to death that day, that Scalise and Anselmi had accepted the secret commission from Capone to take Genna for a ride. This claim was based upon an alleged statement made during that month by an unnamed prominent Italian to a detective friend. 'Mike,' he is said to have stated, 'was on his way to execution when the squad car officers were mistaken for enemy gangsters and fired upon. Momentarily, it upset the plans of Scalise and Anselmi, but in the end it was all right, as Mike was killed anyway.'

This theory does not stand up to examination. Genna and his torpedoes were on that day specifically hunting for members of the Weiss gang. The clanging of the gong and the appearance of the police car could not have left them any room for thinking they were being pursued by enemy gangsters. And the loyalty that the remaining Genna brothers showed towards Scalise and Anselmi in their fraught situation would certainly not have been given if there had been the most shadowy suspicion of treachery.

In fact the efforts made – successfully – to save Scalise and Anselmi are an example of the fanatical clan unity that existed among the Sicilian criminals. Scalise and Anselmi became the Sicilians's private Sacco and Vanzetti, an issue of racial honour. For 'the good name of Sicily', contributions to a defence fund were extracted from compatriots, both those in the racket and those engaged in honest pursuits. Anyway, it was quickly evident that it was unhealthy to refuse or to give grudgingly. Henry Spingola, brother-in-law of the dead Angelo, donated ten thousand dollars but jibbed when pressed for more, and on 10 January 1926 he was shot dead after the resulting quarrel. Two wholesale grocers Augustino and Antonio Moreci, who supplied the Gennas with the yeast for their alcohol parted with two thousand dollars each, but made it clear that that was the limit and also expressed the opinion that the murder of Spingola was a disgrace; each was found filled with bullets in his shop within a week.

The killing of Spingola, a respected elder of the community, aroused much spleen, as did that of Vito Bascone, a prosperous and popular wine dealer who had no link with the gang but who imprudently objected when asked for a third contribution. In retaliation Orazzio the Scourge Tropea, a collector for the fund, was killed on almost exactly the spot where Spingola had dropped; three other collectors, Little Joe Calabriese, Eddie the Eagle Baldelli and Tony Finalli, were also killed.

Baldelli, an ex-soldier who had resigned his job as a postal van-driver to turn bootlegger, was given a spectacular military funeral on the last day of February. It was on this day that Vice-President Dawes presented to the United States Senate a petition from Chicago signed by Edward L. Williams, Dean of the John Marshall Law School, and Dr. L. Williams, Director of the Law Enforcement for Better Government Association, which described 'the reign of terror in Chicago' and prayed for Federal action and relief. The petition declared: 'A colony of unnaturalized persons, feudists, blackhanders and members of Mafia, aided by gangs of American citizens – such as O'Donnells, McErlanes, Ragen's Colts and others – have formed a super-government of their own in Chicago which is levying tribute upon citizens and enforcing collection by terrorizing, kidnapping and assassination. Many of these outlaws have become fabulously rich as rum-runners and bootleggers. They are working in collusion with the police and other officials building up a monopoly in the unlawful liquor business and dividing the territory among themselves under penalty of death to all intruding competitors.' The petition pointed out that more than a hundred bomb outrages had been perpetrated in Chicago during the past twelve months and named five breweries being operated by 'a ring of politicians and public officials' through criminals and with dummy directors. Congress was asked to appoint a committee to investigate the 'shocking conditions' prevailing.

This discussion of their activities at national level did not divert the Sicilian community in Chicago from their preoccupation with the plight of Scalise and Anselmi. Despite their internal dissension and fratricide – and perhaps stimulated into a display of unity by the Gennas' guns – they poured 100 thousand dollars into the defence fund.

With his customary fire, which by now the public had learned had as much real ferocity and heat as a penny sparkler, State's Attorney Crowe intoned over the radio: 'These men will go straight to the gallows.' The citizens of Chicago seemed reluctant to take personal responsibility for accomplishing this. When the trial had begun on 5 October 1925, 234 of the 238 veniremen called to provide the jury had all manner of urgently vital personal reasons why they did not feel qualified to form an opinion as to the guilt of Scalise and Anselmi. One of them was franker than the rest. He said: 'It wouldn't be healthy to bring in a verdict of guilty. Pressure is brought to bear on our families. I'd have to carry a gun for the rest of my life if I served and found these two men guilty.' The defendants' lawyers also put difficulties in the way of forming a jury. They refused to accept as juryman anyone who had ever had any connexion with any law enforcement body, and spent forty minutes arguing against the inclusion of a man who had once or twice contributed money to an organization dedicated to reducing crime in Chicago.

The case for the defence was soon made apparent by one of the battery of lawyers engaged with the 100 thousand dollar fund. 'If a police officer detains you, even for a moment, against your will, and you kill him,' he insisted, 'you are not guilty of murder. It's just manslaughter. If the policeman uses forces of arms, you may kill him in self-defence and the law cannot harm you.' On 11 November, after matter-of-fact evidence which established murder of police by criminals actively engaged in crime, they were found guilty of the manslaughter of Olson and sentenced to fourteen years in prison. There was such an outcry of wrath at this leniency that State's Attorney Crowe found it necessary to issue a long explanation, wherein it was stated that now they would be tried for the murder of Walsh. Judge Brothers, who had presided at the first trial, declared that their return to court 'will not be delayed a moment – they will go on trial next Monday'. Delays did occur. It was three months later when they were tried for Walsh's murder. They were acquitted. 'This verdict is an outright disgrace to Chicago,' said Chief of Police Morgan A. Collins. Yet another interlude. On 3 May 1926 Scalise and Anselmi were escorted to Joliet Prison to serve their fourteen years manslaughter sentence, against which they had appealed. On 23 December the Illinois Supreme Court granted them a new trial, and on 9 June the following year – just two years after the gun-fight – their third trial began. They were acquitted. The reason deserves some prominence in this record. They had only, it was pointed out, resisted 'unwarranted police aggression'.

During all this time that the invisible agencies were busy extricating Scalise and Anselmi from their particularly tricky predicament, the larger contention continued. Angelo Genna had been killed in May, Michael Genna in June, and in July a third Genna was eliminated, and it was Tony the Gentleman. This time, it was by direct intervention of Capone. On 8 July 1925 Tony received a telephone call from Antonio Spano, known as The Cavalier, a seasoned killer whom the Gennas had imported from Sicily in 1921 as a recruit to their force, saying he had important information and would be at the corner of Grand Avenue and Curtis Street, on the Near North-West side of the city at six that evening. The information was of his own death. 'Two of the Gennas had been killed in as many months,' a detective said afterwards, interpreting the new killing for the press. 'They were frightened and suspicious. Tony never would have gone there for George Bugs Moran or Schemer Drucci or for any of the Capones, and that included Scalise and Anselmi. But he would go for the Cavalier. And he did.' He drove over in his car and alighted. Spano's hand reached out and grasped his with a warmth reminiscent of that shown in O'Banion's flowershop. While Spano held him firmly two figures with ·38 automatics circled out of doorways and hit him repeatedly in the back.

He did not die instantly. With him during his last hour in hospital was a Baptist minister's daughter from Chester, Illinois, who had graduated from playing the organ and leading the choir in the Loop, and whom Tony had furnished with a monogrammed sports roadster, much jewellery and a hundred dollar a week suite at the Congress Hotel. To her Tony, never the professional gangster, broke the gangster's code by whispering: 'The Cavalier got me.' The police had a fairly convincing excuse for making no arrest by announcing that they were looking for a man named Cavallero.

The Genna family had given Angelo a splendid funeral at a cost of 100 thousand dollars. Mike Genna's funeral had less ceremonial, as Police Captain Stege dampened the drama by declaring that his men would be present to take in every criminal or suspect who showed his identifiable face, and consequently Mike was buried in secrecy with no mourners, no flowers and no attendants except the undertaker. And Tony's funeral was as drab. His burial was a rush job, without even a prayer, denied the rites of the Catholic Church and the graveside lamentations of his friends.

For the Gennas were broken. Three of the six brothers were dead and the remaining three had been acquainted with the fact that they were on the spot. They did not wait to argue the justice of this. Sam and Pete went into hiding outside Chicago. Jim hastened back to the old home town of Marsala in Sicily, being in such a hurry that he left his wife behind to dispose of the fifty thousand dollars' worth of furniture in their Lake Side Place apartment. He was received by the Italian police and spent the next five years in jail.

'Who killed McSwiggin?'

'The most brazen and dastardly murder ever committed in Chicago.'

STATE'S ATTORNEY ROBERT E. CROWE

'I've been accused of every death except the casualty list of the World War.'

AL CAPONE

THE fall of the house of Genna was not monopolizing all the attention of Chicago's underworld. Concurrently there was much other activity. Between the summer of 1925 and the next, Walter O'Donnell was fatally wounded in a roadhouse; George Big Bates Karl was killed by the Saltis-McErlane gang; Bill Dickman was liquidated for knowing too much about the Karl killing; an attempt on the life of Spike O'Donnell was made by the Saltis-McErlane gang; Tony Campagna, Sam Lavenuto and Jim Russo – all independent alky-makers in the Capone territory – were killed; Irving Schlig, Harry Berman, Aniello Taddeo, Machine-gun Joe Granata and Joe Larson were all taken for their separate one-way rides; the Ragen Colts Club House, the headquarters of the Sheldon gang, was raided by Saltis machine-gunners and two men killed; and there were six more killings and four woundings in the mêlée of incessant collisions between the South Side O'Donnells, the Sheldon and Saltis-McErlane gangs – which all made a contribution to the total of 1926's seventy-six killings and almost as many maimings by bullet, which still endures as a twelve-month record in the history of gang-violence in Chicago or anywhere else in the world.

Also during this period three attacks were made upon Capone; twice his car was picked away from his escort cars in traffic and raked with gun-fire, each time slugs ripping his clothing without injuring him, and an attempt was made to poison his food. His chauffeur was kidnapped, tortured to squeeze from him details of Capone's movements, and then his bullet-holed body was stuffed in a cistern in an East Chicago rooming house.

Yet Capone could not, as he would dearly have liked to have done, turn his full gun-power on to the maliciously aggressive Weiss and his band. As so often happens upon the accession of command within a dynasty, at the moment of the change of seat, a hundred old discontents and enmities erupted. Coincident with taking over control from Torrio, Capone found himself surrounded by rebellion, secession, reprisals and sieges upon his authority; his territory was being invaded and trampled over at all points, and even in Cicero the O'Donnell brothers, now allied with Tom Duffy, a booze-runner and Republican precinct captain, and Jim Doherty, a gunman with a murder record, were openly flouting the peace pact; the South Side was in brawling turmoil; serious trouble was developing within the gambling syndicate; and he was fully occupied with trying to extend his political power through the offices of Hinky Dink Kenna and Bathhouse John Coughlin. This was a crucial period for Capone in all respects, the time when, Peterson says: '. . . the vicious criminal elements and their political counterparts became more strongly organized, government was growing more and more disorganized, until it virtually fell apart and capitulated to a ruthless and defiant underworld.' It was a severe testing time for Capone's skill as ruler and administrator, for it called for the most subtle delicacy of judgement – which factions were too dangerously hostile to be wooed and must therefore be crushed; which ones were too strong to be crushed and must therefore be wooed; which ones were too troublesome but too small to be worth wooing, and could therefore be beaten into line; and which ones could be put at each other's throats and diverted from him. At the same time, he was still trying to apply Torrio's philosophy of armed co-existence and, when conflict became too costly in its disturbance of business, to settle differences around a table.

It was in the early stages of these developing difficulties that a question thundered through Chicago and through all the nation: 'Who killed McSwiggin?' In retrospect, it at first appears strange, after the murders of so many policemen and the exposures of so many crooked officials all received with varying degrees of apathy or tolerance, that this particular crime, the shooting of an Assistant State's Attorney, should have aroused such impassioned interest. 'Public excitement and indignation were intense,' records Landesco; 'columns of newspaper space were devoted to the topic for weeks. Every edition carried clues, new angles and developments.' Landesco's explanation for this is: 'In the four months from January to April there had been twenty-nine killings ascribed by the police and newspapers to the booze war. In the preceding four years, over two hundred such murders had occurred – "Gangsters killing gangsters, a good way to get rid of them". But this was the assassination of an energetic young public official in the most important office for law enforcement – no longer gangsters killing gangsters, but an attack upon the State. It dramatized to the public the relation between criminal gangs and the political machine and threw a flood of light upon the world of organized crime and its sinister attempts at controlling elections, public officials and even the courts. The very failure of the grand juries in solving the mystery of McSwiggin's death raised many puzzling and disturbing questions in the minds of intelligent citizens about the reasons for the breakdown of constituted government in Chicago and Cook County, and its seeming helplessness when pitted against the forces of organized crime.' But by 1926 the citizenry of Chicago were hardly in need of tuition in the methods and successes of the gangs. Perhaps the truer reason for the aberrant emotionalism was that it contained, even for the hardboiled and sophisticated Chicagoan, a dismal shock of disillusionment – young Sir Galahad, too, was revealed to be a cheat, the crusader was seen as a faker with a rubber lance, the martyr who deserved his pile of faggots.

The facts are that William H. McSwiggin, aged twenty-six, Assistant State's Attorney of Cook County and a police sergeant's son with a reputation for securing death penalty verdicts, was killed on the night of 27 April 1926. He was slain by machine-gun fire from a moving car in front of the Pony Inn, a saloon run by Harry Madigan on West Roosevelt Road in Cicero, and there died with him those two branded killers, Jim Doherty and Tom Duffy; also in his company at the time, and who escaped by dropping to the ground and shamming death, were Myles O'Donnell, one of the North Side bootleggers who had been exceeding the Cicero concession granted them by Torrio, and Edward Hanley, a former policeman, Doherty's driver. They had arrived together at the Pony Inn in Doherty's new Lincoln sedan.

The tone in which the story was broken next morning was one of outrage and tenderness: as the State's Attorney's office explained, McSwiggin was up in Cicero 'trying to obtain information'. Here was a stalwart young warrior of righteousness, a kind of symbol of the valour and determination that Chicago so direly lacked, thrusting into the thick of the enemy in pursuit of his duty, and cut down by the scoundrels who feared him. It may have been the sort of morale-stiffening idyll that Chicago then needed, but unfortunately it soon turned rotten.

The martyr-clique at first hogged all the attention. Robert E. Crowe, the State's Attorney, Gorman, his first assistant, and Judge William V. Brothers, Presiding Judge of the Criminal Court, chimed mellifluously in praise of McSwiggin, who, they said, had clearly been murdered in revenge for his relentless hounding of Scalise and Anselmi, and for his vigorous prosecution of other gang cases; additionally they suggested, it was probably known that he had a lot of menacing information about the Durkin case, in which a police-man had been killed in a running gun-fight. It was, they said, all the more credit to the brave young Assistant State's Attorney that he had hobnobbed with known gangsters in order to gather evidence. An alternative and slightly more neutral theory put forward was that of Joseph Z. Klenha, Mayor of Cicero, and Captain John Stege, of the Detective Bureau – that McSwiggin had been innocently trapped in a gang-dispute, and that he had been mistaken as a member of the O'Donnell gang whom they were hunting. Yet another theory was that the killing arose out of the recent primary election in Cicero, subsequently investigated by four special grand juries because of vote frauds, and in which Duffy and O'Donnell had figured, together with Hirschey Miller and Terry Druggan, as authorized supervisors for the Crowe-Barrett machine.

State's Attorney Crowe boomed one of his familiar war-cries that seemed always to exhaust him and stultify further action. 'It will be war to the hilt against these gangsters,' he promised. This time there was no bay of approval from the public; in their flare of hot indig-nation they were sceptical; briefly, they appeared really to want a purge of the crooks. Newspapers spoke bitterly of 'Chicago's anarchy'. Emergency groups of prominent club women led a protest movement against the breakdown of public justice symbolized by the McSwiggin murder. Ministers' associations publicized their repeated failures to get the co-operation of public officials in the suppression of vice and crime. Civic leaders openly said they did not trust Crowe's pledge, and Harry Eugene Kelly, then president of the Union League Club, proposed that an independent fund should be raised to set up a special grand jury for the investigation of the murder, contending that if this had to depend upon Crowe or the County Board for financing it would be 'hampered by politics and incapable of free and unbiased action' – a fairly lurid charge to be made against a high public law official, even in the context of Chicago and its record. Kelly explained: 'I have nothing against Mr. Crowe personally, but obviously he is unfit to go into the beer racket because it is mixed up all down the line with politics. He is not only a capable politician but is the head and front of a powerful faction known as the "Crowe Wing". He is the directing head of a faction organized for politics, and politics only. Therefore, the citizens cannot expect Mr. Crowe to prosecute the kind of an investigation this city requires.'

The unpunctureable Crowe puffed an even denser cloud of curdled rhetoric: 'I am engaged,' he said in a formal statement, 'in the investigation of the· most brazen and dastardly murder ever committed in Chicago. Selfish notoriety seekers, who are called by some newspapers "civic leaders", have started a backfire on the State's Attorney of this county, while he is engaged in this arduous and not entirely safe duty. I appeal to the law-abiding men and women of this county for their moral support and sympathy in this crisis; and I appeal to these officious meddlers that if they have any information, to present it to me; if they can be of any assistance, to co-operate with me, and cease giving aid and comfort to gangsters by attempting to divert my attention from the task in hand.'

(Crowe, it is worth noting, later employed the same tactics when there was insistent public demand for a special grand jury to investigate election day violence at the April 1928 primary election. Then, he tried to frustrate the investigation by instructing his adherents on the County Board to refuse an appropriation for the jury. The citizens by-passed him by raising the funds by popular subscription.)

Crowe then quickly petitioned Judge William V. Brothers, a member of the Crowe Wing, for a special grand jury. This did not bemuse Kelly and his campaigners. They pointed out that a special grand jury presided over by Crowe would be precluded from investigating Crowe and the underlying causes of the murder. Nor, they said bluntly, did they believe that Crowe, being a powerful political leader, would allow a grand jury to determine the connexion between politics and booze-running. To create an impression of magnanimous objectivity, Crowe then asked Attorney-General Carlstrom to preside over the grand jury. The Chicago *Tribune* neatly incised this new bombast: 'Mr. Crowe believes he has checkmated his critics. He appears confident that, with one grand jury digging into the gunmen, the chances for the creation of another will be nil, and that those who have been calling for a Special State's Attorney will not assail the ability or fairness of Attorney-General Carlstrom or charge that he is a member of the same political faction.'

In fact, Carlstrom was used by Crowe and Brothers to divert the labours of the first grand jury into uncovering the scandals surrounding the recent killing of Deputy Warden Klein at Joliet Prison and to the administration of the Governor's pardon and Parole Board.

Crowe and Carlstrom flooded many columns in the newspapers with their discoveries of a syndicate for the sale of pardons and paroles, listed the names of notorious criminals who had bought parole, and claimed that Chicago's crime was solely caused by paroled convicts.

And the parole scandal, which engaged almost the whole time and attention of this first jury, was dropped without the voting of a single indictment. By 5 May the newspapers learned that the police 'had no more actual evidence as to the motives of the shooting and the identity of the killers than they did when it happened'.

The only point upon which the jury seemed able to satisfy themselves was that McSwiggin had been tracking down a stolen bulletproof vest made by Mr. Albert Dunlap, 'a reputable citizen and authorized representative of the manufacturers of the article'.

Then, after a few days, the pro-McSwiggin glow died. Just why *had* he been with that quartet? was the question that began to be asked in newspaper editorials and by the general public. The first horrid disenchantment came from the lips of Capone himself. Speculation as to the identity of the killers had finally circled around and rested upon him. Madigan, the owner of the Pony Inn, in an interview with Chief of Detectives Schoemaker, filled in the background with this personal story: 'When I wanted to start a saloon in Cicero more than a year ago, Capone wouldn't let me. I finally obtained strong political pressure and was able to open. Then Capone came to me and said I would have to buy his beer, so I did. A few months ago Doherty and Myles O'Donnell came to me and said they could sell me better beer than Capone beer, which was then needled. They did and it only cost fifty dollars a barrel, where Capone charged me sixty. I changed, and upon my recommendation so did several other Cicero saloon-keepers.'

That Capone had sound reason for wishing to bump-off the O'Donnells began to emerge, and the case against him strengthened. First came the discovery that a Mr. A. V. Korecek, a West Side hardware merchant, had the week before sold three Thompson submachine-guns to a 'John' and a 'Charlie', who described themselves as bankers, but he failed to identify John Capone and Charles Fischetti of the Capone gang, and begged not to be forced to disclose his customers for fear of his life. Later, he testified that he had sold Thompson machine-guns to Charlie Carr, manager of the Four Deuces, the Capone house of prostitution; he said that he had obtained them through a Valparaiso firm 'under duress'. (These stubbily handy portable assault weapons were made by the Thompson Company of New York, the vice-president of which was Colonel W. H. Thompson, machine-gun aide to General Pershing in World War One. The gun weighed nine pounds, carried two magazines – one holding a hundred bullets and the other fifty – and fired at the rate of 150 rounds a minute.) Then a citizen came forward with the story that on the evening of 27 April he had been in a Cicero restaurant and had seen Al, his brother Ralph and three other gang-members in urgent conversation, at the end of which Al had gone to a panel in the wall, taken out a machine-gun and revolvers, and that they had then all left – at seven o'clock, an hour before the assault.

The third allegation implicating Capone was that McSwiggin had been wrongly identified as Weiss, whom he resembled, and that, receiving the tip that Weiss was in Cicero with the O'Donnell gangsters, Capone had hurried forth to seize the opportunity of disposing of him and all the old scores.

So completely satisfied were the authorities that they had solved the crime that they issued a formal statement, carried on the front pages of the newspapers on 5 May. It read: 'It has been established to the satisfaction of the State's Attorney's office and the detective bureau that Capone in person led the slayers of McSwiggin. It has become known that five automobiles carrying nearly thirty gang-sters, all armed with weapons ranging from pistols to machine-guns, were used in the triple killing. It also has been found that Capone handled the machine-gun, being compelled to this act in order to set an example of fearlessness to his less eager companions. The five automobiles, it has been learned, were used in hours of patient trailing of the doomed O'Donnell gang and later to make sure of escape.'

There is no reason to suppose that Capone would either admit to this charge or speak even partial truth, yet there was a hideous ring of likelihood about the statement he made in an interview with a local newspaper, and it began the sudden twinges of doubt about McSwiggin's guiltlessness. Capone said: 'Of course I didn't kill him. Why should I? I liked the kid. Only the day before he got killed he was up to my place and when he went home I gave him a bottle of Scotch for his old man. I paid McSwiggin and I paid him plenty, and I got what I was paying for.'

Capone then vanished and was missing for four months. He eventu-ally, after discussions between his lawyers and the State's Attorney's office, surrendered himself on the Illinois-Indiana state line to Federal officers. He gave this testimony: 'I'm no squawker but I'll tell you what I know about this case. All I ask is a chance to prove that I had nothing to do with the killing of my friend McSwiggin. Just before he was killed I talked with McSwiggin. There were friends of mine with me. If we had wanted to kill him we could have done it then and nobody would have known. But we didn't want to; we never wanted to. Doherty and Duffy were my friends too. I wasn't out to get them. Why, I used to lend Doherty money. I blew out of this town because I was being made the goat. I've been accused of every death except the casualty list of the World War. I didn't want some fat-headed cop to shoot me on sight, just to make a snappy entry on his record.'

Capone was officially exonerated of any complicity in the murders on 28 July and was dismissed by Chief Justice Lynch, when Assistant State's Attorney Gorman withdrew the charge. He was re-arrested on a charge of conspiracy in the primary election frauds, only to be discharged when all the indictments were cancelled because the primary law was declared unconstitutional by the Supreme Court.

But the McSwiggin scandal did not end with the dismissal of Capone from the case. In spasms of fervour and renewed indignation, it continued until September and yet the public mood had changed. The ardour had been doused by the old cynicism. There would be no prosecutions, it was accurately forecast – 'Too much dynamite in it' – and the original solemn question 'Who killed McSwiggin?' came to be used banteringly like 'Who killed Cock Robin?' and 'Why did the chicken cross the road?' Altogether seven juries – a coroner's jury, five special county grand juries and a Federal grand jury – were empanelled; former Judge Charles A. McDonald and his two assistants drew 34,125 dollars from the county in salaries, and a further 150 thousand dollars were paid out to members of the police department and the State's Attorney's staff for the special work; evidence was heard from hundreds of witnesses – including two hundred subpoenaed Cicero saloon-keepers – and the result was a fog of baffled words.

The investigation bristled with puzzles and inconsistencies. There was only one eye-witness to the killing, a Mrs. Bach who lived above the Pony Inn, who said: 'It was daylight still and I saw a closed car speeding away with what looked like a telephone receiver sticking out of the rear window and spitting fire,' yet there was the curious official statement speaking with apparent certainty about the 'five automobiles', and further confusion was added by the introduction of two sixteen-year-old Cicero boys who said they were playing near by and saw the victims come out of the saloon followed by the murderers. It is also interesting that after the shooting, Hanley and O'Donnell, who had survived, picked up the bodies of McSwiggin and Doherty, put them in the car and then tossed them out at Berwyn, afterwards abandoning the car at Oak Park; Duffy was left where he was, behind a tree where he had crawled to die; in his waistcoat pocket was found a letter demanding the transfer of a police sergeant. A further note of melodrama was added by Mc-Swiggin's father, Sergeant Anthony McSwiggin, of the Chicago Police Department, confronting Capone in the Hawthorne Hotel. Sergeant McSwiggin had been quoted as saying: 'I know who the murderers are – they are Al Capone, Bob McCullough, Frank Rio and Frank Diamond. They killed me too, when they killed my boy.' Yet when Sergeant McSwiggin – it is said – accused Capone to his face, Capone pulled out his automatic and handed it to the distraught old man, demanding: 'If you think I did it, shoot me,' and McSwiggin turned away sobbing. This episode ends with the strange closing words of Judge McDonald, presiding over the last grand jury. 'I know who killed McSwiggin,' he said, 'but I do not know it legally and am unable to present it conclusively.'

What did emerge from the welter of allegation and contradiction, however, was at first a misty, then gradually clarifying, picture of the complicity between gangsters, politicians, police and officials – a situation that everyone had known about and which had incessantly been revealed piecemeal during the previous years, but which had not hitherto been given cohesion: suddenly a hundred loose links in the chain of conspiracy flew magnetically together, and there for all to see was the corporate pattern, leading from gambling parlour to committee room to City Hall to detective bureau. Yet even then, the course of justice was frustrated. Witnesses retracted and disappeared. The judge said: 'It is necessary to keep the witnesses' names secret. The moment that any of them learn that they are wanted they disappear or are even killed.' Even after the fourth grand jury voted twenty indictments involving forty election judges and clerks of the Forty-Second Ward, the proceedings were sidetracked into hearing evidence on the murder of Mitters Foley. (Two members of the gang were indicted – and immediately acquitted by the Criminal Court.) The labours of the grand juries resulted in this finding of momentous hollowness: 'It appears to us that the causes for the gang may be summarized as follows: 1. Profits obtainable from illegal traffic in beer and alcohol; 2. The ease with which deadly weapons are obtainable at small cost and the light penalties for their possession; 3. Widespread violation of the Volstead Act. On the whole a review of the years past gives no special occasion for alarm at the present moment. Crime, in volume and type, wheels and rotates in cycles. In the last thirty or forty years there have been periodical outbursts of gang activities in the criminal groups. The one through which we are now passing has been peculiarly vicious and has produced many murders by gangsters because the stakes played for have been great. Gang after gang has been wiped out by internecine warfare. Remnants of gangs have fled the city and the situation is well enough in hand to encourage the hope that there will be no outbreak on any such scale as the recent past.'

It was soon demonstrated who had the situation well in hand. During all the McSwiggin pother and public fuss, which disturbed the hard core gangsters little and deflected them from their bootlegging and private feuding not at all, Capone, after waiting months for the best opportunity, on 10 August 1926 struck back at the Weiss gang. Weiss, and Drucci were on that day to complete a financial settlement with Morris Eller, Trustee of the Chicago Sanitary District Department, and John A. Sbarbaro, Assistant State's Attorney and the undertaker who buried O'Banion. Weiss called for Drucci at the Congress Hotel, on South Michigan Avenue, and breakfasted with him in his suite. At ten o'clock they left for the Standard Oil Building, where the Sanitary Department had its offices. Drucci was carrying 13,200 dollars in bills. They were also both carrying automatics tucked under left arms.

They got safely to the junction of Michigan and Ninth Streets, at that hour ajostle with businessmen in cars and on foot. As they were about to cross, a car which had presumably been following them, swerved into the kerb, and three men craned through the windows and opened fire with two guns apiece.

Weiss threw himself down on to the pavement, as did every other pedestrian within earshot: in five seconds the hurrying throng had melted away into doorways and alleys. Traffic stopped dead and drivers dived under their dashboards. Drucci ducked behind a mailbox, pulled out his gun and returned fire. Two of the attackers jumped out to get into closer range. For several minutes the crash of reports ran together in a sustained clamour, the only sound that could quell the street noise and bustle of Chicago. Thirty bullets were fired, breaking shop windows and perforating the bodywork of cars. None of the gangsters was hurt, the only casualty being an office worker, James Cardan, of South Aberdeen Street, who was hit in the thigh.

The skirmish was abruptly ended by the arrival of a police patrol. The assailant car roared off without waiting for the two gunmen fighting it out on the sidewalk. Weiss got away. Drucci scuttered, bent low, to a car at whose wheel was a terrified Mr. C. C. Bassett, of Calumet Avenue. Drucci jabbed his gun at Bassett and shouted: 'Take me away and make it snappy.' Before he could get in the door, he was surrounded by detectives and arrested. Also arrested was one of the stranded fighters, Louis Barko, a gambler and Capone gunman, who gave his name as Paul Valerie, of 3533 Walnut Street, a non-existent address. He was pushed forward for Drucci's inspection. Drucci said: 'Never saw him before. It wasn't no gang fight. It was a stick-up, that's all. They were after my roll.'

A week later Weiss, Drucci and one of their legal advisers were driving down Michigan Avenue, again at a peak business hour, when a car rammed them into the kerb in a grinding of locked metal and a hail of bullets showered them with glass. And again they were unhurt. They leaped out and ran for cover into the Standard Oil Building, which was becoming a public shooting gallery.

Having displayed that he could be as tigerish as they if he wished, Capone, still striving to maintain Torrio's policy of pacification, instigated a peace-talk. Antonio Lombardo, Capone's appointee to the Unione Siciliana presidency, was the mediator, and he brought together a meeting a few days after the Michigan Avenue ambush, in the Morrison Hotel. An unnamed police official was present as referee. Weiss came, in a belligerent and unaccommodating spirit, and immediately laid down his terms for talking: that the men who had in such a beastly way attacked Drucci and himself should be put on the spot. To this demand Capone replied, with towering indignation but with not too fine a sense of accuracy: 'I wouldn't do that to a yellow dog.' The peace conference aborted.

Three weeks later Weiss made the boldest assault of all upon Capone's authority – and the most brazen intimation to a cowed and subjugated community that the gangs were arbitrarily going to do what they pleased.

12

The Assault upon Cicero ... and the
Robber Barons' Council

'Here I am in Chicago, and I'm doing very well.'
BIG MACEO, Kid Man Blues.

O N the sparklingly sunny afternoon of 20 September Cicero
had an air of festive expectancy, for the autumn meeting at
the adjoining Hawthorne Race Track was about to begin.
The town had filled with punters, horse-owners and holidaymakers,
who mixed with the usual crowds of women shoppers with prams and
small children. The section of Cicero where the Hawthorne Hotel
stands was then, and still is, a prototype American suburb: an
eighty-foot broad boulevard which at that time had a double street-
car track running down the centre; the Hawthorne Hotel block –
4823–27 on West Twenty-second Street – also contained a radio
shop, a paint shop, an ironmongery, a grocery, a laundry, a delicatessen and a barber; nearby was the Anton Hotel, run by the
Capone combine, and beyond that a fifty-foot vacant lot used as a
car park. Opposite was a garage, a florist, a women's hairdresser, the
Pinkert State Bank, a lingerie shop, a cigarette shop, a chemist, a
café and a confectioner. Above these were the offices of doctors,
dentists, estate agents and lawyers. There were traffic lights at the
intersection, and the area had the general air of raw Main Street
brightness.

On that afternoon at 1.15 Capone was sitting at a white-tiled
table in the Hawthorne Restaurant, facing the front window, with
his bodyguard Slippery Frank Rio; they were finishing lunch and
sipping coffee. It was at this moment that Weiss arrived on his sally
deep into enemy territory.

In the lead of the eleven-car machine-gun caravan was a decoy
black tourer equipped like a detective bureau squad car with a gong
on the left-hand running-board. It came down the street at fifty
miles an hour with the gong jangling and a man beside the driver
firing a tommy-gun loaded with blank cartridges.

As was intended, every one of the sixty customers in the Hawthorne Restaurant jumped up excitedly when the decoy car had passed and the shooting faded – including Capone. He banged down his coffee cup and started for the door. He was grabbed, pressed again to the floor, and dragged under a table by Rio, who was thinking quicker. That saved Capone's life, for a moment later the real onslaught began. The following ten cars came slowly behind, at ten-foot intervals. When the first drew level with the Anton Hotel a machine-gunner began firing, lacing his shots methodically up and down and across like a fireman spraying a hose. It stopped in front of the Hawthorne, and the first stream of bullets was supplemented by volleys from the other cars, now drawn up in a concentrated line. From the ninth car stepped a man in a khaki shirt and brown over-alls. He walked composedly up to the entrance of the Hawthorne with a Thompson sub-machine-gun nursed against his chest. He knelt, brought it level and released a whole drum of a hundred bullets into the restaurant. The gun was set at rapid fire and the fusillade took ten seconds to deliver. While he squatted urbanely sweeping the gun from side to side, the occupants of the tenth car stood on the sidewalk guarding him with sawn-off shot-guns. The din ceased suddenly. The men walked back to the cars, there was a triple honk on a horn as signal, and the caravan drove off east down Twenty-second Street back towards Chicago.

They left devastation behind. The police calculated that a thousand bullets had been fired. The windows of the Hawthorne and Anton Hotels, the barber shop, the laundry and the delicatessen were shattered; the woodwork, walls and ceilings of all of them were gashed and splintered; furniture was cut to pieces; across the lobby of the Hawthorne Restaurant were neat horizontal patterns of ·45-calibre bullet holes, a double frieze the height of a man's head and breast. Thirty-five cars parked along the kerb were holed. Yet, oddly enough, no one was killed. The only casualties were Louis Barko, the Capone gunman and one of the ambushers of Weiss and Drucci the previous month, wounded in the shoulder, and a Mrs. Freeman. Mrs. Freeman, her husband, Clyde, a Louisiana racing man, and their five-year-old son were sitting in their parked car when the attack began. The car was riddled. One bullet sliced through Mr. Freeman's hat, another grazed his son's knee and tore his coat, and a fourth struck Mrs. Freeman in the arm and her right eye was pierced by flying glass from the windscreen. (Capone, it deserves to be stated, paid out five thousand dollars to specialists to save her sight and also reimbursed the shopkeepers for the damage they suffered.) Barko had been about to enter the Hawthorne Restaurant to meet Capone when the attack began. He was struck by the bullet as he ran into the entrance. Chief Schoemaker knew that Barko had seen the raiders, took him to headquarters and paraded Weiss, Drucci, Moran and Peter Gusenberg before him. 'Never seen them before', said Barko, thereby reciprocating his own non-identification by Drucci in August.

Twenty days later Capone retorted. Weiss had spent the afternoon on 11 October 1926 at the Criminal Court, where Joe Saltis and Lefty Koncil were on trial for the murder of Mitters Foley, one of a minor gang who had been trespassing on the South-Western territory. Weiss was concerned in seeing that they were acquitted – as they were despite the evidence of five eye-witnesses – and had been making an inspection of the jury to ensure that they were taking a sensible view of the matter. He had raised a hundred thousand dollar defence fund.

He left the courtroom at three o'clock in the company of Paddy Murray, his bodyguard and beer salesman, Sam Peller, his driver, W. W. O'Brien, a criminal lawyer, and Benny Jacobs, an investigator for the lawyer and a politician of the Bloody Twentieth Ward.

Weiss had retained O'Banion's flower shop on North State Street as his headquarters, and had his office over the premises. At about four o'clock Weiss's car pulled up and the five men got out and strolled, talking, across the pavement towards the door. There was the clatter of a machine-gun and Weiss fell dead with twelve bullets in his body; he had died at about the average age for a gangster – twenty-eight – and left an estate of 1,300,000 dollars. He was taken, with rosary and gun undrawn from his clothes, to be laid out on a slab in the mortuary of that last friend of so many gangsters, John A. Sbarbaro. Murray was hit fifteen times and toppled dead beside him. O'Brien, with four wounds, crawled across the street, sensibly to a doctor's surgery, and, like Jacobs and Peller, who were also seriously wounded, eventually recovered. They were interrogated in their hospital beds by the police, but naturally could offer no assistance; they had seen nobody, could not identify the killers, and had no idea what the attack was all about.

The police, however, had no great difficulty in reconstructing the plot. They established that a few days after the Weiss raid on Cicero a young man giving the name of Oscar Lundin applied to rent a room at 740 North State Street, next to the flower shop. He asked for the second floor front, but it was occupied, and he took a hall room until it should become available. The tenant in the front room moved out on Tuesday 5 October and Lundin changed his quarters. At the same time a woman had rented a third floor back room at 1 West Superior Street, which intersects State Street to the south of the flower shop. The man's room had an L-shaped window which provided a satisfactory diagonal arc of fire across the front of the shop and could even reach inside the doorway; the woman's room commanded a sweep of the back door and alley leading to it. Neither the man nor the woman took part in the ambush. After paying the rent in advance they vanished and their identities were never discovered.

But the rooms did not remain empty. Six ambushers had been assigned to the task, three to each room – for left behind were three chairs grouped around each window and carpets of hundreds of cigarette butts in semicircles on the floors. Enquiries revealed that the men had been in the building for a week. For seven days the vigil had been kept, until, presumably, the street was reasonably empty of other pedestrians and cars. For seven days Weiss had been an irrevocably condemned man as he came and went from the shop, for time after time fingers must have tightened on the triggers in readiness for the propitious moment. And the killers were prepared for a pitched battle. Abandoned in Superior Street was a Thompson sub-machine-gun and drums holding a hundred ·45-calibre steel-jacketed bullets; in both rooms were revolvers and sawn-off shot-guns. More than fifty bullets flew across the street and spattered the stonework of the Holy Name Cathedral.

It had been a particularly dangerous assignment, for the chances of escaping from an upper storey after the slaughter were not good. Yet it was done; and they left taking with them one of the machine-guns, which was later found discarded, behind 12 West Huron Street. No one came forward to report the flight of any one. Obviously the assassination had been elaborately discussed and planned, and it had been decided that there was no hope of getting Weiss by the orthodox method of attack in the street or taking him for a ride; there might also have been in the mind of the originator of the idea an attraction towards Weiss dying almost in the bloodstains of his predecessor.

Not unexpectedly Capone was called upon next day. He was in carpet slippers and shirt sleeves at the Hawthorne Hotel where he received his visitors from the newspapers. 'I'm sorry Weiss was killed,' he said, handing round cigars and drawing upon one himself, 'but I didn't have anything to do with it. I telephoned the Detective Bureau that I'd come in if they wanted me to, but they told me they didn't want me. I knew I would be blamed for it. There's enough business for all of us without us killing each other like animals in the streets. I don't want to end up in the gutter punctured with machine-gun slugs, so why should I kill Weiss?'

No one there troubled to list the reasons, and Capone was left to finish his cigar. Chief of Detectives Schoemaker however supplied the answer. 'He knows why and so does everyone else – he had them killed.' Chief of Police Morgan A. Collins also appeared to have no doubts that Capone's was the finger put on Weiss and his companions. He alleged that recently Capone had been on a recruiting mission in New York and had returned with fifteen hired gunmen to increase his personal bodyguard to eighteen. For this particular job, said Collins, 'Capone played safe first by importing killers, expert machine-gunners, and then hurrying them out of town.'

So, the two heads of Chicago's law-enforcement were both convinced of Capone's guilt, but he was not discommoded. 'The Chicago police department had surrendered to Capone unconditionally,' says Pasley. 'Its morale was sapped.' Collins, asked why Capone was going free, said dispiritedly: 'It's a waste of time to arrest him. He's been in before on other murder charges. He has his alibi.'

This fresh barbarity in the city's streets was mentioned during the trial of Saltis and Koncil. In its final report the grand jury remarked: 'A number of unusual and significant circumstances arose both prior to and during the progress of the trial. Prior to the trial two of the State's important witnesses disappeared, the immediate members of their families either refusing or being unable to give any information or clue as to their whereabouts. After the selection of the jury and the introduction of some of the State's evidence, one of the jurors selected to try the case became violently insane, necessitating the discharge of the entire jury and the selection of another in its stead. During the progress of the trial and immediately after the selection of the first jury, one Hymie Weiss, a notorious character in this community, was murdered in North State Street, a short distance from the Criminal Court Building where the trial was in progress. One of the counsel for the defendants was also shot and wounded at the same time and place. In the possession of the said Hymie Weiss were found a list of the jurors selected to try the case as well as the identical copy of the list of the State's witnesses that had been furnished counsel for the defendants by order of the Court. In addition to these significant facts, certain of the State's witnesses testified to having been threatened with violence in the event they testified against the defendants, and of having been approached with offers of bribery for either withholding their testimony or testifying falsely.'

But the measures succeeded. On 9 November Saltis and Koncil were pronounced not guilty. 'I expected a different verdict on the evidence,' Judge Harry B. Miller commented plaintively. 'I think the evidence warranted a verdict of guilty.'

Weiss's funeral lacked the grandiosity of most 'big shots' and there wasn't a single glittering name among the wreath-labels. The Catholic Church continued its policy of withholding its last rites from the more notorious sinners among its flock. Weiss's old school friends stayed faithful. All the pallbearers were classmates from St. Malachy's School. Police cars prowled about ready to arrest any recognized gangsters, but among those who staunchly saw Weiss to the grave were Eisen, Kaulman, the Gusenbergs, Drucci and Big Ed Vogel. The funeral was also exploited as a shop window for some improvised electioneering. Each of the mourners' cars carried placards, front and rear: 'JOHN SBARBARO FOR MUNICIPAL JUDGE', 'JOE SAVAGE FOR COUNTRY JUDGE', and 'KING-ELLER-GRAYDON, SANITARY DISTRICT TRUSTEES'.

It was all a bit sluttish for gangland.

Capone was not present, and doubtless felt no inclination to be, as the document found on Weiss's corpse could not have endeared him to his memory. It revealed the state of collusion between O'Banion's old mob and that of Polack Joe Saltis, who had been representing himself as a faithful follower of Capone. There had been a previous hint at an association between the Saltis-McErlane and O'Banion mobs – in September, when Vincent McErlane and Peter Gusenberg, an O'Banion man, were arrested for the Grand Trunk train robbery – but that could have been attributed to a passing collaboration in one freelance undertaking outside the province of booze. But Deputy Commissioner of Police John Stege interpreted this new situation succinctly: 'Weiss and Saltis had joined force to put Capone out of business.'

The significance of this unpleasant leakage did not escape Saltis, even though his was not the keenest of intelligences. He was a Pole, a huge landslide of a man, dull-eyed, lumbering of movement, but not entirely stupid. Until Prohibition he had been a low-grade saloon keeper in the Back o' the Yards area, where the Bohemian population lived around the slaughterhouses and meat-canning factories. He had formed a friendship and business partnership with John Dingbat O'Berta, a vivacious, fox-faced political spiv who was Republican committee man for the Thirteenth Ward, and had run for alderman as well as for State senator. The Volstead Act forged their partnership: Saltis knew the beer business and O'Berta had the political drag, and together they began supplying the market of 200 thousand thirsty Slavs in the zone south-west of the stockyards. Within a year Saltis had become a landed gentleman, with an estate in the Eagle River country of Wisconsin, hunted over by rich sportsmen, and O'Berta's popularity, standing and bank account flowered.

The two hundred saloons operated by O'Berta, Saltis and Frank McErlane were an important financial tributary of Capone's main stream of booze profits: he augmented their home-made supplies from his own breweries and distilleries, and also supplied high-level protection in return for a percentage of income. Saltis knew that Capone would be gravely displeased at the news that he was reneging to the enemy, and, while still safely in prison during his trial for the murder of Mitters Foley, talked to O'Berta in the hope that he could find a solution to the dilemma. O'Berta recommended that it should be discussed with Maxie Eisen. Eisen, bootlegger, labour terrorist and fish-racketeer to whom every stallholder in the Maxwell Street open market paid disbursement, and regarded as one of the sagest brains in the business, had been loosely associated with O'Banion, but upon his murder had prudently eased away.

Capone, in a further interview with the press, had indicated that, having again paraded his potency, he was open to an approach for an armistice. 'Hymie Weiss is dead,' he had stated, 'because he was a bull-head. Forty times I've tried to arrange things so that we'd have peace in Chicago and life would be worth living. Who wants to be tagged around night and day by guards? I don't, for one. There was, and there is, plenty of business for us all and competition needn't be a matter of murder, anyway. But Weiss couldn't be told anything. I suppose you couldn't have told him a week ago that he'd be dead today. There are some reasonable fellows in his outfit, and if they want peace I'm for it now, as I have always been.'

Eisen's inference was that the moment was right for a renewal of peace-talks, and although Bugs Moran, as tough and stubbornly surly a character as his late boss, at first rejected the idea of compromise with 'them Sicilians', Vincent the Schemer Drucci, Weiss's successor as chief, was amenable; and so were Myles and Klondike O'Donnell, whose vaulting ambition in Cicero had been quietened by the McSwiggin killing, and Ralph Sheldon of the South Side gang. Eisen, armed with so much good will, remembered that Antonio Lombardo had been the mediator in the first fruitless meeting at the Morrison Hotel in August, and sounded him out.

Lombardo was optimistic and that same day reported the Eisen feeler to Capone. Capone told Lombardo to get a round-table conference organized.

There were two ministers' *pourparlers* to agree upon the agenda for the summit conference, and it eventually took place on 20 October 1926, at the Hotel Sherman appropriately, perhaps, hard by both City Hall and the Chief of Police's office. It was a convention of Ali Baba and the Forty Thieves, a gaudy gathering of robber barons, the merchant aristocracy of the Chicago of this macabre epoch, murderers, ex-convicts, hoodlums, pimps, swindlers and terrorists. 'Here they sat,' recalls Pasley, 'partitioning Chicago and Cook County into trade areas, covenanting against society and the law, and going about it with the assurance of a group of directors of the Standard Oil super-trust.'

Eisen took the chair, with Lombardo at his side. The company fell into four separate groups: 1. Capone himself, Jack Guzik, his manager of the bootlegging and brothel syndicate, and Ralph Sheldon who had earlier split from the Saltis-McErlane gang; 2. Drucci and Moran, and their allies Ed Vogel, Julian Potatoes Kaufman, Frank Citro, Bill Skidmore, Barney Bertsche and Jack Zuta, smallholders but whose friendship was desired; 3. Eisen, representing the incarcerated Saltis and McErlane; 4. Myles and Klondike O'Donnell, now eager to re-enter the aegis of Capone after their hapless incursion on to his ground.

The implicit understanding with which everyone attended was that Capone was henceforth overlord, and no more quibbling. One of the provisions of the conference had been that all armament and bodyguards should, for the first time in years, be left behind. Eisen's opening appeal was: 'Let's give each other a break.' There was a hearty murmur of concordance. Capone then presented the five terms of the treaty. They stipulated: 1. A general amnesty; 2. No more shootings or beatings between the parties to the pact; 3. All past killings and shootings to be disregarded and forgotten; 4. All ribbing – deliberate malicious gossip by newspapers and police to foster discord – to be ignored; 5. All leaders of the represented groups to be responsible for discipline within their ranks and for punishment of transgressions of the treaty. 6. All gangs henceforth to stay strictly within the new boundaries and to eschew muscling-in and poaching.

Capone then announced the future delimitation of Chicago. Drucci and Moran would be restricted to the Forty-second and Forty-third Wards. All their territorial and beer-trade gains south of the Madison Street boundary, in the battle for which O'Banion and Weiss had

died, would revert to Capone; but they were left with a rich range –
from Lake Michigan in the east and north to the suburbs, and on the
south and west from the river to the Wisconsin line, this including
the exclusive beer and spirits rights for both wholesale and retail
trade; their North Side prostitution and gambling concessionaries,
Bill Skidmore, Barney Bertsche and Jack Zuta, were told that their
operations would now be under Capone's control. Saltis and Sheldon
would divide the South Side, extending south from the river to the
Indiana line and from the lake on the east to the suburb on the west;
Saltis, in fact, was being ordered to stay on his own plot in the stockyards. No specific provision was made for the O'Donnells: it was
assumed by the others there that after their bad behaviour, they
would be dependent upon Capone's personal patronage for a living.

It was a horridly hard deal that Capone was driving, but it was
accepted. The appetite of everyone for murder seemed temporarily
satiated, and although this left Capone supreme in the heart of
Chicago – the ruler of breweries, distilleries, transportation systems,
night-clubs, restaurants, race-tracks, gambling-dens, brothels,
assorted rackets and twenty thousand speakeasies, from the Loop
to Cicero, on the south from the Des Plaines River to the Indiana
line, and from the lake on the east to the suburbs on the west – the
mood of the meeting was relief that the rat-race was halted.

Hands were wrung warmly all round, and this time they were not
O'Banion handshakes. Shoulders were slapped. Large, satisfied
smiles were smiled. They left the conference room to eat a celebratory supper together. A newspaper man who had got the wind
of the mass betrothal gained entry to the supper. He afterwards
described it as the most hideous party that had come to his attention.
'Thugs who had taken a shot at each other with murderous intent
admitted the effort to the proposed victim, laughing heartily,' he
said. 'Thugs who had actually killed explained the details of the
killing to friends of the deceased and gave their version why there
was no way of getting out of it. The most frightful things in violence
were discussed and chuckled over.'

Nevertheless, a great deal of chianti was drunk, and everyone was
happy – in varying degrees – and no one there more so than Capone,
whose sense of accomplishment was heightened by the knowledge
that this was not only precisely the state of affairs which Johnny
Torrio had always desired, but that he, Capone, was now at the
pinnacle. 'The Mayor of Crook County', as he had been tagged in
the newspapers was at last the Big Fellow that his followers had
taken to calling him.

Comfortably and complacently, in the terms that one might expect a bomb-disposal expert or a lifeboatman to use, he next day informed reporters: 'I told them we were making a shooting gallery of a great business and that nobody profited by it. It's hard and dangerous work, aside from any hate at all, and when a fellow works hard at any line of business, he wants to go home and forget about it. He don't want to be afraid to sit near a window or open a door.'

The proof of his power was that for the next two months not a bullet was fired. For the first time since Prohibition began Chicago's coroners had the unique experience of seventy days passing without an inquest on a gangster.

13

The Siege of the Detective Bureau

'A policeman murdered him but we sure gave him a grand funeral.'

VINCENT THE SCHEMER DRUCCI'S WIDOW

AT least, it was time to draw breath – and reload guns. Until the re-election of Big Bill Thompson in April 1927 – which heralded a new cycle of saturnalia for Chicago, the wildest binge of all when even the theoretical checks on gang-controlled vice were kicked away, when Chicago became the widest open of wide open towns – the Capone Peace Plan worked tolerably well. The signatories kept, in the main, to their undertakings, but there continued to be a fairly uninterrupted flux of bickering, cheating and gun-play at the lower levels of the underworld among those who benefited little from the master plan, and therefore had no strong inducement to behave like little gentlemen: they continued to grab when they could the squanderings from the big men's treasure chest.

The seventy-day silence that hallowed the armistice survived over Christmas and was broken on 30 December. On that night Hilary Clements, a Ralph Sheldon rank-and-filer, was killed – and on the direct orders of Saltis, it was learned. This was merely a routine incident in the long sequence of thrust and counter-thrust between Saltis and the Ragen Colts, but it transgressed Capone's conditions. Ragen's Colts were members of The Ragen Athletic, an association drawing its two thousand members from within the quadrangle formed by Halsted Street and Cottage Grove and Forty-third and Sixty-third Streets, many of them Irish-extraction tykes of singular clod-hopping roughness and rowdiness. Founded in the 'nineties, the Ragen Club fulfilled a familiar American multiple function of running football and baseball teams, holding annual picnics, training boxers and wrestlers, and operating as the ward political centre for the Democratic party. The Ragen Club was also during Prohibition a booze-running cell, and produced such fearsome Colts as Danny Stanton, Hughey Stubby McGovern, William

Gunner Padden, Frank Dutch Carpenter, Ray Cassidy and Tom
Johnson, all of whom served as Capone gunmen or musclemen. It
also supplied most of the local troops for the bootleg gang of Sheldon,
himself a prominent Colt. The Colts' stamping-ground adjoined the
territory of Saltis, whom they had known from the time when he was
Polack Joe, a neighbourhood bar-tender and a good butt for their
twitting and horseplay. Again, at the back of much of the later
violence was the old racial antagonism, the reciprocal Irish-Slav
tauntings and street-fights. During the race-riots of July 1919 – 'five
days of terrible hate and passion let loose', as the coroner's jury
described it – there was strong evidence that the whites who went
bombing, shooting and beating-up Negroes were members of
political clubs, and the Ragen Club in particular in the Halsted
Street area. Passionate patriotism for the United States and the
American way-of-life was always the banner under which the Ragen
Colts acted, whether it was fighting in the army (five hundreds Colts
enlisted in the first world war), breaking up an anti-papist meeting,
punching a Negro unconscious, or keeping the local Polacks in line.

When beer and big money intensified these inherent enmities,
murder began to supplant kickings and nose-bustings. In 1925 Joey
Brooks, a remarkably beery and loutish Colt, was killed with County
Highway Policeman Edward A. Harmening as they sat talking in his
car. The following April two Sheldon bootleggers, Frank De
Laurento and John Tucillo (Diamond Joe Esposito's brother-in-law)
began peddling their merchandise in Saltis-McErlane territory. They
were taken for a ride in their own car, which was later left in front of
Sheldon's home containing his two salesmen with their brains blown
out.

So when Clements's body was found, Sheldon took the matter to
Capone for arbitration. Capone ordered swift and meaningful
reprisal against Saltis. His friend and left-hand man, Frank Lefty
Koncil, but recently extricated with Saltis by Weiss at high cost in
dollar payments from the Mitters Foley murder charge, and another
Saltis man, Charlie Big Hayes Hubacek, were shot dead in a car
ambuscade. Saltis took note and lived at painful peace with the
Sheldons.

It was not entirely quiet on all fronts. Among the lesser and out-
lying mobs intermittent fighting went on. One of the more profitable
of Capone's subsidiary companies was the small Near North-West
area run on his behalf by the Guilfoyle–Winge–Kolb syndicate. A
rewarding little business in beer and spirits – worth two million
dollars a year by 1928 – had been built up to serve the saloons

between Armitage Avenue on the north and Division Street on the south, and Larrabee Street on the west and Kedzie Street on the east. The founders of this were Al Winge, a former police lieutenant, and Matt Kolb, and into this, with Capone's benison upon him, had come Martin Guilfoyle. Guilfoyle put in as sales supervisor Joey Fisher, an old Volstead hand, who built up a staff of fifty salesmen and persuaders. The smooth operating of this brisk corner of the booze trade was spoiled by the ugly attitude taken by Lewis and Max Summerfield, who until the advent of streamliner Guilfoyle had plodded along modestly but prosperously. During 1925 the Summerfields, finding their business withering beneath their eyes as more and more speakeasies acceded to Fisher's importuning – and to his guns and blackjacks – resorted first to counter-slugging of two-timing saloon-owners and then to the use of firearms and hijacking sorties against the Guilfoyle beer-running crews. This minor uprising in a backward area of Capone's empire was settled when, in 1927, a squad of pineapple-tossers – that is, professional dynamiters – drove slowly past the Summerfield headquarters, at 1910 Milwaukee Avenue, lobbing in a bomb as they passed. The Summerfield premises rose behind them in a thunderous black cloud; the disagreement was settled.

The mayoral election of April 1927 – a crucial one for Capone, for it marked the end of Dever's ineffectual but irritatingly niggling reformist administration and a return to the free-for-all politics of Big Bill Thompson – was preceded, with symbolic aptness, by a killing on its eve. Vincent the Schemer Drucci died, and for a gangster in a rare and humiliating way: he was shot by a policeman. With the term of Dever, memorable more for its pink-cheeked indignation and Boy Scout pledges than for its victories in the campaign against crime, floundering feebly to its close, Capone threw all his weight behind the Republican machine that was again sponsoring Thompson, 'Big Bill the Builder, Chicago's greatest son', as he was lauded in the campaign song. It seemed evident that the mercurial public sentiment of the city was ready for another bout of piratical living. In reply to Dever's doggedly conscientious promises to continue to try to rid the city of its bootleggers and speakeasies, Thompson trumpeted with belligerent gaiety: 'I'm wetter than the middle of the Atlantic Ocean.' Capone supported this concept of realism, and change from the interference of a mealy-mouthed pedant holding the quaint belief that Prohibition should be enforced, by personally contributing what has been assessed at 250 thousand dollars to the Thompson fighting fund. He was also, as ever in these circumstances, ready to lend physical as well as spiritual support. On the day before the election, Drucci and his men were assigned to ensuring that the Forty-Second Ward hindered the Dever administration. One of their ideas was to kidnap Alderman Dorsey R. Crowe, a Dever supporter, and his staff, and wreck their offices. News of the plan reached Chief of Detectives Collins, and he ordered a round-up of all hoodlums on the streets.

Drucci was almost immediately sighted from a patrol car commanded by Lieutenant William Liebeck cruising down Diversey Parkway. Drucci was talking with Henry Finkelstein, a night-club operator, and an Albert Single, of Peoria. The three were surrounded, Drucci frisked and relieved of his ·45 automatic, and all were taken to the detective headquarters. Within twenty minutes Lieutenant Liebeck was telephoned by Drucci's lawyer, Maurice Green, to say that he was at the Criminal Court with a petition for a writ on habeas corpus.

Accustomed to the monotonous efficiency of this release-mechanism, Liebeck wearily led the prisoners out to the car for the trip to the Criminal Court Building. As escort went Policemen Danny Healy and Matthew Cunningham, with Policeman Dennis Kehoe as driver. Drucci was handcuffed to Healy, a policeman who appeared to have an heretical prejudice against gangsters – he had killed one bandit and emerged the master in a brush with Saltis. This is his account of what happened when he put Drucci in the car at the point of his gun: 'Drucci said, "You ——, I'll get you. I'll wait on your doorstep for you." I told him to shut his mouth. Drucci said, "Go on, you kid copper – I'll fix you for this." I told him to keep quiet. Drucci said, "You take your gun off me or I'll kick hell out of you." He got up on one leg and struck me on the right side of the head with his left hand, saying, "I'll take you and your tool. I'll fix you," grabbing hold of me by the right hand. I grabbed my gun with my left hand and fired four shots at him.'

When Green, at the Criminal Court, learned that his client was now in the county morgue, he demanded that Healy be arrested on a charge of murder. Chief of Detectives Schoemaker ignored this, saying mildly: 'I don't know anything about any one being murdered. I know Drucci was killed trying to take a gun away from an officer. We're having a medal made for Healy.'

This did not check the usual processes of political subordination going into motion on behalf of Finkelstein. State Representative Harry Weisbrod, Alderman Jacob M. Arvey and Moe Rosenberg, brother of Sanitary District Trustee Michael Rosenberg, interceded and Judge William J. Lindsay obtained his release on bond.

And the processes of gangland homage went into motion for Drucci. For a day and a night he lay in state in a ten thousand dollar silver and aluminium coffin in Sbarbaro's funeral chapel. He was denied the rites of the Catholic Church, but alternative pomp was appropriated for him. On the tenuous ground of his brief service in the army, he was given a military funeral. Five of the pallbearers were in uniform. Across the coffin was draped the Stars and Stripes.

There was a revival of the earlier profligacy of flowers, thirty thousand dollars' worth piled upon twelve cars preceding the hearse. There were wreaths and bouquets and Bibles of flowers, and set-pieces including an empty chair woven from white and purple blooms inscribed 'Our pal' and a heart of red roses inscribed 'To my darling husband' from Mrs. Cecilia Drucci, the blonde widow.

Among those who attended the funeral and wake were Capone, Moran, Eisen, Frank and Pete Gusenberg, Potatoes Kaufman, Bennie Jacobs (the politician wounded in the machine-gunning of Weiss), Joe Saltis and his wife, John O'Berta, Frank McErlane and Jim Fur Sammons. The widow of O'Banion was there consoling the widow of Drucci.

The body was placed in a vault at Mount Carmel Cemetery until a mausoleum had been built. As she left the cemetery Mrs. Drucci told reporters: 'A policeman murdered him but we sure gave him a grand funeral.' She could afford it. Her late husband's estate amounted to more than 400 thousand dollars.

Despite the lull in warfare that followed the October 1926 peace treaty, 1927 proved to be a trying year for Capone, and most of his anxieties were due to the dogged efforts by the Sicilian Aiello brothers, once his associates, to kill him.

The Aiellos' gang was a family business. There were nine of them – Joe, Dominick, Antonio and Andrew ruled the roustabouts – and also numerous cousins of the same name. Their entry into bootlegging was via supplying wholesale sugar for the Genna brothers' alky-cooking syndicate. After the Gennas had been cut to pieces and disbanded in 1925, Joe Aiello pieced the organization together again to keep Chicago's worst and cheapest rotgut liquor flowing, and the brothers ruled the illiterate peasant families who were their scab labour force with the same kind of harsh paternalism that the Gennas had practised. But an obstacle to their complete domination of the Little Italy community was the nomination of Antonio Lombardo, by Capone, to the presidency of the Unione

Siciliana following the deaths of Angelo Genna and Sam Samoots
Amatuna.

The difficulty in this hot, claustrophobic world of kinship and
secret society is to keep accurate track of the capriciously volatile
relationships, for blood-brothers of one day were pledged to destroy
each other the next, and the maze of family and gang allegiance
dutifully vacillated towards the new, transitory shape. For example,
during the régime of Mike Merlo, the founder of the Unione, who
was venerated by his first-generation countrymen whom he both
exploited politically and also helped in a vainglorious way, Joseph
Aiello and Lombardo had been partners in various business enterprises ranging from cheese-importing to commission brokerage. But
Joseph had his own political ambitions and his resentment at
Lombardo's meteoric ascendancy under Capone's patronage became
so bitter that they quarrelled.

The Aiellos brewed a conspiracy to dethrone Lombardo, and sent
family agitators to New York, Cleveland, Milwaukee, Pittsburgh,
St. Louis and Dayton to undermine the present branch leadership
of the Unione and form underground splinter-groups. In the autumn
of 1926 two Aiellos were cornered in a roadside café near Springfield,
Illinois, on their way back to Chicago from one of these missions in
St. Louis, and were left with their heads lolling in their plates of
spaghetti; this set in a chain reaction of murders in St. Louis, where
a dozen of the opposed Unione factions were shot.

In Chicago the Aiellos continued their foolhardy but audacious
bid for power over both the Unione and the booze business. They
had had their differences with the old O'Banion gang in the past,
but now that the intransigently rebellious Moran was in command,
they held private talks with him, and also with Bill Skidmore,
professional bondsman and gambler-politician, Jack Zuta and
Barney Bertsche, a triumvirate of gunmen-gamblers in whom
Capone's peace-pact orders had rankled and who did come to the
conclusion that they were sufficiently powerful in their North Side
citadel to snub him. A new covert coalition was formed, and the
Aiellos felt lusty enough to finish what they had started.

They began their siege of Capone with four separate attempts to
have him assassinated by imported killers. At the time, this episode
formed an apparently isolated little mystery in the newspapers,
which began with the discovery on the evening of 25 May of a body
in an alleyway in the squalid purlieu of De Koven and Des Plaines
Streets. Not startlingly odd in itself, there were several puzzling
features about the murder. The body, which was unidentifiable, was

expensively dressed and still had upon it 1,200 dollars in notes, so that the original assumption that the motive had been robbery was not tenable; there was a shoulder holster containing a gun; and also, clutched in the cold fingers of the right hand was a nickel which, it was taken, expressed the murderer's contempt for his victim.

Between then and October, three more corpses were found in similar circumstances – and on each was an unfired gun and in each right hand a nickel.

Eventually Machine-gun Jack McGurn, then Capone's chief bodyguard and torpedo, was questioned by the police, to no avail whatsoever. Yet their hunch was right. It was not until much later that this little series of side-line murders became intelligible within the pattern of new intrigue. The four corpses were all professional killers and Mafia men. They were Antonio Torchio of New York, Anthony K. Russo and Vincent Spicuzza of St. Louis, and Samuel Valente of Cleveland. They were entrants in the open competition broadcast by the Aiellos during their proselytizing trips about the country – 'Fifty thousand dollars to anyone who can show us a Capone notch' – but they had each run up against a defence ring too tight to penetrate.

The Aiellos, resourceful but rash, then tried another tactic, and it was this that first gave Capone the certain information that it was they who were hunting him. They offered the chef of the Little Italy Café, one of Capone's favourite eating places, ten thousand dollars to put prussic acid in his soup; the chef, either unable to bring himself to do that to his soup or to Capone, denounced them.

Capone reached out and plucked some of the Aiellos' flowers. In six weeks his gunners reduced the gang by six — Lawrence La Presta on 1 June, Diego Attlomionte on 29 June, Numio Jamericco and Lorenzo Alagno on 30 June, Giovanni Blaudins on 11 July and Dominic Cinderella on 17 July. 'Slayers not apprehended' was the conclusion the coroner wrote at the end of each of the first five inquest records. In the killing of Cinderella, a barman who died with his slippers on – he was found, roped into a ball and stuffed inside a sack, in a ditch – McGurn and a companion, Orchell DeGrazio, were suspected, and were even arrested, then freed 'for lack of evidence'.

With the mechanical energy of a chorus-line prancing through its three-hundredth performance of a musical comedy, the Chicago police force put on a show of indignation and zealousness. Chief Detective William O'Connor asked for volunteers from the detective squad who had fought in France and had experience of using machine-guns – the intention was, he announced, to mobilize a force of five hundred who would patrol the city in armoured cars and exterminate the rival gangs. He addressed the assembled panzer force thus: 'Men, the war is on. We have got to show that society and the police department, and not a bunch of dirty rats, are running this town. It is the wish of the people of Chicago that you hunt these criminals down and kill them without mercy. Your cars are equipped with machine-guns and you will meet the enemies of society on equal terms. See to it that they do not have you pushing up daisies. Make them push up daisies. Shoot first and shoot to kill. If you kill a notorious feudist you will get a handsome reward and win promotion. If you meet a car containing bandits pursue them and fire. When I arrive on the scene my hopes will be fulfilled if you have shot off the top of their car and killed every criminal inside it.'

That, even in the extraordinary state in which Chicago was at that time, was an extraordinary clarion call to unbridled bloody warfare in the city's streets to come from the lips of a police officer obliged by his position at least to pretend to an observance of the processes of arrest, proof of guilt and punishment. In fact, the armoured cars and the detective machine-gunners accomplished no striking conquests. That same day they raided the offices of the Chicago Candy Jobbers' Union, killed Frank Herbert, bodyguard to Joe Saltis, as he tried to escape, and arrested and charged forty-five gangsters with shooting, stabbing and bombing to force candy dealers to join the union. They also prevented Capone's death at the hands of the Aiellos, who were proving resolute as ravenous wolves. They received word from a stool-pigeon that it would be worth their while to pay a call at 4442 Washington Boulevard and at a house ten miles distant on North Western Avenue. At the Washington Boulevard apartment they found a room empty but for a machine-gun nest which looked down directly on to the entrance to Lombardo's home. At the North Western Avenue house they uncovered a cache of dynamite and percussion caps. There, too, carelessly left behind, was an hotel registration slip in the name of Angelo La Mantio, who had recently booked in at the Rex Hotel, at 3142 North Ashland Avenue.

To the Rex Hotel the squad went, and there they captured La Mantio, a twenty-three-year-old Milwaukee gunman, and four of the Aiello gang, including Joseph Aiello himself. La Mantio was more garrulous than most gangsters, and after a short interview with the police he admitted that he had been engaged by the Aiellos to bump off Capone and Lombardo, and he parted with the address from which Capone's surprise was to be despatched. In room 302 in the Atlantic Hotel, at 316 South Clark Street, facing Hinky Dink Kenna's tobacco shop, where Capone called each day for his cigars and for a political gossip, was another machine-gun nest.

Meanwhile Joseph Aiello and La Mantio had been removed to the Detective Bureau, where there occurred yet another surpassingly insolent demonstration of the gangsters' scorn for public opinion, the incident that became known as the Siege of the Detective Bureau.

About an hour after Aiello and La Mantio were brought in a policeman, glancing out of the window, saw a procession of six taxis pull up opposite and disgorge twenty-five men. The policeman's first thought was that there had been a raid and that a bunch of prisoners were being herded in. But, as he watched, the party dispersed; some began strolling up and down the street, as if patrolling, others took up positions in shop doorways and at intervals along the kerb; and another group crossed the road and hurried down the alleyway beside the Bureau and in which the back entrance stood. The policeman called a colleague, and at that moment three of the men came straight up to the Bureau's front door, and as they did one of them pulled a gun from an armpit holster and slid it into the side pocket of his overcoat. The second policeman recognized him as Louis Campagna. 'That,' he said with amazed disbelief in his voice as they both realized that they were being surrounded, 'is the Capone crowd.'

The fantastic situation was reported and a posse of officers were despatched to break up the ring. There was a rapid dispersal as they appeared, but they got their hands on Campagna, Frank Perry and Sam Marcus, three of Capone's recent import of escorts from New York. They were searched. Both Campagna and Perry were carrying a brace of ·45 automatics; Marcus at first appeared to be modestly accoutred with only one gun – until, while he was being questioned in the chief detective's office, he snatched from inside his shirt a Colt revolver with its barrel sawn down to a stub, evidently with the intention of shooting his way out of the building. He was overpowered before he could aim it.

The three of them were put together in the next cell to Aiello. An Italian-stock policeman in rapidly donned rough clothes was thrown into the opposite cell, where he could hear any exchanges made. Campagna was giving Aiello some rough talk in Sicilian dialect. 'You're dead, friend, you're dead,' said Campagna. 'You won't get up to the end of the street still walking.'

Aiello, badly frightened, pleaded for leniency. 'Give me fourteen days and I'll sell my stores, house and everything, and quit Chicago for good. Can't we settle this? Think of my wife and baby.'

There was no perceptible melting of hearts, and when he was released from custody Aiello demanded police protection. He was escorted to a cab and got away unharmed.

The next morning's newspapers screamed of the latest outrage. 'GUNMEN DEFY POLICE: INVADE LAW'S STRONGHOLD.' The story began: 'Chicago gun-fighters almost achieved the ultimate in assassination yesterday when they silently encircled the Detective Bureau and waited patiently for the opportunity to kill Joseph Aiello, hitherto only a modest claimant to gang honours, who became by this stealthy swarming of the clans a new and astonishing figure in the stratum of bullets, booze, gambling and vice. . . . Summed up from police information, the situation is one involving perhaps seventy-five million dollars a year, the profits of gambling and vice and booze in Chicago. It is for control of these profits that there has been launched a new war between one group headed by William Skidmore and Barney Bertsche and another group ruled by Al Brown and Antonio Lombardo.'

It is interesting that even at this late point, 1927, Capone was still being referred to in the press as Al Brown, his cover-name when he first arrived in Chicago. The curious omission from that newspaper outline of the new battle assemblage was the name of Moran.

Joseph Aiello laid low, but did not abandon his campaign to oust Capone. But Capone proved too powerful and invulnerable, and finally Aiello decided to quit. On a night in October 1930 he deemed it safe to make a run for it. It was not. He emerged from a suburban backwater on the far West Side and with a ticket for Brownsville, Texas, in his pocket he telephoned for a taxi to take him to the station. As he hurried from the doorway to the waiting taxi a machine-gun opened up on him from a second-floor apartment across the street. He swung round and ran back—to be met by another burst of machine-gun bullets from a window in the building he had just left. He dropped with fifty-nine slugs, weighing one pound, in his body. The hidden execution squad had been waiting for weeks for that moment of emergence. Meanwhile his brother Dominick, who stayed behind to wind up his affairs, had also been shot to death. The Aiellos had been temporarily stamped down – but Capone later found a use for them, as scapegoats in his own struggle for continued control of the Unione.

14

St. Valentine's Day, 1929

'The place was full of dead men.'

A CHICAGO HOUSEWIFE

'Nobody shot me.'

FRANK GUSENBERG, dying with fourteen machine-gun
bullets in his body

D RUCCI's death in the April election had thrust George Bugs
Moran into the leadership of the O'Banion gang. Moran had
consistently been lukewarm about accepting Capone's
dictated peace terms, and now that he had power of decision on the
North Side he soon showed that he did not take the truce seriously.
He was a big, morose Irishman, with a pouchy, battered face and the
long criminal career of a case-hardened toughie. His first prison
sentence had been received in 1910, when, under the name of George
Miller, he served eighteen months for robbery; he was back in 1913
for burglary and larceny; in 1917 he forfeited bonds in another
robbery case, but this case was eventually struck off the records; and
he went to prison again in 1918 for another botched robbery. Until
then he had been a paltry, and not very successful, footpad. When
he was paroled in February 1923 he returned to find Chicago's
underworld transformed, swimming with easy money for smuggled
liquor and safer than ever before beneath the umbrella of official
protection bought by the huge profits from booze. His contribution
was muscle rather than brain.

The surviving nucleus of the gang Moran inherited from Drucci
were Willie Marks, his bodyguard and second in command; Frank
and Pete Gusenberg, burglars and train-robbers; John May, safe-
cracker; Ted Newberry, in charge of the whisky sales-staff; Al
Weinshank, overseer of speakeasies, and an official of the Central
Cleaners' & Dyers' Association; Jim Clark (real name Kashellek),
Moran's brother-in-law and gunman; and Adam Heyer, owner of the
S.M.C. Cartage Company, the garage at 2122 North Clark Street
where the gang kept its fleet of lorries, vans and cars, and stored

consignments of booze, and which was to become the scene of one of the world's most blazoned and savage crimes of carnage, a gang massacre on a scale hitherto not attempted and not repeated since.

For more than a year Capone had been in loose cartel association with the Detroit Purple Gang, who had been furnishing him with a brand of whisky named Old Log Cabin. This was the whisky apportioned to Moran for his area; the whisky was all right but the price was not. Moran thought it excessively high, and when he was offered a steady supply of a cheaper Canadian brand, he brusquely notified Capone and the Purple Gang that he was discontinuing dealing with them. This was not thought to be a friendly act, but it was accepted and Capone arranged an alternative market for the Purple Gang with Paul Morton, brother of the late Nails Morton.

Moran found he had blundered. His customers – who were paying the same price for the Canadian brand, for it was Moran who was pocketing the difference – preferred Old Log Cabin. Some reluctantly took the substitute, but orders began to shrink. Moran sullenly went to Capone and said he would like to resume dealing with the Purple Gang, to be told, with not much attempt at concealing amusement, that the supply was now bespoken.

Moran's mind worked in crude leapfrogs of logic: the liquor was there; he was being stopped from getting it; therefore he'd get it another way. The North Siders were, by training under O'Banion, adept hijackers. When, during the next months, trucks stacked with crates of Old Log Cabin began with increasing frequency to be held up and either stolen or stripped of their freight, the Purple Gang – and Capone – had no proof but a biased conviction that Moran's night-raiders were dishonestly active or that he was buying what he knew to be hijacked goods from free-lance highwaymen.

The inevitable crisis came when a particularly big and valuable cargo came by ship from Detroit to Chicago – and was seized before it reached its consignee, Paul Morton. Capone and the Purple Gang had had enough of Moran's sneak-thieving and a trap was laid. An agent of theirs represented himself to Moran as a hijacker's mate and tip-off man, and ingratiated himself into the North Siders' confidence by turning over as promised several loads of Purple Gang whisky in as many weeks. On 13 February 1929 the *agent provocateur* telephoned Moran to say that he had a truckload 'right off the river, fifty-seven dollars a case'. Moran said he would have it and told him to bring it to the North Clark Street garage at ten-thirty the next day, which happened to be St. Valentine's Day, the time for delivering tokens of tender regard.

This particular incident, and it was really no more than an incident in the protracted violence between this most emancipated generation of criminals, has been so often and so variously described that it has almost lost its dimensions, become blurred with the successive layers of over-rich paint. In magazines and newspapers the world over it has been dramatized and exalted; it has been re-enacted, in sombrely shadowy cinema photography, even, in one film, *Some Like It Hot*, made the subject for slapstick comedy. The three significant points about the reality are that it was accomplished in eight minutes, and was therefore one of the most neatly efficient planned operations of its kind; that, classically, no one was ever arrested for it; and that it marked high-tide in Capone's career, a blow that destroyed, morally more than physically, the last serious bloc of opposition to his authority.

February 14 1929 was a seasonal midwinter Chicago day: cold with powdery snow blowing in the westerly wind streaming down the ravine of Clark Street, which is a drab nine-mile clutter of small shops, flat-blocks, filling stations and the higgledy-piggledy straggle of a growing city's accretion along what had been Green Bay Trail when Chicago was an Indian tribal range. There was nothing to distinguish the premises at number 2122 from its neighbouring buildings: a cramped narrow-shouldered frontage sandwiched between two taller flanking buildings, with the uninformative name S.M.C. Cartage Company set upon its brick facing. The local residents accepted, without any reason to question the thought, that it was a furniture removal firm. Its appearance revealed nothing beyond the name. There was a wide plateglass window which admitted a view no farther back than an office wooden partition. The garage behind was entered by a door giving on to a passage twenty feet long, running between the garage's north wall and the office partition. The entrance for vehicles was from an alleyway at the rear. It was this concealed rear entrance which was used by the Moran gang's booze lorries, which maintained a busy service to and from the central liquor cache, which the garage primarily was.

No one who could avoid it was out in the bitter weather of that day; even traffic was lighter than normal on that busy artery. It was probably for this reason that the arrival of an ostensible police car was noticed by several people – by Mrs. Alphonsine Morin, a boarding house keeper at 2125 opposite, by Mrs. Jeanette Landesman who was dusting and making the beds in her three-storey flat building at 2124, next door to the garage, and by Mr. and Mrs. Sam Schneider

who were pressing and sewing in their tailoring shop on the ground
floor of No. 2124.

The car was a black Packard tourer with the top raised and the
side curtains drawn; it had a blackened bell on its running board. It
looked to be the kind used by the detective bureau squads. The car
drew into the kerb two doors north of the garage. Five men alighted,
three in police uniforms, two in civilian overcoats and hats, and
entered the front door. It was about 10.50 a.m. when the visitors
arrived. Shortly after, the Schneiders, Mrs. Morin and Mrs. Landesman heard a sustained clatter, followed by two dull explosions.
They took the noise to be the backfiring of a lorry in the garage, but
were sufficiently curious to go to the window and watch the departure of the five men at two minutes before 11 a.m. – although this
time the two civilians came out first with their hands up, followed by
the 'policemen' with guns trained on them. They all boarded the car
and drove away.

The Schneiders assumed, although vaguely puzzled by the circumstances, that there had been a police raid. Mrs. Landesman was less
easily satisfied. She watched the car vanish south down Clark Street,
then went downstairs and tried the door of the garage. It was jammed
shut. She called Mr. C. L. McAllister, a lodger, who thrust the door
open with his shoulder. He walked down the passage and into the
garage. Later Mrs. Landesman recalled: 'Mr. McAllister came
running back. He said the place was full of dead men. I called the
police.'

If not exactly full of dead men, the premises were littered with six
and one dying man. They were among tyres and tarpaulins, at the
foot of a wall hung with saws, files and electric flex. Five of the
corpses were those of Pete Gusenberg, John May, Al Weinshank,
James Clark and Adam Heyer, all Moran mobsters; their diamond
tiepins and rings were undisturbed, their bankrolls (Heyer had 1,135
dollars on his person, Weinshank 1,250 dollars and May 1,200
dollars) had not been removed, their guns were in their holsters. The
sixth body, still dapper with a carnation in its button-hole, was that
of Dr. Reinhart H. Schwimmer, a young oculist, a crony and admirer
of Moran, who lived at the Parkway Hotel on Lincoln Park West
and who, like other citizens of the period, hung around with the
gangs and enjoyed the raffishly romantic reputation that this gained
him among his respectable friends. Three of the bodies, one with a
hat in place, were in a neat line, sharing the cold concrete floor as if
it was a warm bed; a fourth was crosswise at their feet; a fifth was
huddled across a chair; the sixth was a few feet away, as if spun

round by a heavy swipe from something, the seat of his trousers rather obscenely ripped open by a bullet.

Indeed the swipe had been considerable. Post mortem examination showed that they had been sliced back and forth by more than a hundred machine-gun bullets; the line of fire, it was reported, had not deviated and had been 'accurately sprayed between the ears and thighs; all were wounded in the head and vital organs'. So thoroughly had the task been carried out that heads, bodies and limbs were almost severed by the slow and methodical stitching movement of the gun. To ensure the adequacy of the job, a shot-gun had also been employed. Clark and May had received a charge of buckshot apiece in the head. These were the sounds – the backfiring followed by the two thuds – that had been overheard by the neighbours.

Remarkably, there was still life existing within the execution chamber. An Alsatian dog owned by Heyer was howling and yelping under one of the seven beer trucks there and to which it was chained, and the seventh man who had been present had temporarily survived the torrent of bullets. When the police squad under Sergeant Thomas Loftus, of the Hudson Avenue Station, arrived fifteen minutes later, they found that Frank Gusenberg was still breathing in the lake of blood released by the fourteen slugs in his body. He was taken to the Alexian Brothers' Hospital and Sergeant Clarence Sweeney, an old North Side officer who knew him well, sat beside him as his life flickered out.

'They never gave you a chance, Frank,' said Sweeney. 'Who shot you?'

'Nobody shot me,' Gusenberg muttered inaccurately.

'Which gang was it?' persisted the sergeant.

Gusenberg did not bother to reply, and he spoke only twice again before he died at 1.30 p.m., when the sergeant put what was obviously the final inquiry that could be made: 'Do you want a preacher, Frank?' The answer was: 'No'. Then he added: 'It's getting dark, Sarge – so long.'

It was dark, as murkily dark as ever, in these inquiries. The police went formalistically about their duty of collecting evidence. But for once, there were a few people ready to describe what they had seen and to supply information – the scale and callousness of this strike briefly shook Chicago out of its cynical torpor. The Schneiders, Mrs. Morin and Mrs. Landesman gave their accounts. Mrs. Morin told how she watched: 'Two men coming out of the garage, with their hands high above their heads. Behind them were three other men in what looked like police uniforms. They had guns on the first two men. They were walking slow, easy-like. I thought an arrest had been made. I watched them get into the squad car.'

Mrs. Michael Doody of 2119 North Clark Street and Mrs. Mary Atkinson of 2135, both keepers of boarding houses that overlooked the garage, came forward to identify photographs of men who a week earlier had arrived with baggage, taken front rooms in the houses, leaving abruptly on the morning of the massacre. Mrs. Doody recognized her tenants as Harry and Phil Keywell of the Detroit Purple Gang, and Mrs. Atkinson picked out Eddie Fletcher of the Purple Gang, and also Phil Keywell, who seems to have vacillated restlessly between the addresses.

This lead accorded with what the police already knew of Capone's affiliation with the Purple Gang, and the dispute that had arisen from Moran's reckless looting of the Old Log Cabin whisky consignments from Detroit to Capone's agent, Paul Morton.

One of the many initial theories tentatively discussed with reporters by Frederick D. Silloway, assistant administrator of the Chicago Prohibition force, was that the killers were genuine policemen who had been in trouble with Moran. There had been sound reason to suppose that this might be true, for a month earlier five hundred cases of liquor destined for the Moran garage had been seized by unidentified robbers on the Indianapolis Boulevard. The Prohibition agents alleged that crooked police took part in the hold-up, that Moran ferreting out their identities, had threatened to expose them, and that the police had plotted to kill the gangsters before they themselves were either killed or disgraced. Police Chief Russell did not flinch away from this theory. 'I'd as soon hang coppers as gangsters for this murder,' he declared to the press.

The discovery of the presence of Purple mobsters at the scene shifted the direction of the inquiries. The interesting question implicit here was why the killers, whose preparations and patience were becoming clearer, had jumped before Moran himself was in the bag. In fact that was not understood until more than a year later when the full story of the events of that day became known. Lured by Capone's planted spy, the Moran gang had lined up their seven lorries and three motor-cars promptly to distribute the fictitious load of liquor which, Moran had been informed, had been hijacked from the Detroit-Chicago run. The killers knew that the bait of this important business deal would bring about a full gathering of the Moran gang at the garage, and indeed the six who were struck down were then awaiting the arrival of their chief. It was luck that extended Moran's life by another twenty-eight years. He was late arriving. Had he been five minutes earlier at the garage he would have died against the wall and the St. Valentine's Day Massacre would have been even more luridly elephantine a legend, for ten men would have been the toll.

As it was, Moran, together with Willie Marks and Ted Newberry, came walking down Clark Street as the touring car drew to a halt and the 'policemen' alighted. The three unobtrusively sidled into a shop doorway, watched for a moment, and, although suspecting nothing worse than a routine call, melted away from the proximity until the visitors had departed and the heat was off. But already in the garage was Al Weinshank, a man of heavy build and height similar to Moran's, and who was wearing an olive brown hat and brown overcoat closely resembling Moran's. It seems probable that the killers supposed they had the leader cornered with his henchmen.

Next day, having read in the newspapers that the police wished to interview him, Moran presented himself. He was asked, without much hope of help, for his theory of the massacre. Moran stood silently for a minute or two, swivelling his eyes about unhappily, and then he made a statement that astonished the police and which continues to be astonishing in the context of the gangster sealed-lips policy. 'Only the Capone gang kills like that,' he exclaimed viciously, but then would say no more.

The police department finally issued its official reconstruction of the massacre, which continued to monopolize the front pages each day. 'Two of the crew were in police uniforms,' ran the statement, 'and the seven victims, thinking it was only another routine raid, with perhaps an arrest and a quick release on bonds, readily yielded to disarming and obeying the command to stand in a row fifty feet from the Clark Street door, facing the north wall. It was a clever trick. Otherwise the Morans would have sold their lives dearly.'

While the 'policemen' lined up the gangsters purportedly to search them, the statement continued to theorize, the executioners in civilian clothes, who had stayed quietly out of sight in the passage, brought forth the Thompson sub-machine-gun and the twelve-gauge sawn-off double-barrelled shot-gun that they had carried from the car under their overcoats. The machine-gunner strode softly forward, levelled his weapon, and, with it adjusted for rapid fire, moved it evenly down the line from east to west with the delicate deliberation of a painter sweeping his brush across a canvas. The shot-gunner added the postscript for Clark and May, who, presumably, were still twitching. Carrying the plan through to its termination, the executioners then passed over their arms to the 'policemen', raised their hands and were marched – 'slow, easy-like', said Mrs. Morin – at gunpoint from the building to allay the suspicion of any passers-by who had heard the detonations.

There could not long have been much doubt in the minds of police or pressmen that, once again, the key figure in the gory little mystery was Capone. But, once again, Capone was demonstrably out of reach. He was wintering at his Florida villa, and, by the most happy of coincidences, had been deep in conversation with the Miami District Attorney at the very hour of the massacre. Subsequent investigations, and a subpoenaed telephone record from the Congress Hotel, revealed that Capone's aide, Jack Guzik, had recently been making daily long-distance calls to his chief; these had been suspended three days before the massacre, to restart on 18 February.

On 14 March the police at last came to a conclusion: they named three men who, they said, had been members of the execution squad. They were Joseph Lolordo, brother of Pasqualino Lolordo who occupied the parlously dangerous presidency of the Unione Siciliana from September 1928 until Moran gunmen, performing a chummy act for the Aiello brothers in their internal Mafia feuding, killed him on 8 January, 1929; and Fred Burke and James Ray, both of the St. Louis Egan's Rats gang. Burke was a bank-robber and murderer, wanted at that time in Ohio for the killing of a policeman and by Federal authorities for a national bank hold-up. Ray had been named as his confederate in the robbery at Jefferson, Wisconsin, in which 350 thousand dollars' worth of bonds were carried off. The value of Burke and Ray in the plot, apparently, was that, as strangers in Chicago, they were able to masquerade as policemen without being recognized by the Moran men. In further detailing the operation, Assistant State's Attorney David Stansbury stated that Burke and Ray had been paid ten thousand dollars each by Jack McGurn; that the tommy-gun had been operated by Lolordo, who had put to practical peacetime use the training given to him in a United States Army machine-gun detachment and who had been especially gratified to be able not only to earn a fee but to avenge himself upon the murderers of his brother Pasqualino; and that the remaining members of the party were those two ominous buddies Albert Anselmi and John Scalise.

There followed a scurry of arrests, chases, evasions and the customary dust-cloud of concealed negotiations and conflicting announcements. Lolordo had vanished. Arrested were Rocco Fanneli, a Twentieth Ward Capone representative, and Joseph

Guinta, a Brooklyn-born Five Points product brought to Chicago in 1925 by Lombardo to help him run the Unione, and who himself succeeded Lolordo in the office, the fifth president since Mike Merlo's death in 1924.

The evidence against Anselmi, it was decided by the State's Attorney's office, was not strong enough to make a charge worthwhile. McGurn and Scalise were already in custody and were indicted on seven charges of first-degree murder. If this should be supposed to be a sufficiently stout array of indictments to keep them inside, it must be stated that they instantly met their bonds of fifty thousand dollars each (McGurn's surety being South Side hotel property valued at 1,300,000 dollars) and rode back to their homes. In fact Guinta and Scalise never had to bother with the wearisomely repetitive ritual of making a monkey out of justice, for before they could be tried they and Anselmi were, as will be shortly seen, disposed of by their colleagues. McGurn was left to face the charges alone and, under the guidance of the astute legal loophole-wrigglers that the gangs employed for such huge retainers, elaborately extricated himself from the unpleasantness. An Illinois statute laid down that if a defendant demanded trial at four separate terms of court and the State was not prepared to prosecute, the State must enter a *nolle prosequi*. McGurn was brought up for trial on 28 May. The State requested an adjournment until 8 July. On that date his attorneys demanded an immediate trial, but the State asked for, and received, a further adjournment until 15 August. On that date the State was still not ready. When the case was again begun on 23 September McGurn's attorneys made their fourth demand for trial, but Assistant State's Attorney Harry S. Ditchburne told the judge that the State needed still a further adjournment to permit continued investigations. The same plea was repeated on October 28. Judge George Fred Rush granted another adjournment but rebuked Ditchburne and stipulated: 'The State must be prepared to go on trial at that date. If it is not I will discharge the defendant.'

On 2 December Ditchburne rose in court and said: 'We are forced at this time to *nolle prosse* the case against McGurn.'

McGurn stepped free, his character officially unblemished. There was no explanation sought why the State had allowed itself to be put through this blatantly clumsy pavane, dancing to the tune which would inevitably by legal process, release the man who had been explicitly identified by the State's Attorney's office as the organizer of the massacre. No explanation was given, but, then, perhaps none was necessary.

McGurn was an important figure in Capone's organization, the most trustworthily deadly of his hard cadre of killers, and his release was obligatory. That Celtic name should not be allowed to mislead. He was faultlessly Sicilian. He was born James De Mora, eldest of six children of a Little Italy grocer. He showed aggressive courage as a boxer at school and, in his teens, became a professional welterweight with the ring name of Jack McGurn. But he had one hand deeply embedded in the booze racket. Angelo, his father, was a sugar-supplier to the Gennas' alky-cooking industry, and as a result of this marginal implication with gangland was shot to death in front of his Vernon Park Place shop in January 1923. McGurn was then nineteen. He abandoned the ring and became a full-time mobster. From then on the police records contain the narrative of his career: arrested in the Loop carrying a gun; arrested in a West Side hotel in the company of his fifteen-year-old brother, Antonio, and a submachine-gun, a .45 calibre automatic pistol, a rifle and a box of dumdum bullets; wounded by a machine-gun burst while talking in a North Side hotel telephone box; attacked by shot-gunners while driving his car. At the time of the St. Valentine's Day Massacre he was accredited with twenty-two murders.

This flirtation with a trial of McGurn was the only partial pretence made at retribution for a crime which caused these contemporary words to be scorched on to paper: 'Chicago is aroused . . . The reform movement is under way in Chicago with a driving force it has never known before.'

No, the driving force was still in the hands of the gangs, which tacitly meant, now, Capone alone and his political and businessmen accomplices, and Chicago was supine.

While the McGurn case serpentined its way through the court's shadowy antechambers and out into the open, events had twisted dismally for Anselmi, Scalise and Guinta. Scalise and Anselmi had a big and sinister reputation in the Chicago underworld: they were known as the Homicide Squad, respected as the accurate, ruthless gunmen who had killed Mike Genna, Police Officers Olson and Walsh, participated in the O'Banion and Weiss killings, and in addition, it seems probable, in many of the countless other Capone-directed murders of the previous five years. Guinta's rise had been as rapid, but in a different, although neighbouring, field. He was also a gunman, but his talent for persuasion had been employed by Unione Siciliana in a quasi-political capacity. In 1929 he was single, aged twenty-two, and known affectionately as the Hop Toad because of his enthusiasm for dancing. After nightfall he was habitually clad in evening clothes and patent leather pumps and, unless business intruded, usually ended the day in a dance-hall or night-club where the jazz was most boisterous.

Between St. Valentine's Day and 7 May his business came more intimately to concern also Scalise and Anselmi. Guinta appointed Scalise as assistant to himself as Unione president, and Scalise, with 250 thousand dollars capital, a fat income from his beer interests, a reputation satisfactorily evil enough to inspire deference in all about him, and now the coveted incumbency in the Unione, than which no symbol had more status, had grown suddenly huge in his confidence. He was reported to have said, soon after the massacre of the Moran men, and it was a remark that was swiftly brought to Capone's attention: 'I am the most powerful man in Chicago.' Further information that reached him was that Scalise had been trying to bribe a Capone gunman with fifty thousand dollars to kill the Big Fellow, and that the triumvirate were plotting a *coup d'état* which would give them control of both booze and the Unione. Less than three years earlier, when Hymie Weiss had demanded that Anselmi and Scalise be put on the spot for O'Banion's murder, Capone's reply to the ultimatum had been: 'I wouldn't do that to a yellow dog.' Now he relegated them to a category lower than yellow dogs.

On the evening of 7 May the three friends were invited to be guests of honour at a Sicilian stag-party in a private room at a roadhouse at Hammond, across the State line. It was the prescriptive Mafia killing, in which a certain ritual solicitude is observed by dispatching the victim from this life languorous and heavy with food and wine, and in an emotional atmosphere of good will and the glow of brotherhood. No definite facts are known about their last hours, but the side-of-the-mouth story that circulated, together with the post-mortem diagnosis by Dr. Eli S. Jones, the Lake County coroner, suggested that the three honoured guests were allowed to reach coffee and brandy in comfort, whereupon they were from behind bludgeoned to death with a sawn-off baseball bat and then shot to make sure.

Their bodies were found early the next morning on a road beside Wolf Lake, Indiana. Scalise and Guinta were in the rear seat of a car which had been rolled into the ditch, and Anselmi was lonely on the damp ground twenty feet away. Dr. Jones gave his opinion that the particular kind of mess the bodies were in suggested that: 'The three men apparently were seated at a table when their killers surprised them. Scalise threw up his hand to cover his face and a bullet cut off his little finger, crashing into his eye. Another bullet crashed into his jaw and he fell from his chair. Meanwhile, the other killers – there must have been three or four – had fired on Guinta and Anselmi, disabling them. Anselmi's right arm was broken by a bullet. When their victims fell to the floor, their assailants stood over them and fired several shots into their backs.'

And that was the requiem for Scalise, Anselmi and Guinta. The Hop Toad tidied up and in his best evening clothes and dancing pumps, was buried in Mount Carmel Cemetery; Scalise and Anselmi were shipped back to their native Sicily.

15

The Short, Sweet Martyrdom of Jake Lingle

*'I have given orders to make this town so quiet that you
will be able to hear a consumptive canary cough.'*
POLICE COMMISSIONER WILLIAM F. RUSSELL

'Kismet.'

The Chicago *Tribune*

THE early months of 1930 were an interlude of eerie peace –
except for two nonentities, William Clifford and Michael
Reilly, who were taken for a ride on 13 April.

The St. Valentine's Day Massacre had induced a frozen lull in the
feuding and finagling among the beer-runners. Capone was palpably
in control now; there was a manifest tardiness on the part of all his
remaining open and secret antagonists to challenge that control.
During 1929 there were only fifty-three gang murders, to be sure no
figure to be bragged about in Chambers of Commerce leaflets, but
it was an appreciable drop below the previous year's seventy-two
and well below the all-time record, 1926's seventy-six. There was,
during the summer of 1929, even time for relaxing and enjoying the
social life, and the gangs' political supporters began to feel free again
to come out of their hidey-holes and mix gregariously with their
friends and financial partners. When a relative of Jack Guzik was
married, there was a splendid and jolly gathering at the church, one
which included Bathhouse John Coughlin, alderman of the First
Ward, William V. Pacelli, alderman of the Bloody Twentieth Ward,
Captain of Police Hugh McCarthy and Ralph Capone. Al himself
could not be present, for he was then detained in Philadelphia, the
outcome of a brush with an unco-operative court while visiting there
on his way back from Atlantic City gangsters' convention (see Chapter 24).

Then, on the last weekend in May 1930 the guns roared again,
starting pistols for what became tagged as Slaughter Week. On
Saturday Peter Gnolfo, who, having had the Genna organization
shot away from under him, had enlisted with the Aiellos, dropped

143

dead with eighteen shot-gun pellets in his back, a spiteful act that was attributed to a Druggan-Lake patrol acting on Capone's orders. Within a few hours the Aiellos struck back and three died in the reprisal. A party of five were sitting in the early hours of Sunday morning drinking on the glass-screened terrace of a small resort hotel on Piskatee Lake. They were Joseph Bertsche, brother of Barney, and who, since his release from the Atlanta Penitentiary, had been working with the Druggan-Lake mob; Michael Quirk, labour racketeer and beer-runner; George Druggan, Terry Druggan's brother; Sam Pellar, election strong-arm man of the Bloody Twentieth Ward who had previously narrowly escaped death when the bullets cut down Hymie Weiss outside the flower shop; and Mrs. Vivian Ponic McGinnis, the wife of a Chicago lawyer. A full drum of machine-gun bullets shattered the glass and mowed down the party round the table. Peller, Quirk and Bertsche died. Druggan and Mrs. McGinnis were wounded. It took a few seconds. The hunters drove off in a car.

No arrest was made; the newspaper explanation was that a quarrel had developed because the Druggan-Lake salesman had been muscling in on the Fox Lake area, which was then being supplied by the Moran-Aiello breweries.

The tit-for-tat continued. The next Tuesday, Thomas Somnerio, an Aiello ranker, was found in an alley at the rear of 831 West Harrison Street in Chicago. He had been garotted. A deep groove running around his neck indicated that a wire had been steadily tightened in an attempt to make him talk. His wrists had also been bound with wire. Four days later a tugboat passing along the drainage canal at Summit, on the South-West side, nosed out the body of Eugene Red McLaughlin, a Druggan-Lake associate, four times named as a murderer and twice identified by the victims of diamond robberies, but who had never been received inside a prison. He had been shot twice through the head and dumped in the river, wrists lashed behind his back with telephone cable and with seventy-five pounds of iron bars stuffed in his pockets. Two weeks later his corpse was identified in the city morgue by his brother, Bob McLaughlin, president of the Chicago Checker Cab Company, who had taken over the office from Joe Wokral. Wokral had run into a nasty accident while campaigning for re-election: he had been shot through the skull. Before he died he had named Red McLaughlin as his attacker, a lead that seemed to have been altogether ignored by the police. Said Bob McLaughlin to reporters, after the mournful task of inspecting his brother's swollen and mutilated corpse: 'A better kid never lived. He was friendly with all the boys, the West Side outfit, the North Siders, the bunch on the South Side, Capone, too . . . I don't know, I don't know . . .'

The day following the churning-up of McLaughlin's weighted body from the river-bed, a car driven by a man named Frank R. Thompson swerved erratically into the only filling-station at New Milford, an Illinois village in Winnebago County ninety miles north-west of Chicago; the door opened and Thomspon, bleeding all over the place, fell out on to the ground at the feet of the attendant, mumbling: 'Get a doctor.' Little was known about Thompson. He was a general dealer and arms-smuggler around gangland who – ballistic tests suggested – had supplied the machine-gun used in the St. Valentine's Day massacre and in the killing of Frank Yale in Brooklyn. He was taken, gravely wounded, to Rockford Hospital, where he was interviewed by Sheriff Harry Baldwin. Thompson's dying words were: 'Listen, Harry. I've seen everything, done everything, and got everything, and you're smart enough to know I won't talk. Go to hell.'

Nineteen-thirty had opened boisterously with a January gun-battle in which Frank McErlane received partial payment for the treatment he had given to at least nine victims of gang slayings – nine times he had been named by coroners as the cause of death; he was also indicted in the double killing of George Spot Bucher and George Meeghan, this charge being dismissed; he was tried for murder in Indiana, and acquitted. McErlane had recently been professionally restless. He had quarrelled over share-outs with his partner Saltis and transferred to the South Side O'Donnells. On the night of 28 January he was attacked and his right leg fractured by a bullet. That was not a satisfactory reprisal, and late the next month as McErlane lay in his flower-fragrant room of the German Deaconess Hospital he had two unexpected visitors. A pair of men walked through the door and opened fire with guns. McErlane, imprisoned by splints and crane, did the best he could: he reached under his pillow, where there happened to be a ·38 revolver, and fired back five times, which drove the intruders out. Nobody's aim was particularly good on this occasion. Out of two full chambers the gunmen hit McErlane only three times, and not fatally.

He was interviewed by the police, but, consistently, would name no one – but he did hint angrily that this was not the end of the matter. Nor was it. One of the gunmen had been John Dingbat O'Berta (an Italian who had inserted the Irish apostrophe into his name), a ferocious little man built like a fighting-cock who was

Saltis's chief torpedo, a newsboy at the age of eight who battled his way up in the tough Back-o'-the-Yards district to become an influential young politician who spoke at civic luncheons and business men's associations.

On 5 March the Dingbat and his driver, Sam Malaga, were taken for a ride in his own Lincoln sedan. The Dingbat had fired three bullets out of his sawn-off revolver before dropping under a hail of dumdums and shot-gun pellets. His funeral was a splendid two-day wake, attended by fifteen thousand of his admirers and political supporters from the Stockyards. His widow had previously been the wife of Big Tim Murphy, racketeer controller of the Street Sweepers' Union, machine-gunned in front of his home in June 1928. She and the Dingbat had met at the funeral. Now, with a melancholy sense of form, she had her second husband buried next to her first in the Holy Sepulchre Cemetery, each with a rosary in his gun-hand. 'They were both good men,' said the widow.

But all the foregoing were routine internecine clapperclaw wrangles, down-page stories which the average Chicago citizen flicked his eye over before passing on to the sports reports. It was on Monday, 9 June 1930, that a new and apparently different incident became the talk of the town, an outrage that detonated in the front-page headlines of all Chicago's papers. This was the killing of Alfred J. ('Jake') Lingle, a thirty-eight-year-old crime reporter on the Chicago *Tribune*, who was shot to death while walking, smoking a cigar and reading the racing news in a crowded underpass at Randolph and Michigan during the lunch hour. A noteworthy detail in the plot was that one of Lingle's killers was apparently dressed as a parson.

His death created a furore, the parallel of which it is difficult to imagine in Britain. An American reporter – that is, a reporter on the general news-gathering staff, a position which has a different connotation from the British title, for the American reporter may be merely a leg-man, a fact-gatherer who telephones in his information to a desk re-write man – is not startlingly well paid. Yet he has a place in public regard, a compound of glamour, respect and authority, that has no counterpart in Britain. The murder of Lingle instantly assumed the importance and gravity that had attached to the murder of McSwiggin and other police and Federal officials – and, as in the case of McSwiggin, it was an uprush of moral indignation that plunged in as precipitous a slump of disillusionment.

Lingle's duties on the police beat for the *Tribune* earned him sixty-five dollars a week, a poor sum. He had never had a by-line in the paper; his name was unknown to its readers. Posthumously, when his name was famous (and fast becoming notorious), he was revealed to have had an income of sixty thousand dollars a year. He owned a chauffeur-driven Lincoln limousine. He had just bought a sixteen thousand dollar house at Long Beach, on the Michigan Riviera, where his wife and two children, Buddy (six) and Pansy (five) were to spend the summer months. He had recently taken a suite of rooms at the Stevens, one of Chicago's most stylish hotels. He was an addicted gambler at horse and greyhound tracks. All this was known in a general manner among his colleagues, and the discrepancy between his meagre newspaper salary and his lavish spending was understood to be possible because of a big legacy he had received.

On the day of his death he was on the way to the races. He left his wife packing for her departure to the lake. He himself was that afternoon to go to the meeting at Washington Park, Homewood. Another significant point about that day, 9 June, was that the Sheridan Wave Tournament Club, a society gambling parlour at 621 Waveland Avenue, where the champagne, whisky and food was distributed with the managements's compliments during play, was to reopen that evening, an event of some interest to Lingle.

Retrospectively, it seems certain that Lingle knew he was in trouble. Attorney Louis B. Piquett, former City Prosecutor, later volunteered to tell the police that twenty-four hours before Lingle's death he had met Lingle in the Loop. They stood on Randolph Street talking of the discovery of Red McLaughlin's body from the canal. Lingle was giving Piquett his theory of the killing when 'a blue sedan with two men in it stopped at the kerb alongside us. Lingle stopped in the middle of a sentence, looked up at the two men in a startled way and they looked back at him. He apparently had forgotten what he had been saying for he turned suddenly, walked back the way he had come, hurriedly said "Good-bye", and entered a store as quickly as he could.' And again on the day of his murder, after lunching at the Sherman Hotel he met Sergeant Thomas Alcock, of the Detective Bureau, in the lobby and told him: 'I'm being tailed.'

He was. After buying cigars at the Sherman kiosk, he walked the four blocks to Michigan Avenue to catch the 1.30 p.m. train for the Washington Park race-track, and descended the pedestrian subway to enter the Illinois Central suburban electric railway in Grant Park. At any time of day the subway is as busy a channel as the killers could have chosen, and at lunchtime on this Monday it was swirling with two opposite streams of shoppers and office workers.

A strange aspect of what followed is Lingle's apparent uncon-
cern. He knew he was being followed, and a man of his experience
must have known that there was only one purpose in that. Yet, on the
evidence of witnesses, he arrived at the entrance to the subway walking between two men. One had blond hair and wore a straw boater
and a grey suit. The other was dark in a blue suit. At the entrance
Lingle paused and bought a racing edition of an evening paper, and
as he did so a roadster swung into the kerb on the south side of
Randolph Street and blew its horn to attract Lingle's attention. One
of the men in the car called out: 'Play Hy Schneider in the third!'
According to Armour Lapansee, a Yellow Cab superintendent who
overheard the exchange, Lingle grinned, waved his hand and called
back 'I've got him'.

Lingle walked on into the subway. He was seen by Dr. Joseph
Springer, a former coroner's physician and a long-standing
acquaintance. 'Lingle didn't see me,' Springer stated. 'He was reading the race information. He was holding it before him with both
hands and smoking a cigar.'

Lingle had almost reached the end of the subway. He came abreast
of the news-stand twenty-five feet short of the east exit, and the dark
man who had been walking at his side diverted as if to buy a paper.
As he did, the blond man dropped behind Lingle, levelled his left
hand which held a snub-barrelled ·38 Colt – known, cosily, among
police and mobsters as a belly-gun – and fired a single bullet upward
into Lingle's neck, which penetrated the brain and left the forehead.
He fell forward, cigar still clenched between his teeth, newspaper
still in his hands.

Throwing away the gun, the blond killer ran forward into the
crowds, then doubled back past Lingle's body and out up the eastern
staircase. He jumped a fence, changed his mind again, ran west into
Randolph Street, through a passage – where he threw away a left-
hand silk glove presumably worn to guard against fingerprints –
and, pursued by a policeman, ran into Wabash Avenue, where he
escaped into the crowds.

Meanwhile in the subway, a Mr. Patrick Campbell saw the dark-
haired accomplice hurrying towards the west exit. He went to inter-
cept him, but his movement was blocked by a priest who bumped
into him. Campbell said: 'What's the matter?' and the priest
replied: 'I think someone has been shot. I'm getting out of here.'

Later Lieutenant William Cusick, of the Detective Bureau, commented brusquely: 'He was no priest. A priest would never do that.
He would have gone to the side of the stricken person.'

The pattern pieced together. It seemed clear that Lingle had walked into a trap formed by perhaps a dozen men. But what was never put forward as a theory, and which seems the likeliest explanation of his meek and unhesitating advance into the trap, was that, during his progress along the pavement, down the stairs and along the subway between two men, he was being nudged along by a gun hidden in a jacket pocket, under orders to walk naturally and keep reading the paper.

That evening Colonel Robert R. McCormick, proprietor of the Chicago *Tribune*, summoned his news staff together and addressed them on the death of a reporter whom he had never seen and whose name he had never before heard. Pasley, who was there, says he talked for forty-five minutes and pledged himself to solve the crime. Next morning the front page scowled with an eight-column banner headline announcing the sudden end of Lingle. The story read: 'Alfred J. Lingle, better known in his world of newspaper work as Jake Lingle, and for the last eighteen years a reporter on the *Tribune*, was shot to death yesterday in the Illinois Central subway at the east side of Michigan Boulevard, at Randolph Street.

'The *Tribune* offers twenty-five thousand dollars as a reward for information which will lead to the conviction of the slayer or slayers. An additional reward of five thousand dollars was announced by *The Chicago Evening Post*, making a total of thirty thousand dollars.'

Next morning the Hearst Chicago *Herald and Examiner* also offered a twenty-five thousand dollar reward, bringing up the total to fifty-five thousand dollars.

McCormick continued to take Lingle's death as an affront to him personally and a smack at the press which transcended in seriousness all the other hundreds of cases of physical violence and the network of nefariousness. Two days later the *Tribune* carried an editorial headed 'THE CHALLENGE' which read:

'The meaning of this murder is plain. It was committed in reprisal and in attempt at intimidation. Mr. Lingle was a police reporter and an exceptionally well-informed one. His personal friendships included the highest police officials and the contacts of his work made him familiar to most of the big and little fellows of gangland. What made him valuable to his newspaper marked him as dangerous to the killers.

'It was very foolish ever to think that assassination would be confined to the gangs who have fought each other for the profits of crime in Chicago. The immunity from punishment after gang murders would be assumed to cover the committing of others.

Citizens who interfered with the criminals were no better protected than the gangmen who fought each other for the revenue from liquor selling, coercion of labour and trade, brothel-house keeping and gambling.

'There have been eleven gang murders in ten days. That has become the accepted course of crime in its natural stride, but to the list of Colosimo, O'Banion, the Gennas, Murphy, Weiss, Lombardo, Esposito, the seven who were killed in the St. Valentine's Day massacre, the name is added of a man whose business was to expose the work of the killers.

'The *Tribune* accepts this challenge. It is war. There will be casualties, but that is to be expected, it being war. The *Tribune* has the support of all the other Chicago newspapers . . . The challenge of crime to the community must be accepted. It has been given with bravado. It is accepted and we'll see what the consequences are to be. Justice will make a fight of it or it will abdicate.'

Police Commissioner Russell was galvanized into at least making a statement. It went colourfully: 'I have given orders to the five Deputy Police Commissioners to make this town so quiet that you will be able to hear a consumptive canary cough,' but he added, as a preliminary explanation for any further action: 'Of course, most of the underworld has scuttled off to hiding-places. It will be hard to find them, but we will never rest until the criminals are caught and Chicago is free of them for ever.' An editorial next day remarked bleakly: 'These gangs have run the town for many months and have strewn the streets with the lacerated bodies of their victims. Commissioner Russell and Deputy-Commissioner Stege have had their opportunity to break up these criminal gangs, who make the streets hideous with bleeding corpses. They have failed.' Instantly Russell replied: 'My conscience is clear. All I ask is that the city will sit tight and see what is going to happen.'

All that actually happened was that Russell and Stege, in the words of a newspaper, 'staged a mock heroic battle with crime by arresting every dirty-necked ragamuffin on the street corners, but carefully abstained from taking into custody any of the men who matter'. Meanwhile some of the blanks that until now had remained gaping oddly in the accounts of Lingle's character and circumstances began to be sketched in.

It is fair to infer that up to then the *Tribune* management was genuinely unaware of them. Some of the facts that had so far remained unmentioned were that he had been tagged the 'unofficial Chief of Police'; that he had himself hinted that it was he who had

fixed the price of beer in Chicago; that he was an intimate friend of
Capone and had stayed with him at his Florida estate; that when
he died he was wearing one of Capone's gift diamond-studded belts,
which had come to be accepted as the insignia of the Knights of the
Round Table of that place and period; that he was improbably
maty, for a newspaperman of his lowly status, with millionaire
businessmen, judges and county and city officials; that he spent
golfing holidays and shared stock market ventures with the Commissioner of Police.

By the time a week had passed certain reservations were beginning
to temper the *Tribune*'s anger. It is apparent that more details of
Lingle's extramural life were emerging. On 18 June there appeared
another leading article, entitled 'THE LINGLE INVESTIGATION GOES
ON'. In this the *Tribune* betrayed a flicker of uneasiness about the
character of its martyr. 'We do not know why this reporter was
killed,' it admitted, 'but we are engaged in finding out and we expect
to be successful. It may take time; the quicker the better, but this
enlistment is for duration. It may require long, patient efforts, but
the *Tribune* is prepared for that, and hopes that some lasting results
will be obtained which will stamp justice on the face of the crime.'
To endorse its new crusading resolution, two days later the *Tribune*
added to its Platform for Chicagoland on the masthead of its centre
page 'END THE REIGN OF GANGDOM'. Appended was an explanatory
editorial: 'The killers, the racketeers who exact tribute from businessmen and union labour, the politicians who use and shield the
racketeers, the policemen and judges who have been prostituted by
politicians, all must go.'

Ten days elapsed, and there had obviously been some concentrated
rethinking by McCormick and his editorial executives. The word-of-
mouth buzz about Lingle's background and liaisons that was meanwhile racing around Chicago, supported by somewhat less reverent
stories in other newspapers, evidently induced the *Tribune* to take a
revised, frank, let's-face-it attitude. On 30 June a column-and-a-half
editorial was published. Under the heading 'THE LINGLE MURDER',
it read: 'When Alfred Lingle was murdered the motive seemed to be
apparent . . . His newspaper saw no other explanation than that his
killers either thought he was close to information dangerous to them
or intended the murder as notice given the newspapers that crime
was ruler in Chicago. It could be both, a murder to prevent a
disclosure and to give warning against attempts at others.

'It had been expected that in due time the reprisals which have
killed gangster after gangster in the city would be attempted against

any other persons or agencies which undertook to interfere with the incredibly profitable criminality. No one had been punished for any of these murders. They have been bizarre beyond belief, and, being undetected, have been assumed, not least by their perpetrators, to be undetectable – at least not to be punishable.

'When, then, Lingle was shot by an assassin the *Tribune* assumed that the criminals had taken the next logical step and were beginning their attack upon newspaper exposure. The *Herald and Examiner* and the *Chicago Evening Post* joined the *Tribune* in offering rewards for evidence which would lead to conviction of the murderers. The newspaper publishers met and made a common cause against the new tactics of gangland. The preliminary investigation has modified some of the first assumptions, although it has not given the situation a different essence.

'Alfred Lingle now takes a different character, one in which he was unknown to the management of the *Tribune* when he was alive. He is dead and cannot defend himself, but many facts now revealed must be accepted as eloquent against him. He was not, and he could not have been a great reporter. His ability did not contain these possibilities. He did not write stories, but he could get information in police circles. He was not and he could not be influential in the acts of his newspaper, but he could be useful and honest, and that is what the *Tribune* management took him to be. His salary was commensurate with his work. The reasonable appearance against Lingle now is that he was accepted in the world of politics and crime for something undreamed of in his office, and that he used this in his undertakings which made him money and brought him to his death . . .

'There are weak men on other newspapers and in other professions, in positions of trust and responsibility greater than that of Alfred Lingle. The *Tribune*, although naturally disturbed by the discovery that this reporter was engaged in practices contrary to the code of its honest reporters and abhorred by the policy of the newspaper, does not find that the main objectives of the inquiry have been much altered. The crime and the criminals remain, and they are the concern of the *Tribune* as they are of the decent elements in Chicago . . .

'If the *Tribune* was concerned when it thought that an attack had been made upon it because it was inimical to crime, it is doubly concerned if it be the fact that crime had made a connexion in its own office . . . That Alfred Lingle is not a soldier dead in the discharge of duty is unfortunate considering that he is dead. It is of no consequence to an inquiry determined to discover why he was killed, by whom he was killed and with what attendant circumstances. *Tribune* readers may be assured that their newspaper has no intention of concealing the least fact of this murder and its consequences and meanings. The purpose is to catch the murderers . . .

'The murder of this reporter, even for racketeering reasons, as the evidence indicates it might have been, made a breach in the wall which criminality has so long maintained about its operations here. Some time, somewhere, there will be a hole found or made and the Lingle murder may prove to be it. The *Tribune* will work at its case upon this presumption and with this hope. It has gone into the cause in this fashion and its notice to gangland is that it is in for duration. Kismet.'

Kismet, indeed. For during this revisionary interim McCormick's investigators and the police had uncovered transactions of a ramification that could not have been anticipated in the affairs of a slum-boy baseball semi-professional who had wormed his way into bottom grade journalism. Lingle's biography, in fact, accords with the career of any under-privileged opportunist who finds in the gang a reward for endeavour. His first job after leaving a West Jackson Boulevard elementary school was as office boy in a surgical supply house, from where, in 1912, he went as office boy at the *Tribune*. He was at the same time playing semi-professional baseball, and met at the games Bill Russell, a police patrolman, with whom he struck up a friendship, and who, as he progressed through a sergeantcy upward to deputy commissionership, was a valuable aid to Lingle in the police-beat feed work he was now doing for the *Tribune*. Pasley, who worked on the *Tribune* with him during the 'twenties, has described Lingle's relationship with the police and the underworld: 'His right hand would go up to the left breast pocket of his coat for a cigar. There was a cigar for every greeting. They were a two-for-a-nickel brand and Lingle smoked them himself. He knew all the coppers by their first names. He spent his spare time among them. He went to their wakes and funerals; their weddings and christenings. They were his heroes. A lawyer explained him: "As a kid he was cop struck, as another kid might be stage struck." The police station was his prep school and college. He matured, and his point of view developed, in the stodgy, fetid atmosphere of the cell block and the squad-room. Chicago's forty-one police stations are vile places, considered either aesthetically or hygienically. I doubt if a modern farmer would use the majority of them for cow-sheds. Yet the civic patriots put their fledgling blue-coats in them, and expect them to preserve their self-respect and departmental morale.

'In this prep school and college, Lingle learned a great deal the ordinary citizen may, or may not, suspect. He learned that sergeants, lieutenants, and captains know every hand-book, every gambling den, every dive, every beer flat and saloon on their districts, that a word from the captain when the heat is on will close any district tighter than a Scotsman's pocket in five minutes, that they know which joint owners have "a friend in the hall or county", and which haven't. Few haven't. He learned that the Chicago police department is politics-ridden.'

Pasley's view is that Lingle's undoing was gambling – 'he was a gambling fool'. He never bet less than one hundred dollars on a horse, and often a thousand. In 1921, when he was earning only fifty dollars a week, he took a trip to Cuba and came back loaded with gifts for his friends and colleagues, including egret plumes then coveted by women for hat decorations. His big spending and general prodigal way of life began to attract comment, and he gave it to be understood that he had just inherited fifty thousand dollars under his father's will (examination of the probate court records in June 1930 showed that the estate was valued at five hundred dollars). Later he invented a couple of munificent rich uncles. Pasley's deduction is that it was in 1921 that Lingle 'began living a lie, leading a dual life', that the course of his income was not at this time Capone but possibly someone in the Torrio ring – gambling rake-off, slot-machines or police graft. Additional information about his life after office hours was given by John T. Rogers in a St. Louis *Post-Dispatch* series. Pointing to the 'mysterious sources of the large sums of money that passed with regularity through his bank account', Rogers wrote: 'If Lingle had any legitimate income beyond his sixty-five dollars a week as a reporter it has not been discovered . . . He lived at one of the best hotels in Chicago, spent nearly all his afternoons at race-tracks and some of his winters at Miami or on the Gulf Coast . . . At his hotel he was on the "private register". His room was No. 2706 and you could not call it unless your name had been designated by Lingle as a favoured one . . . All inquiries for Lingle were referred to the house detective. "Sure, he was on the private register," the house officer said. "How could he get any sleep if he wasn't? His telephone would be going all night. He would get in around two or three and wanted rest." "Who would be telephoning him at that hour?" the writer inquired. This question seemed to amaze the house officer. "Why!" he exclaimed, "policemen calling up to have Jake get them transferred or promoted, or politicians wanting the fix put in for somebody. Jake could do it. He had a lot of power. I've known him twenty years. He was up there among the big boys and had a lot of responsibilities. A big man like that needs rest.'

This sketch of Lingle's function seemed to be confirmed by a check made of outgoing telephone calls from his suite. They were mostly to officials in the Federal and city buildings, and in city hall.

That Lingle had operated as liaison officer between the under-world and the political machine was the conclusion of Attorney Donald R. Richberg, who said in a public address: 'The close relationship between Jake Lingle and the police department has been published in the Chicago papers. Out of town newspapers describe Lingle even more bluntly as having been "the unofficial Chief of Police". But Lingle was also strangely intimate with Al Capone, our most notorious gangster. Surely all Chicago knows that Samuel A. Ettelson,[1] Mr. Insull's political lawyer, who is corporation counsel for Chicago, is also chief operator of the city government. Thompson is only a figurehead. Are we to believe that there existed an unofficial chief of police associating with the most vicious gang in Chicago, without the knowledge of Mr. Ettelson – who is neither deaf nor blind but on the contrary has a reputation for knowing everything worth knowing about city hall affairs?'

That he had been on intimate terms with Lingle, that Lingle was 'among the big boys', was readily conceded by Capone himself. He was interviewed on the subject at Palm Island by Henry T. Brundidge of the St. Louis *Star*, who on 18 July 1930 published this report of their conversation:

'Was Jake your friend?'

'Yes, up to the very day he died.'

'Did you have a row with him?'

'Absolutely not.'

'If you did not have a row with Lingle, why did you refuse to see him upon your release from the workhouse in Philadelphia?'

'Who said I didn't see him?'

'The Chicago newspapers.'

'Well, if Jake failed to say I saw him – then I didn't see him.'

Asked about the diamond-studded belt Lingle was wearing, Capone explained: 'A Christmas present. Jake was a dear friend of mine.' And he added: 'The Chicago police know who killed him.'

Who in fact had killed Lingle? That aspect of the case seemed to have been temporarily shelved while the fascinating data of his financial state was, bit by bit, exposed for examination. By 30 June

---

[1] Who wrote the lyrics of Thompson's campaign song 'Big Bill the Builder'.

1929 two-and-a-half years of business with the Lake Shore Trust and Savings Bank was on the public record. In that period he had deposited 63,900 dollars. But, obviously, many of his deals had been in cash, for only one cheque for six thousand dollars related to the purchase of his sixteen thousand dollar house. He also carried a large amount of cash on his person – he had had nine thousand dollars in bills in his pocket when he was killed. In March 1930 he paid insurance premiums on jewellery valued at twelve thousand dollars, which was never located. During that two-and-a-half years he drew cheques for the sum of 17,400 dollars for horse-track and dog-track betting.

Another interesting branch of his activities that came to light were his 'loans' from gamblers, politicians and businessmen. He had 'borrowed' two thousand dollars from Jimmy Mondi, once a Mont Tennes handbookman, who had become a Capone gambling operator in Cicero and the Loop – a loan, the report read, which had not been paid back. He had five thousand dollars from Alderman Berthold A. Cronson, nephew of Ettelson, who stated that the loan was 'a pure friendship proposition'; it had not been repaid. He had five thousand dollars from Ettelson himself, who could not be reached but who sent word that he had never loaned Lingle anything at any time, although he 'had a custom of giving Lingle some small remembrance at Christmas time, like a box of cigars'. He had a loan of 2,500 dollars from Major Carlos Ames, president of the Civil Service Commission, and Ames stated that this loan 'was a purely personal affair needed to cover market losses'. He had three hundred dollars from Police Lieutenant Thomas McFarland. 'A purely personal affair,' declared McFarland, as he had been 'a close personal friend of Lingle's for many years.' Additionally it was alleged that Sam Hare, roadhouse and gambling-parlour proprietor, had loaned Lingle twenty thousand dollars. Hare denied it.

Yet further enlightenment thrown by the investigation upon the private operations of Lingle was that he had been in investment partnership with Police Commissioner Russell, one of his five separate accounts for stock-market speculations. This particular one was opened in November 1928 with a twenty thousand dollar deposit, and was carried anonymously in the broker's ledger as Number 49 Account. On September 20 1929 – preceding the market crash in October 1929 – their joint paper profits were 23,696 dollars; later, a loss of 50,850 dollars was shown. On all his five accounts his paper profits at their peak were eighty-five thousand dollars; with the crash these were converted into a loss of seventy-five thousand dollars. Russell's losses were variously reported as 100 thousand and 250 thousand dollars.

'As to the source of the moneys put up by Lingle in these stock accounts and deposited by him in his bank account,' the report commented with grim formality, 'we have thus far been able to come to no conclusion.'

But the Press and the public had come to conclusions – and they were the drearily obvious ones, the ones that again confirmed that they were the inhabitants of a city that lived by spoliation, that they were governed by dishonourable leaders and venal petty officials. As had happened so monotonously before, the dead hero changed into a monster in this fairy-story in reverse. The newspapers continued to theorize why Lingle had been eliminated, and the public were, flaccidly, interested to know; but the fervour, the righteous wrath, had waned. Both the most likely theories identified Lingle as a favour-seller, and both circumstantially indicted Capone's opposition, the Moran and Aiello merger. One story which had percolated through from the underworld was that Lingle had been given fifty thousand dollars to secure protection for a West Side dog-track, that he had failed – and kept the money. Another implicated him in the reopening of the Sheridan Wave Tournament Club which had been operated by the Weiss-Moran gang, but which, after the St. Valentine's Day massacre, and the fragmentation of the gang, had closed. After recouping, Moran had for eighteen months been trying to muster official help for a reopening. It had been in charge of Joe Josephs and Julian Potatoes Kaufman. It was stated that Kaufman, an old friend of Lingle, had approached him and asked him to use his influence to persuade the police to switch on the green light. The Chicago *Daily News* alleged that then, Boss McLaughlin – who on another occasion had threatened Lingle for refusing to intercede in obtaining police permission for the operation of another gambling house – was commissioned by Moran to make direct contact with the State's Attorney's Office. Kaufman and Josephs separately approached a police official, who agreed to let the Sheridan Wave Tournament open, if Lingle was cut in.

Following this, according to the report, Lingle called on Josephs and Kaufman and demanded fifty per cent of the profits. Kaufman abusively refused. So the club remained closed.

Another newspaper, the Chicago *Herald and Examiner*, carried a similar story. According to their version Lingle demanded fifteen thousand dollars cash from Josephs and Kaufman, and when this was refused, retorted: 'If this joint is opened up, you'll see more squad cars in front ready to raid it than you ever saw in your life before.'

Three days before Lingle was killed, State's Attorney Swanson's staff of detectives, on the orders of Chief Investigator Pat Roche, raided a gambling house in the Aiello territory, the Biltmore Athletic Club on West Division Street. Within an hour after the raid, Lingle was repeatedly telephoning Roche, who refused to talk to him. Next day Lingle accosted him in person and said: 'You've put me in a terrible jam. I told that outfit they could run, but I didn't know they were going to go with such a bang.'

Meanwhile, Kaufman and Josephs had made up their minds – doubtless after consultation with Moran – to restart the Sheridan Wave Tournament Club in defiance of Lingle. It was widely advertised that it would be opening on the night of 9 June – the day on which Lingle set out for the races for the last time.

An equally plausible theory was that he had got too deeply tangled up in the struggle for money and power in the gambling syndicate. For years there had been bitter war between Mont Tennes's General News Bureau, a racing news wire service which functioned entirely for the purposes of betting, and the independent news services. As an appointed intermediary, in January 1930 Lingle brought the two opposed factions together and a two-year truce was agreed upon. The truce may not have extended to Lingle, whose services perhaps did not satisfy all the parties.

Possibly all are true: it was simply that Lingle, like so many before him, had gone too far out in these barracuda waters of gang-business.

16

Zuta's Private Papers

'Chicago is on the way to becoming the first great city in America to rid itself of gangster influence and gangster assassination.'

The Chicago *Tribune*

'This is virgin territory for whorehouses.'

AL CAPONE, *surveying the suburbs*

MEANWHILE, the question 'Who killed Jake Lingle?' that had been hammering at the Chicagoans' ears with the clamorous insistence of that earlier one, 'Who killed McSwiggin?' remained unanswered. Familiarly, as the investigators plodded up the course of this particular river of events in search of the source, they found a bewildering number of muddy tributaries angling off until it became increasingly hard to know which was the main channel. At least one of those side streams led into interestingly new country.

Among the suspects sought (but not in every case caught) were nine notorious characters. There was Frank Foster, a Sicilian despite this name and his other alias of Frank Frost, brother of John Citro and a founder-member of the O'Banion gang. The gun found beside Lingle's body was identified as one of five ·38 Colts bought by Foster from Peter von Frantzius, a Diversey Parkway trader who described himself – with no conscious irony, one supposes – as 'a sporting goods dealer' and who had been named as the supplier of the machine-gun used in the St. Valentine's Day massacre; Foster vanished but was picked up in Los Angeles three weeks after Lingle's murder, extradited to Chicago and indicted for complicity in the crime. There was Ted Newberry, identified as Foster's companion when the five revolvers were bought, the whisky salesman who was with Moran and Willie Marks when the three of them arrived just late enough not to be lined up against the wall of the North Clark Street garage eighteen months previously. There was James Red Forsyth, at one stage believed to be the actual triggerman on that occasion, who had once been arrested in a police swoop on a Moran rendezvous – to be released with alacrity when it was pointed out that he was on the staff of Corporation Counsel Ettelson.

There was Grover C. Dullard, a member of the management of the Sheridan Wave Tournament Club, one-time bodyguard and driver for Terry Druggan, and who had known Lingle since childhood. There was Simon J. Gorman, a union official and proprietor of a transport company. There was Frank Noonan. There were Julian Potatoes Kaufman and Joey Josephs, Moran's appointees at the Sheridan Wave; Kaufman, a bookmaker's son, had already been marked as the receiver of stolen property and as concerned in O'Banion gang-murders.

There was Fred Burke, late of St. Louis's Egan's Rats, wanted on a variety of charges ranging from bank robbery to the murder of a policeman, and who was thought to have been one of the men dressed in uniform in the St. Valentine's Day plot and probably to have been the 'priest' in the subway when Lingle was shot.

And there was also Jack Zuta, from whom developed a fresh labyrinth of revelations of graft and political pork-barrelling, an aspect of the case which attracted as much attention as the original slaying. Zuta was to Moran's North Side administration what Jack Guzik and Mike de Pike Heitler were to Capone's: he was business manager and organizer of brothels and bawdy night-spots. For when the more fastidious O'Banion had been removed from the scene, Drucci, Weiss and Moran had not felt the same compunction about trading in women, and had hastened forward into this new enterprise under the seasoned guidance of Zuta. Zuta had previously been in conflict with Capone. Under the 1926 Peace Pact, he, together with Bill Skidmore and Barney Bertsche – then a West Side faction – had been relegated to the Forty-second and Forty-third Wards north of the Madison Street territory-division; but Zuta had soon formed a covert alliance with the Aiellos and, in armed squads, had made pirate raids into Capone country, exacting cash handsel from speakeasies and cabarets. Capone discouraged them: he had a bomb lobbed into their headquarters at 823 West Adams Street. The building fell down. Zuta, henceforth, stayed deep inside the North Side – until, as later seemed highly probable, he was appointed by Moran to put Lingle on the spot.

Zuta was the first to be taken in by the police. He was held for questioning at the South State Street detective bureau for twenty-four hours; he was released on bond late in the evening of Tuesday, 1 July. He was called for by Solly Vision, Albert Bratz and a Miss Leona Bernstein. After talking to them, Zuta seemed not anxious to

leave the building. It appeared that, even if the police had not
finally concluded that Zuta had planned the Lingle killing, Capone
had and Zuta's friends were aware that Capone intended to express
his displeasure. Zuta approached Lieutenant George Barker, a
33-year-old ex-Marine and the youngest officer in the city force,
who was going off duty, and asked for police escort through the
Loop as far as Lake Street, where he was catching an elevated train.

Barker grudgingly agreed to drive him and his friends to the
station. They all got into Barker's Pontiac sedan. Vision sat in front
with Barker, Zuta in the back between Bratz and Miss Bernstein.
The distance to be covered was thirteen blocks. From State Street
Barker drove north. He entered the Loop at Van Buren Street, its
southern boundary, heading towards Madison and State. This is the
heart of Chicago, as busy as Piccadilly Circus or Times Square; at
this hour it was brilliantly lit, thickly thronged by crowds leaving the
cinemas, bars and restaurants, pedestrians and motorists dawdling
about the bright lights of the summer night. As Baker passed Quincy
Street, moving slowly, at fifteen m.p.h., behind a street-car, Zuta,
who had been nervously peering out of the rear window, suddenly
cried: 'They're after us.'

Vision threw himself over the back of the front seat and on to the
pile formed by the other three who were already embedding themselves into the floor of the Pontiac. In his mirror Barker saw a dark
blue saloon with two men in the rear seat closing on them. The car
swerved to the right to get between Barker and the kerb. It spurted
level and one of the passengers, a tall man in tan suit and Panama hat,
opened the door, hoisted a ·45 automatic from an armpit holster and,
standing on the running-board, leaned forward and emptied a seven-
cartridge clip of bullets into the Pontiac. Simultaneously his companion opened up from the rear window and the driver also drew a
gun and began popping away.

Barker slammed on his emergency brake and jumped out of his
car firing his revolver. For thirty seconds there was a sustained exchange. As a north-bound street-car shuddered to a stop because
the Pontiac was blocking the tracks, the driver, Elbert Lusader, of
Berwyn Avenue, the 38-year-old father of three children, collapsed
mortally wounded with a bullet through his neck. Another bullet
wounded Olaf Sventse, a 69-year-old night-watchman on his way
to work at the Standard Club. Policeman William Smith came
running along the sidewalk brandishing his gun, and, believing it
to be an inter-gang squabble, aimed at Barker who – being in
civilian clothes – just in time flashed his star and shouted that he

was a police officer. In the confusion the Zuta party, unharmed, had scrambled out of the Pontiac and fled along with the crowds scattering in panic, jostling up side-turnings or huddling down in shop doorways.

Joined by Policeman Smith, Barker jumped into his car and pursued the gunmen, who were accelerating north up State Street. There was a further shock of melodrama. From the exhaust pipe of the assault car there suddenly belched a dense black shroud – a smoke-screen expelled by a plunger fitted beside the foot-controls. Although blinded, Barker jammed down his foot on the accelerator and shot through the fog belt at fifty miles an hour, and as he emerged he saw the blue sedan turning at Madison Street. It swung east, proceeded for a block and then dodged north again into Wabash Avenue, with Barker overtaking it. He was only fifty yards behind when his engine died, for a bullet had pierced the petrol tank. The gunmen vanished.

What residue of dismay remained unused in decent Chicago welled up at this latest desperate impudence of gunmen who were ruthlessly prepared to fight out their quarrels at the most public of places and times, to turn the city's centre into a cockpit. The newspapers shrilled; protests and horror were voiced at citizens' meetings and at luncheon clubs; both assailants and assaulted went unapprehended. At least, there was no apprehension by the police. But the incident reached its stylized gangland climax. Precisely one month later, on the evening of 1 August, Zuta was pleasantly whiling away the hours in his hide-out at the Lake View Hotel on the shores of Lake Nemahbin, a summer resort near Delafield, Wisconsin, where he was known as Goodman and a big spender. Parties were swimming from the beach; couples were dancing in the hotel's music pavilion; Zuta was idly slotting nickels into the electric piano.

Five men walked in, in single file like a military patrol. The leader was cradling a tommy-gun, the second was armed with a rifle, the next two with a sawn-off shot-gun apiece and the last with a pistol. They arrayed themselves in front of the piano, facing Zuta's bent back. He turned, a tentative smile on his face. The piano was playing 'It May Be Good For You But It's So Bad For Me', a current hit from the musical *Flying High*. The jangling melody was drowned in the sudden hideous uproar as all five guns ruined Zuta's suit.

Zuta was of no remarkable importance or charm, and no one was cast down by his death or would have held this to be one of Capone's most heinous crimes. Yet, as may be seen at this distance, it was one of Capone's most serious errors. For Zuta turned out to be that rare kind of racketeer, a methodical accountant, a bureaucrat bootlegger. The moment the news of his death reached Chicago, the detective bureau pounced upon his premises. They took away with them records that again aroused the public ire, and which, by circuitous sequence, led to the toppling of Capone.

That banditry, illicit alcohol production and retailing, gambling and prostitution were organized commerce, and that there was collusion between the gangs on the one hand and private business and public officialdom on the other, could not have come as a startling revelation to any Chicagoan over the age of ten. But, despite the incessant dribble over the years of newspaper exposés, accusations by various commissions and grand juries, and piecemeal disclosures by the police, not until now had the bare, factual book-keeping of crime been opened to inspection. The documents, said one newspaper, 'reveal for the first time in the history of gangdom the operations of a mob'.

Four safety-deposit boxes were found in Zuta's Loop office. They contained balance sheets, memoranda, cancelled cheques, promissory notes, letter files and records of transactions. In the ledger were entries of weekly payments – which rose as high as 108,469 dollars in one week – to 'M.K.', identified by the detective bureau as the syndicate's bribe-doler. It was 'M.K.'s' duty to distribute honoraria (which never dropped below 100 thousand dollars a month) to police and city and county officials. In return, protection, or rather non-interference, was guaranteed to the syndicate's slot-machine con-concessions and booze plants and bars. The wage structure was neatly divided into county districts. And there, named and in each case with the appropriate fee appended, were the stalwarts appointed as the trustees and administrators of good government.

Perhaps the only mild surprise in glancing down that list is the paltry sums for which these men were prepared to barter their reputations.

Among other miscellaneous souvenirs in this memory box were a couple of picture postcards sent from Hot Springs, Arkansas, by Alderman George M. Maypole. One was a photograph of the Maypoles on horseback and read: 'Regards from the Maypoles'; the other ran: 'I hope when this reaches you, you will be feeling much better.'

Another item from the correspondence file was a letter from Louis La Cava, who had acted for Capone and Torrio in their invasion of Cicero, but who had since dropped from favour and gone into exile. This letter, sent from New York in June 1927, was proposing an anti-Capone alliance, and offered: 'I'd help you organize a strong business organization capable of coping with theirs in Cicero. You know you have lots of virgin territory on the north side limits border line, and they are going to try and prevent me from lining up with you and thereby keep starving me out, until I go back to them begging for mercy.' There was a second letter from La Cava containing the bitter line: 'I have heard the Big Boy is stopping my brothers from making a living.'

Among the filled-in cheque stubs was one for five hundred dollars to Camille Lombardo, widow of Antonio; one for 560 dollars to Tony Mops Volpe, one-time Capone personal gunman; and one for a thousand dollars to Diamond Joe Esposito, the Twenty-fifth Ward Republican Committeeman and political lieutenant of Charles S. Deneen, the Prohibitionist United States Senator. Money-gifts had also been made to Dago Lawrence Mangano and Hymie Levin of the Capone gang.

Lump-sum emoluments included this item: 'East Chicago, 3,500 dollars', identified as referring to East Chicago Avenue Police Station, guardian of the district encompassing the Forty-second Ward and where Zuta controlled a string of brothels, gambling-parlours and shebeens.

Shining brightly from this maze of business minutiae was the central fact that the income from this branch of the Moran-Aiellos-Zuta syndicate – the proceeds of slot-machines, speakeasies, handbook offices, brothels, nightclubs, and the Fairview Kennel Dog Track – was a weekly average of 429 thousand dollars. And this was scratch-farming, the relatively rubbishy crops scraped up by poor-white squatters on the marginal land adjoining Capone's rich estates.

The publication of the above details agitated Press and public. The *Tribune*, still doggedly demanding retribution for the murder of its disgraced reporter, in an editorial beside a McCutcheon cartoon entitled 'At last a breach in the walls', declaimed: 'Progress has been made in solving the murder of Jake Lingle. Foster has been indicted for the murder. The business records of Jack Zuta, the murdered racketeer, have been located and the prosecuting authorities are examining them in detail. They provide evidence for the first time of the relations of gangdom with politics and the police. This is a tremendous advance over anything that has been accomplished hither-to in any American city towards the suppression of the universal threat to society. The Zuta journals may throw light on the Lingle murderers, and, more than that, they promise exposure and prosecu-tion of gangsters and their allies who have hitherto enjoyed immunity.' And it concluded, in a flush of euphoria: 'Chicago is on the way to becoming the first great city in America to rid itself of gangster influence and gangster assassination. The energy and resourcefulness which uncovered the Zuta papers will follow through. The day of reckoning is measurably nearer.'

Actually the day of reckoning was still immeasurably far off. Roche, of the State's Attorney's Office, remarked crisply on the day that the Zuta material was published: 'A lot of men will be leaving town.' There was no noticeable rush. Explanations were demanded of the named men, and a few proffered feeble and unconvincing stories – such as the judge who denied that the many separate cheques amounting to five thousand dollars, and each one signed by Zuta and endorsed by the judge, came from the gambler. But no legal action was taken against any of them, although they might be thought to have been open to charges of graft and corruption.

Stimulated by this unexpected leakage, other people began to volunteer information. Acquaintances of Zuta from Middlesboro, Kentucky, where he had a house, stated that many Chicago politicians, including judges, had been his guest there, and a former county prosecutor said that Big Bill Thompson had once been a visitor. Zuta had bragged around in Middlesboro that he had raised fifty thousand dollars for Thompson's campaign funds in the preceding Chicago mayoralty election. Then Senator Starr, during Probate Court hearings, came up with the news that in 1926, during a confidential chat at the Hotel Sherman, Zuta had told him that he was forming an organization to support Thompson's candidacy. 'I'm going to be a power in city politics,' Zuta had declared, 'and I'm going hook, line and sinker for Thompson because Thompson will go hook, line and sinker for me.' That was top-level operating. Zuta's interests were multifarious: his hand was manipulating at humbler levels, too. The mistress of a police patrolman said she had received 1,500 dollars from Zuta to buy her lover's promotion to sergeant.

The Probate Court hearings were initiated to inquire into Zuta's real estate holdings. What pricked their curiosity was that after he was already dead, City Hall put through a cheque for 2,500 dollars for what was registered as 'balance due' on property under process of being condemned.

For the rest of that summer and autumn and through into the New Year, the Lingle case, with its Zuta case sequel, ran in the newspapers with no more than a few days' break. In January of 1931 testimony was still being heard in the Probate Court about Zuta's operations for the Thompson administration and the Republican machine in general. The only tangible outcome of the proliferating scandal and uproar begun by the shooting down of Jake Lingle was that a St. Louis gun-fighter named Leo Brothers was convicted of murder. He was sentenced to fourteen years in prison; he served ten. Brothers was probably the only man handed over to justice by Capone. Roche, convinced that Capone was implicated in the murder, nagged at him so long for information that finally Capone said that he would have his execution squad deal with the killer and then pass on the information for Roche to close the book on the case. Roche refused to bargain for a dead body, and, to bring an end to the matter, Capone at last grudgingly revealed that he had discovered it was Brothers.

Nevertheless, although the repetitive rallying cries and bugle-blasts declaring that Chicago was aroused, that Chicago was exor-cising its daemons, were more mettlesome than materially true, a number of separate movements of revolt were at last beginning to fuse into the beginning of a positive anti-gang crusade.

The Chicago Crime Commission, which had grown from a recommendation of the Association of Commerce committee, and had been founded by a group of civic leaders in 1919, in 1930 devised a scheme and a phrase that had a phenomenal success. The Commission, under its president Frank J. Loesch, composed a list of the most menacing figures in Chicago's underworld. Twenty-eight were named, with Capone at the top, and the list was sent to judges, to the State's Attorneys, to the Sheriff of Cook County and to the Commissioner of Police with a letter urging that these specified men be unpityingly harried in every legal way – as tax-evaders, as aliens, as patrons and proprietors of prohibited drinking and gambling-houses, and as vagrants. Explained Mr. Loesch: 'The purpose is to keep the light of publicity shining on Chicago's most prominent, well-known and notorious gangsters to the end that they may be under constant observation by the enforcing authorities and law-abiding citizens apprised of the hazards to be encountered in dealing with those who are constantly in conflict with the law.'

The Commission had – and has – no power to prosecute or enforce its recommendations. It was founded with the purpose of excavating and putting on public display facts of Chicago's crime that the official bodies charged with this duty were unable or unwilling to do. It is a harsh reflection upon the rotten state of Chicago's whole structure of justice that a private concern had to be formed to perform this function; at the same time, it is a reflection of the spirit of integrity that persisted within the rotten structure that it was done. In its yearly reports the Commission surveys the present crime scene and, in a way that would be legally impossible, and largely unnecessary, in Britain, starkly attacks named men, judges and other officials, whose activities are suspect. During the Prohibition Era it succeeded in forcing upon the city many invaluable reforms and improvements. It undertook an examination of the police department, which brought out many dismissals and a general reorganization. It induced the city's financial department to provide for a thousand more patrolmen. It inspired the anti-crime drive of the Illinois Manufacturers' Association, the start of the Evanston Crime Commission and the sponsorship by the Industrial Club of Chicago of a state survey of crime and the administration of justice. It brought about the creation of a bond department in the State's Attorney's office, which circumscribed horse-trading by dishonest bondsmen. It pushed through an act to stem the immunity of gangsters on charges of vagrancy and carrying concealed weapons. Its drive against car-thieves and receivers brought a reduction of twenty-six per cent in Illinois theft insurance premiums. It gave relentless publicity to the brief time spent on the bench by individual judges and the small number of trials brought before juries, as a result of which the average time spent by judges in court rose up to four hours a day, with a corresponding increase in the numbers of jury trials.

Its 1930 Public Enemy campaign was a triumph – at least, as an advertising campaign. The phrase instantly caught the imagination of the nation. Throughout the United States newspapers grabbed at it. It was borrowed for the titles of books. Its concrete results in reducing crime were less percusssive, but there were some. This capsule brand upon the foreheads of so many casually notorious characters seemed to stimulate the law-enforcement agencies into re-focusing sights and concentrating efforts. Even the Chicago law moved itself. Four years after the inception of the campaign, the Crime Commission announced that fifteen Public Enemies had been convicted, nine had died, one was awaiting deportation and eight more were booked for appearance in court. The rest, said the Commission (but this time with less justified optimism) were 'on the run and in hideouts because of the existence of various warrants against them'.

The spell of fear and inertia had been punctured. The gangsters no longer ruled so invincibly, so arrogantly, so despotically. Nevertheless, during the four years that the Crime Commission's successes were registered, another 194 gang murders were committed. And that itself was another influence upon the changing public attitude: the glamour that had partially thrown a protective haze around the gangsters was soured; they had finally sickened and frightened the public by their violence. In October 1930 in Evanston, a residential suburb of Chicago, Mr. James G. Barber, a justice of the peace, founded the Business Men's and Women's Pistol Club under the joint presidency of Mayor Charles Barrett and Chief of Police William O. Freeman (both of whom had had correspondence with Zuta). The slogan of the club was 'Citizens! Present – fire!' and its purpose, announced Freeman, was to combat the crime wave with an armed citizenry. 'We are equipping merchants and professional men and women for war against crime,' he said. 'There will be regular practice on the police pistol-range. We are arming the members with ·38 calibre police automatics, and they will also be instructed how to disarm gangsters.'

There is no record of the pistol-packing housewives of Evanston having sent the gangsters scurrying intimidated into cover, but Capone as king was nearing the sunset of his reign. For in the summer of 1931 that least probable of menaces, the tax office, put upon him the detaining hand that all the more obvious agencies had failed to do. There were other new factors arising, and the one that was most direly to affect the Capone syndicate was a combination of Mayor Anton J. Cermak and Roger the Terrible Touhy, head of the powerful Des Plaines beer-pushing gang.

Touhy was the son of a Chicago policeman. He began work as a Western Union telegraphist, with a private sideline in handling racing bets. His downfall came, he explained in his book, published just before he was bumped-off after release from prison in December 1959, was that he 'was too damn honest'. He joined a union and was sacked. In 1926 he bought two trucks and, controlling it from the suburb of Des Plaines opened up in the illicit beer-running business in partnership with Matt Kolb, the one-time Capone mobster who had withdrawn when the blood began to spout too freely in central Chicago. By the late 'twenties he and Kolb were grossing a million dollars a year from beer, and an additional 500 thousand dollars a year from slot-machines. During this period Touhy had peripheral dealings with Capone, on one occasion supplying him with five hundred barrels of beer after Federal agents had closed two of his breweries, and he claimed that Capone tried to swindle him on the payment. According to Touhy's account, Capone's resentment and jealousy against him increased, for he 'was making a pile of money and was practically unknown to the newspapers. My partner, Kolb, had the reputation of being the top man in beer running and slot machines in our part of Cook County. He sort of liked the limelight and I didn't mind his having the notoriety. I enjoyed being a quiet family man.'

In 1931 Capone, still the empire-builder, turned the heat on Touhy's Cook County territory. He despatched Frank Rio and Willie Heeney to persuade Touhy into submitting to the syndicate's plan to fill the suburbs with taxi-dance halls, gambling games and brothels. 'Al says this is virgin territory out here for whorehouses,' said Heeney in a memorable phrase. Touhy stalled. He had further calls from Capone emissaries – in turn from Louis Little New York Campagna, Machine-gun Jack McGurn, Frank Diamond, Sam Golf Bag Hunt, Murray the Camel Humphreys and James Red Forsyth Touhy went to the local police chiefs and told them: 'If the Capone mob gets into your towns there'll be no law left. The mobsters will be killing each other on your streets. You'll have a cat-house in every block. I'm trying to bring up two sons out here in a decent way, and you law enforcement people have families, too. We must protect ourselves.' Touhy did not want his reputation as a citizen damaged – 'I had a pretty good standing in the community. I lived quietly, paid my taxes, contributed liberally to charities and was a leader in the Des Plaines Elks Club.'

Capone did not like the lack of co-operation. He had Kolb kidnapped and collected fifty thousand dollars from Touhy in ransom, and then in November two gunmen walked into the Morton Inn, a suburban speakeasy, and shot Kolb dead. In 1933 by remote control (for he was by then in prison on a tax conviction) Capone framed Touhy – or so Touhy continued to protest – in the kid-napping of Jake the Barber Factor, a financier. Touhy served twenty-five years – and was murdered by shot-gunners after his release.

Touhy's presentation of his destruction by Capone was a quietly modest and appealing account of a peace-loving husband and father who just wanted to carry on drawing a million dollars a year and troubling no one. But what was omitted from Touhy's book was a slightly more complicated and impure matter, a series of events that would have given Capone more reason to wish to see Touhy removed from the scene. After Touhy's death, Saul D. Alinsky, the sociologist who was a member of the Joliet Prison classification board at the time of Touhy's commitment there, came forward and made public a story that he said had 'been commonly known for many

years in many circles in Chicago'. In 1931 when Anton J. Cermak
was elected Mayor of Chicago gang-killings suddenly spurted
upward – in two years nearly a hundred hoodlums died in ambushes
and street assassinations, and for a period the murders came at the
rate of one a day. And most of those who died were Capone men.

What caused this? An.alliance, said Alinsky, between Cermak,
who in his campaign speeches had pledged himself to drive the
Capone mob out of Chicago, and Touhy. Touhy maintained that
Cermak offered him the Chicago Police Department as 'soldiers' in
the war and said that by December 1932 the Capone gang 'was
ready to throw in the sponge'. But in 1933 Cermak was himself
killed, as he stood beside Franklin D. Roosevelt, then president-
elect, in Biscayne Park, Miami. It has always been accepted that
Cermaks death was accidental, that he was hit by a bullet intended
for Roosevelt and fired by Giuseppi Zangara, a deranged anarchist,
who was later electrocuted. No, said Touhy. In the crowd near
Zangara was another armed man – a Capone killer. In the flurry of
shots six people were hit – but the bullet that struck Cermak was
a ·45, and not from the ·32-calibre pistol used by Zangara, and was
fired by the unknown Capone man who took advantage of the
confusion to accomplish his mission.

Whether this is the whole truth will probably now never be
established satisfactorily, for all those who could have known are
dead. If Touhy's story was true, then, even if his plot with Cermak
had succeeded, there would have been little likelihood of a cleaner,
corruption-free Chicago. The only cheer that could justifiably have
been raised would have been: 'The gang is dead – long live the
gang!' Yet during all these furtive scuffles for power, new and
ungovernable transforming factors were looming closer. Prohibition
was running out of whatever supporters it had ever had. Depression
was blighting Chicago. The party, really, was over: the Belshazzar's
feast was ending in indigestion and hangover, in self-disgust and
despair. Gang-rule was not finished, but it would never be quite the
same again. Nor would it be the same for an ephemeral little industry
– some would say an art – that had flourished under the casual
patronage of the gangsters: jazz.

17

The Jazz Baby

*'At the Triangle Club the boss was shot in the stomach one
night, but we kept working. After that he walked sort of
bent over.'*

GEORGE WETTLING

*'While there were some musicians who did a fair amount of
boozing and whoring around and marijuana smoking, there
was also a hell of a lot of damn good honest jazz being
played around.'*

ARTIE SHAW

B EN HECHT's pet name for Chicago in the 'twenties had been
'the jazz baby'. It was 'that toddlin' town that Billy Sunday
could not shut down' of Fred Fisher's 1922 hit, it was the
griddle on which some of the best hot music of the decade was
cooked, for the stimulus given to jazz was one of the benigner by-
products of Prohibition, and for that reason is worth a place on the
record. The gangs' entertainment establishments, together with the
legitimate dance halls which thrived on customers with flasks in
their hip-pockets and some preliminary lubrication from near-by
speaks, provided a booming market for musicians. They arrived in
Chicago in large numbers from all directions, but mostly from the
South. 'Al Capone and his lieutenants replaced the madams of
Storyville as sponsors for the new music,' says Thomas Sugrue.

It is true, but only a segment of the picture. A myth that should
by now have been disposed of, but which still adhesively lingers, is
that jazz did a dog's-leg assault upon the world, that it was invented
in New Orleans in the early years of the century, a piece of instantaneous legerdemain, that there it remained as a local *patois* until
the U.S. Navy had the red-light houses of Storyville closed down in
1917 to protect the sailors' health and morals, that the Negro and
Creole jazzmen, their places of employment shuttered, climbed
aboard trains and river-boats and migrated north to Chicago, that

there the revolutionary music detonated upon the astonished ears
of the outside world, and that from there it advanced upon New
York and universal fame.

It was a far less simple history. Jazz, semi-jazz, near-jazz and
tributary jazz were being played in a racket of local idioms from 1900
onward throughout America – beyond the city limits of New Orleans,
far beyond the Mississippi Delta. Various forms of honky-tonk piano-
playing – piano-roll ragtime, fast Western, overhand bass, barrelhouse, sock style, and even a type derived from Appalachian gospel
shouts – had been evolved by itinerant Negro entertainers who criss-
crossed through the turpentine and railroad construction camps of
the South and West. Syncopated music had for years been played
in travelling minstrel and vaudeville troupes, brass-band street
parades, country fairs, circuses, tent shows and prize-fights, and there
were many minstrel guitar-pickers such as Leadbelly and Blind Lemon
Jefferson earning their erratic living by rambling around the Deep
South singing blues and dance tunes. For a decade and more
before Prohibition this music had been reaching Chicago, for
Chicago, with its huge coloured population and its tumultuous
night-life, was even then thriving territory for the working
musician.

Three hundred and fifty thousand Negroes migrated north from
the Mississippi Delta in that period, most of them escaping from the
poverty of the cotton states (where conditions had been drastically
worsened by a boll-weevil plague) to the plentiful jobs in Chicago's
steel mills, meat-packing plants and railway shops. They crowded
into the 'frail, flimsy, tottering, unkempt' tenements of the South
Side between Twelfth and Thirty-First Streets, as the Chicago
Commission on Race Relations described the housing, most of
which contained a room 'where an automatic piano thumps
throughout the night until closing hours'. The Negro poet, Langston
Hughes, described State Street in 1918 in this way: 'A teeming
Negro street with crowded theatres, restaurants and cabarets. And
excitement from noon to noon. Midnight was like day. The street
was full of workers and gamblers, prostitutes and pimps, church
folks and sinners . . . For neither love nor money could you find a
decent place to live. Profiteers, thugs and gangsters were coming
into their own.'

Between 1905 and 1915 Jelly Roll Morton had appeared often
at the Pekin Theatre-Cabaret, a New Orleans group named The
Original Creole Band had during 1913 been wildly popular at a
series of engagements at the Big Grand Theatre and the North

American Restaurant, and the following year the first all-white
ragtime band, Tom Brown and His Dusters arrived from New
Orleans to introduce their 'jass' at the Lamb's Café in the Loop,
where the new name, derived from a colloquialism for copulation
used in the Twenty-second Street brothels, was revised to jazz.
Between 1914 and 1918 a steady flow of musicians had been initiat-
ing Chicagoans in New Orleans style – The Lousiana Five (which
had Nick LaRocca as cornet-player, and who split away to form
his own Original Dixieland Band), and groups led by the New
Orleans trombonist George Filhe, by Jimmy Noone and by Manuel
Perez, whose band included Sidney Bechet and Lorenzo Tio,
toured such night-spots as the Fountain Inn at Sixty-third and
Halsted, the DeLuxe Café at Thirty-fifth and State, the Royal
Gardens (later the Lincoln Gardens) at Thirty-first and Cottage
Grove, and the Midnight Frolics on the Twenty-second Street levee,
which were beginning to specialize in this rowdy, novel customer-
attraction. According to Frederic Ramsey, Jr., by 1920 there were
more than forty outstanding New Orleans jazzmen in Chicago –
who in the beginning had difficulty in getting regular work, because
the Chicago musicians who controlled the local union obstructed the
invaders, but the public's sudden ravening appetite for the new noisy
sound-track of the times soon broke open the attempt to build a
dam.

Chicago's golden age of jazz began in 1918 with the arrival of
Joe King Oliver, the renowned New Orleans cornetist. In 1920
Oliver formed his own band, moved into the Dreamland Café, on
Thirty-fifth and State, and sent for Louis Armstrong, who had
been on Fate Marable's show-boat in New Orleans. This was the
genesis of what later became known as Chicago style jazz, for
young local white boys – Eddie Condon, Muggsy Spanier, Pee Wee
Russell, Mezz Mezzrow, George Wettling, Red McKenzie, Joe
Sullivan, Dave Tough, Bix Beiderbecke, Art Hodes, Jimmy McPart-
land, Bud Freeman and Frank Teschemaker – began haunting the
South Side cafés and speaks and listening open-mouthed and open-
eared, and began trying to make similar sounds themselves.

The jazz they played was similar, but distinctively different from
the buoyant, swinging and essentially happy music of the New
Orleans Negroes. Perhaps because of a lack of the fundamental
experience from which the Southern jazz had grown, the indigenous
Chicago jazz had a striving and edgy character. Wilder Hobson's
phrase was 'hardboiled eloquence': it had a frenzied drive, a harsh
and brutal excitement, and a form that discarded both the trombone

(which was replaced by the saxophone) and the integrated ensemble playing of the New Orleans men – this was 'hot solo' jazz, every man for himself, the music that Scott Fitzgerald heard and which seemed to him to synthesize the atmosphere and mood of the times, the tension and hectic living that was nowhere more intense than in Chicago.

The first ten years of Prohibition in Chicago was a dizzyingly productive period for jazz. Thirty-fifth Street between State and Calumet became a congestion of sawdust-floored twilight gin-mills fuming with jazz – the Sunset Café, the Dreamland, the Panama, the Plantation, the Fiume, the Elite, the New Orleans Babies, the DeLuxe. Condon claims that the midnight air on that street was so full of music that if you held up an instrument the breeze would play it. Many of the jazz pieces of that period commemorate the sleazy setting in which they were born – 'Friars Point Shuffle', 'Chicago Stomp Down', 'Twenty-ninth and Dearborn', 'Wabash Blues', 'Sunset Café Stomp', Thirty-fifth and Calumet', 'Armour Avenue Stomp', 'Saratoga Strut', 'Royal Garden Blues', 'Chicago High Life' – all named for the city or particular brothels and night-life quarters in which the composers were working. It was out of this turmoil and ferment that those corner-stones of jazz, the famous Armstrong Hot Five and Hot Seven series of records were made with pick-up studio bands for the Okeh Gramophone Company between 1925 and 1929. The pops of the day, 'Sugar', 'Nobody's Sweetheart' and 'China Boy', in the new style bellowed out alongside the tunes that were already being regarded as part of the traditional New Orleans repertoire, 'Working Man Blues', 'Froggie Moore' and 'Didn't He Ramble'. And the blues was being heard in a profusion of forms. Bessie Smith, the great blues contralto, sang her 'Empty Bed Blues' and 'Nobody in Town Can Bake A Jelly Roll Like Mine', at the Avenue Theatre and caused a riot. Alberta Hunter, another great blues singer, introduced 'Loveless Love', W. C. Handy's version of the old 'Careless Love', at the Dreamland Café in 1921. Another revered blues performer of the period, String Beans, was a big draw at the Monogram Theatre, where his tunes were arranged by the pianist Lovie Austin. At the Pekin Inn, Tony Jackson, who had also worked at Pony Moore's and the Everleigh Club, used to play his broken-octave style walking bass and sing:

> *I got an all-night trick agin,*
> *So keep a-knockin' but you can't come in.*

Jimmy Yancey, the fine boogie pianist who had left vaudeville in
1913 and taken a job as grounds keeper for the White Sox baseball
team at Comisky Park, was wandering from bar to bar on State
Street and Wabash Avenue. Two other pianists in this idiom,
Meade Lux Lewis and Albert Ammons, who drove for the Silver
Taxicab Company, were also becoming known as men with a tire-
less, beefy, two-handed technique for the rent-parties spreading
throughout the South Side coloured quarter, which had trebled in
population between 1910 and 1920. Also known as skittles (and
later skiffles), kados, calicohops, breakdowns, stomps, house-shouts,
chitterling rags, too-tight parties, too-terrible parties, their original
purpose was to combine some fun with raising the rent by inviting
around friends who paid a quarter and brought along a jug of bootleg gin. During the 'twenties the pianists who contributed the
music for house-rent parties formed a distinct but at that time
mostly ignored school of jazz. They included men like Yancey,
Lewis, Ammons and Pete Johnson, but also lesser known formidable
keyboard-pounders such as Jack the Bear, Tipplin' Tom, the Tooth-
pick, Montana Taylor, Cow Cow Davenport, Cat-Eye Harry, the
Beetle, Speckled Red, Doug Suggs, Aaron Sparks, Blind Leroy
Garnett and Cripple Clarence Lofton.

'Night spots never had it so good,' a 1950 Chicago *Tribune* article
recalls. 'There were cabarets with twenty and thirty girls in the
chorus line, and floor-shows starting at 4 a.m. and dawn; jazz in
Friars Inn and in the Loop and Bert Kelly's Stables and on the
Near-North Side.' George Johnson, saxophonist in the Wolverines,
reminisces: 'Enthusiastic dancers to play to, dancers who understood
our music as well as we did, whole days spent playing golf, and a full
purse to supply anything we wanted. Those were merry days, with
no end of gin to drink, horses to ride, and a grand lake to swim in.'

But they were not such merrily halcyon days as Johnson's nostalgia
tinted them. The gangsters' booze premises provided the jazzmen
with jobs and an outlet for the music that dominated their minds,
but there were disadvantages attached to this benison. Bootleg gin
killed Bix Beiderbecke; he died at the age of twenty-eight in 1931.
Jimmy McPartland says: 'I think one of the reasons he drank so
much was that he was a perfectionist and wanted to do more with
music than any man possibly could. The frustration that resulted was
a big factor.' Mezz Mezzrow describes visiting a State Street speakeasy with him in 1927: 'A peephole slid open, an eye appeared in
the hole and gunned Bix; then the door swung open like a switch-
blade. I guess the mug of that bottle baby was known to every peep-

hole attendant in the Western Hemisphere.' Pee Wee Russell says: 'As for what caused Bix to destroy himself, well, in that era, naturally where he started, around Indiana, there was that thing with the hip-bottle and the gin – the 'twenties and all that stuff. Later, when he had acquired a name, he could get a bottle of whisky any time of day or night.'

Their purses may have been kept full, but it was a tough environment in which to fill them, and one which took an abundant toll in nervous strain, in physical injury and in lives. In October 1923 the Wolverines – the Chicago group in which Beiderbecke played – was engaged for a daily 9 p.m. to 5 a.m. stint at the Stockton Club near Cincinnati, on the Dixie Highway leading to Hamilton, Ohio, an ostensible dancing-dining roadhouse which also provided alcohol and gambling. On New Year's Eve of 1924 table reservations were given to a Hamilton gang and also to a rival Cincinnati gang – on the understanding that a truce would be observed. But in the early hours, after many bottles had been emptied, a squabble broke out. To preserve an air of normality the Wolverines were instructed to keep playing: while bottles and crockery splintered around them they doggedly beat out 'China Boy' for an hour. Another gangster-operated establishment where Beiderbecke played was the Valentino Café, and Condon wrote, of the time he was working 'in the heart of the tenderloin, five blocks almost solid with cabarets', at the Palace Gardens in the six hundred block on North Clark Street: 'Between midnight and dawn in those days you met all sorts of people in Chicago. You might be sitting quietly in a speakeasy and be informed that for the rest of the evening drinks were on the house: Capone, the owner, had wandered in, ordered the doors closed, and settled down to enjoy himself.'

Dave Tough, the drummer with the Austin High School band, worked in a Capone-owned club that had a clientele composed almost exclusively of baseball players, gangsters and detectives. One night, on his way to the bandstand, Tough jostled a man out of the way. 'Don't you care how long you live?' asked a friend. 'That's Bottles Capone.'

When liquored-up and pleased, gangsters were lavish with their tips to the jazzmen – but they also indulged in such pranks as flipping lighted cigarettes at the band as it played and occasionally using it for target practice. Once when Jim Lannigan, the bass-player, was at the Friar's Inn – a basement in the Loop, 'the hangout of the big money guys, Al Capone and Dion O'Banion', recalled **Paul Mares** – after the New Orleans Rhythm Kings had left, a party of Capone mobsters arrived, dismissed the other customers, closed the doors and took the place over for the night. One of them became fascinated by the shiny expanse of Lannigan's instrument, and finally pulled out a gun and hit the fiddle dead on the seam. It burst open like a seed pod. The band kept on playing. The gangster having satisfied his whim, asked Lannigan how much a replacement would cost. Jimmy McPartland told him 850 dollars – its price had been 225 – and the gangster peeled the roll. 'These Prohibition guys were loaded with loot,' McPartland explains.

The understanding among the jazzmen was that you kept on blowing, no matter what happened around you. Muggsy Spanier, the trumpeter, had two men shot to death in front of him one night. He kept on playing, but afterwards could not remember what the tune had been: his clothing was so saturated with nervous sweat that he had to change even his shoes. Spanier was liked by the Capone men. They would occasionally commandeer him for the evening, transporting him from place to place to play at their table. 'Jazz has got guts,' one of them told him. 'It don't make you slobber.'

Joe E. Lewis, who started as night-club comedian at the Midnight Frolics on Twenty-Second Street, got his throat cut almost fatally when he transferred from one gang-controlled North Side club to another in 1928, and in the same year the eight-to-the-bar pianist Pinetop Smith was shot to death during a masonic hall celebration on the West Side. George Wettling's posy from that period was: 'We would see those rods come up – and duck. At the Triangle Club the boss was shot in the stomach one night, but we kept working. After that he walked sort of bent over.'

Tiny Parham, Jimmie Noone and Lucky Millinder all played in different Syndicate clubs, Millinder's band being resident in a Bottles Capone Cicero establishment. Jimmy McPartland also worked in Cicero, at Eddie Tancl's, at the time that the Capone mob were moving in there. 'One night,' he remembers, 'a bunch of tough guys came in and started turning tables over to introduce themselves. Then they picked up bottles and began hitting the bartenders with them, also with blackjacks and knuckles. It was just terrible . . . The mobsters would break a bottle over some guy's head, then jab it in his face, then maybe kick him. They made mincemeat of people. I never saw such a horrible thing in my life. But we kept playing – period. A couple more nights of work and they came and did it again, much worse. That was the finish. Tancl got rid of the band, and two days later we found out he had been shot dead. That was the beginning of the mobs' moving in on night-club business.'

Marty Marsala also remembers 'plenty of rough stuff'. At one night-spot 'Capone would come in with about seven or eight guys. They closed the door as soon as he came in. Nobody could come in or out. Then he gets a couple of hundred dollar bills changed and passes them around to the entertainers and waiters. His bodyguards did the passing. We got five or ten bucks just for playing his favourite numbers, sentimental things.'

Capone also visited the Grand Terrace when Earl Hines was playing there. 'Scarface got along well with musicians,' Hines says. 'He liked to come into a club with his henchmen and have the band play his requests. He was free with hundred-dollar tips.'

Mezz Mezzrow worked at the Arrowhead Inn in the Syndicate's Burnham brothel quarter, and used to play 'Melancholy Baby' and 'The Curse of an Aching Heart' at the request of the girls who dropped in on their way home from the 8 p.m. to 4 a.m. shift. 'I never in my life saw a flock of chicks who could turn on the weeps so fast when we played their favourite tear-jerkers,' he remarked. Mezzrow also struck up a – brief – friendship with a redhead named Marcelle, employed in the Roamer Inn, a Syndicate whorehouse on 119th Street, until he was advised that she was Capone's reserved girl. 'I used to see Scarface around there and jawblock with him sometimes,' writes Mezzrow. 'He was sharp, young and ready in those days, with a couple of trigger men always trailing along at his elbows. He was friendly enough, and that was how I wanted him to keep on feeling.' He did, however, later have an argument with Capone during his time at the Arrowhead Inn. Capone's young brother, then eighteen, had been assigned to convoy the beer trucks out to Burnham in a Ford coupé with another gunman named Little Dewey. During an official visit to the Arrowhead Inn, Mitzi met one of the singers, a blonde named Lillian. Al heard of his brother's infatuation and ordered Mezzrow to sack her. Mezzrow refused, and Capone's scowl turned into a grin: 'The kid's got plenty of guts,' he said. Mezzrow disapproved of the gangs' patronage of jazz. 'I was surrounded,' he writes in the apoplectic style of his book, 'by a race of gangsters running amuck, a hundred million blow-tops born with ice-cubes for hearts and the appetites of a cannibal . . . Nobody was safe in this funky jungle. It was all one great big underworld, and they'd put their dirty grabbers on the one good thing left on earth, our music, and sucked it down into the mud with them.'

Flying bullets and beatings-up were an occupational hazard for the jazzmen of that era. Wingy Manone, the one-armed trumpeter, was in the middle of his solo of 'Clarinet Marmalade' one night at the Manley Club when a man at a table pulled a tommy-gun from under his overcoat and raked the front of the bandstand in an attempt to stop an acquaintance who was hurriedly leaving. Beiderbecke inadvertently challenged the mob when he joined Bing Crosby (then vocalist with the Paul Whiteman orchestra) at a private engagement at The Greyhound in Cicero. The party proved to be 'made up mostly of blue-jawed young men in dark double-breasted suits with blondes to match'. One of them took to yelling at the band and Beiderbecke offered to get off the stand and punch him in the nose if he did not shut up. The heckler glowered but shut up. Condon later pointed out to Beiderbecke that he, like Dave Tough, had been aggressive with Bottles Capone.

There were those jazzmen who, despite the easy money and the excitingly creative atmosphere of Chicago, felt they could be happier in duller surroundings. Albert Nicholas, the New Orleans clarinettist who in 1924 joined King Oliver and Louis Armstrong in Chicago, two years later turned down an offer to tour the Orient. That night there was a shooting in his club. He went out to the telephone, despatched a wire 'HAVE CHANGED MIND STOP WILL GO', and left for China.

Art Hodes, the pianist who worked first with the Wolverines, and then in various groups with Gene Krupa, Muggsy Spanier and Wingy Manone, drew in the magazine *The Jazz Record* a pungent little vignette of playing for a living in Prohibition Chicago. 'The joint was jammed,' he writes. 'The boss brought us a gallon of wine and that set the pace from then on in . . . Murf finally broke all his banjo strings trying to play as loud as the rest of us and had to play his guitar . . . All of a sudden, from behind me I heard what sounded like a pistol shot. So did the boss. Out he ran from his office with his two pearl-handled revolvers unholstered, ready . . . Murphy was holding his guitar, its neck broken. He'd gotten so mad at the damn thing that he busted it on the piano bench. Murf took to wearing a gun, a small affair, because some guy was out to get him over some chick . . . Another time the night club was full, people getting drunk and celebrating. Upstairs, unknown to many of the customers was a gambling joint. Johnny Craig, a drummer, and myself were playing downstairs, when all of a sudden, pop, pop – the Fourth of July, pistols and all. And me with my back turned! Man, was I scared! . . . And how about the time we were all leaving the Rainbow Gardens, 4 a.m., when three hoods jumped the boss. He fought them single-handed all over the sidewalk until they beat it, one by one. And when someone asked him why he didn't use his gun, the boss said: 'Waste lead on them punks?'

Louis Armstrong about this time changed managers – and was consequently threatened with gang violence. For many months he had two bodyguards accompany him everywhere, on and off the job. Jelly Roll Morton was another New Orleans musician who did not care for the overcharged and over-competitive atmosphere of Chicago, but his basic reason was a different one. He had always profitably engaged in pimping on the side, and to his chagrin he discovered that there was no chance in Chicago for an unknown freelance to muscle-in on this highly organized business. 'For the first time in years,' points out Alan Lomax, 'Jelly Roll was forced, to his great annoyance and to our good fortune, to devote himself exclusively to music.'

But even in this field he was black-balled. 'Jelly Roll was not a good old-time darky like Joe Oliver,' a Chicago music publisher observed. Lomax writes: 'He must have talked loud and long to the racketeers. If they were too fond of his music to kill him, they were not so charitable as to allow him to make his mark in the gin-mill circuit. The word went round that it was unhealthy to work with Jelly . . . Most old time Chicago jazzmen remember working for Capone or one of the mobsters. They recall that it was often unhealthy to quit one of those jobs if the boss said stay. They tell about the trumpetman on a job where business was good. A bid to Hollywood came. The boss said "No" and the horn-blower stalled the offer for six months. When he was finally allowed to resign, the mobsters presented him with a diamond-studded watch. As he was packing in his hotel room, two of the gang came by, beat him up, and retrieved the sentimental memento.'

Jelly Roll thought that the frantic noise of the Chicago imitators had cheapened jazz: 'Some people play like they want to knock your ear-drums down.' But the customers flocked in. 'Back in the shadows sat even more blasé white listeners,' writes Lomax, 'gentlemen who travelled in casual but wary bunches, wore sharp clothes and snap-brim hats, bulged at the hip and armpit and drank only "the amber" . . . The music suited them fine. It went down with them, for gangsters, too, are outcasts. Besides, they had a proprietary interest: they owned or protected the joints that the hot men were packing with customers.'

On the other hand, as Charles Edward Smith points out: 'In the nineteen-twenties, to be sure, jazzmen were frequently blowing out their brains, figuratively speaking, but usually in gin-mills of their own choosing.' Otis Ferguson is quoted in *Jazzmen*: 'They were boom years all along the line and any good music show could support a band in the pit; the radio was going great guns; records were being stamped out as fast as wheatcakes in Child's.' Artie Shaw recalls: 'In those days the South Side of Chicago was one of the foremost jazz conservatories in the world . . . That section of Chicago was a whole musical world in microcosm; and while there were some musicians who did a fair amount of boozing and whoring around and marijuana smoking, there was also a hell of a lot of damn good honest jazz being played around.'

The end of Prohibition killed the lush years for jazz. In any case, clever show-business people, who had listened attentively to the new music and then diluted and sweetened it for easy consumption had closed in on the available dollars. Ruth Etting and Rudy Vallee (it was Vallee who described jazz as 'the weird orchestral efforts of various coloured bands up in Harlem . . . Most of the time there is no distinguishable melody') were more popular than Bessie Smith and Jack Teagarden had ever been. The bands that sold were those of Guy Lombardo and Wayne King, and no longer the New Orleans Rhythm Kings and the Austin High Gang. The word jazz had filtered through into general consciousness, but while it remained pure at heart, what was perpetuated in its name had become as adulterated and artificial as the liquor: jazz meant to most people the emoting of Al Jolson, the triteness of George Gershwin, and the flatulence of Paul Whiteman ('the King of Jazz', he called himself). As the Depression worsened, there was a draining off of the stubbornly puritan jazzmen from Chicago in the direction of New York and Hollywood – Condon, Armstrong and dozens of others had gone East. Others had gone semi-commercial: Beiderbecke had joined Whiteman, Spanier had capitulated to Ted Lewis; many had found posts with radio companies and 'Mickey Mouse' recording bands. Sidney Bechet opened a shoeshine stall and Tommy Ladnier a tailor's shop. Some of the big orchestras – Ellington's and Noble Sissle's – followed the jazz trend to Europe. In Chicago Capone's Cotton Club still served jazz, and the Boyd Atkins band played at a Bottles Capone place on the North Side. But the public mood had changed; the bubbles had gone flat in the synthetic champagne of the 'twenties; the hungover public wanted no more of the overheated bootleg music, but instead bromides such as 'Let's Put Out The Lights And Go To Sleep' and 'Smilin' Through' to soothe their shredded nerves, and deaden the crash of collapsing banks.

PART THREE

'A Government of Bombs and Bums'

'Cops like dough and law is just tricks.'
CHICAGO BOOTLEGGER

18

Good Will, Fellowship and the Ennoblement of Mankind

'The Athens of America.'

CHICAGO PUBLICIST

CHICAGO NOT CRIME RIDDEN.

CHICAGO HEADLINE

'We are busted.'

CHICAGO BANK PRESIDENT

'I'm wetter than the middle of the Atlantic Ocean.'

CHICAGO'S PROHIBITION ERA MAYOR

IN September 1930 the Women's 'Chicago Beautiful' Association sent a letter to the New York State Chamber of Commerce expressing the citizens' resentment at Chicago being labelled 'the gangsters' playground', and asking for help in correcting this slanderous impression. The Association claimed, proudly, that Chicago had dropped to seventh crime place among American cities and was thirty-ninth in homicide; contrary to the general misconception, Chicago was a rapidly developing centre of art, music and culture. The Association added – without, perhaps, reassuring those still retaining squeamish doubts as to whether culture had entirely ousted carnage – that its members would willingly meet timid tourists at railway stations and see them safely placed in reputable hotels. The weakness in the plan seemed to be that even if the timid tourist safely reached his reputable hotel, would he ever put his nose out of it? If he had, he could not have been heartened by the notice in the window of a Loop invisible-mending firm: 'Bullet holes rewoven perfectly in damaged clothes – low prices.'

At about the same time, the *Chicago Visitor*, a hand-out sheet, published an article by a Harry Edward Freund entitled 'Chicago, the City of Destiny'. Mr. Freund wrote, in untrammelled ecstasy: 'Chicago holds paramount the supreme advantage of education,

placing intellect and intelligence on the building of character with
spirituality as the true assets of life, for by the kind of man and
woman produced will each civilization be judged in the future. At
all times fostering and encouraging education and culture, supporting liberally all worthy movements for the arts and willing to lend a
helpful hand for those purposes which ennoble mankind, Chicago
maintains a foremost position. Democracy without class distinction
or religious discrimination against race, colour or creed, is shown in
its highest form in Chicago in the unity of its people working for a
common cause to make their beloved city the greatest in the world.
Faith is the mainstay of the people of Chicago, faith in the future of
their city. From the bank president to the huckster in the street, from
those living back of the yards to the Gold Coast, there is but one
sentiment. This is our Chicago and we love it. The real life of Chicago
is evidenced in its human relations and its homes, for in this wonderful city every phase of life is represented, and its people meet on the
equal basis of goodwill, fellowship and understanding.'

Human relations in Chicago were precisely the point about which
the timid tourist might reasonably have felt most misgivings, but
such niggling details as the city's twenty thousand speakeasies, gun-
battles between speeding cars, and Capone's acknowledged ownership of judges and police were not being allowed to taint the tender
aquatint of Chicago, City of Destiny and Athens of the Arts. For,
simultaneously with the manifestation of those who believed that
their city's besmirched reputation could best be cleansed by such
practical measures as prosecuting criminals and enforcing law, there
arose a body of whitewashers staunchly ready to issue denials at
the drop of a corpse. Gangs? What gangs? It was an adaptation of
the Coué formula that had been the national chant in 1923: 'Day
by day in every way I am getting better and better.' Now the dedicated boosters, the Chambers of Commerce smilers, the Chicago
Beautiful Association women, the blithe politicians who echoed the
Hoover administration's verbal, if not actual, dismissal of economic
catastrophe, hypnotized themselves, and, they hoped, others, with
the formula: 'Day by day in every way Chicago is getting better and
better.' One Chamber of Commerce magazine darkly implied that
the publicity about booze and bumpings-off was deliberately organized
by New York businessmen to discredit Chicago and hijack her trade.

It was a time of bluff and hidden persuasion. In April of that year
an elaborate event, which had all the characteristics of a tribal
witchcraft rite complete with incantation, had been arranged. A
banquet was held at a Chicago hotel, at which the principal speaker

was General Dawes, American Ambassador to Great Britain, whose voice was relayed across the Atlantic by wireless telephone to the hotel and to all the United States. His speech was designed, it was announced, 'to defend the city's good name and refute those who describe it as a happy hunting-ground of gunmen and other criminals'. The dinner opened a campaign to 'establish the truth about Chicago as a good place in which to live and do business'.

There were many voices stentoriously to support this contention. Earlier, Police Chief Hughes had broadcast his pride in his department's record. 'Scotland Yard detectives would be as helpless as rank amateurs if they moved into Chicago to suppress crime,' he said heatedly after his attention had been drawn to the Yard's recent successes. 'I could name twenty of our men who could accomplish more in a given time than a hundred of the best men of Scotland Yard.' Chicago, he added, had less crime *per capita* than any other city in America; its streets were the safest and the police department the most efficient in the United States.

It was at this time that *The Detective*, official United States Police journal, carried the double-column advertisement: 'Murdered! Seven hundred and twenty-seven police officers in 1927. Sheriffs and Chiefs, if you equip only your emergency and motor-cycle officers with our bullet-proof vests you will stop five hundred murders each year.' In September 1928 ex-Chief Detective-Inspector Arrow, retired Scotland Yard officer, described in the *Daily Express* how he would go about cleaning up Chicago. 'Start with Washington,' he advised. 'Politics should be divorced from police work. There should be an end to graft in high places – it clogs the wheels of the machinery of justice.' Arrow then proposed a force such as the Canadian North-West Mounted Police to chase the criminals out of Chicago and urged the value of 'the lash', quoting in support Judge Marcus Kavanagh of Chicago: 'No underworld lord can retain the respect of his followers after he has winced under the pain of a whipping. The cat-o'-nine-tails is more feared by the moron racketeer than a gaol sentence.' The only common ground in the viewpoint towards Chicago's crime problem between those who wanted to solve it with Mounties and the cat-'o-nine-tails and those who said there was no problem worth bothering about was their unreality. At least, the University of Chicago had attempted positive action. In May 1929 it established a Chair of Police Administration, charged with studies of crime investigation.

When it was known that Edgar Wallace's play *On The Spot* – about Chicago gangsters and built around a Capone-figure, and written on board the ship bringing him back from a 1929 *Daily Mail* assignment in Chicago – was to open, Anton Cermak, Big Bill Thompson's successor as mayor, declared that if it proved to be 'injurious to Chicago's reputation' he would not allow it to continue. Cermak said that he would attend the first performance. If it showed the city in an unfavourable light, he would have it taken off. He added that he intended to suppress all plays and pictures which showed Chicago as a crime-ridden city.

In March 1930 the *Daily Mail* published an article by a Louther S. Horne, Jun., headed 'Chicago Is Not All Gunmen'. Mr. Louther began banteringly: 'Chicago! City of dreadful reputation, whose business men wear bullet-proof vests and cower in fear at the explosion of an automobile tyre.' He conducted the reader on a tour of the 'second largest community of the Western Hemisphere'. It was, he assumed, a sunny day with an azure sky. 'We are in Evanston, a suburb known through the culture of its people and the beauty of its buildings as the Athens of America' – that comparison had to come sooner or later – and then on the lake-side boulevard where 'a little girl is romping with a Scotch terrier on the lawn', and onward past beaches, golf links, tennis courts and parks. Finally, Mr. Louther asked: 'Where, then, are the scenes of the savage murders, the enormity of which has shocked the nations?' Way over there, Back o' the Yards, 'a warren of dingy streets lined with squalid tenements', he revealed, and concluded: 'To the law-abiding Chicagoan who reads of a murder in his morning newspaper the crime would be something remote and far removed were it not that such killings have injured the name of the city.' During that period the local newspaper headlines maintained a steady litany: 'CHICAGO WAKES UP'; 'NEW SPIRIT IN CHICAGO – MURDERERS BROUGHT TO BOOK'; 'CHICAGO NOT CRIME RIDDEN – PROUD CLAIM BY NEW MAYOR'; 'SWEEPING CHICAGO CLEAN'; '"SHOOT TO KILL" ORDER – CLEAN-UP IN CHICAGO'; 'SMOKING OUT THE HORNETS'; 'THE NEW CHICAGO'; 'CHICAGO CRIME IS EBBING – IT IS BETTER AND SAFER PLACE'.

Compared with most of the exoneration, varnishing, blind-eye turning, glozing and flat lying that went on at this juncture, Mr. Louther's article glowed with candour.

The immediate motive behind this concerted springing to defend Chicago's honour was the 1933 Centennial Celebration and World's Fair. It was feared by the business community that the protracted world-wide publicity given to gangsters and killings would act as a deterrent upon the influx of visitors and trade. And never had Chicago been more in need of a financial fillip.

During 1930, 1931 and 1932 Chicago tottered drunkenly about on the brink of bankruptcy. All the boosting and braggadocio enjoined in one great symphony could not entirely smother another strain of publicity, an ominous bass to the strident trumpets. In January 1930 a Mr. Silas Strawn, a civic finance expert was rushed in to head a Rescue Committee, which had been formed under an emergency measure to save the city from ruin. 'Mismanagement by Mayor Big Bill Thompson and his friends, and lethargy on part of the public, have reduced Chicago to bankruptcy,' it was reported. 'The chaotic plight of all the public services is now revealed. Unless citizens put money in the till on a large scale, hospitals will shut, inmates of lunatic asylums will be left without food, heat and light, prisons will be unable to house their tenants, and the police and fire brigades will have to be disbanded.' After examining the situation at close-quarters, Mr. Strawn confessed publicly that this was one civic financial problem which had him licked. 'I'm at my wits' end,' he said frankly. 'This is the most serious situation ever confronting an American city – and everybody stays asleep.'

At that point Chicago was in debt 300 million dollars. In November 1931 the President of the First National Bank of Chicago, appealing for economical government said: 'We are busted in the United States.' By August the following year unemployment had soared to half-a-million and the seven million dollars raised for poor relief had been spent – but another twenty million dollars had been raised for the fair, which was to mark Chicago's 'century of life and progress'. The city had no credit left; it was without resources to pay the salaries of its schoolteachers, firemen and police. There was an outbreak of tax-strikes. John McConaughty commented: 'Citizens already paying heavy taxes to racketeers, who can deliver what they promise, are refusing to pay taxes to a city government which cannot.'

In January 1932 an S O S was despatched by Mayor Cermak to the State Legislature of Illinois from Florida, where he had been 'recuperating from overwork and worry'. The message, imploring the guarantee of bonds on behalf of the city, read: 'Our plight is desperate; no time must be lost in relieving it.' Unless 250 million dollars was raised within a few days, it was stressed, policemen's and firemen's wages could not be paid and the sanitary services would be paralysed. The schools would have to be closed, which would mean that the children of the 700 thousand workless, then being fed on midday sandwiches supplied by relief corps, would face starvation. Already, at that point, twenty million dollars was owed in wages to

Cook County teachers – twelve thousand of them and four thousand school attendants had received only six weeks' salary in nine months.

The situation had been worsened a fortnight earlier by a pronouncement by the Law Courts on Chicago's tax assessment. Cermak had been told that the assessments for 1928 and 1929 'reeked with fraud', and they were struck out as invalid. Cermak's reaction to this was a dramatic: 'We may have to close up the City Hall.' He called a meeting of the City Council, at which hefty cuts were made in the salaries of all city employees. At a special session of the State Legislature it was suggested that the only solution might be to place Chicago under martial law.

Following the emergency meeting of the City Council, Cermak whisked away to Washington to attend a Democratic Party banquet, at which he promised a 200 thousand dollars contribution from the theoretically empty city political funds towards the coming Presidential campaign. The party decided to hold its Presidential Convention in Chicago; a month previously, the Republicans – in return for a 150 thousand dollars' contribution towards convention expenses – had reached a similar decision. Illinois was then considered the key state of the National Elections, and neither party was dissuaded by the threat of martial law and civic collapse from there entertaining their thousands of delegates and tens of thousands of supporters.

Nevertheless, on a single June day of 1932 six Mid-Western banks, with deposits totalling five and a half million dollars, shut up shop – bringing the number of Chicago banks closed in one month to thirty-eight.

The great fair – the Century of Progress Exposition – came and went. The site at Soldier Field stretched along the lake front from Twelfth Street South to Thirty-ninth Street. It was run by a Public Protection department to keep the events within bounds which would accord reasonably with the advance publicity of allurement. But there was a good deal of the traditional Chicago 'human relations' alongside the art and music, and as much ingenuity expended on gypping mankind as on those purposes, praised three years earlier in the *Chicago Visitor*, which ennoble mankind. The gambling games at the Exposition were as rumbustiously crooked as when it had been a frontier town. A priest who arrived with 170 dollars was instantly fleeced of it all at the first chance-your-luck stall he encountered. Strip-tease booths, with attendant more private facilities, were a prominent feature; Sally Rand – the girl who needed another hand – was the star attraction of the Streets of Paris show (those drawn there by the promises of culture could also attend half-a-dozen Shakespeare plays every day, as they were trimmed down to snappy thirty-minute versions). There were sporadic outbreaks of squabbling between refreshment-stall concession-holders and Capone representatives eager to pipe their beer into the Exposition.

The Exposition was, nevertheless, a dazzling and carnival success; it even made a profit; but it was rouge on a chancre. The fundamental deterioration in Chicago's fortunes had not meanwhile been deflected or eased. By the end of 1933 the city's bonded indebtedness amounted to 133 million dollars, and obligations to municipal employees exceeded 100 million dollars. A law suit was instituted which threatened to put the entire city in the knacker's yard. Banks rejected tax anticipation warrants and city bonds – they did not consider them worth the parchment they were printed on. The Park Boards' bonds were defaulted. Property values had slumped and, fair or no fair, industries were removing elsewhere from the site of the Century of Progress, removing from both the pressure of the rackets and the swamp of economic depression. Dustbins went unemptied, streets unswept: Chicago began to have the aspect of a mediaeval town scoured by Black Death.

Mayor Cermak, who seemed to be running short of emotional appeals to human administration, said: 'God help Chicago.'

It was during this period of chaos, civic crack-up and ravaging hunger that Capone's personal fortune was estimated to be forty million dollars, that the income of his crime-empire was 100 million dollars a year, that 7,500 protected gambling-houses were operating in the city, that racketeering alone (excluding bootlegging) was costing Chicago an annual 150 million dollars. We have already seen how, by the exercise of their highly specialized talent for implementing the American creed of competitiveness and free-enterprise, the gangsters attained their positions; we have seen, in passing, how they aided and manipulated the politicians and political parties that gave them their best advantage. But what sort of a society is it that puts into office and either supports or submits to an administration that permits a rule of gangsters; what, specifically, was Chicago's political background during the Prohibition Era?

Under the section 'The Reach of the Business Spirit' in *America As A Civilization*, Lerner points out that it is a paradox of America's 'business civilization' that there has been less political corruption in America than in many pre-capitalist societies such as in Asia, the Middle East and South America. Political corruption is most rampant in the cultures where for many it is the only road to wealth and status, whereas in America it is only one of many.

None the less, the business principle has given 'a synthetic cohesion to the far-flung diversity of American life,' says Lerner, and the advance of business power and values weakened the hold of the democratic idea, while translating both the pioneering sense and the nationalist pride into the boom terms of growing industrial power and profit. 'In the realms of politics, the political boss has come to run his domain (the machine) very much as an industrial boss (business-man or corporate manager) runs his ... The difference is that where the businessman delivers commodities for profit, the politician delivers votes for power ... The new (party system) model is the corporation, with the voters in the role of the owner-stockholders, the national committeemen in the role of the corporate directors, and the professional politicians in the role of the corporate managers, who are in theory the trustees and employees of the owners, but in fact the decision-makers and the power-wielders.

'It is not the periods of business decay but the periods of business expansion and vitality which play havoc with moral principles, because they fix men's aims at the attainable goals of the Big Money ... Where the impact of business has been most destructive for morality has been perhaps less in its open corruption than in the incalculable prestige that business success and power have in the eyes of city magistrates, city judges, state legislators, Congressmen, Federal administrators ... Even crime and racketeering in America have taken over some of the organizational structure of business ... Racketeering is the pre-capitalist feudal spirit, using the techniques and structures of business enterprise and thriving because business has spread throughout America the dream of the easy-money bonanza.'

It follows from this that Americans speak of 'the business of government'. At its lowest local level they scorn politics as a racket, and also see it as a competitive sport. Yet there is a polarity here. Ardently possessed by the ideal of freedom, the American is contemptuous of government; at the same time, he respects a strong White House. The schizophrenia runs like a fissure right down to the suburban district. The voter imprisons the state governor in a strait-jacket of restrictions, duplicates many times over the existing agencies and offices instead of interlocking new powers in the old agencies, and tries to balance the authority of every official with the counter-check of another official. The voter dislikes bureaucracy so much that he creates an auxiliary bureaucracy to control the first bureaucracy.

All that is anarchic and resentful of official interference in the American voter, he expresses by openly despising the politician; therefore, the able and honourable citizen eschews politics, and politics is abandoned to the professional politician. In America there is no tradition of political office-holding as in Britain: the professional power-wielders are not the office-holders but the party managers, the men behind the platforms who secure the fixes, bring off the deals, and negotiate with those who are influential and strong in the community – who are often the gangsters. The office-holders themselves – the governors, state legislators, mayors, Congressmen, and the army of county and state officials – are likely to be stooges of variable motives and standards, who will serve a few years and then return to private business. In the vacuum created by the voters' mixed apathy and cynicism, the professional political manipulators are – except during the erratic outbursts of moral aspirations and reformist clean-ups that are a cyclic part of the pattern – left free to steer their great machines of profit, patronage and power in whichever direction the yield is greatest. The system of electing judges, district attorneys, city prosecutors, and the surrogates who administer estates and supervise bankruptcy proceedings, inevitably entangles the administration of justice in the political machine: these jobs are regarded as some of the fatter plums of party patronage. In the big business expansion, politics has become more vulnerable to bribery, has made more attractive the direct sale of political influence to businessmen concentratedly in pursuit of money and not inhibited by any inherited or acquired awe for the ethics of politics, and met half way by the officials who share the respect for money and have seen little in their personal experience of political administration to weigh them down with guilt at co-operating in dispensation of favours.

There may be some significance in that the British publication, Roget's *Thesaurus of English Words and Phrases*, gives thirteen synonyms for politician, all in the respectable vein of 'statesman', 'legislator', 'administrator', etc. In *The American Thesaurus of Slang*, by Berrey and Van Den Bark, there are ten pages devoted to Politics and Government and containing 115 sub-divisions. The general tenor is one of derision and cynicism (the first synonym suggested for 'politician' is 'arm waver'), and there is a section headed Political corruption: graft Here are seventy-eight separate phrases, ranging from 'boodleism' (obtaining money by political corruption) to 'sprinkling the flowers' (distributing bribes), which would seem to indicate a widespread familiarity with official dishonesty. Frank Tannenbaum writes: 'It would probably be too much to expect that we could do a great deal to the criminal groups in our society without doing a considerable amount to the other elements in our social organism. We cannot seriously change the incidence of crime in American life without changing our police, our politics, our morals, our values. There is no reason to assume that in dealing with the criminal we are dealing with something extraneous. We are really dealing with all of society even when we begin dealing with the problem of crime.'

Within this historical context the three terms as mayor of William Hale Thompson, that oafish and grotesque buffoon who openly declared his faith in the principle of an open town, becomes more explicable. Thompson was born in Boston, Massachusetts, in 1869, the son of a rich man who moved to Chicago. Thompson hated school and his indulgent father had allowed him to migrate to the West, in those years still fairly wild. The young Thompson worked as a brakeman on the Union Pacific Railroad, and then became a ranch cook, when he learned to use a lariat and to shoot. While still in his teens he returned to Chicago with an acquired cowboy personality which he nurtured and exploited during the rest of his life. After an interlude as a free-spending playboy, Thompson began associating with the shady Billy Lorimer Republican wing. In 1915, to everyone's surprise except perhaps his own, he became Chicago's mayor, thrown into office by the public's reflex action against the Democrats' attitude to the European Great War.

Big Bill the Builder, as the slogan defined him, had not been hindered by such problems. Flaunting his cowboy Stetson and a fluid versatility that was to characterize all his political gymnastics, he promised everyone anything. To the sporty element he pledged himself to throw the town wide open; to the sober citizenry he promised a law-enforcement rule of unparalleled severity. To the half-million German population he was ferociously anti-British; to other more mixed audiences he was the implacable All-American. He got in, with 147,477 votes to spare.

One of Thompson's first acts as mayor, and one which pitched him into a tub of trouble, was to close the saloons on Sundays. This was done under pressure from the grand jury then inquiring into crime conditions (and in all of Chicago's history there has not often been a time when there wasn't a grand jury toiling away at that assignment). Immediately even stronger pressure was brought to bear on him from the opposite direction – from United Societies group led by Anton J. Cermak, later to become mayor himself. The United

Societies, voicing the broad-minded outlook on liquor of the politically-powerful foreign-born contingent, had forced through the Illinois State Legislature alcohol ordinances of a liberality that pleased not only the foreign-born, but, more significantly, the saloon and brewing blocs. Enlightened on this point, Thompson hurriedly forgot his Sunday saloon promise.

He soon recovered the trust of the open-town lobby and demonstrated that the error had been merely the fumbling of a new boy. Soon slot-machines, more familiarly known as one-arm bandits, were jangling musically throughout the city, and before much more time had elapsed various commissions were investigating shares extracted by politicians from the slot-machine syndicate, the growth of a gambling industry which involved payments of graft to officials, Thompson's own implication in a brothel-ring, and the round-up of a police bribe-taking brotherhood. As may be seen, such side-line pastimes were not a novel invention of the Prohibition era. Thompson's dearest friends and intimates at this time included a gambling king who later became a Capone executive, America's biggest slot-machine manufacturer, a prominent gambling-joint operator, Big Jim Colosimo, the First Ward vice tycoon who brought Torrio to Chicago, and a police chief.

In 1917, when the United States declared war on Germany, Thompson – looking the German-born voters straight in the eye – vociferously opposed the decision and protested against conscription. His enemies dubbed him Kaiser Bill, a smear that still stained him a year later when he unsuccessfully stood for the United States Senate. In the 1919 election Thompson skilfully milked the increasing political importance of the Negroes who had swarmed into Chicago from the Mississippi Valley during the war to work in the armament factories. He was re-elected with a 21,522 majority. His Negro supporters, however, did not get much tangible return for their faith in him. In July of that year, after an incident on a segregated beach, racial riots raged for five days. Houses of coloured families were fired, and shootings and stabbings occurred. Not until the sixth day was the State Militia summoned to check the marauding gangs of white nigger-hunters.

Thompson alone cannot be blamed for the extravert gunman rule that flowered during his long run as mayor, but he certainly scattered profusely the humus in which it rooted. He first cut back the appropriation to the Morals Division and then abolished it altogether; an inspector of the division was dismissed when he entered a report showing that the more elegant and expensive brothels did business without police intrusion; he re-distributed police department personnel so that each ward committeeman had stationed in his zone a captain who could be relied upon to facilitate the open-town policy; and under the new régime, dance-halls, wine-taverns and call-girl establishments that had been closed down during the previous mayor's office all reopened. It was at this point, and with the connivance of Thompson, that Big Jim Colosimo flowered fully as Chicago's prostitution czar. Colosimo was recognized as an invaluable vote-swinger in the First Ward, and was therefore encouraged and furthered by those two gamey aldermen, Michael Hinky Dink Kenna, who ran the Working-Man's Exchange, a saloon where a beer was served in a tumbler the shape and size of a goldfish bowl for five cents, and the scarlet-waistcoated John the Bathhouse Coughlin. Under the aegis of Kenna and Coughlin, Colosimo organized the neighbourhood Republican faction into a social and athletic club the membership of which he delivered as a voting package-deal in elections. In reward he was appointed a precinct captain – which carried virtual immunity from police attention – and rapidly progressed to ward boss. The one-time street sweeper was now gorgeous in embroidered shirts and a stellar system of diamonds – diamond-set watch, diamond watch fob, diamond rings, diamond tie-pin, and diamond-patterned braces. Kenna seconded to him Dennis Duke Cooney, his personal aide, to run the disorderly 'hotels' (rooms on a fifteen-minute booking schedule) of the First Ward, with the Rex Hotel on South State Street as the G.H.Q. Without stretching the logical sequence too far, to Thompson may be attributed Capone's eventual terrorization of Chicago, for it was to protect the new prosperity conferred upon him by the Thompson ring that Colosimo imported Torrio, who in turn imported Capone.

Nineteen-twenty was the crucial year for Chicago, in all the aspects of politics and crime, for it was then that Colosimo was assassinated, that the shrewder and longer-sighted Torrio acceded, that liquor became the new cornucopia for the rapidly evolving business-gangs, that Chicago became the nation's gambling centre, and that Thompson was romping around in his cowboy hat, rhapsodizing about his wide-open town policy and the happy splurge of money that it had induced. Thompson uttered not the mildest tut-tut that the nation's liquor laws were being flamboyantly flouted, and his chief of police, Charles C. Fitzmorris, cheerfully conceded that a big proportion of the city's police were actively engaged in keeping the booze tap turned full on.

Thompson was tumescent with power. His machine appeared unbeatable. In the April election his candidates captured the key position of ward committeeman in thirty-four of the city's thirty-five wards. The Republican Party's national convention was held in Chicago and it was there that Warren G. Harding received the presidential nomination – the genesis of his election and the eventual Teapot Dome oil scandals, a multi-million dollar swindle which, if it did not exactly horrify an America seasoned in such experiences, caused some indignation when it was learned, in F. L. Allen's words, 'that the Harding Administration was responsible in its short two years and five months for more concentrated robbery and rascality than any other in the whole history of the Federal Government.'

It was during the 1920 political campaign that Thompson lit upon the British monarchy as an escape hatch from any political tight corner. His customary reply to any criticism made against him and the administration – and both were then being denounced by the Chicago *Tribune* and *News* as corrupt and unworthy of support – was that such attacks blackened the city's fair name. In one such tirade against his opponents, he boomed: 'I wouldn't sing "God Save the King" in return for complimentary newspaper articles.' He realized he had a good line there. Thenceforth, whenever accusations of corruption and gang-rule were made, he swelled into a red haze of fury against Perfidious Albion, its colonial record in general, and King George in particular. His pledge to 'punch King George in the snoot' if he ever dared set foot in Chicago evoked a spanking response among the voters, especially those of German and Irish ancestry. One of Thompson's most spectacular successes was to bully the Illinois Legislature into expunging the English language from the state. A law was passed which solemnly declared that 'The official language of the State of Illinois shall be known hereafter as the American language'.

The *eminence grise* – or, rather, *noir*, for he dressed in funereal frock coats and black tie – of the Thompson administration was Fred Lundin, an ex-fairground pedlar of soft drinks who had ingratiated and plotted his way up the political scale to Congress. He was a political schemer of unparalleled foxiness. It was Lundin who put Thompson into power, and in collaboration, in November 1920 they inserted their two nominees into two prized seats of influence. Robert E. Crowe, Chief Justice of the Criminal Court, became State's Attorney of Cook County, and Len Small, a farmer-politician from Kankakee, became Governor of Illinois.

With these two posts pocketed, the Thompson-Lundin machine became one of the most formidable juntas that have ever controlled an American community. There did come a minor setback when, in 1921, they made a bid to seize the judiciary. Nettled by the occasional recalcitrance of individual unsold-out judges, Thompson and Lundin prepared to thrust their own panel of candidates into office in the June judicial election. There occurred one of those spasmodic eruptions of public indiscipline. Warned by the press that City Hall was about to take over the courts, the electorate mutinously rejected every one of the Thompson-Lundin candidates, and in the backwash of this a transportation bill which Thompson was trying to barn-storm through the Illinois General Assembly was booted out.

But under the Thompson umbrella, local political issues were being fought out in more vicious terms – the bomb and the gun were becoming the weapons of persuasion. The first explosion, in all senses, was in the Nineteenth Ward, where Democratic Alderman John Powers had had uninterrupted rule since 1888. Gradually there had come about a population shift from the predominantly Irish voters who had kept Powers securely in control, and by 1916 the Italians were strong enough for Anthony D'Andrea, an unfrocked priest and prominent pimp who had gained political strength by assuming the leadership of both the Hod Carriers' Union and the Unione Siciliana, to oppose, with Thompson's backing, Powers's nominee. The battle hotted up in 1920 when a bomb was hurled at Powers's house in McAllister Place, and telephone calls began to be received by Powers's friends acquainting them with the fact that they were down on the list for being bumped-off. Two weeks before the election a retaliatory bomb was flipped into a meeting hall on Blue Island Avenue, where D'Andrea's supporters were gathered. Five of them were badly hurt. There followed two more bombings, one in the window of a D'Andrea lieutenant's home and one in the D'Andrea political headquarters. In the result, D'Andrea was defeated by 435 votes, which caused bitter wrangling over the count and charges of fraud. Shortly after the election two Powers supporters were murdered.

The verdict at the polling stations had not settled the issue, D'Andrea gangs, armed with sawn-off shot-guns, patrolled the streets in search of Powers men. D'Andrea received letters threatening to wipe out the whole of his family and it was certainly reduced in numbers. In May, D'Andrea was ambushed and chopped down by shot-guns, and by the end of the year three of his followers had been similarly admonished.

With no retribution by the police, and with bland neutrality on the part of the city's political authority, these methods of ensuring that muscle prevailed were rapidly extended. During 1921 open warfare broke out between building employers and the unions. Housing was abominable; rents had rocketed; and Federal Judge Kenesaw Mountain Landis, arbitrator in the dispute, pronounced that Chicago's building industry had become 'rotten with manipulative combinations, uneconomic rules and graft, which caused the stagnation in building'. Landis decided against the unions and recommended wage-cuts. The reply was the crunch and blast of bombs. During the Building Trades War of 1922 fourteen buildings were blown up and two policemen mown down. Big Tim Murphy, Frenchy Mader, Con Shea and Dapper Dan McCarthy, a Torrio storm-trooper, were named as the instigators of the terrorization. Mader had at gun-point got himself made president of the Building Trades Council, and whenever disputes between employers and unions arose, he called in Murphy and his men to negotiate a settlement, their simple faith being that nothing settles anything quite so emphatically and flatly as a bomb. They were arrested, released on bonds of 150 thousand dollars, and stayed free. In the April primary election – in which Anton J. Cermak, a Bohemian ex-miner, became president of the Cook County Board of Commissioners, in effect 'mayor' of Cook County – there was finagling at the polls of such flagrancy that the recount ordered by City Judge Frank S. Righeimer led to prison sentences being pronounced upon many election officials, who were instantly released. A perceptible pattern of bold collaboration between politics, business and gangsters was becoming apparent, and the attention of the whole nation was drawn to the harum-scarum cowboy mayor and his New Frontier rough-neck rule by the roar of bombs and the bark of guns. It was not that until then political parties and official quarters had been unblemished by dishonesty and five-percenting, but the culmination of a man like Thompson, half-fool, half-rogue, and the moneybags provided by Prohibition was that now a syndicate of gunfighters had the yoke on City Hall. In a publication entitled *Crime and the Civic Cancer – Graft*, Chief Justice Michael L. McKinley of the Criminal Court in 1923 denounced the 'alliance between predatory politics and professional crime that reaches into every quarter of community life . . . The police department,' he declared, 'is at the mercy of ward bosses who deliver the vote of the vicious elements in return for protection. The criminal syndicates deliver a percentage of their profits to the ward bosses and exert all their influence to the organization whose political partners they are so long as the status quo continues.'

For eight years Thompson ran – or rather used – Chicago, and there was barely a check upon his policy of laxity and licence. But in 1923 during his second term, his career began to skid off track. His former complicity with Lundin and Crowe fell apart in bickering and double-cross about who was going to control the Chicago Police Department, always the most rigged of civic departments and whose chief-of-police post was the most valuable to wallet-stuffing politicians. Thompson's appointment of Charles Fitzmorris to that position in 1920 angered his partners, and, while a violent struggle ensued within the party, while the police force stood inert out of a nervous uncertainty about in which quarter its loyalty lay (the public not looming prominently in that quandary), the burgeoning bootleg gangs plied their trade and fought out their own squabbles as publicly as wild dogs around a carcass.

Thompson, either displaying unsuspected shrewdness, or subjected to invincible dictation from high within the Republican organization, announced that he would not seek a third term in the spring election. The Republicans nominated Postmaster Arthur C. Lueder, whose support came from the anti-Thompson wing of the party. The Democrats played it safe. Having been twice defeated, they chose a candidate of proven respectability and good repute, Judge William E. Dever, who had held aloof from the bribery entanglement within the judiciary, and who in April 1923 became Chicago's new mayor.

But, from the point of view of his sponsors, Dever was to be a stuffed white knight; all that was required of him was to glow with integrity while the Democrat McDonald-Sullivan-Brennan machine occupied itself with manipulating the city in a manner indistinguishable from the preceding period. Dever was undoubtedly sincere when he promised, a few months after his election that he interpreted the duty of his new office to be to dedicate himself and the police department to crushing the war between the 'hijackers, rum runners and beer pedlars'. He saw no reason, he said, why it could not be ended, and swore that nothing would cause him to deviate from this mission. Yet, with inordinate unsophistication, he had given a promise upon his nomination that, if elected, he would leave all appointments to Boss Brennan, George E. Brennan, the Democratic 'grey wolf' who was guided in his choice by such local vote-merchants as Anton Cermak and Hinky Dink Kenna. So, after Dever's election, into the government offices went another clique of gerrymanderers and puppets eager and willing to keep the bandwaggon rattling along.

The ties between gangland and the political parties grew stouter. In 1924 the Torrio-Capone gang was requested, as a deliberate and discussed part of the campaign plan, to send in their gun-squads to ensure victory of the Republican candidate.[1] After Torrio's abdication in 1925, Capone consolidated and developed his affiliations with politicians. He established intimate relations with Kenna and Coughlin, and Kenna's cigar kiosk on South Clark Street became one of his favourite rendezvous. He also recruited Duke Cooney, brothel-supervisor for Kenna in the First Ward, as an executive member of the gang in charge of prostitution. This was reciprocally beneficial. Capone profited financially and in influence from the experience of Kenna and Cooney in organizing the girl trade, and new chains of brothels were founded; both Kenna and Cooney profited politically from their friendship with the gangster whose status, fame and reputation was ballooning as fast as his wealth. In 1927 Dever's term as mayor expired. It had accomplished little. Toiling earnestly within the shrunken area left for his authority, he did succeed, sporadically and trivially, in harassing the odd delivery of liquor, in bringing off the occasional successful police raid: but, although he himself made no deals with the gangs and stayed almost uniquely pure of crooked financial transactions, he was a helpless mite within the web of conspiracy that now enmeshed the whole of the city.

During his four years out of office, Thompson had recovered his confidence and had been cavorting through the headlines in an incessant din of publicity. Preparatory to a carnival come-back as Chicago's mayor, he ostentatiously split with Lundin and allied himself with Billy Lorimer, the one-time streetcar conductor who became congressman and almost United States Senator. In pursuit of public attention, Thompson built a diesel-powered twenty-five thousand dollar yacht, which was named *Big Bill* and had his own likeness carved in oak as figurehead, and announced that he was off on an expedition to the South Seas to capture a colony of tree-climbing fish for Chicago. *Big Bill* was launched at Riverview Park before a huge gathering of spectators. The fish-hunters joined the Mississippi River and headed south, with Thompson making

1 See Chapters 4 and 5.

blazing speeches from the deck at every town en route. He did not get even as far as New Orleans, but he did receive column-yards of publicity. The Fish Fans' club-house in Lincoln Park became his headquarters, where, it soon became known, there was an unstemmed flow of best-quality hooch for anyone ready to join in the new 'Big Bill for Mayor' movement. Another stunt that spluttered in the headlines for a few days was his renowned Rat Show. In, April 1926 he booked the Court Theatre for a campaign meeting, and carried on to the stage a cage containing two rats. Their names, he stated, were Fred and Doc, his former pals: Fred was Fred Lundin and Doc Dr. John Dill Robertson, health commissioner in the previous Thompson administrations, and who was now being entered by Lundin in the mayoral contest as an independent. Thompson then addressed his remarks direct to the rodents. To the rat named Fred he reminisced about how he had saved him from jail. 'Don't hang your head, now, Fred,' he said. 'Fred, let me ask you something – wasn't I the best friend you ever had? Isn't it true that I came home from Honolulu to save you from the penitentiary?' Pointing to the other, he said: 'I can tell this is Doc because he hadn't had a bath in twenty years until we washed him yesterday. But we did wash him, and he doesn't smell like a billy-goat any longer.' Turning to the audience, he recalled how he had lived up to the cowboy code by standing by his old buddies when they were in need of a character witness during a school-board graft trial. And, he added, earlier the cage had contained six rats, the other four representing Lundin-Robertson supporters – but Fred and Doc had gobbled them up.

It was the sort of razzmatazz and slapstick campaign that Chicago loved, and Thompson's popularity began again to pile up from the trough into a new wave. The acrimony splashed about like custard pies. Lundin's reaction to the Rat Show was to express the opinion that Thompson was using 'the guttersnipe talk of a hoodlum'. Robertson resurrected the emotion-charged cry 'Who killed McSwiggin?' and accused Thompson of founding 'a multi-millionaire crime ring' with the aid of Fitzmorris, his chief of police. Thompson swung back: 'The Doc is slinging mud. I'm not descending to personalities, but you should watch Doc Robertson eating in a restaurant – eggs in his whiskers, soup on his vest. You'd think the Doc got his education driving a garbage wagon.'

Thompson's bull-charge back into the affections of Chicago was not confined to these hooks at Lundin and Robertson. He was again energetically vilifying King George and the British, whom he pictured ready to launch a fresh invasion of the New World; he was for America First and for Home Rule; he was against the World Court and 'treason-tainted histories', the school text-books then in use; he was for alcohol and bragged: 'I'm wetter than the middle of the Atlantic Ocean.' He was, he repeatedly declared, Big Bill the Builder, and was responsible for every improvement and new kerbstone that Chicago now had. He again extolled the good business and the good times implicit in the wide-open town concept; Dever may have closed down speakeasies and sporting houses, but Thompson promised that when he was elected he would 'not only re-open places these people have closed but open ten thousand new ones' – a pledge which, his opponents maintained, was an invitation to every crook on the face of the earth to migrate to Chicago and set up illegal establishments. When he was again mayor, Big Bill the Builder swore, there would be no more irritating police activity against 'minor infraction of the laws' – and he would see that the cops concentrated on the hold-up men and bank-robbers.

All this was glad tidings for Capone and his associates, and they showed their approval and gratitude by raising a huge sum – it was put at 250 thousand dollars – for his campaign funds. Jack Zuta, the North Side gambling boss and partner of Bugs Moran, chipped in with another fifty thousand dollars. As he confided to friends, Thompson's wide-open town policy would speedily recover that for him.

The crime plank of Thompson's platform read thus: 'The people of Chicago demand an end of the present unprecedented and appalling reign of crime. The chief cause of this condition is not at the bottom, not with the mass of the police department, but it is at the top, with the powers, seen and unseen, which rule the force . . . When I was mayor I was held responsible for crime conditions and properly so, and I accepted that responsibility without trying to shift it to the courts or to other governmental agencies. With practically the same men as are now in the police department, I drove the crooks out of Chicago, and will do so again if I am elected mayor.'

Whenever he was asked by hecklers to define in detail his position on specific local problems, his large and scornful reply was that he stood for America First and No Entangling Alliances. With a magnificent arm-sweep his election address said: 'I stand for the principles laid down by George Washington,' but at one meeting he did bring this lofty credo down to that one particular local and immediate issue that nettled him. 'I've got a lot of stuff I've been bottling up on the University of Chicago,' he thundered. 'The University is in a conspiracy to destroy American history on behalf of the King of England.'

He pounded onward and upward, apparently untrammelled by setbacks or brickbats, on a ferocious campaign planned by his election manager, Homer K. Galpin (former chairman of the Cook County Republican Central Committee, who later left Chicago when ordered to testify before the grand jury on sources of campaign funds). He also had the support of Oscar Carlstrom, Attorney General of Illinois, who introduced him to an audience of ex-soldiers: 'My friend, Big Bill the Builder, who loves little children, Big Bill the American who stands for America First.' (A year later, after a disagreement between them, Carlstrom was to discover that Thompson 'has been chasing a phantom King George up the alleys, and turning the city over to crooks and gamblers until today's conditions are anathema in the eyes of Chicago'.)

In the face of Thompson's hurricane of irrelevancies, Dever asked in irritated bewilderment: 'How can I campaign against a brain like that? I have tried to confine this campaign to the issues and the interests of Chicago, but in that I have found no combatant. I thought the square thing to do was to get into the ring with Bill with the gloves, but he would not come into the ring. He has been throwing tacks from the outside. I have never respected him. I do not respect him now. I shall not respect him whether he wins or loses.'

Judge Harry B. Miller, of the Superior Court of Cook County, entered a terser evaluation. 'If Thompson wins,' he said, 'Chicago will have a Fatty Arbuckle for mayor.'

Undeterred by such petty meannesses, Thompson exhorted on his posters: 'Vote for Big Bill the Builder. He cannot be bought, bossed or bulled.' He was photographed, braces dangling, blowing a trumpet – his own, of course. On election day Capone gunmen patrolled the West Side polling booths to demonstrate their loyalty and their wishes. That evening there was a wild and whooping gathering of fifteen hundred Thompson supporters in the Louis XIV Room of the Hotel Sherman. Together they sang the campaign anthem as the results tumbled in:

> *America first and last and always;*
> *Our hearts are loyal, our faith is strong;*
> *America first and last and always;*
> *Our shrine and homeland, though right or wrong.*

Chicago got its Fatty Arbuckle. The vote was Thompson 515,716, Dever 432,678, and Robertson 51,347. His followers paraded with brooms – indicating the coming clean sweep – and shouting: 'Big Bill is back!' Into the Louis XIV Room the victor strode whirling his sombrero and roaring: 'Tell 'em, cowboys, tell 'em! I told you I'd ride 'em high and wide.' He then led his faithful band away in a convoy of motor-cars to the celebration party on board the Fish Fans' schooner in Belmont Harbour.

The fifteen hundred hard workers swarmed aboard to where the champagne and whisky awaited. Under its unprecedented load of cheer and cheerers, the schooner sank to the bottom of the harbour. The guests got ashore without loss of life, and Big Bill the Builder was saved to start his third term.

Thompson proclaimed a new slogan, the motto of the administration, which was 'Make Chicago Hum!' He elaborated this into a kind of plain-song: 'Open the waterway, to make Chicago hum. Settle the traction question, to make Chicago hum. Get rid of the bread lines, to make Chicago hum. Speed the great public improvements, to make Chicago hum. Chase out the crooks and gunmen, to make Chicago hum.' Presumably Capone and the boys accepted the last line good-humouredly, as necessary to scansion.

At the victory banquet at the Rainbow Gardens Thompson had been presented with a 5,500 dollar Lincoln sports coupé. He exchanged this for a touring-car into which was fitted a raised left-hand section of the rear seat and a spotlight. On summer nights, Thompson mounted his throne, commanded the chauffeur to press the switch, and his face and torso were bathed in bright light as he rode through the streets. He explained: 'The people like to see their mayor.'

19

Big Bill the Builder

'Vote for the flag, the Constitution, your freedom, your property, as Abraham Lincoln and William Hale Thompson would like to have you do.'

WILLIAM HALE THOMPSON

'The bad breath of Chicago politics.'
Newspaper reference to WILLIAM HALE THOMPSON

As soon as he was back in office, Thompson projected himself towards the glittering objective on which he now had fixed his eyes, the Presidency of the United States. He inflated his America First mania into a national organization. It became the America First Foundation and he was president of that, at least. Its aims: 'To teach respect for the flag, train youth and aliens for citizenship, and instil in the public mind the ideals of George Washington, Abraham Lincoln, and Big Bill Thompson.' To make the campaign hum with music, Corporation Counsel Samuel A. Ettelson, in collaboration with Milton Weil, a music publisher who had already composed *America First* and had been described as 'one of God's noblemen' for his patriotism, wrote a hymn. It was entitled, reasonably enough, 'Big Bill the Builder,' according to City Attorney William Saltiel 'the most inspiring song ever written about an individual'. The first verse and chorus – there were four of each – ran:

Scanning hist'ry's pages, we find names we love so well,
Heroes of the ages – Of their deeds we love to tell,
But right beside them soon there'll be a name
Of some one we all acclaim.

Who is the one, Chicago's greatest son?
It's Big Bill the Builder;
Who fought night and day to build the waterway?

It's Big Bill the Builder.
To stem the flood, he stood in mud and fought for all he's worth;
He'll fight so we can always be the grandest land on earth;
He's big, real and true – a man clear through and through;
Big Bill the Builder – We're building with you.

The carolling of this song by a Chicago Police Department octet, while he was presented with a silver scroll engraved with an attestation to 'one of the greatest living Americans', was the moving climax to his meeting in New Orleans with Huey King Fish Long, the ex-lard salesman who lied and swashbuckled himself into the dictatorship of Louisiana, and who, had he not been assassinated, might have delivered America to fascism. Not amazingly, these two gaudy demagogues took a shine to each other – and it is surely no coincidence that such creatures as Thompson, Long and Capone were able to flourish and become regnant in America at a time when in Europe Mussolini was established and Hitler was rising. For the official visit to New Orleans's Mardi Gras, the Thompson entourage occupied three trains, which themselves resembled carnival floats. At a glittering banquet at the Roosevelt Hotel, Long draped Thompson with garlands of praise. Soon after his return to Chicago, Thompson set off on an even more elaborate tour, a seven thousand mile speech-and-hand-wringing junket. In a private train, with a freight-car stacked with leaflets proclaiming him the natural next president, with the police barber-shop group, and with a platoon of helpers, secretaries and propagandists, he visited Minnesota, Omaha, Denver, Kansas City, Los Angeles, Cheyenne, Wyoming, San Francisco and Albuquerque, addressing huge gatherings at Chambers of Commerce luncheons, fairs, party headquarters and special receptions. His addresses were the usual forest fires, which raged indiscriminately across America First, national flood control, farm relief, the World Court and the League of Nations.

Back in Chicago, he scorched on with his campaign to purify the city of foreign subversive propaganda, especially that which he sniffed out as emanating from Britain and King George. School history books, he discovered, were rotten with sly pro-British sentiments. His book censor in the Chicago Public Library, U. J. 'Sport' Herrmann, yacht-owner and proprietor of the Cort Theatre, had found 'a course for pro-British, un-American propaganda'. All seditious volumes, announced Herrmann, would be purged from the library shelves and burned in a lake-front bonfire. However, he encountered a snag. He discovered that one of the founders of the library was Queen Victoria. When Chicago was in ruins from the fire of 1871, Londoners had donated towards the restoration of the city, and the Queen had led the movement to restart a library. She wrote in one of the many volumes she sent: 'Presented to the City of Chicago towards the formation of a public library after the fire of 1871 as a mark of English sympathy, by Her Majesty Queen Victoria.' Tennyson, Carlyle, Disraeli, Gladstone and many other eminent Britons made gifts of autographed books. So did the British Museum, the Royal Geographical Society, the Patent Office, the Duke of Argyll, the Earl of Kimberley, and Oxford and Cambridge Universities. Herrmann found to his consternation that a hundred of the seven thousand volumes dispatched across the Atlantic were still on the library shelves. 'It would not,' he hummed and haa'ed, 'be fair to accuse the Queen of disseminating propaganda. She was probably acting from the best of motives.' Newspapers throughout the world ran the story, and the upshot was such a wave of derision and indignation that Thompson realized he had perhaps rampaged a shade too far. He repudiated the order to put a torch to the 'tainted' books, and the two separate petitions for injunctions to restrain him were unnecessary. But Thompson pursued his clean-up in the schools. There was another motive here. He intended to depose William McAndrew, a worthy City Superintendent of Schools who had been appointed by Dever, and Thompson wanted him not only out but disgraced. McAndrew, he charged, was a 'stool-pigeon for King George'; he had 'encouraged the circulation of unpatriotic propaganda in our schools to poison the minds of our children against the founders of our country'. Charges concerning Britain's sinister and stealthy indoctrination of young Chicago through the history books were constructed, and the long and preposterous trial of McAndrew began. Finally, McAndrew ignored the order to attend court, and it petered out.

By the spring of 1928 Thompson had come near the point of declaring war on the Federal Government, who were impudently pestering the city with Prohibition enforcement agents who were actually harrying the illegal drink industry – and it is true that some of these officers were as quick on the draw and as snappy with the trigger as the bootleggers they were hunting. In March that year a special squad of them had been drafted in by Washington, at the same time that George E. Q. Johnson, a supporter of United States Senator Charles S. Deneen – whom Thompson loathed – took up his appointment. The squad conducted a raid on a South Side saloon, and there they shot William Beatty, a municipal court bailiff, in the

Above *Capone's car. The shell of the car was armour-plated and the glass bullet proof*

Below *Rear window opens on hinges, for the convenience of passengers wishing to fire at pursuers*

Above *John Scalise* Below *William Hale (Big Bill) Thompson*

Above *Jake Lingle* Below *Body of Jake Lingle*

St Valentine's Day, 1929

back. The mutilated Beatty stated that he, naturally, thought the Federal men were a hold-up gang when they came in with guns drawn, and ran. One of the Federal men, Myron C. Caffey, was accused of armed assault, but when he testified that Beatty had pulled a gun, Beatty was indicted by a Federal grand jury for resisting a Federal officer. If there was anyone left unaware of the fragmentation of law and order in Chicago, the sequel to this strange farce wrote it up for him in big block capitals. Chief of Police Hughes said he wanted Caffey delivered to his authority, whereupon George E. Golding, head of the Federal squad, replied that this was no concern of the police department. Hughes took out a warrant and despatched his men to storm the Federal building and bring out Caffey. Golding forbade them to enter. It did not happen, but an armed battle between Prohibition agents and policemen must have been within a degree of exploding.

Thompson was not slow to capitalize on the situation. In a bellowing speech at a huge South Side meeting, he swore: 'I will do all in my power to save Chicago citizens from any more suffering at the hands of the thugs and gunmen sent here by the Federal Government to further Deneen's political influence. Deneen is filling this town with dry agents from Washington, who run around like a lot of cowboys with revolvers and shotguns. Our opponents would have us believe we don't know how to run our town. Vote for the flag, the constitution, your freedom, your property, as Abraham Lincoln and William Hale Thompson would like to have you do.' And he added: 'We took out a warrant and we'll throw every damn dry agent in jail.' Uproarious applause from Chicago patriots.

The situation was saved from comic disaster by the intervention of Federal Judge James H. Wilkerson, who ruled that Caffey should be turned over to the police – but not until after the primary election in April.

It is possible that even Thompson was, at this stage, worried about the rampant lawlessness that his policy had released, admittedly a slender possibility, but one which may be measured by his vehement efforts at this time to divert the attention of the citizenry to any issue other than the bootleggers and their violence. It was like trying to distract a man from a cyclone by blowing in his ear. There was conflict between the major gambling interests, those of Capone and those of the established loosely-linked independents who bitterly resented the attempt by Capone's agent, Jimmy Mondi, to extort from them cuts varying between twenty-five and forty per cent of takings. Thompson's machine backed the established gambling bosses in this conflict. Capone expressed his regret at this decision by having bombs tossed into four premises owned by Thompson men. Police guards were summoned to protect Thompson's house and those of his advisers. On 23 February, 1928, a Chicago *News* editorial said: 'Now that leading city and county officials of this community are in a state of siege, with police details guarding their homes against assaults by bomb-throwers, the long continued farce of law enforcement which does not enforce manifestly must have the curtain rung down upon it . . . If the law-enforcing agencies of this community have no moral reason for fearing the foes who strike at them so viciously why do they not strike back with all the force of outraged virtue armed with all the powers of orderly government?'

There were moral reasons for fearing the bombers, and there was no orderly government to call upon, for the bombers were ruling. It was a feverish spring. Three weeks before the election Diamond Joe Esposito, the Republican ward leader, was hacked down from between two bodyguards by garlic-poisoned slugs; a few days later Big Tim Murphy, another mobster, fell full of bullets. At the end of the month the houses of Senator Deneen and John A. Swanson, who was nominated for State's Attorney, were bombed, which brought the total bomb attacks to sixty-two in six months.

Shortly before the election the Chicago Federation of Churches issued a resolution not remarkable for its revelationary nature. It seemed clear, it postulated, that there was 'evidence that a partnership exists between the criminals and some officials', and a Day of Prayer was proclaimed by the Union of Ministers. On Sunday, 8 March, 100 thousand Chicago churchgoers in five hundred places of worship jointly entreated God that the city 'might be delivered from graft and corruption at the April primaries'. Clerics also prayed for a large registration of voters 'a happy outcome of the primary and final elections, and a quickening of civic conscience'. One Methodist Episcopal minister compared Chicago to Nineveh and asked that 'this young and strong, good and bad city' might be spared, even as Nineveh had been. A Presbyterian minister prayed that there might be 'put into the hearts of those in authority a desire to cleanse our city of all crime and corruption'.

The collective conscience of the Catholic gangsters seemed not to be reached by this roundabout spiritual appeal, for 1928's statistics were seventy-two gang murders.

To restore one's perspective, it helps to remember that the number of murders – of all varieties – in the whole of Great Britain for 1920–24 was an annual average of sixty-three and for 1925–29 an average of sixty. An Illinois Association for Criminal Justice Survey published in the May declared with a restrained horror rare in official documents: 'The reign of power of the real leaders of organized crime in the city is longer and more secure than that of many of our college presidents – much longer than that of many of our public officials. Administrators come and go, but the overlords of vice continue in power.'

During that year respectable Chicago, disenchanted to the point of despair by the failure of civic authority to tackle dishonesty and thuggery, turned to religion in a flush of yearning for better standards. In January the Chicago Church Federation met to discuss the situation, and decided that Mr. Walter R. Mee, the Federation's secretary, should issue a statement that would proclaim to the world that all Chicagoans were not gunmen and racketeers. 'Chicago', declared the statement, 'is ninety per cent religious. There are two thousand churches in the metropolitan area. The denominations include ninety-one thousand Lutherans, ninety-one thousand Baptists, and Protestants, Catholic and Jewish 400 thousand each.' So rigorously was the religious code applied at this juncture that when Miss Maude Ryden, a preacher, was on her way to Chicago to address meetings of the Methodist Episcopal Church, a branch of the Women's Home Missionary Society cancelled her engagement upon receipt of the intelligence that Miss Ryden smoked cigarettes.

Senator Deneen was fastened upon by the better-government campaigners. He was a cautious man who maintained a relationship with Esposito, speakeasy-operator and wholesaler for the wildcat liquor trade, while remaining in public a staunch dry; but Esposito's murder, the wrecking of his own house on West Sixty-first Street, and the bomb-throwing at Judge Swanson, forced Deneen to make one of his few forthright statements. 'The criminal element is trying to dominate Chicago by setting up a dictatorship in politics,' he said, casting no blinding light of illumination. Yet the fact that such as he were coming down on sides had its effect. At a Loop election meeting, Edward R. Litsinger, candidate for the Cook County board of review, said: 'It costs 243 million dollars to run Chicago,' and asked rhetorically: 'What are we getting?'

The answer came loud and clear from the floor: 'Bombs!' 'Pineapples!'

Henceforth the election was known as the Pineapple Primary. Judge Swanson, the Deneen candidate for State's Attorney, narrowed it down. 'The pineapple industry grew up under this administration,' he declared.

Pineapples were a paramount election factor. The pastor of the Elmwood Park Grace Methodist Church, the Rev. Thomas H. Nelson, who had offered the church for Democrat meetings, approached eight insurance companies for policies covering riot and civil commotion – in this context, bombings – and all refused coverage. United States Marshal Palmer Anderson was moved to such urgency that he telegraphed the Attorney General imploring him to commission five hundred marshals to guard the polls on election day. Senator George W. Norris of Nebraska thought the situation of even deeper gravity: he suggested that President Coolidge should withdraw the Marines from Nicaragua and transfer them to Chicago.

Thompson, his attention at last wrenched around by public pressure to the carnage and noise of explosions, blamed it all on the opposition. 'The bombs,' he said, 'are the work of the Deneen faction, because they expect defeat.' Deneen's men, he added, had also bumped off Esposito – 'They sent prohibition agents here and then some of their own people ran to Joe [Esposito] for protection. He couldn't give it to them, and they wanted their money back. Those birds are tough. You can't take their money and the next minute double-cross them.'

Until two weeks before election day the Deneenites seemed helpless against the weight and pull of the America First machine. Again, the old traditional patronage was matted thickly within the issue – County Recorder Joseph F. Haas had died, and it was around him and his ability to dispense six hundred appointments, that their organization was built; at his death, the job-appointments reverted to the Thompson clique. Also, Esposito's death had sorely hit them at ward level. Deneenites were confronted with the most powerful political machine ever assembled in Chicago: it controlled all the city, county and State patronage, with the exception only of Federal appointments, and marshalled an army of 100 thousand campaign workers. It had never yet been beaten in a primary. The general view was that Thompson's candidates would win with majorities of between ninety thousand and 150 thousand.

Yet it proved not to be so simple and foregone. At the start, the issues had been abstract and romantically emotional – Isolationism, Make America Hum, Draft Coolidge, Better Flood Control, Destroy the League of Nations, and other such cherished Thompson passions. Thompson also had a new grouse against King George. 'Bourbon has increased in price from a dollar fifty to fifteen dollars a bottle,' he told an audience, 'and King George's rum-running fleet, eight hundred miles long, lies twelve miles off our coast, so every time you take a drink you say "Here's to the King!" ' But as the bombs bounced thicker, as the shot-guns roared, as the sluggings and beatings-up and pistol-whippings and murders mounted, the central issue became Prohibition and Capone, the domination of City Hall by armed outlaws. Surprisingly, more and more voices were heard raised in protest and in transports of sickened indignation.

Edward R. Litsinger, once Thompson's pal and supporter, but who had now been accused by Thompson of deserting his 'poor old German mother' roared: 'This befuddled big beast should be tarred and feathered and ridden out of town on a rail . . . Low-down hound who degrades himself and the city of which he is mayor . . . The carcass of a rhinoceros and the brain of a baboon. You know the Three Musketeers. They are Big Bill, Len Small and Frank L. Smith. The right way to pronounce it is the Three Must-Get-Theirs. Insull's shadow is over everything in the Small-Smith-Thompson combination.' Thompson was also referred to as the 'bad breath of Chicago politics'.

This was the sort of steaming volcanic lava that Chicago expected to see erupting from partisans on the platforms, but others, who were not so obviously aligned and perhaps whose vehemence counted more, began to be heard. For the first time the churches entered the campaign in a fully committed sense. The Rev. James S. Ainslie, of the Argyle Community Church, put up a placard for his Easter congregation to digest. It read: 'Bad officials are elected by citizens who do not vote.' The Rev. Walter A. Morgan, of the New Congregational Church, told his flock: 'Chicago needs a cleaning. I hope every man and woman goes to the polls.' The Rev. Charles W. Gilkey, of the Hyde Baptist Church, prayed: 'O Lord, may there be an awakening of public spirit and consciousness. Grant that we may be awakened to a sense of our public shame.' The Rev. Asa J. Ferry, of the Edgewater Presbyterian Church, and Louis B. Mann, rabbi of Sinai Congregation, were more temporal, but less temperate. Said Ferry: 'We have a governor who ought to be in the penitentiary,' and Mann: 'Ours is a government of bombs and bums.'

The excitement and tension was not only local. Journalists from all parts of America jostled in. European newspapers had rushed in their reporters to cover the incredible Pineapple Primary which was recognized as being extraordinarily good copy and also as of crisis importance to Chicago and perhaps to the American political system. The reporters must have wondered if they should not have been clad in war correspondents' uniforms and equipped with protective credentials. For that April day was one of kidnappings, motorized gun-duels and ambush by shot-gun parties – and the murder of Octavius Granada, a Negro candidate opposing a Thompson man, whose car was chased and fired upon, Granada dying under a hail of buckshot.

Yet, despite this massed menace, the Chicago voters rose up and tossed out Thompson's candidates. Thompson remained mayor, but his political future was destroyed. His machine was routed. In the privilege wards, where the vice and gambling controllers were too strong to be snubbed safely, the America First ticket prevailed. But it was a solid vote of disapproval of the 'Pineapples and Plunder Administration', a vote against Capone and the Thompson-Crowe régime. The focal point of the results was that Swanson had triumphed over Crowe for the State's attorneyship by almost twice the number of votes. In a hideout in the woods near Manitowish, Wisconsin, Thompson was reported to be in a state of nervous collapse. When Thompson was eventually found for interviewing and bluntly asked if he was going to resign, he said, with partial recovery of the familiar buoyancy: 'Let's analyse the situation. I haven't lost out so much in the election. I've got a majority of the ward committeemen and the sanitary district trustees. You'd think I'd lost the whole fight. Why should I be resigning?'

'But you said definitely you would get out if Swanson were nominated,' said one reporter, reminding him of a widely quoted promise made before election day.

'Well, I'll say definitely now that I'm not getting out,' said Thompson grumpily.

America First had collapsed, but the system behind it had not. Once again, the swell of optimism that the results had stimulated proved dream-like in its unsubstantiality. The press had applauded and predicted a moral revival in the wicked city. The New York Times commented: 'The political revolution in Chicago came as a surprise to most political observers. They had thought that the city was disgraced but not ashamed.' The London Morning Post: 'Evidently the self-respect of Chicago is tired of being made a byword and a laughing stock by its present mayor. It has told him in effect it is his own "snoot" rather than King George's that needs to be kept out of the city.' Even the Chicago Herald and Examiner, a Hearst organ which had championed the America First cause and supported the Thompson-Small ticket with reservations, said: 'The vote was a direct and tremendous expression of protest against the lawlessness and violence of booze runners, the gambling managers, the bombmen and the gunmen of Chicago. The situation had, to the minds of the citizens in general, got past bearing, and they freed their minds in the only way they could – at the polls.' The Kansas City *Star* said, incredulously: 'There is a God in Israel.'

The Kansas City *Star* was presumptuous. Thompson, certainly, was temporarily in the dumps; his presidential aspirations were scuppered; his party caucus was crippled. He was, additionally, being harassed at this time by a nasty little disclosure which did not enhance his reputation. It plainly and publicly indicted him as a swindler. It was an incident that had unexpectedly surfaced from the distant past. In 1921, when the Thompson group had been in urgent need of party funds, they had vamped up a scheme whereby they had paid from the city till, fees totalling three million dollars to real estate experts for recommendations on public works; the chosen 'experts' had then, after creaming off their commission, paid back the bulk of the money into the Thompson private political treasury. After years of rumours and speculation about the true facts, Judge Hugo M. Friend had been appointed to investigate the mystery of the missing three millions. His report was issued just after the election. It stated categorically that Thompson, together with Michael J. Flaherty, president of the Board of Local Improvements, George F. Harding, County Treasurer, and Percy B. Coffin, Public Administrator, among others were 'guilty of conspiracy and should make restitution to the city of 2,245,000 dollars'. The judge's decision brought about another small convulsion in the league of political friends. Thompson dived back into his Wisconsin retreat and lurked there most of the summer of 1928, while Corporation Counsel Ettelson deputised for him as acting-mayor. There were other equally abrupt departures from Chicago as grand jury investigations probed deeper into the sources of campaign funds.

To propitiate public resentment of the money-fiddles, Thompson and his inner-ring counsellors, under Ettelson, decided that a sacrificial ritual was due, and turned again to the police department, always good for the theatre of a shake-up. Unaffected by the fact that Police Chief Michael Hughes was in hospital recovering from an operation, Assistant Corporation Counsel James W. Breen was delegated to visit him and inform him that he was about to be sold down the river. He was presented with a letter of resignation; all he had to do was sign it. In his place was put William F. Russell, who fulfilled his designed function for nearly two years, until he in turn resigned after the killing of Jake Lingle, the Chicago *Tribune* reporter.

The illusion that the election had brought about reform and the twilight of the gangs survived – if it existed at all in the hearts of even the most determined sunny-side-uppers – no longer than the following February, when the slaying of the seven Bugs Moran's men took place on St. Valentine's Day in the North Clark Street garage, the most flagrant demonstration of all of the gangs ruthlessness and contempt for public opinion.

So the time drew closer of the fall into black chaos of Chicago Beautiful. Jobless, joyless and, perhaps, at last sickened of the juvenile knavery of the cowboy mayor, the average Chicago voter finally threw Thompson out. He did not submit compliantly to being despatched. Spurned by most of his own party, without a newspaper to champion him, manifoldly discredited in the eyes of his despoiled and derelict city, Thompson fought the 1931 mayoralty campaign with undiminished flamboyance and villainy. The first stage in his bid for a fourth term was the February primary, in which his opponents were Municipal Court Judge H. Lyle and Alderman Arthur F. Albert, whom he tagged The Nutty Judge and L'il Arthur respectively. Even within the free-for-all, libel-unencumbered terms of reference of the American press, Thompson's attacks upon the opposition were often unprintable. He again put on a kind of political cabaret show at the Cort Theatre, for which he charged admission. He walked on to the stage trailing a rope with a halter on the end – both L'il Arthur and The Nutty Judge wore halters, he explained, Albert's being the Chicago *Daily News* and Lyle's the Chicago *Tribune*. He became obsessionally convinced that the *Tribune* executives were plotting his assassination. The *Tribune* publisher heard that Thompson's gang-associates had sworn to bump him off if any harm befell Big Bill. During the election campaign there was the singular spectacle of the mayor roaring about the main thoroughfares flanked by shot-gunners and armed police outriders, and the publisher of the city's biggest newspaper cabined inside his newly delivered armoured car and accompanied by hired bodyguards. It is not recorded whether the two cars ever found themselves side by side at a traffic light.

Thompson's flame-thrower methods again had a preliminary penetration: he got the Republican nomination. Now began the battle proper. His opponent was Anton J. Cermak, Chicago's Democrat chief, a formidable enemy, heavy with arms and experience. Thompson had another stunt to detonate. During his malaise and misery of the summer, and when it had been rumoured that his health had broken, the Chicago *Tribune* had revised his obituary in readiness for his death. By some devious means Thompson got hold of a galley-proof. It had been written in a spirit of forgiveness, and was kindly and laudatory in tone. That this was to have appeared in a newspaper now vehemently attacking him was a valuable platform-point. Thompson had the article reprinted and widely distributed, and there were signs that there were once more, some grudging grins on behalf of Big Bill, that he was bouncing, a bit soggily but successfully, back into public affection. Then came a further jolt of bad luck. Under orders from the State's Attorney, police raiders entered City Hall and seized cabinets of records from the office of Daniel Serritella, Thompson's City Sealer. After examination of them by a grand jury, indictments were issued against Serritella – an associate of Capone – and his chief deputy, Harry Hockstein, a personal friend of Frank The Enforcer Nitti. They were both charged with conspiracy to appropriate funds collected for Christmas distribution to the poor. They were found guilty – but the decision was reversed by an Appellate Court jury on the ground that evidence did not establish guilt beyond a reasonable doubt.

Although Serritella and Hockstein escaped the consequences, Thompson did not. He was too intimately enmeshed with the Capone gang to avoid implication in this fresh scandal. It made up the electorate's mind. Thompson was defeated; Cermak became the new Mayor of Chicago.

There may have been some satisfaction in discarding a disastrous lout who had made the city both ridiculous and bankrupt, yet it was a sombre change for the worse. Beside Cermak's systemized grand larceny, the Thompson group were a bunch of amateur petty pickpockets. Cermak's organization was modelled upon New York's infamous Tammany Hall, the earliest classical pattern of the American political machine, whose original and worthy function had been turning the feudal immigrant into a responsible voting citizen. Tammany became an apparatus for the exercise of power, privilege and commercialized patronage on an unprecedented scale: for hundreds of thousands of New Yorkers, upon Tammany depended whether you got a job as a street-cleaner or the contract to build a skyscraper. Cermak, who had trained in politics under the master machiavellian, George E. Brennan, had bounded agilely up the steps to the Illinois General Assembly and to bossing a Democratic machine which he indoctrinated with Tammanyism.

Upon his election as mayor, *The Nation* commented: 'Perhaps Big Bill Thompson was as vicious as his defamers pictured him. To the practical and unprejudiced observer it appears that Chicago has simply swapped one evil for another . . . The people of Chicago by electing Tony Cermak have made him the most powerful political boss in the United States today.'

Cermak shared the latter opinion, and he ensured this by throwing his net around organized gambling which he recognized as possessing enormous potential, both politically and financially. Cermak, a planner of long-sighted shrewdness, also saw that bootlegging as a business was about to decline precipitously: the Depression had dampened the whoopee spirit of the 'Twenties and had staunched the easy-money flow; he saw that Prohibition, the ramshackle and catastrophic 'noble experiment', could survive very little longer. The nation had had a bellyfull of fatuous laws, rotten synthetic beverages, and the rifeness of corruption and crime which – inaccurately – were wholly blamed upon Prohibition. On the face of it, Cermak might not have been expected to wish for the end of corsair liquor, for it was an industry in which he had interests and, indeed, he had been accused by the 1931 *Better Government Association Report* of having 'a long record as the ruthless leader of the saloon and brewery overlords in Cook County before the Eighteenth Amendment'. Cermak had his reasons for wanting to see Prohibition scrapped. He sensed that public sentiment was at breaking point with the law it had been ignoring for eleven years; also, he had come to a secret agreement with Tammany Hall to support the presidential nomination of Governor Al Smith of New York, a leading repeal advocate. At the Democratic National Convention held in Chicago Stadium in June 1932 the repeal of the Prohibition Act was the central issue. In back-room conferences it became evident that Smith could not command the support needed for nomination. The alternative choice was Franklin D. Roosevelt, and during the ceremony in the stadium Cermak was up there on the platform at Roosevelt's side to share in the triumph.

With Prohibition doomed, with Capone removed from personal control of his gang by his arrest on tax charges, Cermak moved nimbly to rationalize and control the city's gambling enterprises. During his time-serving as a ward heeler, he had learned the power and political influence with the underworld that gambling provided. In the autumn of 1931 Cermak appointed James P. Allman as Commissioner of Police, his brief being that policy on gambling would emanate direct from the mayor's office. His two area managers were selected: Big Bill Johnson, who had for years and without police hindrance directed gambling in Cermak's West Side stronghold, and Ted Newberry, the ex-Moran-Zuta partner (it was claimed that

Newberry was one of Zuta's murderers) on the North Side; on the North-West Side, Martin Guilfoyle, whose gambling concessions had derived from the Republican régime, was marked for replacement by a pro-Democrat gangster.

So, while the Federal authorities were bending all their energies to trying to rid Chicago of Capone, the city's mayor, with other gang-bosses and political leaders, was plotting to fill the vacuum created with an even more efficiently organized gambling syndicate. Capone, beleaguered by many cares and adversities at that time, must have looked with morose nostalgia back upon those dear, dead days of only yesteryear when booze seemed an endless river of riches, when the mayor was his buddy and when City Hall was in his charge. That City Hall was no longer his, even by remote control from prison, was demonstrated forcefully when, on 19 December 1932, a special mayoral police party, led by Detective Sergeants Harry Miller and Harry Lang, burst into a Capone office on North LaSalle Street. The press were informed that this was part of the mayor's anti-crime drive. It had been a rough assignment. Frank Nitti had been there and had pulled a gun and tried to shoot it out. He had wounded Lang who, undaunted, had returned his fire, hitting him in chest and neck. Lang was made a headline hero. He received a three hundred dollar award for meritorious service, and both he and Miller were given creditable mentions on the police department's roll.

Unfortunately for Lang and Miller, a few days later the body of Ted Newberry was found in a ditch in Porter County, Indiana. He had been torn apart by shotguns. The reason for his murder, it was said, was that in his attempt to seize control of the North Side gambling ring, with the backing of the Cermak administration, Newberry had offered fifteen thousand dollars for the murder of Nitti, who stood in the way of his ambitions. Lang and Miller had, presumably, been expecting to collect the fifteen thousand dollars in addition to Lang's three hundred, but Nitti failed to die. The Capone mob had promptly smitten Newberry. Nitti was placed on trial on charges of assault with intent to kill Lang.

The trial was conducted in an atmosphere of almost monotonous sensation. The first hard confirmation of the stories that had circulated came when Police Officer Chris Callahan, a member of the detail, testified that when they entered the room Nitti was unarmed and defenceless, that Lang levelled his revolver and deliberately shot him three times. When asked how, then, had Lang received his wound, Callahan replied bleakly: 'There was only one gun fired up there. Lang must have shot himself.' In the witness stand Lang insisted that he shot Nitti in self-defence – and then, to the consternation of the prosecution, refused to answer further questions on the plea that his testimony might incriminate him. The trial turned a somersault. In September 1933 – after nine postponements – Lang went into the dock to face charges of assault with a deadly weapon, and Nitti, the defendant, became the chief prosecuting witness. Prior to this, Lang had intimated that if he was proceeded against he would make disclosures that would blow the Democratic party wide open, but he must have been prevailed upon not to do anything so foolish, for he remained stubbornly uncommunicative at his trial. Nitti now filled in the details. He said that when the squad had stormed in he had been grabbed by Callahan, who had held him by the wrists while Lang shot him through the neck and twice more in the chest. Callahan corroborated this. Lang was found guilty, but was granted a new trial. Eventually after repetitive delays and adjournments, it was dismissed. Lang was dismissed from the police force.

Cermak himself was not around to see the outcome of this marginal complication, or the harvest of his gambling reorganization. In February 1933 he left Chicago for Miami to attend a rally for President-elect Roosevelt. In the waterfront park, as Roosevelt drove in, Cermak stepped forward to shake his hand. As he did so, a spectator jumped out of the crowd firing a gun repeatedly and hit Cermak at close-range. He fell, mortally wounded into Roosevelt's arms, gasping: 'I'm glad it was me instead of you.'

He was taken to hospital, where he died three weeks later. It was believed for many years that, oddly enough, his death did not arise out of gang friction, and it was generally accepted that his assassin was a political fanatic named Giuseppe Zangara who was trying to kill Roosevelt. But twenty-six years later, after the killing of Roger the Terrible Touhy, a new interpretation of Cermak's death surfaced.[1]

Cermak's body was put on a train for Chicago and he was given a solemnly sumptuous funeral in the Chicago Stadium. In an encomium, the State Governor praised the memory of Cermak for having redeemed Chicago's reputation.

One month and one day after his death, Prohibition was annulled and in Chicago seen to its grave in an even more elaborate rite than that for Cermak. Capone was in prison. Thompson was beaten and

[1] See page 170.

broken (although he did, eight years later, make an abortive attempt to regain the mayoralty). Crime, corruption and unholy alliances between underworld and government had not ceased. Indeed, the developed Cermak Democratic organization, which became known as the Kelly-Nash machine, fronted by Edward J. Kelly for fourteen years as mayor, was more ruthless and more efficient than any previous régime. Under it 7,500 protected gambling establishments operated openly, the thousands of speakeasies that had existed at least with semi-secrecy under Thompson, after repeal became legitimate saloons – and proceeded illegitimately, but safely under political protection, to flout the licensing laws; the Capone gang, continuing to use Chicago as their headquarters and in a cartel understanding with New York mobsters, expanded their activities into labour unions and immensely varied and interlocked racketeering, including extortion from the Hollywood film industry; and, in Peterson's judgement, 'it is doubtful if any city has ever been the sanctuary for a greater number of major professional criminals than Chicago in the early and middle 1930's.'

Yet it was a different decade, a different atmosphere, different conditions, different techniques, different people with different personalities. Gang murders continued – in 1933, the year the Prohibition ended, there were thirty-five of them and, although the number dropped to the record low level of two in 1942, between 1933 and last year the total was 241 – but these were only a redolence of things past. The climate had changed, and there was no exactly similar modern counterpart to the gangster in white spats, straw hat, diamond-figured belt, with an occupied shoulder-holster bulging bumptiously as a cod-piece under the wide-striped suiting, riding in his armoured car through the Loop, betting 100 thousand dollars on a horse race, taking a bunch of beaded, blonde It-girls into a dive where the Negro band played jazz as rough as the whisky, giving orders to judges and throwing banquets lavish as a caesar's feast and funerals that were carnivals of flowers, and running elections at gun-point. The gangster and the politician also had sobered and adjusted and adopted more caution. There was no particular improvement to be pointed at proudly; nor was there any cause to repine that the change had come. But come it had, and an outrageously odd and garish epoch – the time of slum hooligan as dictator – had gone, for ever in that form.

PART FOUR

Anatomy of a Gangster

'The Americans are certainly great hero-worshippers, and always take heroes from the criminal classes.'

OSCAR WILDE

'Perhaps, after all, America never has been discovered. I myself would say that it had merely been detected.'

ibid.

20

The Tidelands of City Life

'Chicago's the money town.'
What the immigrant heard

'America, my country 'tis of Thee.'
What the immigrant sang

THE gangster of the Prohibition Era was almost invariably second-generation American; he was almost invariably a Sicilian, an Irishman or a Jew.

The reasons for this are diffused within the broad ethnic and social pattern of American city life – and in the history of America becoming a nation of many nations, the racial stew-pot in which some of the ingredients proved to have a gristly resistance against the rendering-down.

Since World War Two this pattern has been perpetuated by the Puerto Ricans, American citizens since their country was ceded by Spain to the United States in 1898 and who need no passport or permission to take up residence in the U.S.A., a situation similar to that of the unrestricted post-war ingress of Jamaicans and other West Indian Negroes to Britain. Now Puerto Ricans, especially street-gang teenagers, provide a disproportionately high percentage of crime and violence in New York, where their adaptation to an alien urban life is taking place in the ghetto congestion of Spanish Harlem and the West Side tenement-slums, and to a lesser extent (because the influx is slighter) in Chicago.

A new factor in the pattern is the Negro, who constitutes fewer than ten per cent of the population and yet figures in thirty per cent of all arrests made by the police and makes up eighteen per cent of the national juvenile delinquency rate, but who does not by exact definition come within the foreign immigrant category, for the Negro is older American stock than most whites. Nevertheless, the outcome is very similar. During the past forty-five years there has been a vast exodus of Negroes from south to north. Until about 1910 the Southern Negroes had been remarkably static. Between 1910 and

1920 the black population of Northern cities almost doubled. It was a time when employment in the cotton states had been blighted by recession and by pestilence, when jobs were plentiful in such industrial centres as Chicago, with its meat-packing plants, railroad shops and steel mills, and when the word went round that 'Chicago's the money-town – if you can't make it there, you can't make it anywhere'. Field and levee labourers from the Mississippi Delta rode up by train and river-boat in search of the dignity and the living denied them in their birthplace; they did not altogether find them in Chicago. They found that they had to cram together in the Black Belt of the South Side, and when they tried to press out into the better parts of the city they were bombed back by their white neighbours – there were fifty-eight such bombings between 1917 and 1920, followed by the 1919 six-day riot in which thirty-eight people were killed and a thousand left homeless. None the less, in the forty years up to 1950 the black population of the South fell by sixty-eight per cent, and the steepest decrease came between 1940 and 1950 when the black population of the Northern states rose by two million. This was caused by the halt in the supply of European labour for Chicago's expanding industry brought about by the out-break of war, a blockage continued by the subsequent post-war adoption of the immigration quota system. A substitute source was found in the Southern Negro. This has dominantly contributed to what has been described by Professor Philip M. Hauser, director of the University of Chicago's Demography Department, as 'a popula-tion explosion', a 'rapidity of growth, a change in population compo-sition and a mushrooming of physical problems practically unique in human history'. Already Chicago's black population has reached 800 thousand, twenty-one per cent of the city's total, and Southern settlers continue to arrive at the rate of two thousand a week, although this figure also includes poor whites. These come from the Appalachian Mountain region of Kentucky and the surrounding remote and backward areas, the declining scratch-farm and coal-pit areas of Missouri, Mississippi, Arkansas, Alabama and Tennessee, and are generally termed 'hillbillies', a tag loaded with both contempt and dislike.

Many Negroes in Chicago today are first generation immigrants from an underprivileged agrarian background, and these rural pioneers in the asphalt jungle are beset by crises of adjustment and assimilation closely similar to those that beset the earlier European immigrants. 'The problem of the Negro,' writes Professor Hauser, 'is one of transition from a folk culture in the rural South to "urbanism as a way of life".' In the same transitional stage in Chicago are Puerto Ricans, Mexicans, and Navajo, Hopi, Sioux and Mandan Indians. By logical progression it is often the non-European new-comers to the city who today are in conflict with conventional society and with the law, who provide the largest misfit-element, the hooligans, the attackers and the killers, the users of reefers, flick-knives and zipguns, and so are the subject of so many anxious inquiries as well as of such contemporary stage dramas as *West Side Story* and *The Connection*, of such novels as Warren Miller's *The Cool World* and Evan Hunter's *The Blackboard Jungle*, and of scores of lurid narcotics-and-sex paperbacks disguised as documentary sociology.

What are the conditions that produce the violence, the hostility, the unwillingness to accept society's regulations? Basically, the immigrant is a person seeking economic betterment. 'If you ask a Sicilian "Why did you come to America?" the answer is always the same: "We came for bread," ' reported a survey of Chicago's Little Sicily in the 'twenties. In 1850 fifty-two per cent of Chicago's population was foreign-born and between then and the early 1900's the surge of newcomers swelled tidally – the Germans, the Irish, the Scandinavians, the Polish, the Italians, the Jews, the Greeks. They fled oppression, famine, poverty, pogroms and religious persecution in their own countries, and they were lured into that abandonment of their own language and their ancestry and their homes by the glittering inducement of the work and freedom that were said to lay three thousand miles distant across the Atlantic Ocean. In Chicago they got jobs in the stockyards and foundries and rail depots of that burgeoning city. It was not always as golden a new life as they had been given to believe in the city rookeries and vineyards of Europe. Wage-rates were undercut by industrialists quick to syphon off the constantly replenished pool of cheap labour; there were periods of unemployment and hunger, of strikes, lock-outs and uprisings known as bread riots; weapons were used, guns by police and strike-breaking squads, sticks by union-organizers and socialists, bombs by the anarchists; but, in general terms, there *was* work and there *was* greater individual liberty. As it was put to me by Nelson Algren, who grew up in Chicago, himself the son of a Swedish father and German-Jewish mother: 'We were poor, but American poor not European poor; that meant we didn't have a car, but we ate well enough.'

With a pencil one can precisely dot on a street map of Chicago the breeding-places of the gangsters of the 'Twenties. There is the tenement tract that was west of the elevated railway, with Sedgwick

Street and Chicago Avenue north of Division at the centre, bounded
on the south by Smoky Hollow, on the west by the Chicago River
and the thick warp of railway tracks and factories, the drab wilderness known as Little Sicily, or Little Hell, which had been an Irish
shantytown named Kilgubbin until the invading Latins thrust in
and occupied it during 1903–4, the peak Italian immigration year.
Here is the Jewish quarter on Maxwell Street, south of Roosevelt
Road. Here is the new Irish section near the northern city limits
at Edgwater and Sheffield. Of these, the richest source of the slum
children who were to become the gunmen and the bootleggers was,
in Zorbaugh's phrase, that 'zone of instability and change – the
tidelands of city life', the Near North Side's Little Sicily, an area only
a mile and a half long and scarcely a mile wide choked with ninety
thousand people, yet overhung by Tribune Tower and the skyscraper
apartment buildings of the 'Gold Coast', the fashionable Lake Shore
Drive, the exclusive enclave of the rich and the merchant aristocracy.
Along the southern edge of Little Sicily the coal barges and tramp
freighters waddled up the chemical-polluted waters of Chicago
River between banks packed tight with gas works, iron foundries,
sheet metal plants, wharves and lumber yards, oil stores and fur
warehouses, cowled over by the smoke and racket of the factories
and the rail sidings; along the eastern periphery, just eight or ten
blocks away, were the parkway boulevards and tree-arcaded
promenades of Lake Shore Drive, and the blue spread of Lake
Michigan, white-flecked with sailing boats, shimmeringly scarred
by the launches and water-ski trails of the rich at play.

This foreign immigrant slum, 'a bleak area of segregation of the
sediment of society, an area of extreme poverty, tenements, ramshackle buildings', was sliced through by North Clark Street and
North La Salle Street, since the end of the Nineteenth Century
garish strips of dance halls, dubious hotels, strip-tease cabarets,
honkytonks, pawn shops, flop-houses, saloons and brothels. From
Sedgwick Street west to the river was the hard-core Italian community, the crammed, decayed apartment houses of Hudson,
Cleveland, Mohawk and Cambridge avenues and Larrabee, Crosby
and Hobbie streets, in which almost entire villages of Italians had
colonized block by block, transplanting their local dialects, customs
and family-feuds, which were to endure for at least another generation and to linger piecemeal for much longer, despite the onslaught
of influences of the society to which they had transferred.

In 1927 Frederic M. Thrasher undertook for the University of
Chicago an investigation of 1,313 local gangs. Professor Thrasher's

subject was not the confederation of professional criminals, what might best be called the business gangs who in that period were specializing in alcohol and the subsidiary enterprises of gambling, prostitution and protection rackets. His material was the neighbour-hood gangs which in the lower age-group were composed of dead-end kids not necessarily committed to a career of crime, and, at the opposite end, of late adolescents and young men, already with police record credentials, who were at various stages of committing them-selves to full-time crime. His survey concentrated mostly in the Little Sicily area – 'a mosaic of Sicilian villages' – and upon gangs with the names of the Beamers, the Plugs, the Coons, the Bicycle Squad, the Night Raiders, and the Buckets of Blood. 'Gangland,' pronounced Mr. Thrasher not altogether astoundingly, 'is a pheno-menon of human ecology. As better residential districts recede before encroachment of business and industry, the gang develops as one manifestation of the economic, moral and cultural frontier.'

In other words, Mr. Thrasher had reached a conclusion that has since become a commonplace: that metropolitan delinquency and anti-social attitudes can most often be directly linked to degenerate living conditions, disrupted and insecure family life, and the over-stimulated competitiveness of the city scramble.

What was more interestingly revealed by his investigation was the racial composition of the gangs. In Chicago, he reported, the gang was 'largely though not entirely a phenomenon of the immigrant community of the poorer type'. Of 880 gangs ethnically only forty-five were wholly American, and sixty-three were Negro, twenty-five mixed colour and white, 351 of mixed white nationalities, and 396 dominantly or solely of a single national group.

He continued: 'A few of the members of these gangs are foreign born but most of them are children of parents one or both of whom are foreign-born immigrants. Polish, Italian and Irish furnish many more gangs than might be expected from their population groups, while among Swedish and Germans there are relatively few gangs.' He also found that the motivation of many gangs was basically racialism: the consolidation of one neighbourhood race-group so as more strongly and effectively to express aggression against another adjacent race-group. He found odd alliances, especially in the industrial and riverfront zone around Western Avenue and Twenty-sixth Street, for many years a frontier between hostile immigrant colonies. Here Poles and Greeks were in *entente* against Italians, Germans and Hungarians against another community of Italians, Jews against Poles, Syrians against Assyrian-Persians. Commerce did not ever eliminate the strong racial overtones in the activities of the business gangs, the adult confederations of killers running the drink racket. Although there was a great deal of fluidity in allegiances during the booze wars, although there was internecine conflict and murder among the nationalistic groups themselves, particularly in the Italian-Sicilian sector, and although the Capone gang was, because of its size perhaps, unusually heterogeneous, its eight hundred gunmen being, according to the Chicago journalist James O'Donnell Bennett, ninety-five per cent foreign, and of that ninety-five per cent, eighty-five per cent Italians or Sicilians, ten per cent Jews and most of the remaining five per cent Irish – yet broadly the gangsters did hang together with their own kind. Pasley, discussing the Capone-O'Banion conflict, says: 'Racial feeling was undoubtedly involved' – the Irish resented the arrogance and envied the success of the Italian Capone. O'Banion summed up his feelings towards his competitors with: 'Them damn Sicilians.'

There was also the apparently quite sincere conviction of many gangsters, as referred to by Landesco, that they saw themselves with their newly-acquired power and pull as the guardians of their race, and were reciprocally adored and praised by their compatriots. Samuzzo Samoots Amatuna, twenty-six when he was killed and with a bloody record as gunman and murderer, was honoured for his charity and his strong nationalism; his murder was seen by Little Sicily as a blow by the Irish in their attempt to control the liquor industry – 'The Irish had captured the government, the public officials were Irish, and there were several hundred crooked Irish police sharing the profits of the Italian bootleggers,' was one contemporary interpretation of the situation, and there was bitter resentment because Amatuna had been denied the mass and burial in a Catholic cemetery.

There was similar intensity of feeling among the Jewish community when Nails Morton was killed. The *Daily News* headline of 15 May 1923 was: 'TRIBUTE TO NAILS MORTON: FIVE THOUSAND JEWISH PEOPLE ATTENDED THE FUNERAL ACCLAIMING HIM PROTECTOR.' The story pointed to 'a phase of the gang chieftain's character that few outsiders knew while he was alive. Five thousand Jews paid tribute to Morton as the man who made the West Side safe for his race. As a young man he had organized a defence society to drive Jew baiters from the West Side. Speakers at the brief services extolled Morton for his work for his race and for his gallantry in the World War. The other side of the career that ended was not mentioned.' The Davey Miller gang also had a tradition of defenders of the race –

in that case, defence of the Jews against the Poles. In the Anselmi-Scalise murder trial the entire Italian community rose in consolidated support of the killers because of anti-Sicilian remarks made by the prosecution.

Thrasher pointed out: 'It is not because the boys of the middle and wealthier classes are individually white that they do not form gangs, but because their lives are organized and stabilized for them by American traditions, customs and institutions to which the children of immigrants do not have adequate access. The gang is simply one symptom of a type of disorganization that goes along with the breaking up of the immigrants' traditional social system without adequate assimilation of the new.'

Here may be found the first reason why the prohibition bootlegger-gunman almost without exception had a foreign name, and usually an Italian name. Their parents brought over from the Old World, with their bundles of clothing and crucifixes, a thickly-woven fabric of living, a continuity and momentum strong enough to survive the transplanting and flourish in the new American social climate. The economic pressures which are still operating in the case of the Southern Negro and white Kentuckian directed the European immigrant into the slum, the 'port of entry'. This was not a preference for conditions of squalor (a squalor probably more ingrained and congested than that which he had left) but made necessary because the new settler was entering the Chicago labour market at economic ground-level. Therefore he gravitated to the decaying heart of the city, the least desirable part from which the native Chicagoans and the earlier established immigrants who had assimilated and prospered had moved out to the radially expanding suburbs. Here, logically, was the cheapest housing. It was a stinking ghetto, but not importantly worse than conditions he had always known, and already settled in and waiting to welcome him were his relations and friends, his own people who spoke his language and shared his ways, who meant warmth, familiarity and security. After the terrifying trauma of the adventure westward (from a European village or quarter from which he had probably never before ventured) he found himself comfortingly submerged within his own people and the old traditions. It could have been a walled quarter within a city, a shut-in and self-regarding community. He ate the same food, drank the same wine, kept the same feasts, attended the same religious services, and on a summer evening he moved a chair out on to the sidewalk or squatted on the steps and gossipped with neighbours in his own tongue about people and places they all knew. The only demand upon him, so as to survive economically, was that he should learn a modicum of English – although, perhaps, as a factory-hand or manual labourer, working in a national group and under an established and bi-lingual foreman or charge-hand from his own province, not even that proved necessary. For that first-generation European immigrant the problem of how to integrate was not a severe one: he didn't. The stress of this awaited his child.

The American-born child of the foreign immigrant, or the child who was brought across as a baby, could not stay cosily within the womb of the fabricated homeland. For him, in any case, the homeland was a fable and he could not understand the significance of so much of the older generations' nostalgic simulation. Yet, long before he had reached the point of formulating opinion about this, he had been precipitated out of the colony and was feeling the impact of the new culture that had not impinged upon his parents. He was required by law to go to school, and although it is likely that many of his fellow pupils in the neighbourhood public school were of the same stock and background as himself, there would be an admixture of other races, the teachers would be American, he was being impregnated with a literacy his parents had not known, he was learning facts about this nation of which he was now a nominal member that his parents would never hear of, and his knowledge of English which he could not share with them was making him vulnerable to influences that would never touch them. Long before he was able to analyse and understand the emotion, he was opaquely aware, from earliest childhood, of being different from his parents and all the adults in his colony. Out of bewilderment and disquiet grew a pervading sense of conflict. As he grew older and increasingly sensitive to the culture from which his parents and his colony were insulated, much of his confusion hardened into a furtive, guilt-infused contempt for his own people. Their jabbering in low-class Italian, or Polish, or Yiddish, and, even more shameful, their clumsy grotesquely broken English. Their appearance: his mother's peasant hair-style and dingy black peasant dress, his father's curling mustachios and neckerchief. Their incessant boring reminiscing about places he had never seen, would never see, and had no desire to see if they were as queer and corny as they sounded from the descriptions. Their stubborn adhesion to habits which had no relevance in this different hemisphere, to attitudes and ideas which had either lost their point or had been disproved by his own experience. Their disapproval and resentment of characteristics that were being grafted on to him outside the home, their relentless accusations, either spoken or implied, that he was in some way betraying them and his blood by not growing up like a shepherd on the Lombardy plain, or like a *tollus*-draped boy proudly carrying round the scrolls in a Warsaw synagogue – or even like a steady farm-lad in County Cork, content to court and marry the O'Shea girl from the next hamlet.

All this he felt, but he could not take the step to final rejection because of the simple and fundamental reason that he also loved, or at least emotionally needed, these people he despised, and also many of the things that he now recognized as outlandish and 'un-American' he also liked and needed.

In any case, where else was there for him? For, disturbing the shaping personality of the foreigner's son was the realization that, while he neither did nor could belong to his parents' world, nor could he be an integral part of the environment his parents distrusted but to which he was increasingly orientating. 'If the child conforms to the American definition he is a delinquent in the eyes of the family,' wrote Zorbaugh; 'if he conforms to the family definition he is a delinquent in the eyes of the American Law.' He began to see that he might have broken out of his colony's closed circle but there was an outer perimeter wall through which he wasn't going to break. He began to learn that there were classifications for people such as he, and that they had labels such as Wop, Polack and Mick. He discovered that he was identifiable as a hybrid American: his English certainly wasn't a pitiful mess like his parents', but there was something not quite right about the accent and when he forgot himself he easily lapsed into alien phrases and gesticulations, expressions he had acquired as a child; also he *looked* wrong – swarthy, or big-nosed, or long-lipped, he did not accord with the illusory but obligatory American physical image. And he began to find that all these differences cumulatively became a barrier, a barrier to getting friends, girls, jobs, to being accepted outside the enclave on his own terms as a person. Where did he belong? He began to hate his parents and his blood for making him what he was, and he began equally to hate this external America for not accepting him as he was. He was a divided person, living in two social worlds simultaneously and successfully in neither, like a bad character actor for ever scrambling into not very effective disguises.

In an older and more confident nation there may not be such fierce pressures upon the alien to adapt and conform. The national character

is defined and explicit, a palpable model; the code of conduct is
stable and coherent; and even if the novice chooses to remain
eccentrically unorthodox, this society is sufficiently confident of its
own standards not to become affronted and hostile. The United
States is a country that has undergone a unique process of creating in
a few generations a new race from a polygot profusion of ingredients,
and the pace has been forced by the power and prosperity that have
fallen upon it and thrust it into leadership of the West. An American
face had to be presented to the world and that American face had to
be made. This compulsion constantly to advertise the American
image, the harping on the idealized American way-of-life, the
necessity to prove the validity of the American dream of the Good
Life with an array of bright and gaudy material goods, the zeal to
manufacture American ceremonial and American tribal traditions
has a number of consequences. It produces not only such recognizable
physical emanations as the crew-cut, snub-nosed, beefy American
boy-figure, in T-shirt and crumpled jeans, and the fin-tailed rainbow
automobile, but it also produces the ambivalence in the American
personality: the vacillation between brash self-assurance and the
implicit apologetic humbleness about his lack of history and inherited
experience and wisdom. It produces in more sophisticated – and
often moribund – European countries a snobbish and shallow
amusement at the American's fervour both to display his enterprise
and to be loved by the world. It produces the American's fear and
mistrust of non-conformity, and the organization man caricature of
the good citizen, for the non-conformist is seen as the defiler of the
image. It also produces the American's admiration for the go-getter,
the exaltation of money as a mystical talisman, a symbol of success
and status.

All these developing *mores* and publicized ideals bombarded the
second-generation gangster-to-be when he first ventured out of his
colony, and he was further confused by the evident fallacy of so
many of them. He knew that the American home was not always
the white-fenced, green-lawned, tree-shaded house with a two-car
garage in which film families lived so sunnily, nor the duplex pent-
house of the Manhattan and Lake Shore Drive socialites who figured
in the gossip columns, for he lived in one, and it had bed bugs, no
indoor lavatory and looked out on to a soap factory. He knew that all
Americans weren't the tanned, crisp-haired, white-shirted Anglo-
Saxon types of the cigarette ads, because he never saw people like
that in his neighbourhood. (This situation is as present today in
Chicago, where to talk of minority groups, meaning those miscellan-

eous groupings of people still bearing obvious characteristics of non-white American old stock, is fairly meaningless. Foreign-born still number fifteen per cent of Chicago's population, second generation thirty per cent, non-whites fifteen per cent: a total of sixty per cent. So that the minority is actually the forty per cent native white Chicagoans.) Nevertheless, the demand upon him to take on the colouring of the emblematic American was strong, and not only from these external pressures. For the ambivalence he felt also was present, in a different form, in his father. Margaret Mead's explanation of the mental attitude of the foreign immigrant is: 'His grandfather left home, rebelled against a parent who did not expect final rebellion, left a land where everyone expected him to stay. Come to this country, his rebellious adventuring cooled off by success, he begins to relent a little, to think perhaps the strength of his ardour to leave home was overdone. When his sons grow up, he is torn between his desire to have them succeed in this new country – which means that they must be more American than he, must lose entirely their foreign names and every trace of allegiance to a foreign way of life – and his own guilt towards the parents and the fatherland which he has denied. So he puts on the heat, alternately punishing the child whose low marks in school suggest that he is not going to be a successful American and berating him for his American ways and his disrespect for his father and his father's friends from the old country.'

The father, in that case, is the partial failure: one who represents a step towards freedom but not freedom itself. 'His first-generation father,' continues Miss Mead, 'chose between freedom and what he saw as slavery; but when the second-generation American looks at his European father, and through him at Europe, he sees a choice between success and failure, between potency and ignominy.'

Miss Mead's example is the boy who had the opportunity of choice. The prohibition gangster was the man who had no choice, who was economically a degree lower and therefore imprisoned between the two cultures. But he found that there was an outlet, one remaining tunnel of escape from an intolerable situation: the gang.

Sociologists and criminologists still have not agreed upon a satisfactorily convincing explanation why, of two boys born in the same tenement, products of exactly similar conditions and family discord, one becomes a judge and the other a racketeer. Perhaps the motives are identical, the different means employed being due partly to luck and accidental external influences, partly to individual gradations of personality. But what seems to be consistently overlooked is that whereas in a middle-class environment it is the misfit who becomes a

criminal, in the environment of the immigrant ghetto it is the misfit
who becomes a schoolteacher: he is the outsider. The well-adjusted
insider identifies himself with the vague but strong feeling of the slum-
dweller that he is underneath, crushed by the weight of the city's
élite who, both to ignore and to use him, employ the weapons of the
law to hold him where he is. Hostility, hatred and violence, and a
recourse to the strength in numbers that the gang provides, are
natural and normal results. A Chicago professor, himself the son of
foreign-born parents, expressed the situation to me in these words:
'The typical criminal of the Capone era was a boy who had taken on
the pattern of the successful mobster, the pattern that surrounded
him. He wasn't out of step. He was a regular guy. He'd seen what was
rated as success in the society he had been thrust into – the Cadillac,
the big bank-roll, the elegant apartment. How could he acquire that
kind of recognizable status? He was almost always a boy of outstanding initiative, imagination and ability; he was the kind of boy
who, under different conditions, would have been a captain of
industry or a key political figure of his time. But he hadn't the
opportunity of going to Yale and becoming a banker or a broker;
there was no passage for him to a law degree at Harvard. There
was, however, a relatively easy way of acquiring those goods that he
was incessantly told were available to him as an American citizen,
and without which he had begun to feel he could not properly count
himself as an American citizen. He could become a gangster.'

In 1930, at the peak of the Capone phase of business crime, and
when, of Chicago's population of 3,400,000 more than 2,460,000
were foreign-born or born in America of foreign or mixed parentage,
two-fifths of the girl delinquents and half of the male delinquents
were of foreign-born parentage. Lohman, in his 1957 survey of
American delinquency problems, states: 'The problem has shifted in
recent years to the "new migrants" and new marginal groups within
the American scene: the urban-drifting Negro, the Mexican and the
Puerto Rican . . . Today the vast majority of offenders of both sexes,
i.e. over seventy per cent, are native-born and of native-born
parentage.' The training-ground youth gang is, despite its constant
change of membership, still persistent and continues to display ethnic,
racial and territorial dimensions. Fifty per cent of American delinquents originate from twenty-five per cent of the population. Shaw
and McKay found that in Chicago delinquents were concentrated in
a small number of areas – nine central city districts, which, though
containing only sixteen per cent of the teenage population provided
thirty-eight per cent of the delinquency. Of course these were the

dense slum zones. Lohman quotes an eleven-year-old gang member to show the pride in tradition that exists and to which new recruits are conditioned: 'The old guys, they're married or in the Army or in the joint.[1] The middle guys, they're in Charley Town.[2] The young guys, like me, we're pulling all the jobs.[3]'

So the gang becomes the substitute for that missing solidarity and cohesiveness, and also, in a dimly perceived way, substitutes a 'manly-brotherhood' ethos for the absent love. 'Gangland,' said Zorbaugh, 'is the result of the boy's creation of a social world in which he can live and find satisfaction for his wishes.' In 1929 Thrasher defined the characteristics of the Chicago neighbourhood gang in this way: the embryo gangs had their origins in the fighting between rival streets: 'While many of them are emphemeral, others develop considerable social self-consciousness. They often get a name from their own street or of their own choosing. In this way the embryo gang becomes solidified and permanent, and acquires considerable stability. Boys may hang together in this manner throughout the whole period of adolescence, and when they arrive at manhood they represent a well-integrated group . . . Out of these gangs of boys and young men the criminal gangs develop . . . The Crime Commission of Chicago estimates that there are ten thousand professional criminals in the city. It is more than likely that their training was in such gangs, which, usually unsupervised, are veritable cradles of crime. Besides creating juvenile delinquency and training criminals, the gang acts always as a source of disorder in the community. It is a problem for school, for park, for playground and for settlement. It thrives on conflict. When there are riots, the gang takes a leading part in them; and it easily becomes a nucleus for the mob. In its more mature forms, in unscrupulous hands, it becomes the instrument for evil. It may be used in labour slugging, in strike breaking, or in violent competition. In Chicago, as in other cities, it has become a favourite tool of political bosses, who subsidize it and protect it in its delinquency in return for strong-arm work and votes. Yet it would be erroneous to suppose that the gang is inherently evil. It is simply a spontaneous expression of human nature without social direction. It is a product of neglect and repression. It flourishes like weeds in the formal garden of society.'

Another factor is the effect of city life itself upon these peasants' sons. The hugeness, diversity and anonymity of Chicago, the opportunities it offered to the young Italian or Irish boy to escape from their parents' authority to other neighbourhoods and unknown to

[1] The State Penitentiary.   [2] The State Training School.   [3] Crimes.

them acquire new habits and friends was examined by R. E. Park. This mobility and the accelerated change it offers, Park said, 'makes it possible for individuals to pass quickly and easily from one moral milieu to another, and encourages the fascinating but dangerous experiment of living at the same time in several different, contiguous, perhaps, but widely separated worlds. All this tends to give to city life a superficial and adventitious character; it tends to complicate social relationships and to produce new and divergent types. It introduces at the same time an element of chance and adventure, which adds to the stimulus of city life and gives it for young and fresh nerves a peculiar attractiveness. The lure of great cities is perhaps a consequence of stimulations which act directly upon the reflexes. As a type of human behaviour it may be explained, like the attraction of the flame for the moth, as a sort of tropism.'

Membership of the gang, in these turbulent and twilit zones of Chicago, was the prize for behaviour theoretically condemned by respectable society and at the same time condoned and cynically resorted to by society for its own advantage, and so by visible measurement, richly rewarding.

21

The Sabre-toothed Businessman

'If you're gonna be straight you're gonna be poor.'
Chicago immigrant woman

'What is a pick-lock compared to a debenture share?'
BERTHOLT BRECHT

UNTIL 17 January 1920, the American gangster had been identifiable. Indeed, prior even to that he enjoyed a licence unknown in modern Europe. The fusion and mutual aid of crime and politics was an old American custom; the 'open city' principle was widely accepted, not only by businessmen who argued that an anything-goes reputation was good for local trade, or by those who patronized whorehouses, strip-shows and card-parlours, but by many steady citizens who romantically cherished the idea of the survival of that rumbustious, frontier past of Diamond Lil and the riverboat gambler. So the vice wholesaler of the Colosimo cast, with his splendiferous vulgarity, his bamboozling, his swaggering slyness, was tolerated, even relished as a colourful-scamp character – yet remained beyond the pale of the respectable community. He existed, he was half admired, he fulfilled a function that was maybe – with a shrug of the shoulders – necessary; but he was not consorted with and, when all the excuses and indulgences had been exercised, he was marked down as a criminal outside the boundaries of the decent community.

But, after the start of Prohibition, who was the crook? Millions of people who regarded themselves as upright, law-respecting, dutiful citizens, and who in all other respects may well have been, began, blatantly and habitually, to cheat and lie, and entered into routine conspiracy with the underworld. By late January 1920, writes Asbury, 'women began to invade the speakeasies ... Young people began to carry flasks and to break out in whoopee parties at which a popular game was to see who could first get plastered. They helped their elders handle the distilling and brewing apparatus in their homes, saw them guzzle liquor, making drunken passes at one another's wives and husbands, and nursing hangovers. They heard little conversation that didn't deal with the high cost of booze, the difficulty of controlling fermentation, the proper quantity of yeast, and the sterling qualities of "my bootlegger". Drinking became romantic and adventurous, the correct thing for all up-to-date young folks to do.' In 1923 Justice John H. Clarke, of the Supreme Court, told the alumni of the New York University Law School: 'Respect not only for that law, but for all laws, has been put to an unprecedented and demoralizing strain in our country, the end of which it is difficult to see.'

Capone's hurt complaint: 'All I ever did was to sell beer and whisky to our best people. All I ever did was to supply a demand that was pretty popular,' has often been quoted for laughs; yet, without accepting that was 'all' that he did – for that would rather arbitrarily exclude the murder, extortion, terrorization and corruption contingent upon his simple central purpose – those two statements are true. Capone and his fellow bootleggers had a vast host of accomplices: the public.

The middle-aged Chicagoan today looks back on those wanton years with a surprising degree of personal guilt (a banker told me: 'During the 'twenties my daughter said to me, "You've always taught me to respect law and the Constitution, and here you are making your own gin", and I had no answer.') but with an equally surprising absence of censure upon Capone and the gangs. Among the scores of people I questioned about their own attitude, and their memory of the contemporary public attitude, towards Capone, I met only one, an ex-crime reporter, who flatly condemned him ('He was a rat') and it may be of interest at this point to give a few direct opinions.

A lawyer, son of a one-time Attorney General, expressing an improbable view that almost corresponded with that of Brecht's Macheath ('What is a pick-lock compared to a debenture share? What is the burgling of a bank compared to the founding of a bank?'): 'Capone was relatively innocent compared with some of the men who dominated business and public life then – and I'm thinking particularly of Samuel Insull, who conducted his financial operations like a ruthless brigand. There were businessmen who supported honourable political and civic standards, yet who were seduced and bought by Insull. It was the general abandonment of honesty and integrity in public life brought about by Insull that had as a by-product the moral climate in which Capone ascended.'

A sociologist, who as a young man mixed with the Capone mob

for two years while working on a university social study project, said: 'I couldn't look upon the gangs of the prohibition period as criminals. The people of Chicago wanted booze, gambling and women, and the Capone organization was a public utility supplying the customers with what they wanted. It couldn't have operated one hour without the public's consent. It was the "good" people who kept the gangsters flourishing. The big civic leaders and industrial moguls would get up at a meeting and denounce corruption – and then go straight on to a cocktail party, or back to the office to argue with their bootleggers about the quality of the last delivery of liquor. One thing about the gangsters – they were integrated individuals. Among them there were fewer potential patients for the analyst's couch than I've met in any other group. They knew exactly what they were doing. They may have been wrong about only one thing. Capone and the others really believed that they were running the city, but I don't believe they were. They were the executives and the technicians. The city was being run by the politicians and by City Hall, and the big bosses weren't interested if the gangsters killed each other, providing they kept delivering the money. I had respect for Capone. In the Depression he did wonderful work. Before the New Deal got going they set up block restaurants for the unemployed, free food with the compliments of the Organization – and you didn't have to listen to any sermons or get up and confess. You sat down and they gave you a real meal with tablecloths on the tables, and no one rescued you. Even the union racketeering wasn't as bad as it's been painted. I knew one racketeer well who ran a hotel workers' union. He ran it with an iron hand, but he also provided a health clinic, a psychiatric department and picnics and social outings. And there's something else the gangsters haven't been given credit for,' he added without a smile, 'they did more advertising of the Cadillac as a fundamental part of the American way of life than General Motors ever did.'

A judge who consistently opposed the Thompson administration still qualified the total condemnation of the Prohibition gangster. 'The gangs,' he said to me, 'gained power by corruption; there was a corrupt City Hall and a fertile field in which corruption could grow. But the movie theory that the gangsters were cowards is not true. They had immense physical courage. Also, we Americans are mercurial people. We brought in Prohibition. We tried it. We switched. I personally was an advocate of keeping wine and beer. I think we would have taken prohibition of hard liquor. But the minds of the people were occupied by the question: "Why should they have taken away my glass of beer?" The really big bootleg traffic was in beer.

There were some people who hated Capone, but for many he had the attraction of an adventurous brigand – and from the point of view of many he was engaged in the pursuit of supplying the people with their beer. As I said, we are a mercurial people. In every American city there is a group of businessmen and others who favour having an open city – and that goes back to Rome. They argue that by having an honest mayor certain avenues of revenue are blighted. They long for the free-for-all days back; they get them; then they see their children walking down streets lined with whorehouses and joints, and they decide to clean up the city. So it goes in cycles. The gangster cannot be permanently eliminated when there is that kind of social fickleness.'

A university lecturer said: 'Capone was one of Chicago's bene- factors. I don't say that admiringly, only factually. You couldn't have had organized crime as it was then without a prescription for it from the community, and it was legally and morally consonant with the actual behaviour of the city's inhabitants. The situation was that there was a demand for goods and services not provided legitimately, a demand so insistent that other factors arose – those factors were Torrio and Capone. They undertook their task efficiently. The gang had a real structure. It was impossible to enforce its rules through the courts, so it created its own enforcement agency. They were living in an illegal and amoral order, and the most brutal and calloused became the most successful. But in this context to be successful you had to be the one to machine-gun your opposition first. Once you had this situation of the gang having been created by the public it followed that it was absorbed into the city's legal and moral framework, and there followed from that the most amazing liaisons – liaisons with the responsible parts of the community.'

The political climate of the period importantly contributed to this equivocal attitude towards the gangster, especially to the defiant opposition to the official line of solid-citizen condemnation. The defence arose out of the view that there were at large worse pillagers masquerading as good people – an opinion still in existence and crystallized by Nelson Algren, who said to me: 'Corruption begins at the top. I have known a lot of racket people and people who have done time, mostly people who have a legitimate front but with some- thing else going on underneath it. Morally they are sounder than the "good" people who run Chicago by complicity.' This attitude grew partly out of the resentment felt by so many intelligent non- denominational people towards Prohibition – the feeling that their right of free choice had been quashed by a bigoted religious faction –

but also, more vaguely but equally passionately, out of the belief that the gangsters were the rash erupting from much deeper, organic social disease and that they usefully served the purpose of the real malefactors by diverting public indignation away from the source of the blight.

Algren, now in his early fifties, who grew up in the mixed Polish and Negro district of Milwaukee Avenue, and who still spends a good deal of time there, is typical of the self-made intellectuals, the proletarian (or middle-class identifying with the working-class) writers, painters, journalists and peripheral bohemians, who knew Chicago during the depression of 1921, the splurging 'Coolidge Prosperity' of 1923 to 1928, the speculative dementia of the year 1928, the Wall Street crash of 1929, and the bleak, shocking years of the slump 'Thirties, when there was fear, hunger, suffering and the smell of revolution in the land. They were made by events into either restive, outraged, humanitarian socialists of the non-party kind known in America as liberals, or into converted Marxists and even ticket-carrying Communist Party members.

The destruction of Capone was one demonstration of America's need then to reform herself and make recompense, for it was a time of tormented self-questioning, when there were millions of workless men in the land – the three millions of 1929, which accreted to fourteen-and-a-half million by 1932. This was the time when the whole structure of American thought – the premise that prosperity and progress would ever dynamically grow under *laissez faire* capitalism – collapsed with the Big Bull Market. It was the time of the internal migrations, the new treks westward in scrap-heap cars out of the Oklahoma dust-bowl and the derelict eroded farm-lands of the South; of Steinbeck's *Grapes of Wrath*; of the hoboes riding the rods and the box-cars east and west, north and south across the continent in search of non-existent jobs; of the down-and-outs' Hoovervilles built out of packing-cases and corrugated iron on the weedy spare lots of cities; of soup kitchens and bread-lines; of itinerant radical guitarists like Woody Guthrie singing 'Talking Union Blues', 'Vigilante Man', 'Hard Travelling' and morale-builders from the *Little Red Song-Book* of Joe Hill, the executed Wobbly poet, in the wayside camps of unorganized migrant workers; of plays like *Waiting For Lefty* and films like *Winterset*; of the P.W.A. and Federal Relief; of a new passionate protest school of novelists like John Dos Passos, James T. Farrell and Richard Wright; of the appearance of Party poetry such as Maxwell Bodenheim's 'To A Revolutionary Girl' and Langston Hughes's 'Ballad of Lenin'; of strikes and blacklegs, lock-outs and goon-squads; of the spurt to best-sellerdom, after the initial disinterest, of Maurice Hindus's *Humanity Uprooted*, for it was a book about the planned economy of the Soviet Union, and a planned economy seemed suddenly to have virtues lacking in the American slump-boom-slump cycle; and it was a time in which even the pop-song temporarily wrenched its attention from the shallower aspects of sexual love and cast a moist eye upon the smoking rubble of the whoopee age with 'Remember My Forgotten Man' and 'Brother, Can You Spare a Dime?' No American town had higher unemployment than Chicago. None had a bigger proportion of the working population on relief. None had more violent and bloody riots, labour disorders and hunger marches in which police used guns and shot down strikers and pickets. In one month in 1932 thirty-eight Chicago banks closed their doors. Eighteen months earlier, in January 1930, British papers had carried the macabre headline 'BANKRUPT CITY: COMPLETE CHAOS IN CHICAGO'. The incredible fact was that this virile, bustling industrial centre, under the administration of Big Bill Thompson and his confederates, was 300 million dollars in the red.

The magnitude of the mess and of the cheating by men high in public office and business life placed the booze-racket gangster, in the eyes of many Chicagoans, in a state of relative grace. More central to the crisis were such buccaneer financiers as Samuel Insull and Charles T. Yerkes, just two particularly notorious and flamboyant examples of the Chicago breed of sabre-toothed business tigers. Insull – the son, incidentally, of English temperance crusaders and who himself boasted that he had never touched a drop of liquor, which was probably invaluable propaganda for the anti-Prohibitionists – began his career in Chicago by organizing, and seizing control of, the distribution of electric power. He extended his monopolistic techniques to eleven states and 385 cities, became the most powerful tycoon in the Middle West, and by the middle 'twenties was deep in political machinations. In 1932, after some concealed preliminary shudders, his dollar empire caved in; 300 thousand stockholders lost their savings; Insull fled to Paris, where, after being extradited to stand trial, he returned to die owing fourteen million dollars. Yerkes's beginnings in freebooting business were founded on investing funds, embezzled by a friend from the Philadelphia city treasury, in Chicago enterprises after the fire of 1871. He then opened a broker's office, specialized in wangling streetcar franchises and, in hidden co-operation with the City Council 'Grey Wolves', eventually controlled most of Chicago's transportation network. Finally the multimillionaire's political and financial power, despite the distribution of bribes amounting to 300 thousand dollars, was shattered. Before he also fled for Europe, he unloaded his inflated holdings. After Insull had been brought back to the United States to stand trial for fraud – and acquitted on every charge by jurors who afterwards told reporters that they had known what their verdict would be six weeks before Insull took the stand – the Chicago *Times*, in a leader supporting the advent of President Franklin D. Roosevelt's New Deal, summed up: 'Insull and his fellow defendants – not guilty; the old order – guilty.'

It is not astonishing that, by the moral measurement of many of the younger, intelligent Chicagoans of the time, what Alson J. Smith called the 'colourful mastodons of the La Salle Street jungle' were guiltier of harming society than Capone and his group. Writing of the artistic circles in Chicago and their relationship with 'the neolithic gangsters', Smith says that this was partly due to the fact that many of Chicago's writers were also journalists whose daily work brought them into contact with gangdom, partly that many of the Sicilian mobsters were patrons of the opera, partly that there was a meeting place in the jazz joints operated by the gangs, and partly that 'The gangsters did not appal the writers and journalists the way they did most men; they knew them personally; Chicago was a jungle anyway, and Prohibition was decidedly unpopular. Most of the journalists considered the most dangerous beasts not the prowlers of the underworld but the dinosaurs who holed up in their La Salle Street skyscrapers and sallied forth to hijack streetcar franchises and utilities stock. Yerkes and Insull, they would argue, stole more than Torrio and O'Banion, and hurt more innocent people doing it.'

Nor is it surprising that Capone was in complete agreement with this point of view. In June 1931, while complaining to the press of the way he was being harried by the tax authorities, he said: 'I think the bankers who rob poor people of their money are guilty of a greater crime. The Government have made an example of me and I'm not complaining. But they should get after crooked bankers.' On the other hand, five months earlier he had made it clear that he was willing to reach an accommodating *entente* with the authorities, including big business interests. 'I don't interfere with big business,' he told the Washington *Herald*. 'None of those big business guys can say that I ever took a single dollar from them. I don't interfere with their racket. Why can't they leave my racket alone?'

Capone's flexibility was never inhibited by any worrisome rigid standards; he had the talent of a good military commander, agile in his shifting of ground to meet a change of the tactical situation.

So it may be seen that the formal objurgation of gangsters, customarily expressed with a trumpeting note in reports, public addresses and crime exposé books, that the gangster is a vampire with his wings hooked round the helpless body of the community as he sucks up its life blood, does not accurately reflect all points of view. Nevertheless, I feel that unjustly lacking from this denunciation of public discipline and integrity is a crucial factor. The British are often perplexed and irritated by the matted confusion of state and local laws in America, by what seems to them a chaotically inefficient jurisprudence thick as guerilla country with bolt-holes and escape routes for the criminal equipped with an attorney and speedy to assert his constitutional rights and to shelter behind the silence afforded by a handy Amendment. The British also read much of the violence and dissonance in American society, and much of the McCarthyist and racial excesses which bring about reactions towards timidity, towards bland conventionality, towards a non-committal mediocrity that is deemed safer than vigour and originality, and the puzzled British are often hard put to see any reality in the principles of individuality and personal liberty that occupy so much space in declarations about America's greatness and destiny.

In fact those principles have a most potent reality in the way that they mould the American's outlook and code of behaviour – even if, like human beings everywhere, he often falls below those idealistic standards in practice. It was those principles that contributed to the survival and the success of Capone. At its simplest, it is that such importance is invested in the idea of individual freedom that the criminal is allowed to get away with a lot; administratively, its effect is that, although there are often weighty reasons of personal profit in wanting to keep local affairs run locally, there is a profound and ferocious pride in autonomy of the state, a reluctance to get enmeshed by Washington and Federal officials. Finally, of course, Capone became so powerful – and such a national embarrassment – that it required Federal action to smash him, and Chicago's responsible citizens had reached a point of desperation at which Federal help had to be sought. But much is explained by the remark of one Chicago businessman to me: 'We knew finally that we had to get rid of Capone, but this was a complex matter, with a lot of things like self-esteem, civic honour and a good deal of both shame and arrogance mixed up in it.'

What is not yet entirely explained is the regard in which Capone was held and is still widely held, a regard which in his heyday ranged from the grudging 'you've got to hand it to the son-of-a-bitch' chuckle of the mature to the open hero-worship of the immature. This formed an emotional climate in which Capone blossomed under the sunlight of popularity and glamourization.

What John Gunther calls 'these folk-lore creatures' were celebrities in their lifetime. Pasley described in 1930 the interest aroused by the approach of Capone in his armoured car: ' "There goes Al", would fly from lip to lip, and pedestrians would crowd to sidewalk kerbs, craning necks as eagerly as for a circus parade. It was a civic spectacle to linger in the recollections of strangers within the gates of America's second largest city during 1925, 1926, 1927 and 1928.' Inevitably, too, the gangsters were glamorous swashbucklers in the eyes of the young. In 1928 an Indiana boy was arrested for vagrancy in Chicago. He said he had made the trip expressly 'to see the brave guys who make monkeys out of you cops'. Jane Addams, the sociologist, wrote in 1929 that good citizens were all 'much concerned as to the effect of all this law-breaking upon the young. There is no doubt that a spirit of adventure natural to boys in adolescence has been tremendously aroused by the bootleg and hijacking situation. It is as if this adventurous spirit were transferred from the Wild West into the city streets.' She also pointed to the number of enthusiastic youthful recruits used by the gangsters as look-outs around their wildcat distilleries and breweries and to the increase of arms-carrying by boys, and mentioned a recent incident when five boys who had been drinking hooch had shot and killed a policeman who tried to arrest them.

Today, thirty years after the close of his régime, and of that particular kind of crime empire, Capone has become the central figure of an American Arthurian legend. Chicago of the 'twenties is a neon-flickering Camelot ridden by blue-chinned and slouch-hatted knights in beer trucks and those mediaeval raw-boned touring cars with black hoods pulled like baseball caps over the open iron-lattice-worked sides, through which poked the tommy-guns and automatics, on their jousts through the traffic jams. It is a legend that is not without genuine courage, chivalry and, within its own ethic, grace of conduct. The gangs imposed their racial traditions and ritual upon their way of life, so that it evolved its own protocol and etiquette: the exchange of the 'kiss of death' between a Sicilian gunman squad before they departed upon an assassination; the no-shaving decree which marked with a show of a few days' stubble the

sudden demise of a friend; the considerate Mafia technique of
execution from the back, followed by a *coup de grace* bullet; the pomp
of the funerals and the banquets; the rigid separation of bloody
brutality of professional life from the claustrophobic intimacy of the
family; and the disciplined bravery expected of the gunman whose
pay was that of the member of a warrior elite, but who in return had
to accept a life of haunted tension until his almost inevitable end in an
alley dustbin or the boot of an abandoned car with the back of his
head blown off.

That these men were emotionally abnormal, cold-hearted and
avaricious, does not detract from the fascination of the world they
created for themselves, which was as controlled by its own ordinances
as was the society which it defied. It was a world in which a barbaric
brand of piracy had its golden time because of the intelligence with
which they manipulated modern techniques and conditions: the
anonymity of the city skyscraper, the fast car, the machine-gun and
the bomb, and the methods of modern business.

Also there is the fact that, despite the 'yellow rat' stamp with
which law-enforcement tried to brand the gangster, the public
recognized in him a real kind of bravery: he had, despite the legal
security obtained by bribery and intimidation, chosen a desperate
life. The crash of guns in the streets, the almost daily fatalities, were
audible and visible evidence that these were singular men who had
the daring and resource to live constantly in an extreme situation,
coolly and arrogantly on the edge of death. Just as the fighter pilot
and the spy – whatever the cause they serve – excite the admiration
and surreptitious envy of the sober citizen, so did the gangster have
an irresistible enticement. For, after all, there is a good deal of Walter
Mitty in us all, and these tough, amoral, dangerous-living desper-
adoes flamboyantly displayed qualities that secretly attract us in some
of our moods – boldness, recklessness and the forcefulness to bend
circumstances into the shape they wanted them, instead of submitting
to being bent by circumstances as we so often feel we are. Robert
Sherwood understood this when in his play *The Petrified Forest* he
had his weak, vacillating intellectual, with his self-indulgent charade
of freedom and separation from mass-thought, say with a kind of
sickly envy of the Neanderthal killer (a part Humphrey Bogart in
the film obviously modelled upon John Dillinger, the bank robber)
who has him prisoner: 'You are the last of the rugged individualists.'

The gangster of this period was carefully and not too conspicuously
dressed – the gold-toothed, clamorous-waistcoated Colismo-type had
toned down. The new gangster wore a pearl grey felt hat with black

band – 'the trade-mark of the Capone mobster', noted Ness – dark double-breasted suit and waistcoat with white handkerchief, white shirt, striped tie and spats. When a Harry Doremus was arrested in the summer of 1929 on a larceny charge, he was too proud of the fact that he had been a Capone triggerman to conceal the past; obviously, to the young and striving criminal, membership of the Capone gang equated with a soldier's service in the Brigade of Guards or an airman's time as a Spitfire pilot during the Battle of Britain. Doremus regarded himself as being one of a select and privileged crack troop, and he added: 'The Big Fellow hires nothing but gentlemen. They have to be well dressed at all times and have to have cultured accents. They always have to say "Yes, Sir" and "No, Sir" to him. Capone hires his men with great care, they got to be his own type in dress and conduct.' Pasley wrote in 1930: 'The picture of a furtive, sallow-faced creature, with cap with pulled-down visor and cigarette drooping from listless lip, gives way to that of an upstanding, square-shouldered fellow, in his teens or twenties, keen-eyed, ruddy-cheeked; a smart dresser, with a flair for diamonds and blondes; always occupying choice seats at prize-fights, wrestling matches, football and baseball games, the race-track, and the theatre; knowing the night-club head waiters and receiving their deferential ministrations.' Also Capone was as zealous as a Gordonstoun master that his gunmen and sluggers should keep in peak physical form for their rigorous duties. At his Metropole Hotel headquarters, according to Pasley, were two rooms equipped with punching bags, horizontal bars, trapezes, rowing machines and other gymnasium devices in which his staff were expected to have regular workouts. "They followed a schedule of training as methodical as that of college football athletes,' Pasley said. 'Experience had taught him that their professional value, based on that quality commonly described as nerve, was in direct ratio to their physical fitness. It might be only the imperceptible tremor of a trigger-finger, or the slightest wavering of an eye, or a split second of hesitancy at the crucial moment in any of a score of unforeseen emergencies; yet the cost of the lapse would have to be reckoned in lives and money.' Accuracy of eye was maintained at regular target practice on private machine-gun ranges in thinly populated areas of Illinois.

Efficient and conscientious though they were in their way, humour and a sense of irony were not their most marked characteristics. The extreme to which their spirit of vengeance went is demonstrated by the execution of Nails Morton's horse. Samuel J. Morton, of the O'Banion gang, was a cut-above-ordinary mobster. He had served

with the 131st Illinois Infantry in France as a first-lieutenant, and
had been awarded the *Croix de Guerre* for leading a squad over the
top after being twice wounded. After demobilization, he took up
the civilian occupation of bootlegger, and put his training in warfare
and ballistics to practical use. In 1921 he and Hirschey Miller
killed a pair of policemen in a café, twice going to trial and twice
walking out unhindered. Morton was a stylish liver and rode daily
on the Lincoln Park bridle-paths among the mounted rich. One
morning a stirrup leather broke while he was cantering; he was
thrown and kicked to death. His buddies decided that the normal
processes of retribution should be put into motion. Two-Gun Louis
Alterie went to the stable and rented Morton's horse, rode it to the
spot where the accident had occurred, where a crowd of O'Banion
men were waiting, and there the horse was ceremonially bumped-off,
each gangster firing a shot into its head. Alterie telephoned the
stables. 'We taught that goddam horse of yours a lesson,' he said.
'If you want the saddle go and get it.'

Yet, although there was the obvious, meretricious appeal of these
gunman irregulars, who superficially fitted into the treasury of
quixotic brigands, with the Crusaders, Robin Hood, Dick Turpin,
Blackbeard and Jesse James, there is a deeper, philosophical reason
why the gangster has become an integral part of the American
myth. The foreign-stock youngster was forcibly fed upon the New
World credo of private enterprise, competition and material
success, and his generation melodramatically demonstrated how
well the lesson had been learned. These *entrepreneurs* of the gigantic
booze syndicates, orchidaceously rich and powerful, were living
(although, admittedly, often short-lived) expressions of two characteristics implicit in the American: his admiring respect for the go-
getter who has got there and his enjoyment of the spectacle of
authority flouted and made foolish. To achieve self-advancement
the bootlegger used methods – murder and violence – which the
ordinary citizen stopped a long way short of, yet his attitude to life,
his beat-your-neighbour tactics, his triumph in the competitive
system at its most ferocious extreme, had a kind of romantic right-
ness. He had accepted the prerogatives of the cash-nexus ideology
and pushed them to their farthest point, and the commercial business
he built up was a microcosm of capitalism operating at its logical
ultimate without the checks and controls of government and trades
unions. 'We're big business without high hats,' Dion O'Banion
once said. There for all the United States to watch was the way the
profit motive worked when no holds were barred, and it was difficult

for anyone bred in and breathing the atmosphere of a dollar civilization, taught that ruthlessness and aggression were requisites for success, to do the mental somersault needed to see Capone and his gangsters as evil—especially when the end to which they worked was making available to him a pleasure that he could not regard as sinful. When Jack Greasy Thumb Guzik, who rose from a whorehouse waiter to financial head of the Capone syndicate, was arrested on the suspicion of the murder of James M. Ragen, a rival racetrack wire-service operator, he said to the police: 'I've got more cash than Rockefeller and there's twenty of us with more than I have. No one's going to push us around.' Guzik was stating simply the money=privilege equation, the formula in which he and every other gangster had always seen the American way of life and according to the precepts of which they had lived.

More than fifty years ago Lincoln Steffens, the famous 'muckraker' exposer of civic disorders and author of *Shame of the Cities*, warned America that a society that conditioned people from the cradle to regard power and money as the most important and desirable objectives in life—and to be reached whatever the cost—ensured its own corruption. Max Lerner defines the racket as 'a pattern of extortion and tribute which urban brigands levy' on legitimate commerce; he defines the syndicate as 'a business combine with a feudal structure of authority organized to exploit activities beyond its margin'. But, he emphasizes, these activities are not as marginal to American life as they are to American law. 'One trait on which the rackets and syndicates build is the belief in luck, which is deeply ingrained in a culture that underlines the big prizes. . . . America today, as in the past, presents the picture both of a lawless society and an overlegislated one. America is the type-society of the West in which little is left to loose community action, and the characteristic way of dealing with crime is to set down definite statements of legal transgressions and punishments. Nevertheless, Americans consider crime a problem they cannot master, which will continue to grow because it is an outcropping of some inner disease of society. Recognizing this, they also recoil from it, thus displacing on the criminal their own guilt and powerlessness – which may help explain why the treatment of crime has lagged. To feel mastery over the environment, over things and money, and yet to feel baffled by so elementary a fact as crime, has become a source of frustration.'

Why, asks Lerner, are Americans drawn to the gangster films which they know to be distortions of their urban life? Because 'a gangster is an American "cultural hero" in whom Americans

recognize a symbol of the energy of their culture.' The 'rationality'
of the habitual criminal is explained by his twisted antisocial
premises from which his acts flow logically. So that the criminal
'takes serious the barely concealed premises of the culture itself.
He sees easy money being made and predacity practiced, knows that
the rules are constantly broken, knows that there is an internal
violence in the act of exploiting the market and ravishing the
environment . . . Thus the forms of American disorganization
arise from the more naked drives within the culture itself, with the
workaday masks stripped away that have hidden the sadism
and ugliness which are part of the human condition and are to be
found in every culture.'

The essential truth about the gangster is not that he scorns
property but that he values it so highly as to be ruthless in seeking
short cuts for making it his own. 'The principles by which American
culture lives', continues Lerner, 'are those of freedom and acquisition,
and – where the two meet – the freedom of acquisition. There are
always a number of people who feel themselves left out of the operation of these principles, or who are too much in a hurry to wait, or
who feel resentful because others seem to start with an unfair set of
principles, and who therefore seek some equalizer. Since they feel at
a strategic disadvantage in the competition of life, they feel justified
in ignoring the usual inhibitions and in tearing down the accepted
cement of social relations.'

While deploring these dislocating energies, Lerner considers that
they are inevitably an inherent part of a society in which the pace
of life is set by freedom, competitiveness and acquisitiveness, part
of the price society pays for those principles: A 'society less free and
less dynamic – one of tradition and status, or one of totally state-
directed power – may escape some of these dislocations but be beset
by others. The whole impulsion of American culture is to raise
hopes and claims in the individual and spur him on to fulfil the
hopes and nail down the claims. At the same time it is too young a
society to have developed the kind of inner discipline which – let us
say, in England – can serve to inhibit the full sway of the impulsion.'

It is interesting, again, to find an American, at the final stage of
such analysis, finding it unavoidable within himself to advance a
defence for the gangster – again, the conviction that to expunge the
gangster would, in some almost mystical way, expunge a vital force
from the ethos in America. Examining the source of the gangster,
Lerner says: 'The racketeer is likely to come up from the slums,
reaching for quick affluence by breaking the windows of the mansion

of American success rather than by entering at the door . . . The violence with which intense slum youngsters imitate the values of the culture, even while distorting them, may be seen as their own form of flattery.' And he adds: 'What they do is legally and morally wrong, but instead of being a sign of the decay of American life it may be taken almost as a sign of its vitality.' Even the narcotics pusher 'represents the principle of creating a market, inherent in the market economy'.

In Landesco's 1929 report on *Organized Crime in Chicago* he examined 'The Gangster's Apologia *Pro Vita Sua*'. He wrote: 'The gangster's defence of his mode of life arises only when he comes into contact with the legitimate outside world. Only then does he become conscious of a conflicting way of living . . . The gang youth takes as his pattern the men in the neighbourhood who have achieved success. The men who frequent the neighbourhood gambling houses are good-natured, well-dressed, adorned and sophisticated, and above all they are American in the eyes of the gang boy.'

He quotes the case of a gangster returning on parole to Chicago from a term in prison to see that, as a result of bootlegging, 'Every wop has got a car in front of his home.' One of his friends asked him: 'Do you have a yen for being a poor working sap now?'

After the death of the gunman Angelo Genna an Italian woman and her Bohemian daughter-in-law were discussing the funeral.

'It sure was some funeral,' said the daughter-in-law. 'I was to a party with Mrs. Genna a couple of weeks ago and she wore an ermine coat and she was one sparkle of diamonds. Well, I thought, if you're gonna be straight you're gonna be poor.'

'But you see they get bumped off,' observed the older woman.

'Yeah, but they like to get bumped off,' was the reply and gave as an example a criminal known to them both and who later in an interview by the Landesco team explained that it was fun to be a marked man. To the adventurous young man, the risk itself was an attraction. Even if he has to stand up to police beatings and third degrees, he knows 'that it will bring him the plaudits of his group just as a young soldier does under the baptism of fire'. The young gangster 'contrasts the "easy money" and the "good times" of the gambler, beer runner, stick-up artist and con-man with the low wages and long hours of the "poor working sap". He speaks in flowing admiration of the power, the courage, the skill, the display and the generosity of the outstanding gang leaders. His glorification of the life and the characters of the underworld is complete evidence of the absence of any feeling of inferiority or shame about his own

criminal aspirations.' Landesco then gave the statement of a gambler
and confidence man interviewed during the investigation: 'The
men of the underworld are the brainiest men in the world. They have
to be because they live by their wits. They're always planning
something, a stick-up, a burglary, some new racket. They're constantly in danger. They have to think quicker and sharper than the
other fellow. They have to size up every man they meet, and figure
out what line to use on him. The leading men of the underworld
can move in every circle of society. They're at home in Chinatown,
along the main stem, in gambling dives, or in the best hotels and
the Gold Coast. When they have a lucky break they can live like
millionaires.'

Landesco found that the criminal became 'highly moralistic in
defence of his own criminality'. He would explain that the function
of his gang was that of protecting the interests of his national group
or neighbourhood; that he had got better conditions and wages for
an unorganized group he had absorbed into the racket; that he was
doing the public a valuable service in keeping the liquor flowing.
One interviewed gangster pointed to the black-bordered obituary
notice in a Miami newspaper of a fallen rum-runner named Red
Shannon. 'Look at the risks he took against the coast guard to bring
in genuine imported whisky for the pleasure of all of us,' he said.

'Yes,' objected the interviewer, 'but you gangsters bump each
other off, and a life is a life.'

'Okay,' said the other, 'but they choose that life. They choose to
fight their own battles and bury their own dead.'

Landesco further reported that he had rarely encountered remorse
among gangsters during four years' mixing with them. The gangster
is untroubled about his crimes, but 'he is stirred to the depths of
his feelings and sentiments by any charge of personal treachery to
his friends . . . The welfare, standards and laws of organized society
evoke no response in their hearts and minds. They seem to have no
conception of justice, of laws, and of courts, except as some external
superimposed system of oppression which they must by hook or by
crook obstruct and evade.'

But the Irish, the Sicilians and the Jews were not the only race-
groups who arrived in the United States at that time to be fed into
the mincing-machine of a strange, industrial labour market. Why,
then, was it rare to find a Swede, a German, a Greek, a Persian or a
Chinese in the beer-running trade or involved in the gun-battles?
It is too simple to attribute this to national character, to say that the
Scandinavian and the Asian are stoical, orderly and stable peoples,

and were therefore predisposed to adjustment to the new life and to earning citizenship by conscientious hard work. But the Irish, the Sicilians and the Jews had one experience in common that the other racial-groups had not: European backgrounds in which self-preservation had depended upon fighting and clannish solidarity against an internal enemy – the English land-owners and soldiery in Ireland, the French occupation forces in Sicily, and the anti-Semitism that ringed the Jews in almost every European city. The ancestors of the Prohibition gangsters had survived by using their muscles and their cunning. Their parents came over to America with an ingrained, bitter antipathy towards the theory of justice, which, in their experience, was more often than not used as a truncheon of despotism, and consequently they were not so easily dazzled and drawn by the American lodestar of middle-class managerial respectability. While other immigrant race-groups compliantly submerged into the general working mass and melted into the American spiritual amorphousness, the Irish, the Sicilians and the Jews retained a hard, set-mouthed distrust of the slogans and the exhortations which urged the infatuated to enter grindingly bad working conditions in a spirit of glory; they remained stubbornly embattled. This was especially true of the Sicilians. 'You can't convince a Sicilian that the police, the courts, or the law are on the square,' declared Helen A. Day, head resident of Eli Bates House, a Little Sicily social settlement, in the 'twenties. 'There is no faith in justice, only in the fixer who will talk to the judge. There is no respect for law. The law collects the taxes. It takes your children away when they are old enough to work, and puts them in school. It batters down your door and breaks open your kegs of wine. The Sicilian fails to comprehend all this.' The Irish, the Sicilian and the Jewish settlements produced young men who wanted the fat fruit of American prosperity and were willing to do anything to beat their way up out of the poverty of the slums to grab the plums – anything except the patient toil expected of them.

In the 'twenties there developed in Chicago an inflamed prejudice against the Sicilians, which took the crude form of flagrant wop-hatred, and there were efforts by liberals and the socially conscious to stem this and other currents of racialism. Burgess, in the Summary to the Landesco Report, wrote: 'The lack of full participation on the part of many immigrant communities in general public opinion is only matched by the ignorance of the native American of the lake-front neighbourhoods of conditions of life and thought in the river wards. More effective measures than in the past should be introduced to break through this lack of comprehension. At present the police and the public seem to hold the entire Sicilian colony responsible for any outrage committed by a single Sicilian. This attitude could not exist if there were understanding and friendly relations between immigrant communities and the outside American public.'

That was doubtless true, but it was an exculpation that could not affect the conviction of many people that the Sicilians were savage and dangerous outlaws, for this had foundation in fact. Between 1924 and 1929 – the peak years of slaughter in the beer war – there were 373 gang-killings. From these I have singled out the sixty-four more important mortalities, the inner-circle mobsters of staff-officer status, down from the generalissimo level of Dion O'Banion to the rank of field-commander. Of these sixty-four, forty-four are Italian names ... Genna, Vinci, Granata, Amatuna, Drucci, Scollo, Esposito, Lombardo, Signorelli, and so on. The rest are a roughly fifty-fifty mixture of Jewish and Irish names ... Gusenberg, Weinshank, Murphy, Zion, Feeley, Padden, Heyer, Berman, O'Donnell ... (Although this does not necessarily accurately reflect their racial origins, for the Sicilians had a penchant for adopting Irish aliases – Jack McGurn's real name was De Mora.) The Sicilians, there, suffered the heaviest casualties, but then there were more of them engaged in the feudal battles – and in the supply lines, where much of the illicit liquor was made in thousands of secret back-kitchen stills by working families whose only direct contact with the gangs was with the agent who paid them and the van-driver who collected the produce. The public's total condemnation of Chicago's Sicilians was doubtless unfair to some families who contrived to take the personal decision of holding free of underworld entanglements. Yet the truth is that, while the Irish and the Jews had geographically dispersed themselves more widely through the city and whereas the solid body of them were in honest occupations, the Sicilians belonged to a quite different category.

Until 1914 the Sicilian colony in Chicago was because of its isolated situation due to poor transportation and the barriers of river and industry, relatively untouched by American custom, a transplantation of Sicilian village life into the interior of an American city.

It was an utterly foreign community. The immigrants were mostly from villages near Palermo, such as Milicia, Vicari, Ciminna, Termini-Imerese, Monreale and the city of Palermo itself. Larrabee Street was a little Altavilla; the residents of Cambridge Street were from Alimena and Chiusa Sclafani; those on Townsend Street from Bagheria; those on Milton Street from Sambuca-Zabut. The colony centred around the church of St. Philip Benizi and Jenner School. The colony's principal thoroughfare, West Division Street, was lined with macaroni factories, soft drink parlours and Sicilian restaurants. The groups retained their village identity, living together, intermarrying and celebrating their local feasts. The women lived as they had in Sicily, never leaving their homes except to attend mass and make ceremonial visits. Adjacent garment factories made it possible for them to earn by doing finishing at home. There was no food for sale that was not distinctly foreign and it was impossible to buy butter, American cheese, pumpkins and other native vegetables in the colony. There were no bookshops. Italian newspapers had a limited circulation – because of the total illiteracy of the older immigrants – and Chicago papers none. Few of the immigrants had skills. Many who had worked in the orchards in Sicily got work in South Water Street as fruit packers and sellers, but most men were sent by their leaders – who occupied the same positions of power here as in Sicily – in labour-gangs to the railroads and to building contractors. But, reported Mary Leavitt, after 1914 a change had come about; the colony was disintegrating; old customs giving way. The children, by making contact with the outside world through work and school, 'have a vision of freedom and new opportunity. They are out of patience with the petty interests and quarrels of the older group, and refuse to have their lives ordered by their parents whom they know to be ignorant and inexperienced.'

Even so the Sicilians still remained, compared with all other foreign groups in Chicago an entrenched alien faction, like an invading striking-force encamped securely deep in enemy territory, and held in indissoluble league not only by blood, religion and common experience, but by an element that affected no other racial-group, by fear and secret conspiracy – by the Mafia.

22

The Black Hand

'What's the Mafia?'
Member of the Mafia

A T a 1950 Washington public hearing of Senator Estes Kefauver's Senate Crime Investigating Committee, Salvatore Moretti, a New Jersey gambler and racketeer, was asked: 'Do you know what the Mafia is?'

'What?' said Moretti.

'The Mafia,' repeated Counsel Rudolph Halley. 'M-a-f-i-a.'

'I'm sorry, I don't know what you're talking about.'

Halley said incredulously: 'You never heard that word before in your life? Do you read?'

'Nah,' said Moretti, sardonically. 'Like I says before – I don't read very much on account of my eyes.'

Similar blank puzzlement was encountered by the Committee in other cities. In Kansas City Tony Gizzo (identified as one of the leaders of that city's intensely active Mafia) asked: 'What's the Mafia? I don't even know what the Mafia is.' In Chicago Jack Dragna, a Los Angeles Sicilian resident, had read about the Mafia in the newspapers – but that was all – and Philip D'Andrea, once a gun-guard for Al Capone and President of the Unione Siciliana, conceded that he had heard of the Mafia when he was a child but 'knew nothing' of its current activities. Asked if it was a subject discussed among Italian families, D'Andrea replied: 'Oh, God, no. No, sir! It's not discussed out of the home.'

An indication of the hooded stealth that surrounds the Mafia is that it was not until the Kefauver Committee prised up the lid a few inches ten years ago that it was often discussed, or even heard about, outside an Italian home. 'Some of the witnesses called before us,' Kefauver reported after the hearings, 'who we had good reason to believe could tell us about the Mafia, sought to dismiss it as a sort of fairy tale or legend that children hear in Sicily where the Mafia originated. The Mafia, however, is no fairy tale. It is ominously real, and it has scarred the face of America with almost every conceivable type of criminal violence, including murder, traffic in narcotics, smuggling, extortion, white slavery, kidnapping and labour racketeering.'

Even then there was an understandable reluctance among adult citizens of a modern democracy to accept the idea that a kind of comic-strip secret society, replete with unwritten codes and a Black Hand insignia, was anything more than the rather pathetically infantile compensation-device for under-privileged foreign immigrants, a poor man's Masonry with a twist towards petty skullduggery. The Black Hander? – a mildly comic cartoon caricature with an inky handlebar moustache, a Chico Marx pudding-basin hat and a bomb like a smoking cannonball. It seemed patently absurd that such buffoon characters could form a national network of organized, corporation crime, intangibly but intrinsically in control of the industrial, political and social life of most large American cities.

In fact that was, and largely still is, the function of the Mafia. Some damage was done to the engine of the organization by the famous raid on the Apalachin convention in 1957. It was this that awoke the public at large to the reality of the Mafia, to the fact that it was neither a fable nor a triviality swollen into melodrama by newspaper feature-writers. On a November afternoon in 1957 Sergeant Edgar Croswell, of the New York State Police, was intrigued by the herd of Cadillacs, Chrysler Imperials and Lincolns with out-of-state number plates drawn up at the house at Apalachin, near Endicott, New York, which belonged to Joseph Barbara, proprietor of a soft-drink company. He took the chance of investigating. Inside were found sixty-five dons, the *capo mafioso*, or elders of brotherhood; many of them bolted, lumbering in their soft calf shoes over the fields towards the distant woods, but were rounded up. They sat, white-faced and smoking incessantly, these big, dignified dignitaries, and not talking. Pressed for explanations, each gave a similar one: poor Joe Barbara had a heart condition, and he had just happened to be passing by and had called in to cheer Joe up. Joe luckily happened to have two hundred pounds of steak on the premises to give the unexpected guests all a barbecue snack.

It emerged that these casual callers were from points as far-flung as Los Angeles, Dallas, Tucson, Kansas City, Cuba and Italy; also that twenty-five of them were related by blood or marriage; half of them had been born in Sicily or Italy, the rest were of Sicilian or Italian extraction; fifty-six of them had in aggregrate been arrested 275 times and shared a hundred convictions for serious crimes ranging from homicide and extortion to pimping and narcotics-trading.

The power of the organization may be judged by the fact that even this disclosure was no more than a temporary discomfort. In April 1960 Kefauver said dispiritedly in an interview: 'The gambling syndicates, united by the infamous Mafia, are worse today than they were ten years ago,' and a newspaper asked: 'What's the point of exposing the rackets and the Mafia bosses who run them? It all goes on still, as though the Kefauver Commission had never existed.'

It has had practice in survival. The Mafia may go back as far as the ninth century in Sicily, when the islanders secretly fought as an underground army against the Arab invaders. Another theory is that it was founded in the year 1282 when the Sicilian peasantry rose and slaughtered the French occupiers to the cry of 'Morte alla Francia Italia anela' ('Death to the French is Italy's cry'), from the initials of which the society is said to have taken its name. Historians doubt this. What is certain is that the tyrannizing and torturing by the Bourbon rulers in the middle of the eighteenth century welded the Sicilians together into a tough, consolidated, disciplined and ruthless alliance of families, and the man who could use a gun and knife accurately, and seized every opportunity to avenge his family and his race, was honoured and respected. Gradually the code of omerta evolved. In its general application this means a conspiracy of silence, but the five specific rules of the credo – which still bind the brothers as rigidly today – are: (1) A mafioso must aid his brother in trouble even at the risk of life or fortune. (2) A mafioso must obey implicitly the orders of a council of senior brothers. (3) A mafioso must regard an offence by an outsider against a brother as against himself and the brotherhood, and avenge it. (4) A mafioso must never appeal to the police, the courts or any government authority for redress. (5) A mafioso must never admit the existence of the brotherhood, discuss its activities or reveal the name of a brother. Death is the instant punishment for infringement of any of these rules.

Other characteristics developed. A mafioso is polite, reserved, disciplined – a difficult, and therefore recognizable, rule of conduct in a volatile Sicilian. He lives modestly, no matter how great his wealth; he eschews ostentation; he is abstemious, church-going, and a kind and attentive husband and father.

The later role of the Mafia in Sicily has also produced other characteristics. From being an underground rebel force, a self-protective family structure resisting invaders and oppressive land-owners, it began, for baser reasons, to exploit its power and reputation for implacable savagery. It entered into compacts with the landowners, and in turn began to live off the peasantry, by means of extortion, kidnapping and primitive racketeering. Gavin Maxwell, while living in Sicily to collect material for his book about the bandit Salvatore Giuliano, *God Protect Me From My Friends* and his later *The Ten Pains of Death*, found that today it is impossible there to own land, enter trade, do business or even be a successful criminal without paying 'tax' to the Mafia, that the Mafia takes its percentage on practically all money that changes hands. All produce – meat, fruit and even water – is under Mafia control: it is bought at starvation rates and sold at the highest price in the market.

There were two big migration waves of Mafia members to the United States, first in the 1890s, when the word passed back that the opportunities were glittering, and second in the 1920s when Mussolini, jealous of the authority of the Mafia, tried to stamp it out. They took with them their skill at blackmail, their promptness to murder and their unshakeable loyalty to each other. There is a further, at first knowledge baffling, aspect of the mafioso. His traditional conditioning has created a personality that to the outsider is as weirdly contradictory as the Bushido code of the Japanese officer who was able during the war to perform monstrously degenerate and sadistic violence upon prisoners and his own soldiers, and yet remain, according to his own lights, an honourable man. So with the mafioso. He does not belong to a club; he is the privileged initiate of a philosophy, and a mystique. In this private, esoteric morality he does no wrong even when he kills, violates and bleeds other humans. If he abides by the precepts of *omerta* he is, to himself and his brethren, in grace. He is, as a Catholic, at peace with God – although this may be a less weighty consideration than it would appear to be. Helen A. Day, head of a Little Sicily social settlement, wrote in 1929: 'He (the Sicilian peasant immigrant) is nominally a Roman Catholic. A vein of superstition holds him to the church, but not to the point where it clashes with his own interests. His attitude toward the saints is proprietous and patronizing rather than reverent.'

In America the mafioso found that the land and future were bright. He had immense status, springing from fear and personal experience of his methods, among his prey, the hordes of poor and illiterate peasants settled in the slum zones of New York, New Orleans and Chicago. As a further basic statute of the Mafia is that a brother does not labour with his own hands but lives off others, this he proceeded to do. The Black Hand came into existence. Quickly it was dismal general knowledge that when you received a written demand for money with the *La Mano Nera* insignia at the bottom, you paid up, or had a bomb containing nails and nuts tossed into your shop, or had your child kidnapped, or died yourself.

In Chicago between 1900 and 1925 three hundred Black Hand cases came to the notice of the police – and there were most likely twice as many which did not – from the Italian community neighbourhoods of West Taylor Street, Grand Avenue, Oak Street and Wentworth Avenue. A typical Black Hand letter, in its shattered English and floral phrases, is this one which was run down to its source – Joseph Genite, arrested at 1,001 South Racine Avenue, where a Mafia arsenal of dynamite, sawn-off shot-guns and revolvers was discovered: 'Most Gentle Mr. Silvani: Hoping that the present will not impress you much, you will be so good as to send me two thousand dollars if your life is dear to you. So I beg you warmly to put them on your door within four days. But if not, I swear this week's time not even the dust of your family will exist. With regards, believe me to be your friends. La Mano Nera.' During the 'twenties the telephone began to replace the letter as a means of informing the victim that the Black Hand's finger was on him.

In the early years of the century the Mafia speedily established its parasitic mode of living – and flaunted its pitiless methods of imposing its rule. In 1910 there were twenty-five unsolved Mafia murders in the Italian quarters of the city – stiletto-stabbings, shootings and clubbings; in 1911 forty; in 1912 thirty-three; in 1913 forty-two. In May 1913 the Chicago *Daily News* editorialized: 'In the first ninety-three days of this year, fifty-five bombs were detonated in the spaghetti zone. Not one of the fifty-five, so far as can be determined, was set for any reason other than the extraction of blackmail. A detective of experience in the Italian quarter estimates that ten pay tribute to one who is sturdy enough to resist until he is warned by a bomb. Freely conceding that this is all guess work, then 550 men will have paid the *Mano Nera* since 1 January. The Dirty Mitt never asks for less than a thousand dollars... Well-informed Italians have never put the year's tribute to the Black Hand at less than half-a-million dollars.'

Detectives soon found that inquiries usually led only to an impregnable wall of silence. A sergeant attached to the Chicago Avenue Station said: 'All the reply I could get was "Me don't know".' As early as 1910 it was found to be formidably hard to hold a Mafia suspect, for instantly unlimited money was at his disposal for legal aid, political intervention and the bribing of juries and witnesses.

The Mafia had swiftly perceived the importance, in these new conditions of political dog-fighting, of competing for the favours and prizes available to those cunning and savage enough. The history of this particular minority's struggle for self-determination through political emancipation and successes to political power is a dizzyingly confused one, for between 1916 and 1930 there was a flux of intermediate stages, at which factions of the immigrant Italians were in conflict with others – conflicts between those who had already joined interests with the established groups that preceded them in their wards and those who were rapidly growing strong and big enough to threaten the transitorily dominant. An example of this are the events in the 'Bloody Nineteenth Ward', where Alderman John Powers had been ruler since 1888, riding up on the backs of the Irish who then populated the ward. As the Italians filled the spaces vacated by the prospering Irish, they began to clamour for one of their own countrymen as alderman. The man who arose was Anthony D'Andrea, the unfrocked priest who controlled the red-light district and who had served a prison sentence on a counterfeit charge. In 1916 he was put forward as the candidate in opposition to James Bowler, junior alderman and Powers stooge, for the Democratic nomination. The stiletto and the gun and the bomb began to arrogate for the people's choice. In February 1916 Frank Lombardi, a Sicilian ally of Powers was shot dead in a saloon by D'Andrea's torpedoes. But the contenders were still too young and flimsily organized, and D'Andrea lost the election. During the next three years, D'Andrea tightened his hold on the district by becoming business agent for the Macaroni Manufacturers' Union, and muscled-in on the management of the unions of Sewer Diggers, Tunnel Workers and Water Pipe Extension Labourers.

During the political campaigns of the next four years meetings were bombed, murder threats were received by both sides, houses of the faction leaders blown up, policemen suspended, election results rigged, voters intimidated and several men on each side killed by gunmen. The climax came on 11 May 1921 when D'Andrea's political career was terminated by the explosion of a sawn-off shotgun; his funeral was royal in its splendour, with many public officials as pall-bearers and his own brother, a priest, officiating; the funeral was followed by the slaying of three of his followers, Andrew Orlando, Samuel Laspisa and Joseph Sinacola. D'Andrea's death also created a vacancy in the presidency of the Unione Siciliana, which he had held since 1919.

By the time Prohibition presented unprecedented means of easy money and town-rule, it may be seen that the pattern was already demarcated and the machinery efficiently working: through the agencies of the Unione Siciliana and the Italian Colonial Committee of the Italian Societies of Chicago, the Mafia had hegemonic control over the Italian communities of the city, and was later able to employ them as the labour in its bootleg distilleries and breweries; through the agencies of the ward political machines it was able to secure immunity for the illegal activities performed under cover of these nominally respectable bodies. By an odd paradox it was a group of free-lance Black Hand terrorists, and not Mafia high policy, that set in train the sequence of events that led to the Capone era and its development into the present Capone Syndicate. The diamond-flashing prosperity of Big Jim Colosimo, vice boss of the First Ward, attracted the attention of local extortionists. He received *La Mano Nera* letters threatening kidnapping for ransom, then torture and death. Colosimo's response was to summon from New York a promising young hood, the leader of the James Street gang who operated on the East River waterfront, Johnny Torrio. Torrio handled the situation efficiently for his new boss. The day after he arrived in Chicago, the Black Handers walked into Colosimo's café and told him that unless he instantly paid them twenty-five thousand dollars he would be executed. Colosimo agreed to deliver the money next day at four-thirty in the afternoon under a railroad viaduct in Archer Avenue. Instead of Colosimo and the package, waiting were Torrio and three other men, who met the blackmailers with a mass blast from four sawn-off shot-guns.

Torrio rose rapidly to a position of authority on Colosimo's staff, and in turn he recruited a new employee from New York, young Alphonse Capone. Torrio was a Sicilian, and, as he rose in the gang, rose also in the hierarchy of the Mafia until he was admitted to full status as a *capo mafioso*. Such an honour was not accessible to Capone, for he was an Italian and therefore not eligible to membership of the closed order; but, as his abilities became more evident and his power swelled, the Chicago *capi mafiosi* increasingly were prepared to accept his leadership in the area of practical crime, consult him and work in partnership with him. The point came when Capone sat in at Mafia inner council conferences, supervised the appointment of new dons and controlled, at one remove, the Unione Siciliana.

Yet in the dark depths of these weedy waters there was incessant intrigue and dissension, for it was an unusual situation for a non-Sicilian to have the influence and sway within the Mafia that Capone had. His main antagonist was Joe Aiello, of the Aiello brothers, a partner of Bugs Moran, Capone's main enemy during the beer wars.

The crisis came when in November 1924 the presidency of the Unione fell vacant due to the death of Mike Merlo. After that it became the hottest seat in Chicago. There developed a ferocious internal contest for the position which carried with it so much power in the American underworld. Capone wanted to ensure that the chair stayed under his influence; the Aiellos and the Gennas, fanatically Sicilian, were determined to end the infiltration of racial impurities. Without waiting for guidance to arrive from Frankie Yale, American head of the Mafia and Capone's old Brooklyn boss, Angelo Genna was thrust by his supporters into the office, in defiance of Yale's directive that Torrio should become temporary caretaker until the disagreements had been resolved. Angelo was quickly disposed of, shot down on 26 May 1925. Sam Samoots Amatuna, the next aspirant, was killed that autumn as he sat, peacefully relaxed, having a manicure in a barber's shop. It was this combination of commercial competition in the liquor business and the Mafia rivalry that brought about the internecine flare-up of the mid 'twenties and the attack upon Torrio. Torrio was ambushed by Moran–Aiello gunmen, severely wounded, and abdicated in fright.

Determined not to allow the rebels to grab the seat of power, Capone travelled to New York and urged upon Yale the appointment of Tony Lombardo. Yale, nervous of both spreading the conflagration and bringing the anger of the Aiello–Moran group down upon his own head, refused to become involved in the dispute. Instead, he urged Capone to go back to Chicago and, 'for the good of the Unione,' to settle the matter amicably. Capone returned, but almost immediately reported to Yale that an Aiello–Moran machine-gun nest had been discovered overlooking the cigar store patronized by himself and Lombardo – a plot which, it was then suspected, was manufactured by Capone himself to discredit Aiello to Yale. Finally, despite Yale's doubts, Capone had his way and Lombardo was installed.

Increasingly suspicious of Yale's goodwill, Capone assigned one of his most dependable spies and shadow-men, James De Amato, to feed him information about Yale's activities – especially in regard to the persistent hijacking of liquor which the New York gang had undertaken to channel from the Long Island reception ports by road to Chicago, and which Capone suspected was being short-circuited by the men who were supposed to be getting it safely on its way. Within a month De Amato was dead – shot down in a Brooklyn street. There was no certain proof that Yale was responsible, but Capone no longer doubted that he was being double-crossed.

The breach between them widened and two years later Capone passed death sentence upon the Mafia chief. On 1 July, 1928, Yale was driving along Forty-fourth Street in the Homewood section of Brooklyn in his new Lincoln car, when a black Nash sedan carrying Illinois licence plates raced out of a side turning and spurted alongside, and from it were released a hundred ·45-calibre bullets into his body – the first time that a machine-gun had been used in New York gang warfare. Yale's car, with him dead at the wheel, lurched over the kerb and into the front of a house. When the police examined him, they found his revolver still in his right coat pocket, undrawn. Torrio, back in Brooklyn and long recovered from his wounds, acceded to the national Mafia throne.

As Capone's prime minister, Lombardo had been presented with despotic rule over fifteen thousand Sicilians in his own city, and with far-reaching influence over the Sicilian communities of Pittsburgh, Detroit, St. Louis, Cleveland, Philadelphia and New York through the Unione branches in those areas. His affiliations with the Mafia, with City Hall and with Capone were as plaited as a pigtail. The Unione – renamed the Italo-American Union during the mayoral election of 1928, presumably to diminish its 'foreign', Mafia overtones in the eyes of the voters – had its offices in the Loop, at the Hartford Building on South Dearborn Street, two blocks away from City Hall, conveniently near for the traffic of business that passed between them. By the time Lombardo succeeded, behind its façade as a benevolent and patriarchal body, a kind of miniature Welfare State for Sicilian families, thrived a ten million dollars a year business which controlled the supply of sugar to the wildcat distilleries of Chicago's West Side and extending to Cicero, Chicago Heights and Melrose Park, and supervised the alky-cooking network, the 2,500 home stills which were the source of much of Capone's bootleg spirits. To Lombardo were submitted for arbitration all matters appertaining to the Sicilian community, including breaches of the law. Liaison between the Unione and city administration was smoothly co-ordinated: the city sealer was Daniel A. Serritella, a personal friend of Capone, frequent guest at his Florida house, and Republican committee-man of the First Ward.

In his first flush of exaltation at attaining this proud post, Lombardo had had printed a biographical sketch, straight and glowing from his own pen. It read: 'Chicago owes much of its progress and its hope of future greatness to the intelligence and industry of its two hundred thousand Italians, whose rise in prestige and importance is one of the modern miracles of a great city. No people have achieved so much from such small beginnings, or given so much for what they received in the land of promise to which many of them came penniless. Each life story is a romance, an epic of human accomplishment.

'Antonio Lombardo is one of the most outstanding of these modern conquerors . . . Mr. Lombardo came to America twenty-one years ago. He was one of hundreds who cheered joyously, when, from the deck of the steamer, they saw the Statue of Liberty, and the skyline of New York, their first sight of the fabled land, America. With his fellow countrymen he suffered the hardships and indignities to which the United States subjects its prospective citizens at Ellis Island without complaint, for in his heart was a great hope and a great ambition. After he had landed, he paid his railroad fare to Chicago, and came here with just twelve dollars as his initial capital . . . Mr. Lombardo, however, accepted the hardships as part of the game, and with confidence in his own ability and assurance of unlimited opportunities, began his career . . . He became an importer and exporter . . . His political influence is due largely to his interest in civic affairs and his championship of measures for maintaining and improving standards of living, as well as his activity in the support of charities and benevolent institutions. Like most successful men, he has received much, but has given more to the community in which he lives. It is to such men that Chicago owes her greatness.'

It was a brief spasm of glory. On an afternoon in September 1928, at the height of the home-going rush, Lombardo left the Unione headquarters with his two bodyguards, Joseph Lolordo and Joseph Ferraro, and walked through the Loop. As they passed a restaurant near the corner of State and Madison, two men emerged from the crowds of shoppers and typists, and opened fire. Lombardo sagged with the gaping holes of dum-dum bullets in his skull. Ferraro, hit in the spine, dropped beside him fumbling with his revolver. Lolordo, untouched, drew his gun and raced after the killers into Dearborn, but was overtaken by Policeman John Marcusson who, believing him to be one of the assassins, jammed him against a wall with a gun in his stomach until a squad car arrived. It was one of the most insolently brazen of all Chicago's gang murders. Hundreds witnessed it; scores came forward with descriptions of the killers; but finally a line was drawn under it in the police dossier with the familiar concluding words: 'Slayers not apprehended.' Lolordo had recognized them. In his first anger he had pleaded with Policeman Marcusson to be allowed to pursue them, but at the inquest his mind had gone blank: he could identify no one. Similarly, Ferraro, questioned on his death bed by Assistant State's Attorney Samuel Hoffman, observed *omerta* and would give no information.

It was the eve of 8 September, the festival of Our Lady of Loreto, the American Italians' biggest feast, when a week is spent in carnival and worship. Just east of Halsted Street, in Little Sicily, the streets this September were bare of bunting and banners. Instead, on the church of San Filippo Benizi, Father Louis Giambastiani tacked upon the door a notice in Italian which read: 'Brothers! For the honour you owe to God, for the respect of your American country and humanity – pray that this ferocious manslaughter, which disgraces the Italian name before the civilized world, may come to an end.'

During that year twelve of Father Giambastiani's parishioners had been killed in Mafia and gang warfare, and 75 thousand dollars' worth of property destroyed by bombs. Lombardo was the third president of the Unione to die by gun-fire. Capone, unshaven in the Mafia manner to display his grief, cut short his holiday in Florida and returned to Chicago to take the crisis in hand and to grace the funeral. It was customarily theatrical. Under Cardinal Mundelein's ban excluding gangsters from benefit of clergy and consecrated ground, and their corpses from Catholic churches, Lombardo was placed in a mausoleum at Mount Carmel Cemetery and there his family and friends had to be content with an oration by a civilian, a male voice quartet singing 'Nearer, My God, To Thee', and Capone's tribute to 'an honoured citizen'. But prior to that there had been a two-mile *cortège* – seventeen cars of flowers, and twelve pall-bearers in tuxedos for the bronze coffin, which was crested with a brass eagle and draped with a silk Stars and Stripes and the Italian flag. The centerpiece was a huge floral structure in which T. LOMBARDO was woven in pink and white carnations. Before it started on its way, police frisked the cars for machine-guns and the mourners for revolvers.

At his death the 'honoured citizen' came in for close scrutiny by Frank J. Loesch, president of the Chicago Crime Commission. Following the recent kidnapping by Black Handers of a ten-year-old Italian boy, Judge Frank Comerford of the Superior Court had called for the 'annihilation of the Mafia'. Now, Mr. Loesch said: 'Judge Comerford has acted on a conviction that has been steadily growing among the people: that law enforcement has broken down completely when it comes to the arrest, prosecution, and attempt to convict such gang murderers as the Mafia gunmen. Who are the gangsters seemingly tied up to this family tree? Scarface Al Capone, vice, gambling and liquor king, and the recently murdered Tony

Lombardo. Lombardo is dead, but his organization – the Mafia – is still organized and ready to function uninterruptedly . . . All the kidnappings, blackmail, terrorism, murders, and countless other crimes committed in the name of the dread Mafia sprang from the minds of Lombardo and the men who are now fighting to take the place vacated by his death. It was Lombardo who ruled the alcohol cookers. They bought their sugar from him or they died. The people paid him tribute on their cheese and their olive oil. And part of these spoils, the extortions from the fathers of kidnapped children, the profits of the alcohol sales, went into the political coffers . . . The Mafia must be suppressed here as it was by Mussolini in Italy. The upper hand which the criminals are obtaining in this city by their alliance with politicians not only gives the city a bad reputation, but it will certainly end in anarchy if permitted to go on a few years longer.'

Capone did not allow the grief and the ritual to delay him in ensuring that the Unione remained in his grip. On 14 September Pasqualino Lolordo, elder brother of Joseph, Lombardo's body-guard, friend and associate of both Lombardo and Capone, was inducted into the presidency. He lasted until the following January.

On 8 January, 1929, three men called at Patsy Lolordo's apartment, in a block on West North Avenue. Lolordo welcomed them effusively and took them into the living-room; wine, whisky, sandwiches, pastries and a box of cigars were brought out, and they settled down to amiable chatter. Mrs. Lolordo was ironing in the kitchen. For an hour she heard them talking and laughing, and her ear then caught a shouted toast: 'Here's to Pasqualino', and the scraping of chairs as the guests rose to drink his health. A crash of shots followed immediately. She rushed into the room in time to see one of the men holding a smoking gun in one hand and with the other, in the considerate manner of the brotherhood, gently easing a pillow under Lolordo's head as he lay twitching in a lake of his own blood on the floor; his hand still clutched his wine glass. The three men pushed by Mrs. Lolordo and left.

Sergeants Thomas Foley and Joseph Cullerton, of the Racine Avenue station, picked up a ·38 calibre revolver on the stairs and another in the living-room. Eleven bullets had hit Lolordo in face, neck and shoulders; seven more had missed and struck the wall and fireplace. In his bedroom the police found a sawn-off shotgun and the draft of a new constitution for a North-West Side branch of the Unione, which professed its intention 'to improve the education of its members, morally, economically and socially'.

In her initial distress Mrs. Lolordo identified a police photograph of Joseph Aiello as one of the killers; later, in the return of calm, she remembered her duty as a good Mafia wife, retracted her former statement and said she had never before seen the men who were on such intimate terms of friendship with her dead husband; of only one fact could she be certain – they were not Italians. The coroner's summation was: 'Slayers not apprehended.'

Meanwhile, Aiello, having failed in direct attempts upon Capone's life, including bribing a restaurant chef to salt his soup with prussic acid and offering an open reward of fifty thousand dollars for his murder, had been trying more devious measures. These included the wooing of Scalise and Anselmi. Promising them positions of command once Capone was liquidated and the regional Mafia was under his authority, Aiello persuaded them to urge upon Capone that Guinta would be an admirable replacement for Lolordo in the Unione throne. Such subtleties did not bemuse Capone. He had developed an espionage network of bartenders, waiters, shoeshine boys, doormen and hotel clerks as well as men in key positions in government and police departments, who passed on any overheard information that might interest the Syndicate, and had also a staff of engineers who maintained a wire-tapping service. From these sources, and from general contact men, a dossier on Guinta's background and affiliations was quickly gathered together. His sponsors, and the planned coup, were laid bare. Guinta, together with Scalise and Anselmi, were executed with bizarre ceremonial at the banquet of enthronement, when, hazy with chianti and food, they were brained with a baseball bat and pumped full of bullets.

Unsettled and irritated by these internal diversions from the main object of money-making, Capone then planned the move that was to provide the foundations for the corporate national organization that the Mafia was to become. He called together the senior *capi mafiosi* from all the big American crime centres. That meeting in Atlantic City in May 1929 was of historical interest, for there Capone explained to the suspicious Sicilians his grand design for a nationwide syndicate of business, covering not only bootlegging, which was by then beginning to look a doubtful long-term investment, but of gambling, prostitution, extortion and labour racketeering. Territories were defined, spheres of influence delineated, old feuds healed; there was much handshaking and a general agreement to give the daring and imaginative plan for cartel crime a trial for the common good.

And it worked. Not only was it economically sound, but it was found that punishment of defaulters and the disciplining of intruders could be more safely and effectively carried out. Murder Inc., the name given to the pool of trained professional executioners under the control of Albert Anastasia in New York, operated with cool thoroughness. From then on a Mafia murder was never committed by local gunmen. The executioners were transferred from some other city, and did their job as anonymous strangers, emotionally uninvolved by personal acquaintance with the victim, and providing no links that could help the police. The adoption to the machine age did not affect the old-world ritual of such an operation against a *mafioso*. The 'kiss of death' was still exchanged between the chosen executioners. The victim was still, if possible, lured into a benign state for his last hours: wined and dined until enjoyably soporific, whereupon the gun was raised upon his skull from behind and he was despatched in comfort from this world. In pious respect of his memory, the brethren still allowed stubble to grow on their chins from the day of the demise until the day of the funeral. For a non-*mafioso*, less thoughtfulness was shown: for security reasons, the assault had to be conclusively mortal, but finesse was sacrificed to ferocity. But the traditional rule that a *mafioso* must be killed suddenly and unexpectedly still applied. He must suffer 'the *lupera* sickness'. *Lupera* is heavy handmade lead buckshot filed into pyramidal shape, still used in Sicily executions and which is particularly lethal. Today this tedious handicraft has been replaced by bullets of heavy calibre – but the condemned is still shot in the head and neck. Even if the wounds prove not to be instantaneously fatal, it renders the victim incapable of talking much prior to his death.

Yet more coercive than the ever-present weapon of death for failure or betrayal is the ethic of the Mafia, the desire to remain in grace, to be worthy of the respect of the brethren. Status within the group is the criterion, and that this is achieved by income derived from selling heroin to high-school children or running houses of prostitution is of little relevance. The disciplinarian system, harsher than would be considered supportable in any modern army or business organization, is accepted as essential to the security and purity of the brotherhood. It is an anti-social ideology passed down from father to son and through blood-united families. The Mafia came to America with its warped, sinister traditions intact; from Capone the outsider, the non-Sicilian upstart, it learned how to adapt them to a Western industrialized society. But Capone could never have realized the potentialities of the system he forged.

'Legitimate business is used,' writes Frederic Sondern, 'among other reasons, for the purpose of creating monopolies, the investment of funds from illegal enterprises, and as fronts to cover illegal activities. It is not a coincidence that many members of the brother-hood who are known to be active in the narcotics traffic also control sections of the New York waterfront and have interests in trucking companies, import-export houses, and the wholesaling of cheese, olive oil and other imported produce. This means that a kilo of heroin (about thirty-three ounces) placed in a barrel of olive oil or a wheel of cheese before shipment will be in "safe" hands from the time it reaches dockside in the United States until it is delivered to the buyer.'

Testimony before the McLellan Committee also suggested that the possible reason for the racketeers' interest in both chemical and garment industries is that the common chemical acetic anhydride, used in the manufacture and treatment of rayon, is also used in the conversion of raw opium into the morphine base from which heroin is made.

A simple straight line of progression may be drawn from the brash bootleg days of Chicago's gang warfare under the generalship of Capone. But the problem that is the inheritance of that period is not only the exposure and elimination of the Mafia. It is how America can employ the delicately fine surgery to cut out the rackets – the fingers of the Black Hand – that have intertwined throughout the economy.

PART FIVE

The Big Fellow

'Nobody's on the legit.'

'Hell, it is a business. I'm thirty-two years of age and I've lived a thousand.'

AL CAPONE

23

'Al, We're With You'

'You boys just made a mistake. I'm going to give you a break.'
AL CAPONE *to a police squad*

> *Waiting by the window*
> *my feet enwrapped with the dead bootleggers of Chicago*
> *I am the last gangster, safe at last,*
> *waiting by a bullet-proof window.*
>
> *I look down the street and know*
> *the two torpedoes from St. Louis.*
> *I've watched them grow old*
> *. . . guns rusting in their arthritic hands.*

'The Last Gangster', from GREGORY CORSO'S Gasoline

AT the door of Cook County Jail on an October morning in 1931, which, unbeknown to him then, was the last meridian moment of his singular career, Alphonse Capone paused on his way inside to issue a statement to the press. It was a sentence that, in its poignant bafflement and hurt, classically expressed the attitudes that set the psychotic criminal irreclaimably apart from society.

'It was a blow below the belt,' he said, 'but what can you expect when the whole community is prejudiced against you?'

Capone had just stepped down from the dock after receiving an eleven-year prison sentence for tax evasion, a sentence he managed to postpone until the following May, during which time he remained on bail pending appeal. Until that summer, when, only by the most stubborn persistence had the Federal Government of the United States of America hauled him into court, Capone had been one of the most obviously powerful men in the world. In this year of 1931 Mussolini had been dictator of Italy for nine years; the National Socialists had just won a hundred seats in the Reichstag, and it was only months ahead before Hitler became chancellor and constituted the Third Reich; Stalin had been supreme head of the Soviet Union for seven years. All, in this developing age of rule by violence and victimization, were more sombrely fearsome by far than an American gangster whose ambitions were neither political nor nationalistic, but who used politics obliquely as a means of obtaining money and the power through which more money was obtainable. Yet perhaps all of them were part of the same pattern of that darkening time, an age when enforcement of policy by gun, cruelty and oppression, in contempt of the theoretical canons of law, became naked and ubiquitous. Capone himself seemed hazily conscious of inherent similarities. As he walked, handcuffed, from the courtroom to his cell through volleys of exploding flashbulbs, he said with melancholy pride to Eliot Ness, the F.B.I. prohibition agent who was largely responsible for his conviction: 'Jeez, you'd think Mussolini was passin' through.' And, in 1931, when Hitler was aged forty-two, Mussolini forty-eight and Stalin fifty-two, Capone was but thirty-six. For a comparatively young man, a slum delinquent of foreign birth and little schooling, his accomplishments up to that year had been prodigiously impressive.

The President in status and several hundred industrialists in material possessions were mightier and more influential Americans than Capone, yet not by so great a margin, and, in concentrated autonomy, were much less so. Probably no one man since Cesare Borgia's rule of Rome had so inexorably controlled a city for purposes so piratically self-interested and contrary to principles of government in the society of which he was a member. In his four years of total power, between 1927 and 1931, Capone's authority ramified beyond Chicago and beyond the state of Illinois. 'He was', wrote Paul Sann, 'mayor, governor and machine boss all rolled into one. He gave the orders; the people's elected servants carried them out and kept their mouths shut. His authority was so great it could not be measured.' The gross income of his business in liquor, gambling, prostitution and assorted rackets ran into millions of dollars annually. Chicago's twenty thousand speakeasies operated, with only sporadic and ineffectual interference from the Federal Prohibition squads, openly and busily for years. He ran an organization which owned or had stakes in breweries, distilleries, warehouses, truck-companies, garages, bars, nightclubs, dance-halls, restaurants, brothels, race-tracks and casinos, and which was beginning at the time of his retirement to infiltrate its extortion racket into unions, film production and dozens of trades and industries. He amassed a fortune of twenty million dollars – an incredible sum that is not my estimate but that of the Internal Revenue Office. He was the commanding officer of a private army of seven hundred storm-troops, and for auxiliaries had call upon an estimated sixty per cent of Chicago's police force who were on his pay-roll. In that four-year period there were 227 gang murders; there were no convictions. (In the forty-year period from 1919 to 1959 there were 929 gang murders committed in Chicago. Only seventeen culprits were convicted – and several of those were freed on appeal to the Supreme Court.) He took over the suburban district of Cicero with a military efficiency and converted it into a vice-reservation, a day-and-night resort of 161 cabarets, call-houses and dice-parlours, and when he seized control of the town of fifty thousand people he nominated his own group of bought politicians and posted squads of gunmen at the polling stations to ensure their election. His influence extended into journalism; there was certainly one reporter – Jake Lingle of the Chicago *Tribune* – on his pay-roll, and probably others in regular receipt of patronage in return for sympathetic coverage. Even during his prison term the headlines rang with fond concern: CAPONE GAINS ELEVEN POUNDS and CAPONE DOESN'T GO TO CHURCH ON SUNDAY. He was a celebrity swelling into a legend. Citizens scurried to the kerb to stare when his three-and-a-half ton armour-plated Cadillac, with bullet-proof glass and tail-gunner's movable back window, passed with its escort of two armed scout-cars. Lucky out-of-town and foreign visitors among the crowds had their stimulating glimpse of the famous face, stuck with cigar, in the dim haze of silken cushions, perhaps the quick glint of one of his famous diamonds, behind the bodyguard in the front seat with Thompson sub-machine-gun handily across his knees. Tourist buses had 'Capone Castle' – his Hawthorne Inn headquarters in Cicero – and his Metropole Hotel city headquarters on their itinerary. A press photograph of him with Jack Sharkey, the boxer, and Bill Cunningham, former All-American football player, which was nationally circulated by an agency, was captioned 'Gangland's King'. When he attended a prize-fight or race-meeting the fact was mentioned by the sports columnist. In 1929 the London *Daily Mail* despatched Mr. Edgar Wallace to Chicago to write a series of articles about the Capone régime, and he was only one of many European journalists who were hastening towards a tastily juicy story of smoking guns and brazen daring, an improbable Wild West melodrama here for the harvesting in a modern city. The articles, interviews, biographies and personal reminiscences proliferated, and accuracy of detail was not allowed dingily to stifle the rich potentialities of such material. If one collated all the alleged direct quotations from Capone himself that were printed at that period, a curious portrait of a garrulous but primly stilted Boy Scout would emerge. This watchful and wary crime-syndicalist, who, except when angry (which was rare to see) or relaxed with wine (which was not often in the presence of outsiders), confined his conversation outside the confederate circle to pleasantries with reporters, would seem, from the printed records that remain, to have been able to discourse learnedly upon philosophy or Napoleon's tactical errors ('the world's greatest racketeer, but I could have wised him up on some things'). One 1929 newspaper report of his activities during his short prison sentence in Philadelphia described him as 'a stern highbrow' and cited his 'favourite authors' as Shakespeare and Shaw; another dispatch reported that he was occupying himself by reciting Balzac and Victor Hugo. He was even, in one odd publication in 1931, *Carrying a Gun for Al Capone* by the sculptor-painter Jack Bilbo – who later admitted that he had never been to Chicago – represented as being a reader of Robert Louis Stevenson and Karl Marx, and as talking like a ruminative cardigan-clad don in an English repertory drama: 'Sentimentality is the main danger which threatens us in life. One either has to rid oneself of it or one is entirely in its power. The day will come when our softness will rise up and we will flounder in it.' Most of the myth-making that was then beginning had at least a few more roots in reality, even if it was as fatuous as Edward D. Sullivan's description of him in a 1931 book, *Chicago Surrenders*, as 'the best billiard player in the Greenpoint section of Brooklyn', but there was also a vast quantity of glamour-endowing mawkishness about Capone in Sunday paper serials, in 'detective' magazines and in quick-turnover booklets, lavish with those smudgily sinister pictures of corpses sprawled beside fire-hydrants. One of these, *X Marks The Spot*, published in 1930, is a fair specimen of the tone of excited, fulsome admiration thinly veneered with moralizing that was current then. Beside a full-page frontispiece ran this caption: 'Here is an excellent likeness of Alphonse Capone, the big boy of Chicago Gangland, and the greatest gangster that ever lived. When King Al poses for a photograph, which isn't often, he always turns his right cheek to the camera. The left one is disfigured by an ugly scar. Legend has it that Capone was struck by a machine-gun bullet when he was a soldier in France.' (That, as will be seen later, is one little Capone-inspired legend that collapsed.) Within, the story of Capone's life, which was on the level of the 'official' biography of a film star in a fan-club circular, began: 'He is a glamorous figure, an actual part of the American scene. Legends are already springing up around him. The magazine stands are aflame with underworld stories about the man with the gat who wears a tuxedo and has a liveried chauffeur. With no intention to eulogize him, Capone unquestionably stands apart as the greatest and most successful gangster who ever lived. The difference between him and all other gangsters is that he is possessed of a genius for organization and a profound business sense.' All the documentary comment induced was not quite so banally degenerate as that but there were more sober and grudging tributes to his talent. An internal revenue officer, charged with investigating his tax dues, told Pasley: 'Capone has exceptional business ability and would have gone far in any legitimate line. If he had only been honest, what a hero he would have made for a Horatio Alger tale.' Capone and his régime also brought about novels such as W. R. Burnett's *Little Caesar*, plays such as Ben Hecht's *The Front Page* and Edgar Wallace's *On The Spot*, and a cycle of brilliantly harsh gangster films of which *Scarface*, directed by Howard Hawks and with Paul Muni as the psychopathic hoodlum Tony Camonte, a name with, perhaps, a deliberate onomatopoeic quality, was the best. (In 1932 in America it was billed, deludingly, as 'The Shame of a Nation', when there was, in mass unemployment and hunger, a far more bitter shame abroad. In Britain it was extensively cut, banned completely by the Manchester Watch Committee, and the Council of the Cinematograph Exhibitors' Association recommended that it should be sent back to the censor for 'further consideration because of its morbidity and bloodshed'.)

Fact was inextricably scrambled with fiction. It was fact that this new dignitary, the paunchy pallid-faced Big Fellow who was beginning to tower above the officially eminent with a unique glitter and who was giving Chicago a peculiar global fame, was among the committee appointed to welcome Commander Francesco da Pinedo, Mussolini's round-the-world goodwill pilot in 1927, together with Leopold Zunini, Italian Consul-General, Dr. Ugo M. Galli, Chicago Fascisti President, and Judge Bernard P. Barasa, representing the Mayor. It was a fact that he was lionized by the smart – it was cute to know Al; that he entertained at his Florida estate seventy-five guests at a time, many of them fashionable and famous; that he rebuked and instructed politicians and judges over the telephone from his Metropole Hotel office; that on the occasion of the second Dempsey–Tunney fight he threw the biggest, and wettest, party seen before or since in Chicago – it blinded on for three days, the liquor bill (even at his wholesale rates) was fifty thousand dollars, and it was attended by socialites, movie stars, politicians and theatre and boxing celebrities from all over America.

So it may well have also been a fact that – as he once bragged – in seven years he 'fooled away' ten million dollars pocket money on gambling. He customarily shot craps for fifty and a hundred thousand dollars a throw, and never for less than a thousand unless with impoverished friends; he bet a hundred thousand at a time on a horse race (but would not gamble on the stock market – 'Wall Street is crooked'). Appropriate to his station, he lived a sybaritically luxurious life. His custom-built car cost thirty thousand dollars, his ring, an eleven-carat blue-white diamond from the South African Jagersfontein mines, fifty thousand dollars. His casual munificence with his thickly wadded bankroll became one of the romances of that hard-bitten city where nothing had ever previously been for free. He was once charged – and paid without wincing – a thousand dollars for a round of drinks in the Country Club, an exclusive New York speak run by Belle Livingstone, dubbed by the papers 'the Most Dangerous Woman in Europe' when she was the outstandingly lurid playgirl of the Edwardian age. His personal gratuity rates were five dollars for a newsboy, ten dollars for a hat-check girl and a hundred dollars for a waiter. There were many such heart-warming stories as that of the hard-up hat-check girl who, decent but desperate, pleaded for a position in one of his brothels to support her ailing mother. 'Forget it. Not a nice girl like you,' said Al, peeling off a hundred dollars for her. At Christmas he spent a hundred thousand dollars on miscellaneous gifts. All the year round he distributed diamond-inlet belts to his new friends and ruby-set gold cigarette cases to politicians and business associates, whose cellars were also kept stocked with wine and champagne (not the speakeasy brands). During his only other prison term – a sojourn in Philadelphia in 1929 for carrying a gun – he bought a thousand dollars' worth of the convicts' handiwork, ship models, cigarette boxes, carvings and other *objets d'art*, and posted them to friends as Christmas presents. He sent 1,200 dollars to a deserving Philadelphia orphanage. With probably no traditional knowledge to draw upon, he regarded this huge industrial city as his estate and assumed the function of a squire, a benevolent despot capriciously distributing largesse among his villeins. In hard winters the poor of Cicero could draw all the groceries, clothing and fuel they needed from coal depots and department stores on the Capone account. His individual acts of charity, from a fifty dollar loan to an outright gift to a destitute Italian family, were many. He paid the hospital bills of a woman bystander wounded in a street gun-battle. It is not altogether astonishing that today there are many respectable citizens in Chicago who speak glowingly of Capone's philanthropy and particularly point out that in the early Depression days it was the Capone gang who set up the first soup-kitchens and block-restaurants for the distribution of free food on Thanksgiving Day.

When this real-life Robin-Hood appeared at a North Western University rally, ten thousand Boy Scouts, young eyes a-sparkle with hero worship, spontaneously set up the yell, to the embarrassment of their troop leaders: 'Good old Al'. Older people, too, made Capone what Pasley described as 'the object of a sort of hero worship'. Upstanding citizens sorted out the opportunity in public places of grasping his hand. A Chicago civil engineer, on a business visit to Philadelphia during Capone's stay in the Eastern Penitentiary, requested an interview with him, introduced himself, shook his hand and told him: 'Al, we're with you.'

Perhaps one should remind oneself, however, that this one-man welfare state had at his disposal for his good works the lion's share of the 150 million dollars, which was the sum estimated that marauding and extortion cost the State of Illinois annually.

At one point, around the time that he had been described as 'a cancer' and 'America's Nineteenth Amendment', and was saying mournfully: 'There's a lot of grief attached to the limelight,' Capone considered hiring Ivy Lee, the publicist who pulled off the most formidable assignment in public relations, that of popularizing the loathed, union-smashing millionaire John D. Rockefeller, Snr. This did not come about, possibly because Capone recognized that his own instincts for publicity were as sound as any advice he could buy from Lee. By 1930 he was a celebrity of a size rare in the pre-television age. Pasley, writing at that period, described him as 'America's Exhibit A. Al had grown from civic to national stature. He was an institution,' and Pasley grouped him in a small glorious host in the annals of enduring Americana with Will Rogers, Henry Ford, Rin Tin Tin, Babe Ruth, Charles Lindbergh, Texas Guinan and Al Smith.

As it has turned out, Pasley sold Capone short. I suspect that today although Ford and Rin Tin Tin might be known to many children in Europe, Africa, the Far East and even perhaps the Soviet Union, most would instantly recognize one name only among that list and that, if language was a barrier to explanation, they would be able to communicate their knowledge with a levelled finger and a staccato rat-a-tat-tat.

He outlasted four chiefs of police, two municipal administrations, three United States district attorneys, and a regiment of Federal prohibition agents; he survived innumerable crime drives, grand jury investigations, reform crusades, clean-up election campaigns, police shake-ups, and Congressional inquiries and debates. He killed between twenty and sixty men himself – there is no way of ascertaining any nearer tally – and was responsible by delegation for the murder of at least four hundred others, and was never charged with one of them. His ultimate' arrest and commitment to jail on 24 October 1931 came about from the doggedness of the Intelligence Unit of Elmer Irey, chief of the United States Treasury Enforcement Branch; but it was not really the forces of law and order that defeated Capone. When he was struck down his strength and menace were failing. Capone had been defeated by three unexpected things: the approach of repeal, which was to dissolve his black-market in booze; depression, which dried to a dribble the easy money of the golden days; and disease which was eating him from within.

Now, thirty years after that febrile and predatory era, it is evident that Al Capone will have a more durable, definitive place in history, both popular and serious, than any of those other candidates for immortality with the possible exception of Henry Ford, although even that revolutionary will never be preserved in the same glare of popular fascination.

As the years go by Capone stands out more palpably as a phenomenon and a symbol of a sort. He cannot be summarized by all the conventional terms of disapproval, that he was evil, ruthless or corrupt, although he was all those things. The splendour of his dispensation to the needy and the greedy cannot be allowed to admit him back to grace, although he did practise a flashy generosity which, although doubtless paranoically vanity-feeding, was no mere fable. In only a decade he ascended from squalid poverty to a status, which, if no less squalid, was unique in its power and scope. He was, after all, a pioneer of a kind, for nobody before had done quite what he did, and in him there were undoubted qualities of imagination, forcefulness and ingenuity.

Sources of information about Capone's early life are scanty, even about his first years in Chicago. The reasons are obvious. Most of those who knew him best have died, usually abruptly and with their shoes on, and, because of both a lack of educational training and a deep distrust of volunteering any facts, were not men disposed to leaving behind personal journals and written reminiscences. The Italian-Sicilian circles in which he lived all his life are, in any case, famously tight-lipped about their private circumstances. Capone was watchfully guarded in what he revealed about himself – although it pleased him to hint at romanticized or downright falsified events of his younger days – and during the years of prosperity his family was shuttered out of the blaze of publicity that enveloped his public life, unobtrusive in the marginal shadows of respectable domesticity where a good Catholic-Italian family belongs. Nor is his background appreciably filled out by official police records. In 1929 Landesco remarked upon 'the meagre records of Al Capone and his two brothers, Ralph and John' and elsewhere observes laconically: 'Most Capone men have no records whatever.' It seems deducible that bribes had bought the necessary Orwellian 'memory-holes' down which irritating documentation could be consigned to oblivion.

Capone was born in 1895, although he liked to whittle five years off his age and usually gave 1900 as his year of birth. He was also sensitive about his foreign blood. In 1931 he stated: 'I'm no Eyetalian. I was born in New York thirty-one years ago.' He also declared with bellicose patriotism: 'I'm no foreigner. I'm as good an American as any man. My parents were American-born and so was I.' None of this was strictly correct. Although often described as a Neapolitan, and sometimes as a Calabrian, Capone was born on 6 January 1895 at Castel Amara near Rome and christened Alphonso. His surname was then spelled Caponi. His father was Gabrielle Caponi, a shopkeeper. His mother, who already had a two-year-old son Ralph, was named Theresa. The year after Alphonso's birth his father obtained immigration visas and the family filtered insignificantly, in the great European exodus of the late nineteenth century, into the United States of America, the new world of liberation and opportunity for Europe's oppressed. One immigrant who was spectacularly to fulfil the dream and the promise was the Caponi baby who went steerage to New York.

The family vanished into the congested Italian quarter of slum tenements in Brooklyn, where the father worked variously as grocer and barber, without ever financially getting out of the gutter on to those golden sidewalks of New York. Of the five more children born, four brothers and a sister, all but one also entered the underworld, sister Mafalda's connexion having been to marry one of the Maritote clan who were prominent in Chicago's Italian community. Ralph, known as Bottles, Frank and John joined Al in his Chicago enterprises. John, now known as Martin, still lives in Chicago. Frank was killed in the 1924 Cicero election. Ralph went to jail on a three-year sentence at the same time and on a similar tax-charge as Al's. Matt, the youngest of the brood and for whom Al planned superior things – he sent him to the exclusive Villanova University in Philadelphia – was later tried for murder. The fourth brother, Richard, soon after the First World War detached himself from the family and became a law officer under the name of Two Gun Hart, in Nebraska, where he died in 1952. Gabriel, the father, died in 1920, never to know of Al's world fame to come; but he was not altogether left out of the family bonanza. When the beer profits were foaming in, Al had his father's remains exhumed from their drab Brooklyn grave and reburied with great pomp in the Capone enclosure in Chicago's Mount Olivet Cemetery. Theresa saw the whole rise and fall of her second son: she lived until the age of eighty-five, dying in Chicago in December 1952.

It was a rich harvest of delinquency, bound with family solidarity, that had sprouted in that particular Brooklyn backstreet apartment. The childhood of Al seems to have been classically parabolic in its conditioning and logical in its course: the case of the second son is exceptional merely in that the trajectory of his career described a higher curve than is normal. At fourteen, before reaching top class, Capone was removed from school and put to work to bring in money for the family. During his term in Alcatraz twenty years later he was adjudged to have the mental age of a thirteen-year-old, but this seems to require some qualification: his educational standard may have remained at that stage, but the facts of his career do not support any inference that he was retarded.

Nevertheless, when he left school he read poorly and his spoken English – unaided in a household where Italian was used – was bad. It is a familiar context, and one which is just as relevant today in New York's Puerto Rican ghettos – the dead-end kid, fiercely resenting a sense of inadequacy and oddness that he cannot change or subdue, graduating into the hostile delinquent. Capone, according to the pattern of instability, zigzagged from meaningless job to meaningless job, and in the meantime was integrating with the street gangs that then, as now, found scrapings of self-respect, strength and importance in unity and preservation of territory, their 'turf', their few blocks of decaying buildings and garbage-littered streets, and found substitute excitement in the tensions kept permanently taut by the clashes and rumbles with adjacent gangs. Capone, a hefty thick-set youth with fast boxer's feet, was already developing the calm and deadly shrewdness which later characterized him. Today he would be said to be cool, for it is still the same quality of deadpan, controlled menace that stamps the most successful hoodlum in any Western city teenage gang. But, at this point, Capone had not realized his potential; his gang activities were mostly violence for violence sake, with casual felony exploited when the opportunity turned up for shop-breaking and the looting of parked lorries. At twenty-two he was employed as a meat-cutter in an Atlantic City butcher shop. This was in 1917 and upon America's entry into the war he was summoned to the Army.

In newspaper interviews in later years he attributed to his war experiences the two parallel three-inch scars on his left cheek, of which he was inordinately self-conscious and which earned him the nickname of Scarface (one which was never used by his henchmen and never used in his presence by anyone else who wished to retain his goodwill). 'I got those scars fighting for my country overseas,' he related. 'I was eight months in France with the famous Lost Battalion of the Seventy-seventh Division. A burst of shrapnel caught me in a battle. I was operated on four times in a base hospital and laid up for two months before I got back to the front lines again.' He somewhat modified this account during his trial, when, as he stood under oath, he was directly asked by the prosecuting attorney what his war service had amounted to. More briefly this time, he answered: 'I was certified in the draft but never called.' In fact, the scars were the outcome of a knife-fight in a New York saloon with Frank Gallucio, another Brooklyn hoodlum, after Capone had made a slighting remark about Gallucio's sister. Later Capone resumed his friendship with Gallucio and at one stage employed him as a bodyguard, but continued to the end sensitively to turn his left cheek away from any camera pointing in his direction.

He also on occasions paid tribute to the American Army for planting the seed in his mind of the machine-gun as a piece of business equipment ('The sergeant told me that one man with a machine-gun was master of fifty men with rifles and revolvers,' he told a reporter. 'You know something? That guy was right') but as his only brush with the Service was at his medical-board, that idea presumably germinated later.

Not avidly seized upon by the Army, Capone went back to his odd-jobbing and promiscuous rough-stuff. He was now carrying a gun and a blackjack, and was acquiring a local reputation as a felicitous adept with both. By 1920 he had become initiated into full-time professional criminal society, but still comparatively, when one looks forward only a few years, at the most submerged level. He was then given a job in a Coney Island cabaret with an atmosphere of resounding academic stylishness, since it was named the Harvard

Inn and run by a Mr. Frank Yale. However, Frankie Yale's real name was Uale, and he was the rackets and liquor boss of Brooklyn, a gunman mercenary and national head of the Unione Siciliana, and the Harvard Inn was a tough waterside honkytonk, handily adjacent after Prohibition began for the reception of bootleg consignments from the rum fleet plying off the Long Island coast. Doubtless Capone was happy to be meeting the right kind of people after drifting aimlessly for so long around the edges of quality crime, but nevertheless he was not so young – he was twenty-five – and the job Yale gave him did not have much splendour or status. He became, in the Harvard Inn, a dishwasher and part-time bartender, who operated also as a bouncer if disagreements with customers occurred. During that year he developed promisingly. He was enrolled into the notorious Five Points Gang, which had been formed by an Irish thug named Paul Kelly with a horde of 1,500 young tearaways in the early years of the century and which reigned in the sector bounded by the Bowery and Broadway, and Fourteenth Street and City Hall Park. (Charles Dickens, in his *American Notes*, described the Five Points slums as 'of the utmost depravity', 'all that is loathsome, drooping and decayed'.) The Five Points steel-hardened not only Capone but also such other celebrated cadre men as Gyp the Blood and Lefty Louie (the suspected killers of Herman Rosenthall, the gambler, in 1912) who ten years earlier had been recruited by Big Jim Colosimo, the prostitution tycoon of Chicago, as a bodyguard against Black Hand persecution. In 1920 Capone was questioned in two murder cases. Wary at the attention being paid to him, he wrote to Torrio in Chicago, an eaglet from Torrio's old eyrie asking for the opening to spread his wings in new country.

Capone did not know it then, but the timing could not have been more propitious. It was 1920 and Prohibition was just floundering into existence. Colosimo, the aging, antiquated vice-boss, flabby from too much easy money for too long, bemused by his infatuation for a young girl singer, and unable to see the stupendous bullion waiting to be carried off by organized booze-traffickers, was about to topple. Torrio, the modern man, the murder-planner rather than the operator who pulled the trigger, and now the burgeoning business executive, began to see what might, with the techniques of cartel and organization, be extracted from this new situation. Colosimo was not to be persuaded. 'Stick to women,' he said. 'There's no future in bootlegging.' On 11 May 1920 Colosimo was struck by two bullets in the lobby of his restaurant. When Torrio heard of his death he wept. 'Me kill Jim? Why, Jim and me were like brothers.' According to the police, Frankie Yale, who had been visiting Chicago, left that night just after collecting ten thousand dollars from Torrio.

It was at this point that Torrio received the letter from Brooklyn. He knew Capone's reputation was that of a hard-headed, dependable and ruthless yeoman, and Torrio was building his shock-troops for the imminent action. He sent for him. Capone, with the Irish-American wife, Mae, whom he had married at fifteen, and his baby son, took the train west and to an abundant future.

That this was to be the case was not immediately apparent. The job Torrio had for Capone in one of his Burnham brothels – a unique establishment which straddled the state line and had one entrance from Indiana and another from Illinois – was, once again, as chucker-out. His zeal and dedication made his probationary period brief. Torrio recognized in him business talent similar to his own, and within a few weeks Capone was appointed to the management of the Four Deuces, a vice emporium which took its name from its street number, 2222 on South Wabash Avenue, which contained whores on the third floor, gambling chambers on the second, business offices on the first, and a bar, cabaret and restaurant at street level. It was a tough spot, where twelve unsolved murders had been committed, and was not much visited by socialites from Lake Shore Drive. Capone moved into a corner shop next to the Four Deuces, stocked it with an imaginative range of articles including a piano, furniture, carpets, books (among which was a copy of the Holy Bible) and a glass case displaying leather wallets and purses, and had the sign painted up: SECOND HAND FURNITURE DEALER. It may not have had much turnover but it served as a cover of ordinariness.

It is interesting to look back upon the obscurity of Capone's early years in Chicago. In only four years he was to ascend through a welter of blood, slaughter and conspiracy, to become the overlord of the city's vice, a multi-millionaire and a symbol throughout the nation and beyond the seas of a startling new era of autocracy in which crime and politics were partners. But then, in that first year of Prohibition, Capone still looked the slum tough from the Five Points district. He played pinocle with other rankers in Amato Gasperri's barber shop and ate his spaghetti in Esposito's Bella Napoli Café. He wore a cloth cap and cheap clothes. The unguent urbanity of manner that later characterized him had not matured, nor had he assumed the striped yellow suits, spats, velvet-collared overcoats and white fedoras that were to make him the prototype of all film gangsters. He had by then slightly adapted his name.

Alphonso Caponi had become Alphonse Capone, but he was more widely known – and continued until the end of his life to be generally known in the underworld – as Al Brown. Apart from the hated nickname of Scarface, he also was known to his most intimate associates as Snorky. The Capone, he insisted in his pursuit of complete assimilation, should be pronounced Capohn. How unimportantly he was rated by newspapers and police is indicated by the mistakes that usually occurred on the rare occasions that his name went on to paper. He was more often described as Anthony or Alfred than as Alphonse. It was not until August 1922 that he broke into the news for the first time. He was the subject of a City News Bureau item, which was evidently assessed to be of such trivial moment by the copytasters that only one Chicago paper used it, as an inside down-page story. It ran:

'Alfred Caponi, 25 years old, living at the notorious Four Deuces, a disorderly house at 2222 South Wabash Avenue, will appear in the South Clark Street court today to answer a charge of assault with an automobile. Early this morning his automobile crashed into a Town taxicab, driven by Fred Krause, 741 Drake Avenue, at North Wabash Avenue and East Randolph Street, injuring the driver. Three men and a woman, who were with Caponi, fled before the arrival of the police.

'Caponi is said to have been driving east in Randolph Street at a high rate of speed. The taxicab was parked at the curb.

'Following the accident, Caponi alighted and flourishing a revolver, displayed a special deputy sheriff's badge and threatened to shoot Krause.

'Patrick Bargall, 6510 South Claremont Avenue, motor-man of a south-bound street-car, stopped his car and advised Caponi to put the weapon in his pocket, and the latter then threatened him, according to witnesses.

'In the meantime, the Central police had been notified and they hurried to the scene, arresting Caponi. Krause was given first aid treatment by an ambulance physician.'

Not only did the City News Bureau err with Capone's name but also in the charges preferred against him. In addition to assault with an automobile, he was charged with drunken driving and with carrying a concealed weapon. It made little difference. In the hours between the tipsy fracas and his appointment in the South Clark Street courtroom certain concealed events took place. What representations were made by whom and to whom can be only guessed at, but the case never came to trial, and the charges were dropped.

Capone did not appear in court. The misdemeanours of the Special Deputy Sheriff of Cook County were expunged from the record. (Even as late as 1929 he was still described as Caponi – in reports of March of that year when the Federal authorities were trying to persuade him to return from Miami to be questioned about the St. Valentine's Day Massacre.)

Yet within three years of that first trumpery news item about an unknown hoodlum, there was always a fresh anecdote circulating Chicago about the power and pull of the newly risen boss. There was the story told on the police network of the prisoner who escaped from the Criminal Courts Building and who was searched for in South Side gang hang-outs. A party of young and newly enrolled patrolmen burst into the back room of a café and surprised a gathering of bootleggers, who shed their pistols and sawn-off shot-gun on to the floor. The policemen collected these and delivered them to their chief, who said: 'Take that stuff back. Who gave you orders to confiscate them?' That was not the end of the incident. They were told that Capone was irritated by their brash zeal, and that they had better call and put themselves right with him. He received them at the Metropole Hotel. 'Well,' he said, 'I understand your captain wasn't to blame, and that you boys just made a mistake. I'm going to give you a break. After this, don't pull another boner.' They left chastened and grateful for the kindness. Another story was related by a reporter who was talking with Capone in his office when he was informed that one of his gunmen had just been brought up in court in defiance of his orders for a release. Angrily Capone got the judge on the telephone and yelled at him: 'I thought I told you to discharge that fellow?' The judge explained that he had been off the bench, had written a memorandum to a fellow judge but that his bailiff had forgotten to deliver it. 'Forget!' shouted Capone. 'Don't let him forget again!'

His wealth and influence waxed. After he had bought his Palm Island estate three miles outside Miami – a deal that was conducted without his identity being revealed – that part of the coast became the winter playground of Chicago's gang-chiefs. Terry Druggan and Frankie Lake took a neighbouring estate, and Hughey Stubby McGovern another large villa at which a non-stop house party was held and to and from which bootleggers and mobsters and girl-friends streamed. There were big and convivial meetings at the Hialeah horse-track and the Miami dog-tracks, and much money surged into Florida from the Illinois bar and brothel trade. Capone had also moved his family – his wife, son, mother, sister and brothers John

and Matthew – into a pleasant, plain, quiet residential house
on Prairie Avenue, on Chicago's South Side; he had there as
neighbours two policemen and a police sergeant. The Capones, the
only Italians on the block, were liked by the other Prairie Avenue
householders, who included, as well as the police element, a druggist,
a publisher, a draughtsman, a Presbyterian minister and a clothing
manufacturer. Capone's sister, Mafalda, was then attending a
girls' private school, to which at Christmas time Capone drove up
with his car laden with gifts for all the pupils and teachers, and
turkeys and fruit for the term-end dinner.

He was encouraging, and enjoying, his reputation as a free-spender
and good guy. When he attended a prize fight he bought a hundred
dollars' worth of extra tickets, which he handed out to the youngsters
who milled around him calling 'Hi, Al!' Such munificence was
increasingly easy. The daily – and nightly – scene at the Metropole
Hotel was indicative of his swelling importance. A description by a
reporter who knew it at that time was this: 'It was garrisoned like
Birger's blockhouse in the woods in Bloody Williamson county. The
Capones occupied as many as fifty rooms on two heavily guarded
floors. They operated their own private elevators and maintained
their own service bars. Gambling went on openly and women visited
the floors at all hours of the day and night. The aroma of highly
flavoured Italian foods brought in from the outside permeated the
corridors. Nearly every hotel rule and regulation was violated daily.
On Sunday mornings especially the lobby was a beehive of activity.
Prominent criminal lawyers and high officials of the police department, along with politicians and dive-keepers waited their turn to
consult with the Big Shot. Policemen in uniform streamed in and out.
A blind pig operated in the lobby by a semi-public official did a land-
office business. In an underground vault, specially constructed, was
stored 150 thousand dollars' worth of wines and liquors. The stock
was constantly replenished. It was for the gang's private use. Capone
himself occupied rooms 409 and 410, overlooking the boulevard.
The hallway was patrolled by sentinels, posted at regular intervals
as in an army. In an ante-room of the Capone suite was the bodyguard, equipped with the latest type of fire-arms.'

Two blocks away Capone had more private and intimate quarters,
at 2146 South Michigan Avenue, where there was a small plate on
the door bearing the name Dr. A. Brown. This was the strongroom of
the syndicate, the business cell that was overseen by Jack Guzik, the
financial head and man of solid and weighty status in the underworld (and so he still was twenty-five years later when the Kefauver

Committee examined his gambling activities and reported that the reformed Accardo-Guzik-Fischetti Chicago crime ring was then 'one of the two major underworld organizations in the nation'). Jack Guzik and his brother Harry (a convicted, but unpunished, pimp who was pardoned prior to serving sentence) had been associates of Torrio since 1916. Jack Guzik was Capone's appointed dictator of gambling in Cook County, and accountant for all the prostitution, liquor and assorted rackets. When a relative of his was married in 1929 a report was carried by a morning newspaper under a two-column picture; guests included Bathhouse John Coughlin, First Ward alderman; William V. Pacelli, Bloody Twentieth Ward alderman; Captain of Police Hugh McCarthy; and Bottles Capone. The value Capone placed upon Guzik is indicated by the round-the-clock guard that he stationed at Guzik's bed when he was ill in Michael Reese Hospital. His concern for the well-being of Guzik became understandable after the raid instigated by Mayor Dever on the medical premises on South Michigan Avenue. Behind the reception room was the surgery. It contained rows of bottles, ranging from phials to quarts, containing various coloured liquids. These, a sniffing detective found, contained samples of all the types and brands of alcohol that could be offered to customers by the Capone bootleg organization, and which could be taken away for a chemist's analysis. Under Guzik's administration, an office staff of twenty-five ran the syndicate's auditing system, the machinery of 'a super-trust operating with the efficiency of a great corporation' (Pasley). The records contained the names of more than two hundred well-known Chicagoans and hotels and drug-stores supplied by the syndicate, the names of police officers and Prohibition agents on the bribe list, a transportation plan for running in booze from Canada, Miami, New Orleans and New York's Rum Row, personnel lists of four breweries owned by the syndicate and producing most of Chicago's beer, brothel income ledgers, and an alphabetical register of the Illinois saloons and speakeasies buying the syndicate's drink.

It seemed, fleetingly, as if Dever was right when he announced triumphantly: 'We've got the goods this time.' The evidence of graft among police and Prohibition agents, and of vast illegal trade, was conclusive. Next day, before the documents could be turned over to the Federal authority as the basis for prosecution, they were impounded on the orders of a municipal judge. Sixteen hours after the Federal office at New Orleans asked for a transcript – a request which was not granted – the judge, at a special and un-notified hearing, had them returned to Capone. United States

District Attorney Edwin A. Alson handed to the press his letter of
protest to the judge demanding that he withhold a decision until an
investigation and an inspection of the records. The letter was
ignored. The judge was unscathed – except by public knowledge of
his conduct – and Capone and Guzik continued their business from
safer quarters. It was not until after Capone had been seized for tax
evasion that Guzik was similarly overtaken by belated retribution –
in 1932 he was sentenced to five years in the Leavenworth, Kansas,
Penitentiary and fined 17,500 dollars for non-payment of taxes on
income of 1,538,155 dollars from gambling houses.

24

'Where's Daddy?'

*The bootlegger told me, 'Stop – those G-men have been
    aroun'. . .*
*An' broke up all the moonshine an' poured the mash out on
    the groun'.'*
*We've got to run a new racket, people, we've gotta find a
    better rule.*
An' if we can't get decent whisky, we'll take a drink of mule.

CURTIS JONES, *Alley Bound Blues*

As has been the case of most other conquerors and dictators, Capone's destruction came about by his own hand: his was too thickly studded with diamond rings and too ready to use a gun. The blatancy with which he paraded his wealth, his political power, his violence and his contempt for the law built up an antidote to the tolerance and admiration that had debilitated society into the condition of permissiveness amid which he flourished. It is no credit to the civic administration of Chicago that Capone was finally brought down, for, by its own readiness to be corrupted and Capone's ability so efficiently to organize its corruption, by the late 'twenties the forces of law and order had been emasculated. However, there were scattered pockets of resistance to Capone's autocracy even within the city, and these included the Chicago Crime Commission, a voluntary body financed by the contributions of private citizens and headed by Virgil Peterson.

Capone must have been assailed by melancholy forebodings. Suddenly and catastrophically, the fat golden years were expiring, and the immunity from responsibility and punishment that he had for so long enjoyed, began to be punctured at a dozen different points. The attempts upon his life were increasing in frequency, his closest brush with death being in 1927 when he was driving his car across the mountains from Hot Springs, Arkansas. A car closed in upon him and zipped past with bullets spraying in upon him. He escaped by jamming on his brakes, throwing himself out of the door and rolling down the steep slope into cover.

Although it could not then have been apparent, the point of high tide in the career of Capone was midnight on 16 May 1929. It was than that he had been arrested with his bodyguard, Slippery Frank Rio, as they left a cinema in Philadelphia. They were carrying guns. Capone's presence in Philadelphia has been the subject of much theorizing. It has been suggested that the heat was so intensely on in Chicago that he deliberately made himself vulnerable to arrest so as to obtain the safe refuge of jail until the trouble – revenge by the remnants of the Moran gang for the St. Valentine's Day Massacre – dispersed. Another possibility is that Capone absented himself from Chicago to avoid being charged with the murders of Scalise, Anselmi and Guinta. On the other hand, with the opposition so badly maimed, it seems improbable that Capone's reason for leaving Chicago could have been any especially severe threat of reprisals, but he may have been advised by his lawyers that it would be wise to be inaccessible to police questioning for a while. This, then, was a suitable time for the business talks that had been in a state of preparation since St. Valentine's day and the killing that had alarmed and sobered crime bosses throughout the United States. It seemed clear that internecine slaughter of this wildness could not continue without the entire machinery of illegal profits being crippled. The step towards a pan-gang cartel agreement was taken by the New York racketeer Frank Costello, then extending his interests from liquor, prostitution and narcotics to control of slot-machine concessions in the Eastern states. Costello called an executives' conference and early in May 1929 fifty gang-chiefs from most of the major cities in the United States, and including a thirty-strong Chicago contingent gathered at the President Hotel in Atlantic City. Earlier, Maxie Eisen had said: 'We're a bunch of saps, killing each other this way and giving the cops a laugh.' The St. Valentine's Day Massacre had at last forced upon all this saddening truth. On neutral ground, and in a sympathetic atmosphere, Capone and Moran composed their old hatreds. 'We agreed to forget the past and begin all over again,' Capone later reminisced, 'and we drew up a written agreement, and each man signed on the dotted line. We hoped that this would call a halt to the gun battles and gang warfare in Chicago.'

Conflicts and over-lapping of interests were settled in an atmosphere of reason and compromise, and Chicago in particular was the subject of revision of territorial rights. The formal non-aggression and mutual aid pact was signed by the barons. Corporation interlocking of operations in liquor-supply, brothels and gambling houses were agreed upon, and Torrio was elected chairman of the board.

Feeling that this disarmament treaty was at last the real hope of an era of peaceful money-making which none of his local peace-conferences had achieved, Capone left Atlantic City with Rio. Between trains in Philadelphia, they filled in the hours seeing a film show. As they left the cinema they were recognized by two detectives, stopped and searched, and found to be armed. They were arrested and taken to the night court, where the Magistrate, a Mr. Carney, ordered them to be released on bail of thirty-five thousand dollars each for hearing the next morning. Capone produced ten thousand dollars from his wallet, but could not raise the remainder, and he was booked into a cell for that night. Said Carney, fixing the bail: 'Authorities in some American cities, including some public prosecutors, are afraid of you Mr. Al Capone, but Philadelphia is not afraid of you. My only regret is that you are not before me on charges which would justify me in ridding the United States of you for ever.' He and Rio were removed to the cells, where their belongings were confiscated, including a large diamond ring from Capone. Next morning they were brought before Captain Andrew Emanuel of the Detective Bureau, and charged 'with being suspicious characters and with carrying deadly weapons'.

This was, according to Capone's testimony, only the fourth time that he had been arrested – previously, once in Joliet, Illinois, for carrying a concealed weapon, once in New York on suspicion of murder, and once in Olean, New York, for disorderly conduct – and in each case had been discharged. In fact there had been a number of other arrests, but he had never until now served a single day in prison during a career which, conservatively, included responsibility for four hundred murders.

On this occasion the legal process moved with speed and effectiveness he had not experienced in Chicago. Sixteen and a half hours after his arrest he was brought before Judge John E. Walsh, of the Criminal Division of the Municipal Court, found guilty, sentenced to a year's imprisonment and, a convict for the first time in his life, became No. 90725 in Holmesburg County Jail, soon after to be transferred to the Eastern Penitentiary as No. 5527-C. Interviewed by a British United Press reporter after his sentence, and asked why he carried a revolver, Capone exclaimed: 'I had just come from a conference with rival Chicago gang leaders at Atlantic City, where we negotiated peace terms. But, as for the gun, well, I'm on the mark, you know – marked for death.'

It is odd, in retrospect, that on this occasion Capone almost idly neglected to put into gear his costly protective legal machinery. It may be true, as has been suggested, that he was advised to 'take the rap' as a convenient source of safety while it was seen how the new peace pact worked out in practice, especially in regard to the Sicilian associates of Aiello. Yet it seems likely that when Capone pleaded guilty to the gun-carrying charge he expected only the usual three-month sentence. 'Al figured on taking a rap,' one of his men admitted to a reporter, 'and he took a K.O.'

Still, his sufferings in jail were not unendurable. In July Major L. B. Schofield, City Safety Director, revealed that 'strenuous efforts' had been made to secure his release, and he said: 'Capone has offered fifty thousand dollars or more to any lawyer or group of lawyers who can obtain his release before the end of his twelve-month term.' When this failed, upon high-level direction – obscure in origin but familiar in kind – Capone and Rio were speedily transferred from Holmesburg, which had an unattractive reputation for harsh discipline, to the Eastern Penitentiary. There Capone was allotted his own cell equipped with a five hundred dollar radio, a pair of easy chairs, bookshelf, table and carpet, was given the undemanding duties of file-clerk, and was permitted to make long-distance business telephone calls to his attorneys, Bernard Lemisch and Congressman Benjamin M. Golder, of Philadelphia, from the office of Herbert B. Smith, the warden.

There was regular news of his activities. He was reported to be playing a great deal of handball for exercise. His wife frequently visited him – but left their son behind. Capone told a journalist caller: 'I wouldn't have him come to the prison for anything. My boy thinks I'm in Europe. Whenever he sees a picture of a big boat, he asks his mother if that boat is bringing Daddy home.' There were other stories to pierce the heart of the sentimental newspaper-reader. After being convicted for an attempted hold-up, a young apprentice criminal was brought into the prison hospital with a gun-shot wound. Capone, it was recorded, heard that the doctors were preparing to amputate his arm, and gave instructions to them: 'Save the boy's arm. If it takes money, I'll be glad to pay for it.' In his new relaxation, he treated interviewers to rambling home-spun philosophy, such as his dilations upon the role of the modern woman. 'The trouble with women today,' ruminated Capone, 'is their excitement over too many things outside the home. A woman's home and her children are her real happiness. If she would stay there, the world would have less to worry about the modern woman.'

His behaviour was exemplarily placid, and he earned the admiring commendation of Dr. Herbert M. Goddard, of the Pennsylvania State Board of Prison Inspectors, who removed his tonsils and operated on his nose. 'I can't believe all they say of him,' the doctor said a few days before Capone's release. 'In my seven years of experience I have never seen a prisoner so kind, cheery and accommodating. He does his work faithfully and with a high degree of intelligence. He has brains. He would have made good anywhere, at anything. He has been an ideal prisoner. I cannot estimate the money he has given away. Of course, we cannot inquire where he gets it. He's in the racket. He admits it. But you can't tell me he's all bad, after I have seen him many times a week for ten months, and seen him with his wife and mother.'

Ironically this prison term was a relatively halcyon interlude in the life of Capone: regular sleep, relaxation of tensions, no sound of gun-fire, and, at first, business prospering reasonably well under the supervision of Bottles, with regular commuting between Chicago, New York and Altantic City by his board of directors and Torrio in pursuance of the new inter-state association. It was certainly his last experience of freedom from anxiety.

When he left the Eastern Penitentiary on 17 March 1930 all was altered. Bottles was in prison; business was being badly hit by the depredations of the Untouchables[1]; and in the previous autumn the bottom had fallen out of Wall Street and, with three million men thrown out of work and Depression blighting the whole land, money for bootleg booze was diminishing. For a week before Capone's release the Chicago newspapers carried much comment and speculation about the Big Fellow's return to his kingdom, and there was reflected in the columns a marked change of attitude. Coolidge Prosperity, maggotty in the middle, had caved in; skirts had lengthened and the red-hot baby was demode; there were more men at soup-kitchens than in speakeasies; the big splurge was running out, the jazz age had lost its fervency; the killings had reached a point of extravagance that made even hardboiled Chicago uneasy; and as the new decade opened, chilly and frightening, the mood of indulgence for such giant social anachronisms as Capone was withering. He suddenly seemed less of a swashbuckler than a cheap cheater; his glamour suddenly seemed elusive and the stench with which he had covered Chicago's name more noxious. An election campaign was opening and the World's Fair was imminent: Capone,

[1] See pages 300 and 305.

the brigand figure, did not fit into the picture which Chicago wished to present to the world at that time. Given courage by the tax trial of Bottles and by the brewery-busting of the Untouchables, Police Captain John Stege announced that a cordon of twenty-five uniformed police, with orders to arrest Capone on sight, was being put around his Prairie Avenue home.

The interest in the reappearance of Capone was intense. Despite the growled appeal of a brother: 'Let us have no fuss nor feathers,' reporters, cameramen, newsreel teams and crowds of sightseers began to gather around the Eastern Penitentiary on the day that Capone's commutation papers were expected from the parole board in Harrisburg, the capital. Squads of city police patrolled the streets around the prison, roping off the block to keep the spectators (and possible assassins, for it was reported that his old Chicago enemies had offered fifty thousand dollars to the gunman who managed to kill him) at bay. Motorcycle police were drawn up, ready to marshal the released prisoner. In the morning a tri-engined private aircraft landed at a nearby field and was understood to be collecting Capone (a blind that cost two thousand dollars).

It was all a deception. To thwart the throng, Warden Smith had already driven to Harrisburg to get the commutation signed by Governor John S. Fisher. On the Sunday evening, twenty-four hours before the official time of his release, Capone huddled low in the rear seat of the warden's car and, convoyed by police outriders, was smuggled to Graters Ford, thirty miles away, to await the hour of 4 p.m. Monday when his sentence expired. At 8 p.m. on Monday Warden Smith walked to the prison gate and issued the following statement to the press: 'We stuck one in your eye that time. The big guy's gone. We shot him out in a brown automobile.' The crowd jeered and hooted.

With a start of thirty miles and twenty-eight hours, Capone had been whisked away into temporary oblivion by his men. For four days nothing was seen of him. His mother's welcome-home turkey dinner, it was poignantly reported, had gone cold. The press scurried about in inconclusive gyrations, trying to find him. One story placed him in Baltimore, inspecting a vessel bound for Miami. Another asserted that he had gone to an unnamed destination in Indiana, where he was being given ceremonial reception by his associates together with a new car as a token of their esteem. The Governor of Florida was stated to be in a state of grim apprehension as the delivery of a thirty-six-inch iced cake seemed to portend Capone's return there, but it was later decided that the cake had been an iced red herring. He did not attempt to jump the cordon in Prairie Avenue, which remained in position and in increasing embarrassment for three days and nights.

In fact he was back in Chicago. His whereabouts were learned, but not revealed, the day after his release. The Elliot Ness group intercepted a call on their tapped wire. It was a summons to his brother, a voice saying urgently: 'We're up in Room 718 at the Western and Al is really getting out of hand. He's in terrible shape. Will you come up? You're the only one who can handle him when he gets like this. We've sent for a lot of towels.'

Cooled off and rubbed down after his drunken celebration Capone slipped quietly across to his old headquarters in the Hawthorne Inn, Cicero, and spent three days inspecting account books and the health of business. As the cordon was still stubbornly rooted in Prairie Avenue, there seemed no choice but to confront the authorities and challenge their threat to arrest him again. He appeared, wearing a pearl grey felt hat and gold spectacles, and sucking cough-drops, with his lawyer, Mr. Nash, at the office of Captain John Egan, chief of detectives, and from there went to the State's Attorney's office and then to the United States District Attorney. None held a warrant for his arrest, no charges were outstanding against him, and there was no law – all had to admit – under which he could be held. Stege, the next day's newspapers related, then in despair appealed to the better feelings of the 'prisoner'. He said: 'You've got to get out of this town and stay out. We're not having any more gang killings here and the best way to prevent them is to run you out of the town. Leave for Florida or wherever you are going.' He somewhat reduced the potency of this plea by adding that the Florida police had orders to arrest him on sight. After leaving the building, Capone at his most conciliatory, told reporters: 'Egan couldn't help it, Stege couldn't help it. If they'd let me come back to Chicago and go about my business there'd have been plenty of people saying they were afraid of me. I made it easy for them. I was willing to face any charge anyone had to make, and there wasn't any.' His right hand was bandaged, and he was asked if he had been shot. He grinned: 'I burned it on a piece of roast beef.' He was once more interviewed next day in his office in the Lexington Hotel, where he was found sitting at his mahogany desk 'with an air of injured innocence', writing cheques for charities and issuing orders to his organization: Asked if he was back in bootlegging, he said: 'Sure, and some of our best judges use my stuff.'

But, although the law agencies seemed unable to collect either

their wits or the applicable facts which would enable them to seize
Capone again, there was nothing to stop Stege keeping Capone
under constant watch as a suspected person. For weeks he was
followed wherever he went, not only by his own bodyguard but by
two uniformed policemen. The climate was cold, and a certain
desperation was entering Capone's soul. The Chicago Crime Commission held a searchlight of publicity upon him and all his activities.
Its policy was to hound and harass, and they had invented a label
which instantly caught the public imagination and began to be
applied to Capone in the newspapers and in public speeches. He
was no longer the Big Fellow: he was Public Enemy No. 1.

Another Maquis-type group that had come into existence to
operate as underground saboteurs against the syndicate was the
Citizens' Committee for the Prevention and Punishment of Crime,
a specially appointed action group of the Chicago Association of
Commerce. They had cloaked themselves in anonymity out of self-
protection, and so had won the headline name of The Secret Six.
Their chairman was, in fact, Colonel Robert Isham Randolph, a
prominent businessman and President of the Chamber of Commerce,
and the committee included a couple of millionaires. They formed
themselves in 1929 and appointed Alexander Jamie, a Department of Justice man with a reputation for honesty, as their special
investigator. Jamie was seconded from the Special Intelligence
Bureau but retained his Federal power, to which was added those
of the State and city police – a total authority which superseded
that of Police Commissioner Alcock and State Attorney Swanson.
The newspapers approved the step and Jamie's assignment – 'to
clean up Chicago in the greatest crime drive in our history' – but
reserved an understandable doubt as to whether one man, even
though backed by funds from Chicago's biggest business houses,
could accomplish what three thousand police and three hundred
Prohibition agents had so calamitously failed to do. In fact, Jamie
and the Secret Six, in conjunction with Elliot Ness's special prohibition squad – the Untouchables – did make themselves uncom-
fortably felt, to the extent that in September 1930 Capone directed
a whip-round among all members of the allied gangs to raise a
hundred thousand dollars fighting fund to contest the Secret Six.
'If we can't square the policeman on the beat, we can fix the sergeant,'
he was quoted as saying.

Yet, although all these separate agents of retribution were slowly
gathering momentum, in the end it took President Herbert Clark
Hoover himself to raise the fist heavy enough to smash Capone.

Even for Washington, it was a long, laborious and frustrating bout with Capone, in which the knock-out blow was repeatedly dodged and parried; it required the combined skill of the Intelligence Unit of the United States Treasury and the special prohibition squad of the United States Department of Justice attached to the Secret Six to deliver the blow. The story that was later passed around was that Hoover's determination to get Capone was stimulated by personal pique, because, it was said, soon after his election to the Presidency he went into a Florida hotel and was enjoying the adulation of the foyer crowds when it was suddenly switched *en masse* away from him and directed upon a suavely-smiling man chewing a big cigar who followed him in, this being Capone. Ten years later Hoover flatly denied this to Elmer J. Irey of the Treasury Department Enforcement Branch, who in the spring of 1929 had received the presidential directive, via the Commissioner of Internal Revenue, to put Capone behind bars. Hoover told Irey that he had never met Capone in Florida and that his order went out as a result of a visit from Frank Knox, publisher of the Chicago *Daily News*, and a deputation of Chicago citizens to the White House pleading for Federal action.

The task of placing Capone back in jail was discussed at summit conferences. The Secretary of the Treasury informed Irey that his detail must gather the evidence and that the Attorney General would prosecute. Irey, although baffled why a body whose function was combating tax, customs and narcotics frauds should be assigned to apprehending a murderer, gambler, pimp and bootlegger, opened the investigation. His unit already had some knowledge of this particular crime area because a tax case against Bottles Capone (Al's elder brother, Ralph) had been compiled. It began to seem possible that similar proceedings might work against Al.

That they did, in the end, was considerably due to the brightness and zeal of a young agent named Eddie Waters in the Chicago Internal Revenue Office. He had earned himself a rare reputation for being able to extract tax payments from gangsters. He did this by cornering them in saloons and gambling parlours and, partly by appealing to their civic duty and partly by reminders of the penalties, succeeded in squeezing out occasional sporadic payments. In 1926 Waters yet again nagged Bottles, who, probably out of boredom, agreed to go through the motions of making tax returns. He stated that in 1922 and 1923 he had made fifteen thousand dollars annually and twenty thousand a year in 1924 and 1925, from gambling, his profession, and promised to sign the forms if Waters filled them in for him. This was done and Bottles put his signature to papers showing that he owed 4,075 dollars 75 cents. He then either forgot about it or could not bring himself to pay even this petty sum. It was this oversight, or his inability to overcome the deepest instincts of an inveterate bilker, that was not only to put himself in prison but to bring his brother to ruin.

Bottles ignored all demands for the money that he admitted owing, and in January 1927 the Collector of Internal Revenue had warrants of distraint issued, under which his property could be seized by the government.

Not especially disturbed by this development, Bottles had his lawyer call at the collector's office to explain that his client was in financial difficulties due to gambling losses and to the sickness and death of his race horses. His only remaining assets were a half-interest in two race horses, and his income was being devoted to their training. So, would a payment of a thousand dollars, which he could borrow, be accepted in settlement? The collector recommended acceptance of the offer, presumably, from long experience of defeat, believing that a thousand dollars would be better than nothing. But Washington rejected the recommendation, and the case was referred to Irey for investigation.

It was found that Bottles owned or had shares in not two horses but four, and that the day before he had pleaded poverty he had removed the contents from his safety deposit box. Bottles raised his offer to 2,500 dollars and then, unable to wheedle a compromise out of Washington, at last sulkily agreed to pay the whole 4,065 dollars 75 cents owed. But by this time – November 1928 – a further thousand dollars had accrued in interest and penalties, and, now perversely irritated by all these time-wasting formalities, Bottles stubbornly refused to pay the additional thousand dollars.

By the happiest of coincidences it was during this prelude that a South Side gambling parlour named The Subway was raided and its books seized. The tracing of cheques led to certain banks and brought a number of accounts to the attention of the tax agents. They came upon a curious series of accounts, to which were attached the names of James Carroll, Harry Roberts, Harry White and James Costello, Jr., each of which had in rotation been closed and another opened with precisely the same amount withdrawn from the earlier one. And this rhythmical sequence led back to 27 October 1925, when the account of Bottles Capone had been closed and his name expunged from the bank's records, and an exactly similar sum of money had the same day been used to open the account of Harry White. No one felt any reason to doubt that these were all aliases of Bottles – although that had yet to be proved – and the agents noted with satisfaction, if with no surprise, that on 4 October 1927, the date on which Bottles had offered a borrowed thousand dollars to settle his income tax, the account of James Carter had contained a balance of 25,236 dollars 15 cents. Altogether between 1924 and 1929 1,751,840 dollars 60 cents had passed through Bottles's masquerade accounts.

On the night of 8 October 1929 as he approached his front-row seat at a prize-fight, Bottles was arrested and the same month brought before a grand jury on seven indictments, six of which were routine charges of failing to pay taxes and concealing assets. The seventh was a resurrected Civil War statute, enacted to prosecute war profiteers who 'cheat, swindle or defraud' the American Government – an indictment aimed specifically at Bottles's declaration of poverty when he had more than twenty-five thousand dollars banked.

This ancient and disused oddment of law was being given a testing – not only in the hope that it would convict Bottles, but with the intention that it should be a pilot run for much more important litigation that might soon be enjoined: the trial of Al Capone.

Gang funds ensured that Bottles had representing him the best talent to be bought, and after much abstract argument the defence attempted to negotiate a two-year prison sentence in total settlement, but the prosecution insisted that he should be sent for trial. It lasted for fifteen laborious days, during which Bottles was confronted by bank records which were piled four feet high and wheeled into the court-room on a trolley. He admitted that all the names on the bank records were bogus – necessary, he explained, because he was illegally operating a betting handbook. But he indignantly repudiated the suggestion that any of his income was derived from the sale of liquor. As for Al Capone, he conceded that they were related, but stated that he had no idea how his brother made his money.

Twice during the trial Bottles was roused to fury and indignation. Once when his hat was stolen; the second time when the jury found him guilty on the seventh indictment and he was sentenced to three years in jail and a ten thousand dollar fine. 'I don't understand this at all,' he exclaimed in angry bewilderment.

Washington was pleased by the result, but the greater, secret satisfaction was that, now that the precedent had been established, the way was clear for stalking down the bigger catch, the biggest of all, who was just about to be released from the Eastern Penitentiary, after serving ten months on the gun-carrying conviction.

The assault came from several different directions. Irey conferred with Arthur P. Madden, Chicago Intelligence Unit Agent-in-Charge, and two agents, Frank Wilson, who later became head of the United States Secret Service on atomic research security, and a man whose identity is still concealed under the pseudonym of 'Patrick O'Rourke', an Irishman whose Latin looks had greatly aided his infiltration of Sicilian circles. Wilson and O'Rourke were detailed to assemble a dossier on Al's finances similar to that prepared for the prosecution of Bottles. O'Rourke's method was to draw upon the seventy-five thousand dollars pool supplied *carte blanche* by the Secret Six, buy himself a wardrobe of gangster-style clothes, and, after polishing up his Italian, he went about the slow, devious and dangerous device of joining the Capone mob as Michael Lepito, a gunman from Philadelphia and Brooklyn. Concurrently Wilson plodded systematically through account books accumulated for a decade in swoops upon brothels, distilleries and gambling casinos, following tenuous, fragmented threads through the complexity of figures, disguised entries and internal shorthand. After months of analysis he presented enough evidence to take out charges against Frank The Enforcer Nitti, Capone's aide-de-camp, and Jack Guzik, and produced a great mass of inference about Capone's money that was going to be less easy to prove. It was decided that the first move should be to strike against Nitti and Guzik, and they were arrested. On 19 November 1930 Guzik was put away for five years and Nitti, indicted for possession of 742,887 dollars over a period of three years without paying tax, fled.

Meanwhile the United States Department of Justice Prohibition Detail were also, belatedly, trying to bring pressure to bear on Capone. The record of the Federal Prohibition agents was not one of shining purity. Between 1920 and 1928, when the Department of Justice took over as the Prohibition enforcement agency, the Treasury dismissed 706 of its agents for larceny and prosecuted 257 of them. There were no Civil Service standards for enlistment in the Prohibition squad, and consequently it filled up with motley mercenaries – political appointees, stooges and near-gangsters, who were wet and bribable almost to the last man. The Prohibition agent was, amid the general collapse of standards of that period, held in the most wide and profound contempt: by the average wet citizen who disliked his function and his indiscriminate toughness, by the boot-

Above *George (Bugs) Moran answering a charge of vagrancy*

Below *Genna family of Chicago.* Left to right: *Sam Genna, Angelo Genna, Peter Genna, Tony Genna, Jim Genna and families*

Left 'Machine Gun' Jack McGurn

Below Jack McGurn shot in a Chicago bowling alley

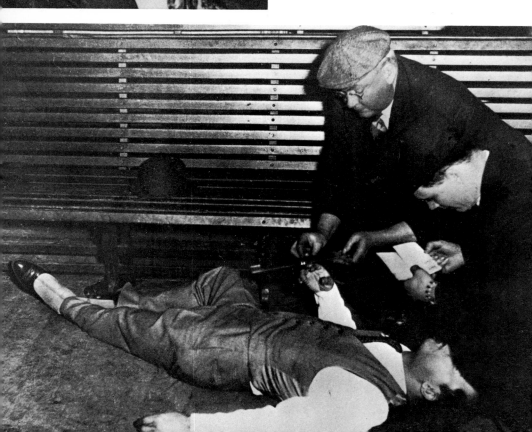

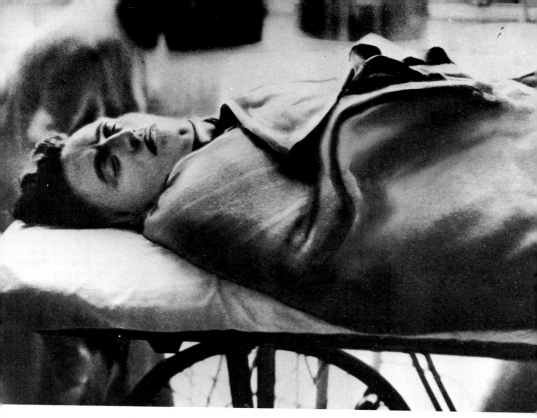

Above *Tony Genna shortly before he died of wounds*
Below *James Genna*

Al's grand exit: the splendid sepulchre marking the place in Mount Olivet Cemetery, Chicago, where Capone in his gold-handled bronze coffin was laid to rest, February 1947

legger who knew him to be dishonest and an expensive nuisance, by the police who resented the Federal intrusion, and he was hated by all combined for his shameless affluence. It is doubtful if all Prohibition agents – whose wages were only about fifty dollars a week – rode about in chauffeured limousines and had show-girls for mistresses, but there were enough of them living on this meretricious scale to support the general contention. Certainly Captain Dan Chapin, chief of the New York prohibition force, once employed a rough-and-ready but simple means of weeding out the bribe-takers. He gathered all his force around a big table and then said: 'Put both hands on the table. Every one of you sons-o'-bitches with a diamond ring is fired.' Half his staff thereupon departed. It was against this background of dubious loyalty that a special, hand-picked and screened squad of Prohibition agents was put under the jurisdiction of the Secret Six. When, in September 1929, this proposal was put to George Emmerson Q. Johnson, the United States District Attorney, by Eliot Ness, a 26-year-old Prohibition agent who believed that Capone's breweries could be closed down by a closely-knit commando of about a dozen detached incorruptibles, Johnson's reflex question was: 'Can we find enough honest agents?' Ness found ten, most of them drawn not from Chicago's three-hundred-strong force, but from elsewhere. The scheme was approved and Ness was told that, while Irey, Wilson and O'Rourke probed the financial underbelly of the Capone caucus, it would be the task of the Ness squad to shut up the breweries and distilleries, to staunch his income at the source and make it impossible for him to pay the graft which gave him immunity. During the six months prior to Capone's homecoming from his prison term the Ness squad had burst through the doors of half a dozen Capone breweries with their ten-ton truck with a steel battering ram jutting from the radiator, had seized lorries and destroyed beer and equipment worth 250 thousand dollars, and taken five prisoners. There were attempts to scare them off and to buy them off; the attempts failed, and the squad became tagged by the newspapers the Untouchables. Attempts on Ness's life followed. One gunman – carrying a pistol with the serial numbers filed off and the cylinder loaded with dumdum bullets – was caught tailing Ness's car. Next came a telephoned promise that he would shortly be found in a ditch 'with a hole in your head and your wang slashed off' – a traditional Mafia expression of extreme contempt being to blow out the victim's brains, and then to cut off penis and testicles with a stiletto and leave them beside the body. Each day the call came: 'Hello, big

shot. How does it feel to be waiting to get it? It won't be long now.'
A dynamite bomb was planted in his car, wired to the starter. As a
demonstration of their achievements to date, Ness staged a mass
parade of forty-five confiscated beer trucks which were slowly
driven past the Lexington Hotel, where Capone was in residence.
Capone threw an Hitlerian fit, broke two chairs over a table, and
rushed screaming round the room. By the summer of 1931 the
Untouchables had accomplished their objective. As well as the fleet
of seized lorries, they had closed more than thirty illicit liquor
plants, broken up millions of dollars' worth of apparatus, and
poured a lakeful of beer and spirits down the drains, and they
finally struck their severest blow against the organization by uncovering on Diversey Avenue a gigantic alcohol plant, masked as a
paint factory, producing twenty thousand gallons a day piped
direct to tank cars on the adjacent railway siding. That Chicago was
running dry was indicated by the ambushing of private cars running
a few kegs at a time along routes where big vans loaded with barrels
had been rolling freely a few months earlier, and by a conversation
overheard on a tapped wire in which Guzik had informed one of
his pay-off men to suspend the monthly gratuities to the police – 'We
just ain't makin' any dough and if we ain't got it, we can't pay it.'

Capone was ruffled, unwell, and his beaming insolence of only
a year ago had been superseded by a look of bleak anxiety. There
were odd expressions of sympathy. A member of the Rapid City
Chamber of Commerce – galvanized, one suspects, more by the
gimmick of getting Rapid City some column-inches than by
genuine regard for Capone's misfortunes – wrote offering him the
hospitality of the West in the Black Hills of South Dakota. 'We
assure you,' he sparkled, 'of the glad hand of welcome into a community practically free from crime. We extend this invitation with
the sincere belief that with the associates you would meet here
you would soon outlive the crimes that have been credited to you
without any proof whatsoever, and soon you would be recognized
as a law-abiding upright citizen and a credit to the community.'

Apparently not smitten by the bucolic peace of the Black Hills of
South Dakota, Capone obstinately stayed in Chicago and attended
to his disrupted industries. Faced with severe erosion of income
from the drop in booze trade and the closure of his plants, he began
seriously to invade the union field as a milker of both organized
labour and of employers.

By 1930 Capone had infiltrated his racket-system into many
industries and unions, and was also taking a personal hand in

political control. Racketeering alone cost Chicago 136 million dollars in 1928, and a good portion of this went into the Capone syndicate's coffers. In a twelve-month period more than two hundred rackets were brought to the attention of the police, and in 1929 a Racket Court was established solely to investigate criminal cases arising out of labour and union rackets. The Court's jurisdiction covered destruction of property by explosives, injury to persons by explosives, malicious mischief to houses, collecting payment as penalty, depositing of stench bombs, conspiracy to do an illegal act, boycott or blacklist, manufacture or sale of explosives, entering premises to intimidate, kidnapping for ransom, mayhem, and intimidation of workmen. Gordon L. Hosteter, Secretary of the Chicago Employers' Association, listed as ultra-racketeering combinations a selection of trade groupings that covered almost every form of commercial activity in the city. These included the Cinder and Scavenger Association, the Soda Dispensers' and Table Girl Brotherhood, the Jewish Chicken Killers, the Electric Sign Makers' Union, the Apartment House and Hotel Association, the Tyre Workers' Union, the Junk Dealers and Pedlars, the Fish Dealers' Association, the Garage Employees' Union, the Chicago Candy Jobbers' Association, the Master Jewish Butchers' Association and the Master Photo Finishers of America. The methods used by Capone's ancillary enforcers to increase their income was that of the racketeer who offered garage-owners a big increase in business in return for a percentage payment – he despatched troops of thugs armed with ice-picks who in one month punctured fifty thousand tyres on cars parked in the streets: there was a consequent rush by drivers to book garage space. Out of gambling Capone, in a new peaceful alliance with racing rings, had organized a betting syndicate of five thousand Chicago bookmakers, guaranteeing them 'protection' at dog and horse tracks in return for weekly fees. And on the political front, Capone was beginning to take his own hold over City Hall independently of his party sponsors. He was sponsoring his own man, City Sealer Daniel A. Serritella, to the appointment of City Superintendent of Streets, thereby seizing control of an annual budget of seven million dollars, three thousand jobs and access to the five million dollars a year allocated to street-repair work. He was also lobbying for a bill that would create a plumbers' pool and give him supervision of another 1,200 municipal jobs.

Meanwhile, he was still fighting for an honest citizen's freedom to live where he wished. In April he returned to his Miami residence, to find that the court officials had been ordered to padlock the house on the ground that it was 'a public nuisance' and escort him to the State border. His lawyers instantly took out an injunction which suspended the Governor's instruction to county sheriffs that he should be arrested on sight. The Governor's rejoinder to this was to issue through a grand jury an appeal to all inhabitants 'to co-operate by all legitimate means towards ejecting a public menace and imposter and to exterminate from the community the cancerous growth of organized crime'. On 27 April Capone's attorneys forced the issue into court and pointed out that their client was charged with no crime and under no indictment, and claimed that, therefore, he had a perfect right to live in Florida. Unmoved by this fine point of law, the Public Prosecutor answered that it was 'just as much a crime to permit Capone to remain in Florida, as it would be to allow a rattlesnake to live in a garden where it could bite children'.

During the next month, the Florida police, displaying a tenacity and toughness that he had never encountered from such quarters up in Illinois, ignored the Federal injunction protecting him from arrest, persecuted him mercilessly. On 10 May his car was stopped and he and his brother John and two companions were taken to the police station and lodged in jail without charges being preferred. Capone gave his age as thirty and his occupation as 'retired'. The other three gave their occupations as 'real estate dealers'. He was quickly sprung, but five days later, while on his way into town to attend a boxing match, was again arrested for failing to obey an injunction to keep outside the city limits.

On 13 May Capone threw a birthday party for his ten-year-old son. Fifty children attended, but, hypersensitively nervous now at infringing any technicality, he insisted that every child should bring with him written parental permission. Within his own walls, Capone seemed to recover a little gaiety. While servants distributed chicken, ice-creams and soft drinks, the social columnists reported, Capone wandered about blowing up balloons and handing around sweets.

On 21 May he was again arrested at a prize fight with his brother and two bodyguards and charged with vagrancy. He had been about to fly off to New York to 'begin beauty treatment' – a twenty-one day surgery course to eliminate those old facial blemishes – but now he stayed on to combat this systematic molestation, made possible by the passing of a special city ordinance against vagrants, but which had been more bluntly expressed by the Mayor's order: 'Pick up Capone.' Late that month he obtained warrants charging the Mayor, the City Commissioner, the Director of Public Safety, and Mr. James

Cox, publisher of the Miami *Daily News*, with 'conspiracy to deprive him of his liberty'. That same day detectives attempted to arrest him for the fourth time, but he beat them to the sanctuary of his attorney's office.

He was fighting back with his characteristic skill and fast-footedness, and succeeded in whipping up some local support. On 30 May he gave a dinner to which he invited the rich and prominent of Miami – and many of them came. During the speeches, one guest gave a graceful welcome to 'the new businessman of the community', and presented him with a fountain pen.

In July he was cleared on technical grounds of a charge of perjury – and was cheered by occupants of the court public gallery when the judge directed the verdict of Not Guilty. He left facing another charge of perjury, but it was obvious that this could not be pressed. As he left the court he made a formal announcement of his retirement as leader of the Chicago syndicate. He intended, he said, to settle down permanently in Florida; he was buying a thirty-five acre estate to the north of Miami, where he would build a new home enclosed by a ten-foot wall. Capone had sat it out, and again won: the fury of the arrest-bail-injunction sequence tapered off and became temporarily quiescent.

Capone's claim to have retired from the rackets was not confirmed by the survey of his recent activities in the Chicago Crime Commission report which was issued in September. That showed that he had succeeded in gaining command of trades unions and employers organizations. The report revealed that his agents had lately been canvassing the ice-cream cafés, promising a big discount if they took their supplies from the firm they nominated, and that the syndicate had just captured the Theatre Ushers' and Ticket Takers' Union, as well as the Theatre Treasurers' Union. This, it was observed, now enabled Capone to appoint ushers at all prize fights and sporting events. It was estimated that Capone now controlled thirty-three per cent of Chicago's labour unions. His staff numbered five hundred men, none of whom received less than a hundred dollars a week, while he himself was drawing between two thousand and five thousand dollars from the new racket enterprises.

It may have been this factual, detailed disclosure of his new undertakings that caused Capone to use them as the basis of negotiations with the authorities. In November Chief Justice J. P. McGourty, of the Chicago Criminal Court, addressing yet another grand jury charged with an investigation of beer-running and labour-racketeering, made this remarkable statement: 'With cool effrontery, overtures were very recently made to the end that Chicago's most widely heralded and powerful gangster will withdraw from labour activities if he is permitted to conduct unmolested by law his racket in beer. His most formidable competitors have been ruthlessly exterminated, and the only apparent obstacle towards his undisputed sway is the law. Such a truce is unthinkable. There must not be any compromise with lawlessness. It is time every citizen should manifest his sense of responsibility and his willingness to unite in establishing the rule of law in Chicago. The time has come when the public must choose between the rule of the gangster and the rule of the law.' Later, the judge was asked by newspapermen to whom he referred. 'Capone,' he answered. The reports added that it was understood that he and the Public Prosecutor were approached on Capone's behalf by Mr. M. J. Galvin, secretary and treasurer of the Teamsters' Union, one of whose agents, George Barker, was then doing time for violation of parole and another, Jack White, awaiting trial for murder. Galvin, who had been repeatedly charged with labour racketeering, was then the principal power within the Chicago unions operating independently of the American Federation of Labour.

There was a conspicuous hardening of heart and diminution of toleration towards the beleagured but still undefeated gang king. It must have been chillingly discomfiting to hear the law, once his mouthpiece and his servant, speak as did Judge H. Lyle, of the Chicago Felony Court, to the Chicago Safety Council in December 1930. 'As soon as Capone is arrested on the vagrancy warrant now in the hands of the police,' said the judge, 'an effort will be made to send him to the electric chair. He will be tried for the murder of Colosimo. We'll send him to the chair if possible. He deserves to die and has no right to live. Capone has become an almost mythical being. He is not a myth, but a reptile who deserves to be crushed.' An order was then issued to Capone to face a grand jury on an income tax inquiry.

Capone beat the vagrancy rap on this occasion. When he was released on ten thousand dollars bail the following February, he told Chief Detective North: 'I'm sick and tired of being made the goat of every politician and reformer.' And, again: 'I guess I will retire.'

He was beyond the point of retirement, and, despite Judge Lyle's attempt to deflate the myth, he had become one and, ironically, it was his garish fame that made it impossible for Capone to submerge into quiet, rich obscurity. The glare of public attention burned upon him from every angle. Warner Brothers, it was said, were going to pay Capone two hundred thousand dollars for acting in their scheduled film *Public Enemy*, and later a second Hollywood company tried to persuade him to play the leading part in a gangster movie. A publisher offered him another huge sum for exclusive rights to his life story. 'I'm not going into the literary business, nor am I going to be a film star,' said Capone, refusing the propositions. 'I'm tired of publicity.' He continued to get it, preposterous or pertinent. In Berlin an elderly Hungarian named Ladislaus Kabovic walked into Grosswardein police station, claimed that he was Al Capone's father and demanded that they should telegraph the Chicago Federal Court insisting upon very severe punishment for having given him so much trouble when he was a boy. 'I will box Al's ears, for all his machine-guns, if I get hold of him,' threatened his improbable parent. In Detroit police raided bookstalls displaying publications 'glorifying Capone's exploits'. In London leading circulating libraries banned Pasley's book on Capone, sub-titled 'The Biography of a Self-Made Man'. In New York it was announced that Capone was negotiating for the Chicago rights of Edgar Wallace's play *On The Spot*, which had opened on Broadway with Crane Wilbur in the part of Tony Pirelli, the Capone-type mobster, played by Charles Laughton in London – a story which received wide publicity but which Capone immediately denied. (On the New York first night, as the play was in progress, an Italian hoodlum named Joseph Riggio was put on the spot outside the Catholic church in Brooklyn.) A two-year-old racehorse was given the name of Al Capone. In Copenhagen police confiscated from saloons and restaurants four hundred gambling machines made in Chicago and said to have been installed by Capone's agents who were taking a sixty-five per cent rake-off. A story appeared that Capone was arranging to send his son to school in Dublin because of threats to kidnap the boy and take him for a ride. In October 1931 Capone, McGurn and bodyguards arrived at a North Western University football game against Nebraska University, at Evanston, Illinois, were recognized and hurried away in a storm of jeers and boos.

Unhappy and dazed, Capone lumbered about like a bomber evading a searchlight cone. He toiled at ingratiating himself back into public admiration. He told a reporter feelingly: 'I've spent the best part of my life as a public benefactor.' He pursued this reputation with the unemployed who were multiplying in the slump-stricken city and to whom he appointed himself a mysterious, veiled Lady Bountiful, but whose veil was tantalizingly lifted just long enough for that bland swarthy face to be seen behind. In November of 1930 a newspaper story ran under the headline 'CAPONE FEEDS HUNGRY: EVEN A GANG CHIEF HAS A HEART'. 'A mysterious benefactor who has been feeding thousands of Chicago destitute at a huge soup-kitchen for a fortnight past was revealed today as Al Capone. A big building bears the sign "Free Food for the Workless". Two thousand were fed there yesterday on stew, soup, bread and coffee. No church or social body are concerned. Inquirers were told that a well-known philanthropist who wished to do good by stealth was behind the project. Today the manager admitted that Al Capone was paying all the expenses, and that his lieutenants were giving their services as relief workers. Capone, it was said, believed that persons of wealth like himself should take the responsibility of feeding the poor in these hard times.' A rather horrid incident intruded upon this *Christmas Carol* atmosphere – when a truck bearing a thousand of the birds destined for his soup-kitchen's Thanksgiving Day turkey dinners was halted on its way into the city by gunmen and the turkeys hijacked.

At the same time, he was not neglecting business. That year the Federal Farm Board had succeeded in its plea that the marketing of grape juice – a liquid lending itself to easy fermentation – was not illegal under Prohibition, and the Government-subsidized Fruit Industries Ltd. of California had inspired a national advertising campaign to dispose of the grape crop and aid employment. Shortly after, Mr. Donald Conn, managing director of the company, received the intimation that Capone was displeased about his announced intention to sell bottled grape concentrate in Illinois, and that his health would doubtless suffer badly if he persisted with the scheme.

However, Capone was, from various points of view, still considered good value by many Chicagoans. A member of one of the oldest and richest Chicago families, tried to persuade Capone to dine with a party that included socialites and writes, 'We offered Mr. Capone a chance to take wine with the *élite* of Chicago,' he said, 'Society would be a lot more fun if Al would join in.'

Al did not, for he was doing his best to rid himself of the taint of gaudy ostentation and excessive habits. Quiet, solid respectability was his lodestar, and he strenuously eschewed public appearances – especially those in police courts. It was also safer, for the peace-in-our-time pact forged so recently was already crumbling. In November police raided the apartment of Terry Druggan, the Irish co-partner in the Druggan-Lake beer gang. The raid revealed an interestingly grand status for those straitened times. His name was engraved in gold on his dinner service; it was also upon the furniture, upon his silver toilet set and upon his sixteen pairs of shoes. Oriental rugs covered the floor. Sets of Dickens, Thackeray and Shakespeare were bound in tooled Levant morocco. The rooms were panelled in walnut, behind which, it was discovered, was a functional cavity containing an arsenal of machine-guns, bombs and ammunition. The detectives also found files of letters from gangsters and gunmen in other parts of America. It was in one of these that plans were discussed for assassinating Capone, news which quickly reached him.

Possibly for this reason he stayed away from the wedding of his sister, an event of great splendour in the December of 1930 and one which was of particular political importance to gangdom. It was, in fact, a classically arranged union for the purpose of alliance between dynasties, such as has traditionally been the pattern of royal families and business empires. In November it was learned that a licence had been issued for the marriage of eighteen-year-old Mafalda to Mr. John Maritote, a twenty-two-year-old labourer. Maritote, the brother of Frank Diamond, was at the time engaged to another woman. The suit was said to have been agreed at a high-level gang conference without reference to either of the parties, Capone's contribution being the gift of a home and fifty thousand dollars. Questioned by the press, Mafalda admitted, after some hesitation, that Al Capone was her brother. The newspapers attributed the match to 'an effort to heal the rivalry between the liquor factions of Chicago'. The wedding, on 15 December, was an all-Italian pageant and it received mass coverage by the press. Four thousand guests attended, and thousands of spectators crushed around the church. A new red carpet was unrolled down the aisle. The bride wore an ivory satin gown with a train twenty-five feet long and carried a bouquet of four hundred lilies of the valley. There were five bridesmaids in pink taffeta and wearing double pearl pendants, gifts from the labourer bridegroom. Mrs. Capone, mother of the boys, was there in a mink coat. Among the uninvited guests were squads of detectives, who quietly removed guns from the frock coats of five of the congregation while a tenor sang 'Oh, Promise Me'. The bride and her groom were reported to look 'rather sheepish' during the ceremony, but there were compensations for submitting to the arrangement, such as the honeymoon spent in Cuba.

Apart from Druggan's animosity, Capone's main reason for remaining absent was probably that, as he was now permanently listed as No. 1 on the Vagrancy File, he would almost certainly have been arrested. His urgent philanthropy and the courtship of the people were not now making the authorities falter in their resolution; he was netted in a web of civil and police proceedings from which the ingenious labours of his legal advisers could not free him. During

1931 he was continuously in and out of court, and denying or dodging accusations that were thickening into a bombardment. In January 1931 he granted a vindicating interview to Eleanor Patterson, of the Washington *Herald*, who was visiting Miami, and who described him ecstatically as 'one of those prodigious Italians with the neck and shoulders of a wrestler, thick chested, almost six feet tall, with gigantic hands which superficially seem soft from easy living; nevertheless, they are beautifully manicured'. During the interview Capone served lemonade, while eight bodyguards hovered silently in the background, padding after them while Capone showed her around his mansion. He talked lengthily about his troubles and the injustices committed upon him. 'Prohibition has done nothing but make trouble for all of us,' he said sorrowfully. 'It is the worst thing that ever hit this country. If I say I give it no more than another five years, then I'm right, you bet. It's like this. I don't interfere with big business. None of those big business guys can say that I ever took a single dollar from them. I only want to do business with my own class. I don't interfere with their racket. Why can't they leave my racket alone? But there they are – always after me, trying to frame me. They got me framed in Chicago now. If I don't answer this framed income tax charge, they're going to try and trump up a charge of vagrancy against me. It ain't fair.' Mrs. Patterson looked into his eyes: 'Ice-grey. Ice-cold. I could feel their menace. The stirring of the tiger. For a second I went a little sick. I had to fight the impulse to jump up and run blindly away.' She sat there. So did Capone – impassive as a Buddha. Then he smiled – 'his thick-lipped, boyish smile'.

During the conversation an aeroplane swooped low down over his estate. Mrs. Patterson asked if he wasn't afraid that he might be bombed from the air. Capone shrugged somewhat despondently: 'Well, one way or the other.'

During the next few weeks, uninfluenced by his apologies, one public man after another spoke out against Capone and his crime empire. The Chicago District Attorney's office revealed that they had raided the Rex Hotel – owned by Dennis Duke Cooney – and carried off records of the Capone gang's pay-roll. It included a Congressman, several high administrative officials, leading politicians and many policemen. 'We found names on Capone's pay-list which we do not even dare to talk about yet,' said one of the District Attorney's staff. Mr. Albert R. Brunker, of the Chicago Civic Safety Committee, visiting Boston made graver allegations. 'There are six thousand city, State and Federal officials in Capone's pay,' said

Brunker. 'Eighty per cent of Chicago's magistrates and judges are criminals. Capone has supplied me with figures that show that two-thirds of the nation's drink bill go in bribes to officials.' Even the Army got into the attack. Major General Smedley Butler, of the United States Marine Corps, said in a speech on 20 February: 'When American public opinion is aroused, Capone will be run out of the States and deported to Italy.' This especially pricked Capone in a tender place. 'The General is misinformed,' he said with dignified indignation. 'I was born in America and cannot be deported under United States Law. Butler says I am a criminal. The only charge I know of against me is one charging me with vagrancy. I have been feeding three thousand people daily in Chicago in the last six months,' he added, casting aside the mantle of the benefactor doing good by stealth. 'If this is the act of a vagrant I want to be classed as one. I leave it to the American people to judge between Butler and myself, and I am satisfied to abide by their verdict.'

Unfortunately for him, he was now vulnerable to the more stringent and implacable verdict of the law. That month he had to return to Chicago to appear on a charge of contempt arising out of his refusal to answer questions. He again put to the gathered newspaper men his case for the right to public judgement. Referring to the previous day's primary election in which Big Bill Thompson had won the Republican nomination for the mayoralty, he said that this had vindicated him, for it was Judge Lyle, Thompson's opponent, who had issued the warrant for his arrest as public enemy. 'The people have given their verdict,' he said, repeating the phrase he seemed obsessively to think exhaled a fragrant fog over his past, 'on the attempt to make me a campaign issue. While Judge Lyle has been spending thousands of dollars trying to get into office, I have been spending thousands feeding the hungry. I am glad our courts are still functioning and I have no fear that the judiciary as a body will become hysterical. The public will one day awaken to the humbug which has been built up around me and my family.'

The humbug continued remorselessly. Two days later he again had to attend court, and there was sentenced by Judge Wilkerson to six months in prison for contempt. Wilkerson said that an affidavit furnished by Capone in February 1929, stating that he was ill and in bed, as an excuse for failing to appear before a Federal Grand Jury was 'glaringly false'. Government witnesses had sworn that he was during this period a regular visitor to the race tracks, and had made several long trips. Capone stood listening to this judgement mopily chewing gum. He was released on five thousand dollars bail and granted thirty days to prepare an appeal.

The old pull had not departed. To get Capone behind bars was like trying to catch fish between fingers. When the vagrancy charge came up for hearing, the judge was forced to dismiss the case as, he was told, no one could be found to testify against him. The prosecutor informed the court: 'We cannot find a single policeman who can furnish evidence on which the State bases this prosecution.' As he left, Capone told reporters complacently: 'Biggest frame-up I ever knew.'

Meanwhile, the legal process ground on down in Miami. For the first and only time Capone's wife took a public hand in her husband's matted affairs. She appeared successfully to secure an order from the Miami Court restraining the Deputy Sheriff from removing furniture from the Palm Island house to meet a fifty thousand dollar claim for legal fees brought by Capone's attorney. The furniture, she swore, was hers. So much in the background did Mrs. Capone live – thereby fulfilling her husband's dogmatic ideals, expressed earlier during the Philadelphia interview, that a woman's place and happiness was in the home – that this step out into the searchlight beam attracted considerable notice. The only previous newspaper publicity she had received had been of the most general tenor, such as the article that appeared three months earlier which had stated: 'Mrs. Capone, a good-looking Irish woman of Brooklyn birth, goes to Mass regularly, and is a member of the Sisterhood of St. Theresa. She seldom leaves her island home except to go to church. Tony, the ten-year-old son, is a bright little fellow. He goes to Miami daily in a roadster driven by one of his father's Pretorian Guards to attend school conducted by the Jesuit Fathers of the Church of the Redeemer, where he was recently confirmed. She lives under constant fear that Tony may be kidnapped or her husband assassinated. More than one bomb has been thrown over the barricade of the Spanish villa by someone in a speedboat.' Capone's recipe for a housewife's happiness seemed distant from his own home.

Six days after the little problem in Miami had been disposed of, Capone was back in court again in Chicago – this time to face the tax charges that had been loomingly gathering in bulk. He appeared in gay garb, in a pale brown summer suit, brown and white shoes, and a straw hat perkily tipped. When reporters chaffed him at the brightness of the ensemble, he wisecracked: 'Yeah, it is loud. I was afraid the judge might not see me, so I had to make sure.' But he was in a sober and meditative mood. Once again he announced his determination to quit and become an ordinary, well-behaved citizen. The Secret Six, he admitted, had killed the racket. 'Any successor will find it doesn't pay any more,' he said. 'I want the public to get me right. I've never done anything worse than sell a little beer and alcohol, and cheat the tax collector. I'm going to take my medicine and then live a respectable life.'

The real medicine, during all the foregoing sporadic buffets and sparring, had been a long time brewing.

Almost as soon as he had left the Philadelphia prison in March 1930 there had come the further shock of Nitti's and Guzik's indictments for failure to pay taxes, and, with his brother already convicted of a similar offence, Capone's nervousness increased. Following his new policy of meek deference to authority, in the summer of 1930 he spontaneously presented himself for an interview with Frank Wilson in the Department of Internal Revenue. With Capone was a lawyer, a tax expert summoned from Washington, who declared that Capone wanted to pay any tax that it could be shown that he owed, and would answer any questions. The first question Wilson put to Capone was if he owned The Subway, the gambling-house from which had been obtained the invaluable records which had convicted Bottles. 'Mr. Wilson,' Capone said humbly, 'I will let my lawyer answer that for me.' The lawyer explained that although Mr. Capone was only too willing to help the government, he wished to be discreet about information that might be used as evidence in criminal proceedings. At the end of the interview, Capone's respectful manner slipped sideways. 'Mr. Wilson,' he said thickly as he rose to leave, 'you be sure to take care of yourself.'

During that summer Capone and his lawyer paid several return visits to Wilson, without being aware that meanwhile Irey and his men were surreptitiously collecting hard facts about Capone's expenditure – such as that he was paying bills of three thousand dollars a year to the telephone company and six thousand to hotel companies – all of which proved that Capone had income, even if, at this stage, it could not be proved where the income came from. At last the lawyer admitted that his client was in receipt of income, although, he said, that never amounted to more than a hundred thousand dollars a year. At Wilson's request this admission was made in the form of a letter, which later contributed to Capone's conviction. This letter sketched a dire situation: Capone was the sole support of his widowed mother, his house was heavily mortgaged, he supported a wife, son and sister, and, additionally, as he was the

member of a firm that had never kept books, it was impossible to
make any accurate statement as to his income, although his share was
one-sixth of whatever profits were made; but certainly until 1926
he had never made more than 750 dollars a week. With all these
cautious qualifications as a preamble, the lawyer then continued:
'Notwithstanding that two of the taxpayer's associates from whom I
have sought information with respect to the amount of the taxpayer's
income insist that his income never exceeded fifty thousand dollars
a year, I am of the opinion that his taxable income for the years
1926 and 1927 might fairly be fixed at not to exceed twenty-six
thousand dollars and forty thousand dollars respectively. For the
years 1928 and 1929 it did not exceed a hundred thousand dollars
per year.'

This did not serve to convince the Internal Revenue, as they
already knew that he spent more than a hundred thousand dollars a
year on horses and clothes alone. It was decided that, although there
were enough admissions in the letter to hang a short prison sentence
on Capone, the secret investigations would be continued to see if
it could not be ascertained exactly what was the sum of which
Capone received one-sixth. Little by little the provable facts
accumulated, aided considerably by a dusty ledger through which
Wilson had at first unhopefully flicked during his night-long
examinations of the stacks seized in gambling and liquor raids.
This, the account book of the Hawthorne betting-shop, contained
records of monthly divisions of big profits and had repeated references to 'Al'. An ex-Hawthorne cashier, a man named Leslie
Shumway, was finally picked up at a Florida race-track and was
persuaded to make a written deposition in which he estimated the
profits during the twenty-two months he worked in the betting shop –
just one of many such establishments – at 587,721 dollars. Even if
Capone got only the one-sixth he owned to, even if this were his only
source of income, his profits had exceeded by far the 750 dollars a
week he claimed to have been getting at that time. The evidence was
at last substantial enough to take action, and on 13 March 1931
Shumway was ushered before a secret grand jury and Capone was in
his absence charged with evading income taxes for 1924. The
indictment was not publicly revealed, for further indictments were
pending, twenty-two of them which were handed down by a May
grand jury charging evasion between 1925–1929 and presenting a
tax bill of 215,030 dollars.

The March proceedings may have been secret but it seems
probable that Capone had news of them. For early in the year he

abruptly left Chicago. When Capone took the train he was already, although he did not know it, a displaced person, a refugee from retribution that had taken an unconscionable time to clank into movement but which was now irresistible. He arrived in Los Angeles and was promptly instructed by the police to be gone within twelve hours. 'We were just tourists,' Capone complained piteously. 'I thought Los Angeles liked tourists. We no sooner got there than the newspapers started writing stuff about me, and then I got the bum's rush. And somebody stole my wine. A swell dump!' All he was looking for, he said, was a quiet place where he could settle down in peace. He did not find his haven in the Black Hills of South Dakota, where he next turned up, for the Governor – repudiating the invitation issued only a year before by the local Chamber of Commerce – threatened to call out the National Guard unless he left voluntarily. Cuba and the Bahamas heard of his intention to descend upon them, and sent peremptory warnings not to. Piqued and bewildered by this calamitous reversal of his fortunes, by the disappearance of the old magic attached to his name that once had the famous and the well-bred eager to meet him, he started out for his island estate in Florida – and was again rebuffed. Governor Doyle E. Carlton alerted each of the sixty-seven Florida sheriffs: 'It is reported that Al Capone is on his way to Florida. Arrest promptly if he comes your way and escort him to the state border. He cannot remain in Florida. If you need additional assistance call me.'

Again Capone, the property-owner, fought. Managing to resurrect two old friendships from the wreckage, he prevailed upon Attorneys J. F. Cordon and Vincent Giblin of Miami to obtain a temporary injunction from Federal Judge Halsted L. Ritter restraining the sheriffs from 'seizing, arresting, kidnapping or abusing the plaintiff, Alphonse Capone', and he was able to reach his Palm Island villa. The injunction was eventually made permanent.

Yet that did not stop the local authorities from discomfiting him in other ways. One of his chief lieutenants, Machine-Gun Jack McGurn, who was staying with him, was arrested on Miami golf course and jailed, the police acting upon the complaint of a neighbour of Capone, Ernest Byfield, a hotel magnate, who had seen McGurn and his friends polishing up their marksmanship by firing tommy-guns at floating bottles. This assault upon Capone at one remove was helped by three prominent Chicagoans vacationing in Miami who telegraphed to Deputy Commissioner Stege demanding that he claimed his own delinquent, and a pair of detectives were despatched south to bring McGurn back.

A new outcry against Capone's presence was set up in the Florida papers, who alleged that he was a deterrent to timid tourists and businessmen fastidious about accidental encounters with such a notorious figure.

In an attempt to disabuse the Miamians' minds of their distorted impression of him Capone issued one of his many proclamations that he had forsaken his old ways. 'I would like to correct the impression,' he said stiffly, 'that my house in Miami is an armed camp and that I live in daily fear of my life. That is not true. I am cut off entirely from the underworld. No one bothers me. I don't believe anyone wants to. People insist that I never sleep without a pistol under my pillow. That is not true, either. The possession of a pistol without a proper permit is a violation of the law. I have not a permit and I do not have a pistol. The reason is simple. I am a peaceful law-abiding citizen and I mean to remain so. I have no desire to break the law. I cut out of Chicago a long while ago and I broke loose from everything connected with it at the same time. Crime and bootlegging hold not the slightest interest for me.'

Capone had stayed on at Miami Beach for several miserable and fretful months. An interviewer who visited him there described the setting he found him in. His twenty-room white-painted villa with a sun-porch faced the moon-flecked waters of Biscayne Bay, the scent of jasmine and hibiscus drugged the breeze. They walked together around the 'estate' – 'nothing finer in the Hollywood movie colony', Capone told the interviewer. Capone tossed biscuit crumbs to the tropical fish in a fern-hung rock pool with submerged lighting, and they walked between marble benches and shrubberies to his private pier where his speedboat and cruiser proudly flying the Stars and Stripes were moored. Capone dilated upon his pleasant life of leisure: he rose at nine-thirty, took a plunge in the swimming pool, had a business session with his secretary, then fished for bonito (a kind of mackerel), or played golf or bridge, or went to the races; there were usually friends in for dinner; in bed by one a.m. But upon the idyll intruded the old pressures. Armed guards patrolled the high-walled perimeter; at dusk the lights went on inside and outside the house, flooding away from the garden and sea-shore the shadows which could accommodate enemies.

There was no peace of mind to be found fishing among the palm trees. One additional worry was that, with his forbidding presence absent from the Chicago scene, the pot-shooting and scrabbling for what he possessed had broken out again. On 24 March he was

telephoned to say that the previous night Johnny Genaro, one of his
chiefs of staff, had been rubbed out. Genaro had been driving with
Joseph Vince to visit his mother, when, in the crowded centre of the
city, a Ford had drawn alongside and, in the ritualistic manner,
bullets had been hammered from it. Genaro was killed; Vince said:
'I can't describe the men, I was so confused.' Suspected was James
Belcastro, who had recently been wounded by Capone thugs. At the
time, Belcastro had said: 'I can't say who they were. I have such
poor eyes.'

In the summer the grand jury was again in session, for a whole
week. Capone must, with increasing anxiety, have been watching
their ominous deliberations, for this time he did not attempt to stall
as he had in February 1929. Then, when he was served with a sub-
poena by a deputy marshal ordering him to return from Miami to
appear before a grand jury, his reply had been an affidavit from his
doctor stating that he had been ill and that 'if he went north his
death might result' (although bullets were not mentioned as the
possible fatal visitation). This time, presumably informed by his
advisers that the gathering weight of legal process was too strong to
be snubbed, in June 1931 in his new state of meekness Capone
travelled to Chicago and took up residence at the Lexington Hotel.
The indictment was returned at 1.30 p.m. on 5 June, handing
down against Capone and sixty-eight others indictments charging
them with five thousand violations of the Prohibition laws, and an
income tax evasion against Capone specifically, which charged him
with failure to pay 215 thousand dollars on an income of 1,050,000
dollars between 1924 and 1929. Three hours later Capone walked in,
smiling in gracious acknowledgement to the words of encouragement
from reporters and sightseers. His voluntary appearance was a
crushing disappointment to at least one officer, one Clarence Con-
verse, an agent on the Capone case, who burst into tears when he
realized that he would not have the deep pleasure of entering the
Lexington and marching Capone out under arrest. Half an hour
later Capone, freed for eleven days on fifty thousand dollars bail,
left – smiling, determinedly urbane – with his entourage of bodyguards and lawyers.

After Capone's return to the Lexington, Frank Wilson, the tax
investigator who had prepared the evidence for the grand jury, had a
telephone call from Pat O'Rourke with information that Capone had
just shipped in five gunmen from New York whose assignment was
to kill Wilson, Madden and Irey, in the hope that this eleventh
hour demonstration of his fire-power would deter anyone else from

continuing with the prosecution, or, at any rate, from voting him guilty. Next day the car with the New York licence plates and its five occupants had vanished. Capone, reported O'Rourke, had been talked out of this desperate measure, for the days had irrevocably gone when such brazen slaughter could have succeeded, and there were men around Capone wiser than he himself, who were sensitively sniffing the new climate of resolution. One more slightly subtler scheme was tried. A dapper young man called upon a New York businessman friend of Irey and asked him to convey to Irey the offer of one and a half million dollars in cash if Capone was pardoned. The offer was not accepted.

25

The Blow Below the Belt

'There was too much overhead in my business.'

AL CAPONE

I'm a real good bootlegger but I done fell poor.
Since good whisky been in, bootleggin' ain't no good no more.

BLIND BLUES DARBY
Bootleggin' Ain't No Good No More

CAPONE'S third and final strategy was now adopted. Surreptitiously negotiations began to take place. Unofficial approaches were made to government representatives by Capone's attorneys, suggesting a secret deal, a token two-and-a-half year sentence, and a financial settlement. Capone had been persuaded to reconcile himself to another short, comfortable sabbatical in jail to end these irritating formalities about which the Federal authorities were now being so stubborn. A Chicago newspaper printed a story early in June alleging that a confidential agreement had been entered into, and Irey, many years later, stated that United States District Attorney Johnson, acting on orders from Washington, had finally decided that the government would be satisfied with a compromise two-and-a-half year sentence in return for a plea of guilty by Capone, rather than run the familiar risk of intimidated jurors and frightened witnesses who would panic at the last moment and turn Capone free. The cautious view was that a limited assured victory was preferable to probable total defeat.

Having been reassured that he could plead guilty safely and expect no more than two-and-a-half years, Capone accepted the situation with the grace of which he was capable. He was seen around town and at the races in his customary front box. Then, acting with traditional pomp, he threw a going-away banquet. It was the final splendour of the Capone gang era, the twilight rite of this particular god. It was held in the New Florence Hotel, a Hogarthian gathering of the Chicago underworld and its allies, emissaries from the race-track, the boxing-ring, brewery firms and ward political circles fraternally assembled with gunmen, brothel-keepers and racketeers for the last supper. During the dinner Capone circulated, accepting condolences and warm wishes, with his arm around Johnny Torrio who had returned for the occasion. 'Johnny'll look after things while I'm away,' he told his friends. There also was O'Rourke, still masquerading as Lepito, the new recruit, sharing a table with Mike Kelly, Machine-gun Jack McGurn and Paul Ricca. When Capone greeted him on his stroll around the company, O'Rourke said loyally: 'Sorry you're going away, Al.' Drinking – but of specially reserved champagne, spirits and wines, and not the stock for general distribution – went on until dawn.

On 16 June Capone presented himself before Judge Wilkerson and, with no arguments, pleaded guilty to everything, to the five thousand Prohibition and one income tax charges which theoretically could place him in prison for twenty-five thousand years. He was a prize, unbelievably inside the law's grasp at last, and he was treated with gingerly concern. A solid phalanx of policemen ensured that there was no swoop upon him by his enemies in this exposed situation, and he was taken up to the fifth floor of the court house in the private elevator. A federal judge who shortly before had tried to enter the elevator had been barred by the attendant and told: 'You can't use this, bud. It's reserved for Al Capone.' After his plea of guilty, his lawyers requested a two-week suspension of sentence so that he could get his affairs into order. The request was granted, and a subsequent application for a further thirty-day delay on the ground of his son's illness with mastoiditis.

On 30 July Capone arrived back at the court house to receive his mild tap upon the knuckles. He received, instead, a dazing body blow. Perhaps at that point Capone sensed it moving massively towards him for he seemed to have last minute misgivings about the trustworthiness of the deal. Although he had been talking confidently to the press about the thirty-month cinch he had fixed, he told newspaper men in the corridor on the way in: 'I'm a little nervous. After all, I'm only human.' He was costumed stylishly for the opening in a dark green suit and brown-and-white shoes. Rhythmically chewing gum, he watched Judge Wilkerson take his seat and instantly put an edge of unexpected tension on the proceedings by stating emphatically: 'I will hear the evidence in this case. The defendant must understand that he cannot have an agreement in this court.'

There were exchanges of apprehensive glances between Capone and his attorney, Michael Aherne, and both listened closely to United States District Attorney George E. Q. Johnson explain that the recommendation for leniency had been arrived at with the approval of the Attorney General, the head of the Intelligence Unit of the Internal Revenue Department, and an assistant secretary of the Treasury.

The judge interrupted with: 'A plea of guilty is a full admission of guilt. The power of compromise is not vested in this court, but is conferred by Congress on other governmental offices. The court may require the production of evidence. If the defendant asks leniency by throwing himself on the mercy of the court he must be prepared to answer all proper questions put to him by the court. While the court may determine the degree of guilt, it must assume on the defendant's plea, that the defendant committed the offences as stated in the indictment. If the defendant expects leniency from this court he must take the witness stand and testify on what ground he expects leniency.'

Aherne protested: 'The defendant and his counsel never considered that this would be an unqualified plea. Prior to the entry of the plea and prior to the return of the last indictment, I conferred with the District Attorney. The District Attorney said if a plea of guilty was entered he would make a recommendation with respect to the duration of the punishment.'

Judge Wilkerson raised his hand. 'I understand that the District Attorney intends to do that,' he said.

'We thought,' Aherne continued quickly, 'that the recommendation would be approved by the court. We believed that the department would have the power to compromise both the criminal and civil liability, that it constituted an inducement for the defendant to enter the plea we made. I am frank to say that we would not have entered those pleas unless we thought the court would accept them as made.'

What Judge Wilkerson then said left Capone in no doubt that his time of privilege and special concession was finished. Wilkerson continued: 'Certainly it is an unheard of thing in court proceedings that anybody, even the court itself, could bind the court as to the judgement which is to be made by the court. The court will listen to recommendations of the District Attorney, but the defendant cannot think that the court is bound to enter judgement according to those recommendations.' And, direct to Capone, he added: 'The defendant must understand that the punishment has not been decided before the close of the hearing. I must have it understood that there can be no bargaining in the Federal Court.'

There was a dismayed, muttered consultation among Capone's

attorneys and his counsel leaped up to withdraw the pleas of guilty. Capone, chewing his gum more rapidly, appeared bewildered. The indictments on the five thousand Prohibition charges could not be substantiated, Wilkerson ruled, but Capone must stand trial on the income-tax charge. 6 October was named as the day.

Even at this late stage Capone was still astutely watchful for any opportunity of gathering good will. During the interlude between Wilkerson's ruling and the start of the trial, John Lynch, millionaire race-track operator and gambler, was during August, kidnapped and held to ransom for 250 thousand dollars. The Chicago police department, private detectives and an organized committee of his friends, failed to trace him; an offer of a hundred thousand dollars was rejected by the kidnappers who sent back the brusque message that either the whole amount should be sent or Lynch would be murdered. Lynch's friends obtained audience with Capone and asked him to use his influence in the underworld to obtain his release. Capone said grandly to reporters: 'A kidnapper is no better than a rat, and I don't approve of this racket because it makes the kidnapped man's wife and kiddies worry so much. I shall be glad to help Chicago in this emergency.'

A few hours later Lynch was tossed out of a car in a street in Kanakee, Illinois, and arrived back at his home at Lake Geneva, Wisconsin, exhausted but unharmed. Capone's intervention, and the latest demonstration of his power, received much publicity; but there were those who were less impressed and sniffed an elaborate kudos-earning plot, whereby Capone could have arranged Lynch's removal and, after letting the authorities sweat helplessly for a few days, attract gratitude and applause by turning the wretched millionaire loose. The police took this cynical view and issued a warrant for his arrest on a charge of being concerned in abduction. Capone had ducked out of sight. His associates, with strident indignation, said that the Big Fellow had been double-crossed. When the excitement had fizzled out and the warrant had been pushed aside out of boredom with the whole thing, Capone reappeared and told the newspapers: 'We shall have to make examples of these kidnappers. I want to get these fellows more than any other criminals.'

Capone had not capitulated in his individualistic fight for human rights. Five days before the tax trial opened O'Rourke came on the telephone to Irey to report that the gang had the list of the hundred Chicagoans to be called in the special panel for jury duty. 'The boys are out talking to jurors with a wad of dough in one hand and a gun in the other,' he said. O'Rourke's report proved true: jurors were being bribed and threatened. Irey hastened to Judge Wilkerson, who listened and said: 'Don't worry.'

On the day before the trial the special panel of citizens was summoned. Five tried to avoid selection. The judge excused a few on legal grounds, and ordered the rest to be present next morning when the trial would begin with the selection of the twelve. None of the prospective jurors complained of the approaches that it was known had been made to them. Irey and his colleagues were depressed and overwrought, secretly almost certain that Capone had won, that the trial would be swung.

There was the atmosphere of festival and high drama next morning outside and within the courthouse. Big crowds were gathered. A network of extra telegraph wires had been installed to carry the news all over the nation and the world. Reporters from throughout America and correspondents of European papers crammed into the press and public benches, and outside the building newsreel cameras whirred and flashlamps exploded as the Capone contingent arrived. In personal attendance upon the Big Fellow was Phil D'Andrea, a sombre and bespectacled gunman, who was carrying a briefcase. He was also found to be carrying a loaded revolver down the front of his trousers, was removed to a cell, and later got six months in jail for contempt of court.

On his way in Capone talked volubly to journalists. 'I was willing to go to jail,' he said, still deep in his character part of the injured philanthropist. 'I could have taken my stretch, come back to my wife and child, and lived my own life. But I'm being hounded by a public that won't give me a fair chance. They want a full show, all the courtroom trappings, the hue and cry, and all the rest. It's utterly impossible for a man of my age to have done all the things with which I am charged. I'm a spook, born of a million minds. Yet if Al Capone is found guilty who is going to suffer – a masquerading ghost or the man who stands before you? You're right – it'll be me who goes to jail. Well,' he ended, with a flourish of vivacity, 'I'd much rather be sitting in a box watching the world baseball championships. What a life!'

The swearing-in of the jury began. Bailiff Frank Otto called the first name. Capone's attorney ran his eye down a list before him and looked up startled. His anxiety increased as he looked vainly on the paper for each of the next eleven names. None was among the hundred citizens the gang had been busy interviewing. Early that morning Judge Wilkerson had been to the court and ordered that the listed special panel should be substituted for the regular jury panel used by the rest of the courts. From that moment on it did seem possible to Irey and the prosecution that there was now an even chance that Capone's misdeeds would be heard and examined objectively.

The trial lasted twelve days. There was a procession of witnesses, called to demonstrate the sums of money Capone had consistently spent. Tailors, shirt-makers, jewellers, butchers, hoteliers, real-estate agents and various other tradesmen disclosed the payments made to them by Capone – usually in cash, but occasionally by cheques bearing Jack Guzik's signature – in return for goods and services. One witness revealed that Capone had bought from him suits of underwear at eleven dollars each made of finest Italian glove silk – 'a material similar to women's silk-knit gloves,' he explained. There was laughter and Capone blushed sulkily. Other traders came forward with the information that he paid 135 dollars for his suits, twenty-five dollars for his monogrammed shirts, and that he had bought thirty diamond belt buckles at 275 dollars apiece. He paid twelve thousand dollars for his automobiles.

Shumway, the one-time Hawthorne Smoke Shop betting agent, and other ex-Capone employees gave evidence of the source of Capone's income. When the defence objected that none of these witnesses could prove that Capone had received a cent, Wilkerson overruled with: 'The defendant purposely maintained no bank account and kept no records so that no information might leak out concerning his income. The defendant has built a stone wall around himself, and the Government must rely on a chain of circumstances.'

The stone wall was, nevertheless, flaking. Despite fierce objections by the defence, the letter written by Capone's lawyer to Frank Wilson the previous summer admitting income was introduced. By laboriously piling detail upon detail during the twelve days, the prosecution cumulatively proved that Capone had income, that he admitted it, that he spent it and that he paid no taxes on any of it. The defence's answer was that the only thing that had been proved was that Capone was a spendthrift.

The jury was retired for ten hours. It returned its verdict at 11.10 p.m. on 18 October, and a curious verdict it was. Capone was found not guilty of tax-evasion during 1924, 1928 and 1929 – a pronouncement which he listened to with spreading glee. What followed froze his wide grin. He was, continued the foreman, guilty of tax-evasion during 1925, 1926 and 1927, and of failing to file returns for 1928 and 1929. So baffled was the prosecution by how

Capone could simultaneously be not guilty of paying no taxes in 1928 and 1929, and guilty of not filing a return in the same years, that request was made for an adjournment in which to decide whether the verdict could be accepted. After a quarter of an hour the prosecution announced that the Government accepted the verdict.

Six days later Capone was brought back into court for sentence. Wilkerson's judgement was even more complicated than the original verdict. The judge's grey touselled head was bent over his notes as he dealt with each charge; as each sentence was announced in separate periods of years Capone reacted visibly: his face worked and his tongue ran around his lips, he twisted his fingers behind his back, then fumbled with the white handerkchief in his breast pocket. He tried to smile but did not succeed notably. As the judge continued, both sides seemed increasingly uncertain precisely what penalty was being imposed by the concurrent and varying sentences arising from the five separate convictions. Obligingly, the judge finally summarized it: Capone would go to prison for eleven years and pay a fifty thousand dollar fine and thirty thousand dollars costs. A murmur of astonishment rose in the courtroom – for this was more than double any penalty previously meted out for any similar offence. Finally, the judge raised his eyes and asked the marshal when he could arrange for Capone's transportation to Atlanta Jail, and the marshal replied crisply: 'At six-fifteen tonight.' Capone turned to his lawyer and shook his hand, saying: 'Well, so long . . . Goodbye.'

Looking weary and bemused, he walked to the elevator. It was no longer reserved for him exclusively. It was crowded with reporters, court officials and police, and there too was O'Rourke, who on the fourth day of the trial had emerged from under his disguise as Lepito, the Brooklyn gunman, to give evidence. Capone looked at him and said: 'The only thing that fooled me was your looks. You look like a wop.' He added with a faint grin: 'You took your chances and I took mine. I lost.'

But the strained composure disintegrated when he reached the swarming crowds outside the courtroom. The news had travelled swiftly. Chicago seemed in a state somewhere between shock and amazement that the Big Fellow had actually been cut down, that even at the very last moment his money and influence had not been able to extricate him. Pale-faced and now visibly distressed, Capone's rage flashed and he grabbed at a bucket of water to throw it over a photographer levelling a camera at him, but was hauled back by the guards. He was walked to receiving cell D5 and put in with a man being held for non-payment of a fine. When reporters were admitted,

Capone was in control of himself again, able to remember his reputation for the royal gesture. Pulling a roll of dollars from his pocket he peeled off some and handed them to his cell-mate, explaining to the press: 'I'm gonna help him out.' He then amplified his earlier complaint that it was a 'blow below the belt', adding: 'But if we have to do it we can do it. I have never heard of anyone getting more than five years for income-tax trouble, but they are prejudiced against me. I never had a chance.' He asked photographers not to take shots of him behind bars – 'Think of my family' – and was then left. At supper that night he drank two cups of coffee, but did not touch the corned beef and cabbage on a tin plate. He refused to give further interviews to the press – he attributed the severity of his sentence to his newspaper notoriety, was the message conveyed.

The bolts had not quite been rammed home on him. Judge Wilkerson had refused to admit him to bail pending an appeal, but promptly on Monday morning Capone's lawyers filed an application for bail with the circuit court of appeals. The battle against his sentence continued for six months, and it was futile. The appeal was denied and on 3 May 1932 Capone was taken from Cook County jail to catch the Dixie Flyer from Dearborn Station for Atlanta, where he was booked in the federal penitentiary as No. 40,866. Eliot Ness later described this departure from Chicago. A pair of United States marshals were escorting him to Atlanta, but Ness was made responsible for his protection until the train rolled off. To guard against any rescue or assassination attempt, Ness organized a five-car caravan for the short trip between jail and station. One car led the way; Capone's next; behind that three more carrying Prohibition agents and police, all armed with sawn-off shot-guns, revolvers and automatics in unbuttoned shoulder holsters.

Capone was led from his cell at nine-thirty although the Dixie Flyer was not to depart until eleven-thirty. As he was taken down the cell corridors to the warden's office, shouts came from other prisoners: 'You got a bum break, Al,' 'Keep your chin up, Al – it ain't so tough', and 'You'll own the joint before you're there long, Al'. In the warden's office Marshal Henry Laubenheimer handed the prison clerk the warrant which instructed the sheriff to 'deliver the bodies of one Alphonse Capone and one Vito Morici'. Capone's companion was on his way to Florida to be tried in the Federal courts there for transporting a stolen car. As they left and Morici began to put on his overcoat, Capone said to him: 'Keep that over your arm so nobody sees the handcuffs.'

An advance party of photographers were in the jail's inner courtyard and the flashbulbs exploded. Capone seemed curiously pleased to be briefly back in the public eye and it was then that he remarked to Ness: 'Jeez, you'd think Mussolini was passin' through.' More pressmen and a crowd of three hundred Chicagoans were at the prison gates, and a much vaster throng at the Dearborn Station, including many of his friends and his two younger brothers, to see him go, and to see the end of an era. But after the initial reintroduction to the old frenzy of limelight, he suddenly became querulous and yelled at the pressmen: 'Go to hell, you lousy rats. You want to take me for a ride some more, huh? Well, I'm not going to talk.'

There were eight cars on the Dixie Flyer and all were searched. Capone was put aboard the second from the end with the two marshals, and the compartments on either side were occupied by armed guards assigned for the trip. Capone took off his overcoat and lit a cigar. He glanced up at Ness. 'Well, I'm on my way to do eleven years,' he said flatly. 'I've got to do it that's all. I'm not sore at anybody. Some people are lucky. I wasn't.' Then he added with the gloomy candour of a bankrupt surveying his mistakes: 'There was too much overhead in my business anyhow, paying off all the time and replacing trucks and breweries. They ought to make it legitimate.'

The doors crashed and the train pulled out.

26

The Biggest of the Has-beens

'We must keep America whole and safe and unspoiled.'
AL CAPONE

Cain't sell no whisky, I cain't sell no gin . . .
I cain't keep open, I'm gonna close the shack.
The Chief of Police tore my playhouse down,
No use in grievin' – I'm gonna leave this town.
MAGGIE JONES, *Good Time Flat Blues*

CAPONE spent the next two years in Atlanta Penitentiary, working most of the time in the tailoring shop cutting out overalls and trousers for seven dollars a month, which later rose to ten dollars. He inside and his followers outside had still not given up all hope of reversing the calamitous trend. In May 1932 his application for a rehearing of his trial, based on the ground that action had been taken against him after the statutory time limit had expired, was dismissed by the Supreme Court. Said Capone disconsolately: 'I'm still the goat. The law didn't treat me fair. I'm a good citizen. Look at all the good I've done in the world, and this is what I get for it.'

Inside the jail he continued to be concerned about his good name. When it came to his notice that Howard Hawk, the Hollywood producer, was making the film *Scarface* he despatched an emissary to Hawk to intimate that he wanted to be consulted on the treatment of the story. Hawk reported: 'The man said that the Big Fellow was opposed to gangster films, particularly those that show underworld characters as rats and not heroes. I told him the Big Fellow would have to lay down his money at the box office if he wanted to see how I was doing the film. I believe Capone is giving funds to the campaign against this kind of movie.'

From the cell he made one last desperate effort to enlist the public sympathy that he believed still survived for him. It was the Lindbergh baby kidnapping that gave him the notion. In April 1932, when the nation was shocked by the seizure of the hero aviator's child, Capone issued an offer to use all his underworld resources to hunt down the kidnappers and recover the baby – if he could be given temporary freedom. He said he would put up bail of five hundred thousand dollars and that his younger brother would enter jail as hostage until his return. 'I believe I can find the baby,' he said. 'I won't run away. I won't doublecross the younger brother I love. If my brother is not acceptable, my son Tony may take his place, provided his mother agrees. What a lot I could do outside! I don't know a thing about the Lindbergh kidnapping, but I'm known to all the racket crowd as an honest guy, an honest guy who would keep his word if it's money they're after. If anyone stole my boy I feel sure I could get him back and I would work just as hard for the Lindberghs, and ask for no pay and no glory. I should soon know whether the child was in the possession of any regular mob that I can connect with, or any individual working his own racket who would know that he could trust me and that it might not be a bad idea to do me a good turn.'

This eloquent petition drew no response from the stony authorities, who now had the honest guy behind walls and intended to keep him there. There was even some speculation whether this was a desperate attempt to hold the baby hostage for Capone's freedom, a plot engineered by his gang.

Lindbergh told reporters that he would be willing to accept Capone's offer, but the official reply was, briefly and emphatically – No, Capone would not be released. He lapsed into depressed silence, broken when in early May the Lindbergh baby was found, dead. Capone had one more try. He declared that if he were set free he would bend all his energies to bringing the criminals to justice, and offered a reward of ten thousand dollars for information.

There continued to be a steady trickle of intelligence about Capone's welfare and progress as a prisoner. In December of that year, United States Attorney Dwight Green, who had helped to put him inside, brought the news to the outside world that Capone wore 'an almost constant smile and had become popular through his good humour'. Green said: 'But he behaves so well in Atlanta that the other inmates are beginning to think he is a milksop. He has been trying unsuccessfully to get a place in the prison baseball team. He is a model prisoner, and obeys every order the second it is given. His face is bronzed and his figure has become trim and lost its paunchiness. He has now become a valuable worker in the prison shoe factory.' He added that Capone appeared not to have been forgotten by his admirers – 'He receives more fan mail than anyone else in prison.

His weight was down from seventeen to fifteen stone, it was further learned, he constantly received letters, many from Britain, requesting autographs, and his cell was decorated with family photographs and pictures of boxers and baseball stars clipped from the papers.

As the months passed rumours began to circulate that Capone was having an elegantly comfortable holiday at Washington's expense, that his shoes were hand-made casuals, that he spent most of his time at sport, that he was even allowed out of prison in the evenings. These questions were raised in the House of Representatives, where a statement was given by the warden, who made it known that Capone wore regulation boots, could play lawn tennis only half an hour a day and was not given evening passes. 'On account of reports that his friends would probably try to smuggle money and guns to him,' added the warden, 'we have not been permitting his interviews to be held with other prisoners, but each interview takes place in the presence of an officer where his movements can be watched and his conversations clearly heard.'

There was still current a nervousness that the Capone who only a year or two previously had seemed capable of getting his own way in any circumstances and through any agency was still not safely neutralized. It certainly seemed clear that, despite the punishment levied upon him, he was not without means for in August 1932 there appeared the startling report that he was planning to turn cowboy upon his release. A Colonel Zack Miller confirmed rumours that Ralph Capone and his associates were negotiating on Al's behalf for the purchase of a famous Oklahoma show-place seventeen thousand acre estate, the 101 Ranch. A local real estate dealer informed Reuter: 'The Capone boys are quitting the racket and are going to take up the active management of the ranch if the deal goes through.' The Mayor of Ponca City, Dan Kygar, was asked for his attitude towards the possible advent of a colony of Chicago killers. He displayed remarkable magnanimity. 'We'll give them an Oklahoma welcome, give them the keys to the city and assure their protection until they become acclimatized,' he said largely. 'After that they must look out for themselves. My welcoming words to Al Capone are "Come to Ponca City, but bring your bodyguards along".'

Bad tidings continued, with rhythmical persistence, to strike Capone about his pummelled head. In July 1933 it was announced that the Federal authorities were proposing to retry him on new charges in order to lob a further stretch of imprisonment on to the end of his present sentence. Then, in the following January, he heard that he was included in a batch of prisoners booked for transfer to

Alcatraz, the lump of rock off the West Coast known as America's Devil's Island. His attorney immediately made it known that he was appealing from the decision of the Federal District Court rejecting his right to petition for release by writ of habeas corpus. The appeal was not allowed.

'He has taken his transfer mighty bad,' his lawyer informed the press after a visit to Capone. 'He doesn't consider that his good prison record merits him being classed as a dangerous criminal.' Nevertheless, in August 1934 a jail-on-wheels took Capone and thirty-nine other graduates of Atlanta to San Francisco. There had been rumours that the Capone gunmen were planning an attack upon the train to release their chief. He went manacled to the seat in a coach with drawn blinds guarded by scores of escorts armed with guns and tear-bombs. Thousands of spectators gathered at San Francisco rail terminal to watch his arrival – or perhaps to see the gangsters' rescue attempt. It is doubtful if the police regarded the rumour seriously, but even so they were taking no reckless chances, and the train was diverted at Martinez, California, on to a route which by-passed San Francisco and led it to Sausolito, directly behind the island fortress. There, it was run aboard the ferry and shipped across the bay, where Capone was received according to plan. The warden, Mr. James A. Johnston, issued a statement to the press which said that the reason for Capone's transfer was that 'the Government wants to break the contact of Capone and the other incorrigibles with the underworld'.

Occasional news about him filtered across the Pacific moat to the newspapers. A rather suspect message of repentance was claimed by one publication to have been passed on to them by lip through a friend. 'If I could have lived the life I wanted to, I would never have been here,' Capone was alleged to have rued. 'For the past ten years I have been trying to break away from the gangs. It wasn't that I was afraid of them, although my life was always in danger. It was really because I wanted to get my wife and child away from it all. I'd like to go back to Italy with my family. The gangs don't like a quitter, and although I don't think I'm one, it would be impossible to convince them that that was not so. As long as the gangs remained in power, it would be impossible for me to get out of America. But now the doom of the gangs is sealed. It's no use our shutting our eyes to the fact that Prohibition is ended in America and with the end of Prohibition the mainstay of gangdom is cut adrift.'

Apart from the somewhat garbled imagery which sounds unlike Capone's customary constricted but pungent language, this does not reflect his commercial needle-wittedness. Prohibition or not, Capone knew that while there were industries and unions to be prodded at gun-point, no gang need join the bread-line – although, of course, this may have been yet another attempt to propagate the suggestion through an emissary that, if he were released, he could be depended upon either to go straight or go beyond the ocean.

In April 1935 a released Alcatraz prisoner named Verrell Rapp made it known that Capone was tottering on the edge of madness, that he had recently started a fight with another convict. Both had been sentenced to solitary confinement and were suspended from the ceiling by chains, with legs held in irons – a tale that the Department of Justice promptly denied. Only a day later another ex-Alcatrazian, an Englishman named William Henry Ambrose, a drug pedlar awaiting deportation, partially confirmed the story that Capone had been in solitary confinement. 'Alcatraz,' he said, 'is a jail of eternal silence. No prisoner may speak except during one authorized period a week, from one to three-thirty on Saturday. It's enough to drive you crazy. Even hard guys like Capone are furious at the silence, at the strict discipline and at the harsh punishment. Capone has three or four times been thrown into the black hole for talking, but he's not losing his reason. He's not giving away an inch.' This chilling melodrama hardly accorded with yet another report from inside. In the September a third former prisoner, W. D. May, who was then under death sentence at Huntsville, Texas, told a newspaperman that Capone had spent 1,350 dollars on jazz band instruments and presented them to the prison orchestra; he had also offered forty thousand dollars for the building of a tennis court for the convicts. 'Al isn't high hat,' said May, 'and seems like a pretty good guy. Most of the men in Alcatraz like him. He's working in the library and gets about among the boys pretty much.'

For the first time for a decade Capone was now sealed off from crime reporters and inquisitive women columnists, but the newspapers continued on the assumption that any Capone news was hot news. During those years there was a continual stream of items, some reasonably credible, others highly and wildly weird. He was playing the banjo like crazy; he had been drubbed with a window-sash weight for refusing to join in a prisoners' revolt; he was practising the violin in a private guarded room; he had been knocked out by a blow to the jaw from Big Harmon Waley, kidnapper of George Weyerhauser, son of the lumber millionaire, after Capone had taunted him with being a baby-snatcher; he had by means of a code arranged for his gang to capture the heavily-armed police patrol boat, cross to the island in the officers' uniforms, and open up a machine-gun barrage under which Capone would escape.

Intermittently, while the public was served with these savoury tidbits about their deposed overlord, the Federal authorities kept chipping away at their capture. In September 1937 David L. Bazelon, Chicago Assistant United States Attorney, announced that he had been authorized to bring an action against Capone for 270 thousand dollars arrears of taxation, interest and penalties, due on income between 1924 and 1929; in August the following year, a fresh demand was made upon him – for a 120 thousand dollars contribution to the Treasury from the trove they were convinced he had cached away.

It appeared that Capone's thoughts had expanded beyond the cash that had until his downfall dominated his life. He was now also deeply concerned with politicial ideologies – and especially with the menace of Communism. The press got hold of a letter he had written to a friend, in which he expressed his anxiety about Soviet Russia. 'Bolshevism,' warned Capone, 'is knocking at our gates. We can't afford to let it in. We have got to organize ourselves against it and put our shoulders together and hold fast. We must keep America whole and safe and unspoiled. We must keep the worker away from Red literature and Red ruses; we must see that his mind remains healthy.' Capone was still the idealist capitalist at heart; prison had not tainted his businessman's ethic with bitterness and disillusionment.

Altogether, he seemed to be living a life of harlequin variety within Alcatraz. On dribbled the hearsay and the yarns: he played his banjo during the services in the Roman Catholic Church; he had blossomed as a solo singer, and among his repertoire was a composition of his own entitled 'Mother'; he was uncharacteristically dealing in stocks and shares, the courier between Alcatraz and Wall Street being his wife; he had once again suffered physical assault, having been felled and savagely beaten by a man named Burton Phillips during a work strike in which he, the anti-Red anti-unionist, refused to participate.

Then, just after Warden Johnston had given a progress report to the press on the change that the system had brought about in the arrogant gunman personality – 'We've taught Capone he's not as big as he thought he was; now he's a mild, skinny little fellow with frightened eyes' – there came the hard and official news that Capone had indeed been in trouble. In June 1936 the headlines screeched that he had been stabbed. A Texan bank robber named Lucas, who

was having a haircut in the prison barber's, had snatched up a pair
of scissors and plunged them between Capone's shoulders as he
walked past the door. Capone was carried, weeping, to the hospital.
Lucas gave his reason for the attack that Capone had squealed on
him, to which Capone replied that Lucas had asked him for money
to help him escape, and he had refused.

He recovered from the scissor-wound, but in February 1938 it
was reported that he had suffered a mental collapse, the reason
given that he had been driven mad by fear of being killed by fellow
prisoners. The San Francisco *News* stated that he had suddenly 'gone
berserk', and kicked and punched other convicts; removed to his
cell in a strait jacket, he had fallen into spells of deep depression
interspersed with singing bursts of arias from Italian operas. For
hours at a time he made and remade his bed. Dr. Edward Twitchell,
the prison psychiatrist, said that after refusing to leave his cell to go
to breakfast he had fallen into a coma. He was, declared Dr.
Twitchell, suffering from paresis.

Shortly after, he was moved for medical observation to San Pedro
Prison, where he stared glassily about him and chattered inco-
herently. One view was that this was religious fervour. The Rev.
Silas Thweatt told the press that he had visited San Pedro to
take the church service. 'I asked if any of the seventy-five convicts
present felt the need of prayer,' he said. 'Al Capone was among those
who raised his hand. We prayed for them. Then I asked "Are any
of you here feeling the need of a Saviour? If so, stand up before your
fellows and confess the fact." Al Capone was the first to rise.'

In October 1939 a British journalist, Trevor Wignall, obtained an
interesting interview with him at the San Pedro institution. He found
him slim and apparently fit, except for a rather alarming continual
winking of both eyes, and dressed in blue slacks and shirt, and green
sun-glasses. He recalled meeting Wignall previously: 'I invited you
to my table that night I gave the party at the Frolics in Chicago, the
night Tony Canzoneri fought Kid Berg. Tony was there with us, and
so was Owney Madden. You wrote about me in your paper and I
telephoned to say it was swell.'

Wignall asked him if he was intending to return to Chicago upon
his release. 'Not likely', replied Capone. 'I've finished with that
burg. I've got a nice place in Miami and that's where I'll spend the
rest of my time. Fishing and maybe a bit of farming. I'll take it easy.'

How was his son? asked Wignall.

Capone smiled widely. 'Oh, swell. He was up here the other day.

He's nineteen now, and quite a fella. He's at Yale, you know, so he's
had a fine education. Might get to be a lawyer some day.' He
mentioned the war in Europe: 'Say, those guys are crazy. Hitler –
pffff! Why can't they get together and talk things over? They're all
crazy over there. There's no need of war, and there's no need for
America to get mixed up in another one. Peace is what we want. All
this shooting and killing is the bunk.'

He was moved to the Federal Correctional Institution at Terminal
Island, California, and eight months later secretly sent from there to
Lewisburg Prison, Pennsylvania. On 17 November 1939 he was
released. 'AL CAPONE DYING, SAY HIS DOCTORS' ran the headlines. He
was, but with haphazard slowness.

He returned to his Miami estate and to his wife and son a sick and
disintegrated man. He entered a Baltimore hospital for treatment. He
was suffering from slowly progressive deterioration of the intellect,
failure of judgement and memory, an increase in suspiciousness and
irritability, sullen depression interrupted by periods of boastful exaltation. The onset of his condition was gradual, and for the first few years
after his release he superficially improved in health. 'He is very happy,'
his brother informed the press in the spring of 1940. 'He spends most
of his time reading the newspapers, and now and again goes out into
the grounds to get the sunshine.' He liked driving on meandering
journeys in his car, often stopping to hand out dimes to small
children, and leaving Miami in the hottest height of the year for
another of his retreats, a house at Mercer, Wisconsin, used by Bottles.
He made no attempt physically to return to the day-to-day running
of his Chicago business enterprises, changed in character now that
Prohibition was dead and discarded, but in which he remained as
sleeping partner. Money was no worry, but the tax authorities had
not finished with him. Although his personal fortune – estimated at
twenty-five million dollars in 1930 – had been heavily eroded, it was
estimated that he still had salted away five million dollars to support
him when he left prison. In 1941 an effort to seize a further portion
was made. In February of that year he was summoned to appear in
court in Chicago to answer questions so as to determine what assets
he had to meet a new 262,500 dollars judgement for income tax. This
suit arose from a specific bootleg item – 250 thousand dollars due for
non-payment of tax on 19,984 barrels of beer handled between 1921
and 1922, an unusually realistic action for a Treasury department to
extract its cut of illegal profits. Eventually, in July 1942, the Government accepted a thirty thousand dollar settlement. During 1941 he
made one of his increasingly rare public appearances at the wed-

ding of his son to a society girl of Chattanooga, Tennessee, and was encouraged by the fond and nostalgic enthusiasm with which he was greeted, personally and in the press. As a result in January 1942 his life-long patriotic fervour of an American citizen – 'I'm no foreigner' – again asserted itself. He announced that he was offering his services to the War Department 'in any capacity to aid the national defence effort'. Despite his proven knowledge of arms and ballistics, his offer was not taken up.

During the next few years men's ears were filled with gunfire grosser and more prodigious in volume than the sporadic puny explosions that had once made Chicago's streets infamous, and Capone the pirate personality was extinguished by larger events, although he still remained, in the memories of people who could not have sworn whether he was alive or dead, a vague legend. The occasional down-page paragraph acted as reminder of the strange days of the war-lord of that distant peace-time of a past decade. In 1943 a wire-service sent out the report: 'Today Al Capone is a sick and broken man in his Palm Island hide-out. He wears dark sunglasses and long side whiskers as a half-disguise. Today he carries about as much menace as a puppy. Stripped of his gang and his gun, he is just an apathetic old relic of a dead era. He is the biggest of the has-beens.' In Britain during the 1940s, that shabby antique armoured-car continued to be trundled around fairgrounds, a seedily dubious pleasure during an austerity-drab period, until protests from American servicemen that it gave a false impression of life in a country 'that no longer had gangsters' caused it to be withdrawn. (Some years earlier, Judge Sir Alfred Tobin at Westminster County Court, hearing a civil claim involving a Mr. Beresford Bennett who was showing the car in a Haymarket amusement arcade, asked: 'Are there not other ways of making money in England than by exhibiting American murderers' cars? You might as well take a trunk from Brighton and exhibit it. Is it for the educational benefit of the English working classes that they should see a car belonging to a murderer?' The last news of the car was in 1958 when it was bought at a Manchester auction for 170 guineas by a Mr. A. Stuart 'for a museum piece', was then displayed at Belle Vue, and then in April shipped from Liverpool for delivery to a Toronto buyer.)

In the first month of 1947 Capone's last big headline was erected over his body, a gravestone of black type. He had had an apoplectic seizure. For five days he lay helpless in bed, and the last rites were

administered by the Rev. Father William Barry, priest at the Roman
Catholic Church of St. Patrick, at Miami Beach; he briefly rallied,
and then contracted pneumonia. Doctors and nurses prolonged his
life by continually administering oxygen. In the early hours of the
morning of 25 January, at the age of fifty-two, he died. Gathered
about his bed were his mother, his three brothers, Matthew, John
and Bottles, his sister Mafalda, and his wife and his son.

The corpse was placed in the hands of Windham Thildrick, known
in Florida as the millionaires' mortician. Throughout the next day
the Thildrick craftsmen worked on the costliest and biggest coffin
they had been commissioned to make – heavily embossed bronze with
six gold handles. Into it was placed Capone, freshly shaved and
washed, and dressed in a newly-tailored dark broadcloth suit, white
shirt and collar and grey tie. He lay in state in the Thildrick funeral
parlour, to which came friends and relatives to look for the last time
upon that suave, pale face, and to kneel and pray. Flowers and
wreaths began to arrive at Miami from all parts of the United States,
including remembrance posies from old friends then resident in
Alcatraz and Sing Sing.

On 1 February, while the body was on its way by train to Chicago,
the United States Treasury were inquisitively inquiring about the
residue of his estate. Abraham Teitelbaum, one of his lawyers,
stated to the press: 'So far as I know Al left no will and no money.
His house was mortgaged and he had been supported by members
of his family in recent years. He still owed the Government money
when he died. I'm sure he died penniless.' It was verified that Frank
Harmon, a Chicago night club proprietor, held a 43,750 dollar
mortgage on the Miami house; it was not verified to the authorities'
entire satisfaction that Capone died intestate and in poverty.

On a viciously cold February day, with a wind scything across the
city from Lake Michigan, forty relatives and friends huddled in a
tent in Chicago's Mount Olivet Cemetery for the private service.
Among them were Al's cousins, Charles, Rocco and Joseph Fischetti,
gambling *entrepreneurs*; the DeGrazio brothers, Melrose Park gambling
bosses; Willie Heeney and Joe Corngold, Cicero gambling bosses;
Joe Aiuppa (alias Joey O'Brien), Claude Maddox and Robert
Ansoni, owners of the Taylor Company, a big company producing
casino equipment; Jack Guzik, Murray The Camel Humphreys,
Sam Golf Bag Hunt, and Tough Tony Capezio in derby hat and
dark glasses. It was a sombre, subdued gathering, with none of the
peacock glitter of the old-style gangster funeral, and with no publicity
wanted. Newspapermen were made most unwelcome; both Matt

Capone and Charles Fischetti bawled at the journalists, and threatened any cameraman who attempted to take photographs. Funeral rites were accorded because of his death-bed repentance, but the Catholic church omitted all ceremonial to mark its disapproval of his past life. Then a gang of Depression unemployed in ear-muffs, scarves and woollen gloves, hauled the gorgeous bronze casket across the snow and lowered it into the hole hacked out of the metallically-hard soil. Capone joined the company of two-hundred-and-fifty-odd earlier arrivals at Mount Olivet who had died before his gang's guns or in his service.

The fifteen years after his recession from untrammelled power had been, if not straitened in circumstances, a bitter twilight of ill-health, harassment and loss of his particular kind of glory, but at least his final achievement was one shared by few of his professional colleagues: he died in bed, with a pillow under his head.

27

'There's a Lot of Grief Attached to the Limelight'

'No more brass bands for me.'

AL CAPONE

'A boy has never wept nor dashed a thousand kim.'
DUTCH SCHULTZ'S *dying words*

'Chicago . . . forever keeps two faces, one for winners and one for losers; one for hustlers and one for squares.'
NELSON ALGREN

WHAT sort of person was Capone? Again, there is scanty personal testimony to be drawn upon in assessing the personality of the man whom his friends, close companions and family knew, nor is much medical evidence available. From time to time, during his period of fame, there was long-distance theorizing about his state of mind, including such specialized interpretations as that made in 1930 by a Dr. C. J. Gaddis, a Chicago osteopath, who declared that Capone's criminal tendencies had been caused by a structural defect in his head and that, had he been treated in childhood, those tendencies would have been eliminated. (Dr. Gaddis added that, as children were now being treated osteopathically, Chicago could sanguinely look forward to the time, only a generation or two ahead, when it would be a crimeless city.) About the same time a newspaper sought the opinion of Dr. William Hickson, a Chicago psychoanalyst, on Capone. His imperturbability was not hard to explain, he pointed out, for the typical gunman committed murder 'with no more emotion than is felt by the average man as he says good day to a friend'. 'Good-bye' might have been a more appropriate example. But Dr. Hickson added percipiently: 'What will be his ultimate fate? No one knows. But it can be safely prophesied that his name in the distant future will be romanticized like that of many a pirate king.'

343

Regrettably, there seems to have been little attempt during Capone's incarceration in prisons in Atlanta, Alcatraz and Terminal Island, California, to put him under consistent psychological observation. He was for a time in Alcatraz under the care of Dr. Twitchell, the penitentiary psychiatrist, but as the mental impairment, caused by the disease that finally killed him, may then have been becoming apparent, the findings at that period would probably not have been relevant to his 'normal' psychology. In any case, Dr. Twitchell is no longer at Alcatraz, and has long ago left San Francisco, and the penitentiary medical and central files are confidential and cannot be examined without a court order.

Nevertheless, there are some tentative and theoretical conclusions about Capone's psychology that may be inferred from the available knowledge of his outlook and conduct. Broadly, in psychiatric terms, Capone was clearly a psychopathic personality, and more exactly a sociopathic personality – that is, one of a category of predominantly aggressive types of sociopath, the 'readily detonating type' which has been defined by Curran and Guttman[1] as 'the often plausible and shameless individual . . . (who) may calmly pursue the evil tenor of their ways'. Particularly Capone's manifest characteristics fitted with almost tailor-made precision into the routine clinical definition of paranoid schizophrenia: the type who 'believes he is persecuted because he is the possessor of remarkable powers', who has highly developed 'sensitivity and suspicion', who suffers 'friction with society', who has 'shallowness of emotional response', who employs 'falsification of memory to fit his past', who has 'illusions of grandeur'. Emil Kraepelin's description of paranoia was the 'insidious development of a permanent unshakable delusional system, with complete preservation of clarity and order in thought, will, and action', which may be considered a fair outline of the framework of behaviour within which Capone acted.

But this kind of labelling is an elusive and often illusorily misleading undertaking, and it seems doubtful if at any time up to the appearance of his mental deterioration Capone could medically have been pronounced insane. And what must be considered are the environmental factors of his childhood, the conditions of deprivation and poverty, and the sense of belonging to an unaccepted minority group, so conducive to the production of an antisocial, antagonistic psychopathic personality.

There was the ineffectual shopkeeper father, the 'poor immigrant' symbol incapable of successful adjustment to the new conditions,

[1] *Psychological Medicine* by Desmond Curran and Eric Guttman.

probably an unadmirable failure in the eyes of his sons; there was the mother, who in rare photographs is a horse-faced woman with hard, humourless mouth and strong, bony jaw, not a bit the prototype fat, warm Italian *mama mia*; there was Capone's early wrenching away from school to fling him into the cruel world of adult economics; and there was probably the discipline of Catholicism in the home.

Yet the anomalies persist. His conditioning did not produce the matrix delinquent that has become a modern urban cliché, the hating, hysterical misfit who so often logically progresses into the dull-eyed dissociate, out of communication with his fellow-men and able to find self-expression only in random violence. Beneath that careful urbanity, Capone was unstable, emotional and vicious, and eruptions of rage unpredictably broke through the controlled calm. He was also vain, egotistical and cold-hearted – a combination often found in people who practise excessive generosity, for the lavish distribution of gifts and favours is the only way they know to enter into relationships with others, to earn love, and at the same time to provide themselves with a substitute sensation of giving love. Nevertheless, Capone had many attributes that the obsessional, destructive killer – of the cast of, say, Dillinger or McGurn – did not have. He seems to have possessed a genuine affability, and a relaxed sociability, allied with a natural talent for leadership and the creation of an atmosphere of *esprit de corps* that a good Army officer has, qualities that made him respected by the group of moody and dangerous neurotics who surrounded him. It is not too far-fetched to see Capone's situation at the height of his dominance as a collateral to that of a front-line company commander in the thick of a bloody action. That Capone retained, at any rate superficially, a genial ease of manner with cannons to the right of him and cannons to the left of him cannot be cursorily dismissed. Look at the kind of life he lived.

He was never alone. The threat of legal reprisal, although theoretically neutralized by the system of bribery and intimidation, was always present, for the fickle passions of the public and the erratic but unfixable Federal authority might at any time and at any point assert themselves and bring about, at minimum, trial and jail sentence. What was much more immediate and probable was reprisal by his criminal associates and enemies. A man in Capone's position lived perpetually with ear cocked for the report of a gun, with body tensed for the thud of a bullet. Consequently, he existed permanently within a human fence. After his first two or three years in Chicago when his apprentice anonymity had been dispersed by fame, he was never again able casually to walk down the street, spontaneously to go into a bar for a drink, to stop on a street corner for a glance at a newspaper, to take an unpremeditated drive, to decide off-hand to see a movie or buy a theatre ticket, to stroll out with his wife on a summer evening, to sit beside a window, take a taxi, go on the subway or eat in a strange restaurant. He lived like Royalty, in all its senses, like the president of a police state – disbarred from normal, gregarious, impulsive life. He travelled, however short the distance, by tank – in that steel-lined limousine with a machine-gunner stationed beside the chauffeur, preceded by a scout-car and followed by a tourer carrying a platoon of gunmen. If he had to walk a few steps along a pavement or cross a road, he was convoyed by a flotilla of destroyers and mine-sweepers. He attended theatre first-nights with an entourage of eighteen men – a bigger bodyguard than the President's – whose dinner-jackets bulged inelegantly around their left armpits, who surrounded him in a block of seats and stood sentry at the doorways. In his Hawthorne Inn and Metropole Hotel headquarters the lobbies were, day and night, scattered with watchful men; the window shutters were armour-plated, the corridors were patrolled. In his Metropole office suite his swivel chair, beneath portraits of Abraham Lincoln, George Washington and Big Bill Thompson (Capone's personal holy trinity of Great Americans), had an armoured back so that when he swung round facing away from the door he would not suffer exposure to any sudden assassin clever or mad enough to have penetrated the garrison. The barber shop he patronized in the basement of a Loop hotel had a chair reversed towards the door for its edgier customers. When a photograph of one of his cars appeared in an afternoon paper showing its licence number he gave it away. 'That picture would have put me on the spot,' he said. Many attempts were made upon his life, from furtive poisoning of his food to the mass obliter-ation daylight raid upon the Hawthorne Inn, and in June 1925 he applied for life insurance. Despite his statement that he was engaged in the second-hand furniture business, which is not high on insurance companies' lists of hazardous occupations, his application was repeatedly turned down.

It may indeed be fundamental justice that the tyranny and fear that Capone created enmeshed him equally, and it is not intended to evoke sympathy when one observes, quite objectively, that it was an unenviably hideous life of anxiety and terror that he must have lived amid the money, the luxury suites and the girls. In one of his franker interviews he told a newspaper man: 'You fear death every moment.'

As his power and reputation ballooned, his bonhomie and expansiveness with reporters increased. In his early insecure years in Chicago, when he was clawing his way upward, he had shunned publicity and maintained a poker-faced brevity with the press; later, when he was the undisputed beer baron of the town, a consort of the city fathers and bright young things, he developed an appetite for being in the headlines. He was not difficult to interview, and indeed was accustomed to demands for a press conference whenever a particularly sensational bumping-off had occurred, upon which occasions he handled the situation with the practised ease of a public figure, glib with the bland denial, the injured indignation, or, if it suited him tactically, with the ambiguous wink. James Doherty, a crime reporter on the Chicago *Tribune* during that eventful epoch, and now retired, accurately sized up Capone's attitude at this time. Doherty told me: 'The *Trib* was a wet paper and its staff were wet too – we were a hard-drinking, hard-working bunch, and we were against Prohibition because of the methods of enforcement. Crime was important news then and we used to give it full coverage. We were in terrific competition with the *Herald and Examiner* on the crime side at that time, and I spent a lot of time with the mob and saw Capone often. I can't say I especially liked the guy, but he was always nice enough with me. I wrote hundreds of stories about him. I'd accuse him of a murder today and meet him tomorrow, and neither of us would mention the subject. I'd see him at a funeral, or in a speakeasy, or down at the D.A.s office, and he'd always give me some quotes. He wasn't very good company, not a very articulate guy. He'd exchange commonplaces but he didn't volunteer information. Still, the more I wrote about him, the more he liked it. He loved the limelight and was always willing to yak a little with reporters. He liked the advertising. It made better business for him. It made it easier to intimidate the customers. We built him up as the big shot in the gang world. They were all racketeers and they liked to be known as good ones – like the politicians used to say: "Just spell my name right and say what you like." I can't feel he was all-evil, like he's been painted since then. Sure he was a cold-blooded killer, but he had his good side I see him as a victim of his time and circumstances. Capone was tolerated by the public because – let's face it – he was giving them a service they wanted. No one minded about them trading booze; it was all the killing that brought about their undoing, although that was between themselves, don't forget.

It was a war, chiefly, between the Irish and the Italians. I'm Irish
and I'd come into the office one morning after another shooting and
say to an Italian colleague of mine: "Well, that's one more Dago to
my side", and next day he'd come in and say to me: "It's levelled,
Jim – we chalked one up on our side last night." I'll say this for
Capone, I wrote some tough stories about him but he never held it
against me. I wouldn't say his men liked him, but they certainly
respected and feared him. He was a big man, you know.'

There are many others to be found in Chicago today who recall
Capone with both affection and admiration. Charles Bianchi, head
waiter at Riccardo's Restaurant, who in the 'twenties ran a speakeasy on Broadway, on the North Side, which was supplied by the
Bugs Moran mob, told me: 'When I first came to Chicago, before I
raised the stake for opening my own place, I used to wait table at a
roadhouse just outside the city. That was a Capone joint. They sold
a lot of whisky there. Every now and then, Capone would come in
with a bunch of the boys. I always found him a regular kind of guy.
You know, he was courteous and quiet. He'd give me a five-dollar
tip just for bringing him a cup of coffee. He was all right.'

A Chicago journalist told me that his mother often had talked of
one evening when she was having dinner at a restaurant once owned
by Colosimo. The waiter came round to each table to inform them
that 'Mr. Brown and his associates had telephoned to say they were
on their way'. Mr. Brown was Capone. The journalist's mother
considered this to be very considerate of Capone. She took it to be an
intimation that they might prefer quickly to pay the bill and leave.
She stayed. On the other hand, another interpretation of this story
may be that the gang had telephoned for table reservations and
that the restauranteur thought it best for his own reasons to let his
customers know the situation.

Nelson Algren said: 'Capone was a very smooth man. He was
honourable and hardly ever made enemies. You never knew what
move he was going to make, because Daddy never said anything
wrong. His outward speech was friendly. People liked him. He was a
good guy. He was very generous. He was what is now known as cool.
The idea that he founded a kind of syndicate of evil is a lot of horn-
swoggle. This city was syndicated by the Anglo-Saxons who founded
it – by the first guy who sold a bottle of whisky to an Indian'.

Conversely, Mike Meredith, an old-hand reporter on the Chicago
American, did not think much of the period or its personalities.
'Everybody thought then that it was a great thing to be able to say

they had a good contact for hooch. It was smart to know the gangsters and to be able to say "Hi, Al!" at a night-club. Cheaters,
cheaters, cheaters. Capone wasn't admired by people, but he was
feared. General feeling was that we'd got Prohibition, so we got him.
He was always well-dressed but there was nothing glamorous about
his appearance. He was a pudgy, greasy, lousy low-life little son-of-a-
bitch. But the hoods never bothered anyone who didn't bother them.
At least, that didn't go for girls with Capone. He didn't drink much,
just a little beer or wine, but he sure liked women, always chasing
them. And especially little girls, thirteen or fourteen. That was told
to me by one of his own boys, a little blond Irishman who was one
of the few people Capone was afraid of. He once hit the Big Fellow
round the face when he was trying to get a little girl into his car.'
  Was he Meredith's 'little son-of-a-bitch' or Doherty's 'big man'?
It may help to assess his size to hear Capone himself talking. During
the late 'twenties and early 'thirties thousands of column-inches
all over the world were filled with words represented as being straight
from the Big Fellow's mouth. Much of this was almost certainly
fictional, and bad fiction at that, in which neither the idiom nor the
atmosphere was remotely captured; but in the dusty and yellowing
pages of the fat papers of that time are scattered quotes from routine
news-stories that have the stamp of immediacy and authenticity –
Capone sounding-off irritably outside a court-house, Capone justify-
ing his trade in scented cumulus of cigar-smoke in his private
chambers, Capone philosophizing sentimentally about his patriotism
and peacefulness while sun-bathing beside his Miami swimming pool.
Discarding the obviously bogus and also the suspiciously eloquent,
what follows is a montage, a spliced-together tape-recording, of
Capone's voice, for seen wholly in this way it is an illuminating
window upon the criminal's mind and mysterious facility for self-
vindication. The advocacy begins with the theme that was seldom
absent from Capone's public utterances from 1929 to 1931, his plea
that he was out of the rackets and wanted only to be left alone to live
the quiet life of a respectable (although actually non-tax-paying)
citizen.

  'I'm out of the booze racket now and I wish the papers would let
me alone. I'm a businessman. I've made my money by supplying a
popular demand. If I break the law my customers are as guilty as I
am. When I sell liquor it's bootlegging. When my patrons serve it on
silver trays on Lake Shore Drive it's hospitality. The country wanted
booze and I've organized it. Why should I be called a public enemy?

'A crook is a crook, and there's something healthy about his frankness in the matter. But a guy who pretends he's enforcing the law and steals on his authority is a swell snake. The worst type of these punks is the big politician who gives about half his time to covering up so that no one will know he's a thief. A hard-working crook will – and can – buy these birds by the dozen, but he hates them in his heart.

'Hell, it *is* a business. I'm thirty-two years of age and I've lived a thousand. All I do is to supply a public demand. I do it in the best and least harmful way I can. I can't change conditions. I just meet them without backing up. When Prohibition came in there were 7,500 saloons in Chicago. This town spent nearly a hundred million dollars for booze every year at the old price. Nobody wanted Prohibition. This town voted six to one against it. Somebody had to throw some liquor on that thirst. Why not me? My customers include some of the finest people in the city, or in the world for that matter, but I'm just a bootlegger. I violate the Prohibition law. All right, so do they. It's hard, dangerous work, aside from any hate at all, and when a fellow works hard at any line of business he wants to go home and forget about it. He don't want to be afraid to sit near a window or open a door. They've hung everything on me except the Chicago fire.

'I want peace, and I will live and let live. I'm like any other man. I've been in this racket long enough to realize that a man in my game must take the breaks, the fortunes of war. I haven't had any peace of mind in years. Every minute I'm in danger of death. Once you're in the racket you're always in it. The parasites will trail you, begging for money and favours, and you can never get away from them no matter where you go. I have a wife and a boy I idolize and a beautiful home in Florida. If I could go there and forget it all, I'd be the happiest man in the world. I'm tired of gang murders and gang shootings. It's a tough life to lead. You fear death every moment, and, worse than death, you fear the rats of the game who'd run around and tell the police if you don't constantly satisfy them with money and favours. I can never leave home without my bodyguard. He's been with me constantly for two years.

'I've never been convicted of a crime, never, nor have I directed anyone else to commit a crime. I don't pose as a plaster saint, but I never killed anyone. And I'm known all over the world as a million-aire gorilla. My wife and my mother hear so much about what a terrible criminal I am, it's getting too much for them, and I'm sick of it myself. The other day a man came in and said that he had to have three thousand dollars. If I'd give it to him, he said, he'd make me beneficiary in a fifteen thousand dollar insurance policy he'd take out, and then kill himself. I got a letter from a woman in England. She offered me £100 and my passage to London if I'd bump off some neighbour she'd been having a spat with. Even over there I'm known as a gorilla.

'I'd rather the newspapers wouldn't print a line about me. That's the way I feel. No more brass bands for me. There's a lot of grief attached to the limelight. Say, if I was just plain Izzy Polatski, living in Chicago, I'd not stand out in the gutter trying to get a peek at Capone. I'd attend to my business and let him attend to his. No use making a laughing stock of the city. Why, the very guys that make my trade good are the ones that yell the loudest about me. They talk about me not being on the legitimate. Nobody's on the legit, when it comes down to cases. Your brother or your father gets in a jam. What do you do? Do you sit back and let him go over the road without trying to help him? You'd be a yellow dog if you did. Nobody's really on the legit – you know that and so do they.

'The funny part of the whole thing is that a man in this line of business has so much company. I mean his customers. If people didn't want beer and wouldn't drink it, a fellow would be crazy for going round trying to sell it. I've seen gambling houses, too, in my travels, and I never saw anyone point a gun at a man and make him go in. I never heard of anyone being forced to go to a place to have some fun. I've read in the newspapers, though, of bank cashiers being put in cars with pistols stuck in their slats, and taken to a bank where they had to open a vault for the guy with the gun. It really looks like taking a drink is worse than robbing a bank. Maybe I'm wrong. Maybe it is.'

When all that is specious, convoluted, spielish, fraudulent and rodomontade is stripped away from the above hanky-panky, it is impossible not to concede that Capone had there some telling truths about the standards of morality and rectitude within which he built his business. And, if all else fails to move, there is a certain affecting melancholy in the valediction of the back-street immigrant hooligan fallen from greatness: 'If I'd known what I was stepping into in Chicago, I never would have left the Five Points outfit.'

EPILOGUE

'We nearly had feudalism.'

STANLEY PARGELLIS

I'm so glad good whiskey has come back again
Don't have to drink no hooch, no more of this moonshine
Now I can drink good whiskey, without being afraid of dyin'
I can walk up and down the street without dodging every cop
  I meet

PEETIE WHEATSTRAW, *Good Whiskey Blues*

Now the kids in Chicago are playing a new game: cops and
cops.

Newspaper report following the 1960
exposure of a Chicago police
housebreaking ring.

As I was shaving and preparing to leave my mews room behind North State Street for a late breakfast of orange juice, coffee and wheatcakes at the corner drug store one summer Saturday last year, across the city a Chicago businessman met with an atrocious mishap. Frederick Evans, aged sixty, proprietor of three companies, the Industrial Garment Service, the Infant Diaper Service and the Crib Diaper Service, was rammed against the brick wall of a car-park at the junction of Lake Street and Lotus Avenue, and hit in the forehead and throat with five bullets.

The late edition of that day's Chicago *Daily News* bore the front-page streamer headline 'CAPONE "FINANCE BRAIN" SLAIN: STOOD AGAINST WALL, GUNNED BY TWO'. Next day's Chicago *Sunday Tribune* also made this the front-page lead. '2 GUNMEN KILL GLIMCO PAL' blared the inch-and-a-half black type. After leaving his office on West Lake Street, Evans had been seen by passers-by to be waylaid, as he was about to board his Cadillac, by a man who ran out the adjoining alleyway brandishing a gun. He was forced to stand against the wall with hands in air while a second gunman, who approached from Lake Street, pulled an envelope from his hip pocket, whereupon both opened fire on him. The gunmen ran to a blue Chevrolet standing in the alley and drove off towards Long

Avenue. Evans staggered the few feet across to his car and collapsed across the edge of the front seat. He was pronounced dead at West Suburban Hospital. One of the witnesses to his murder, Mrs. Alice Griesemer, of North Lotus Avenue, said: 'It was like watching a movie or a television show.'

The newspapers filled in the background detail. Evans was 'the mystery man' of the crime Syndicate. He was the subject of two investigations then being undertaken by the Federal Government, one a study by a grand jury of gang infiltration of legitimate businesses, and the other an investigation by Internal Revenue Service agents into the income tax returns of Joey Glimco, head of Local 777 of the Taxicab Drivers' Union. In 1940 Evans had been identified by the Cook County State's Attorney's office as 'the financial genius of the Capone mob', which at that time was bossed by Frank The Enforcer Nitti. In the same year he was indicted, in the company of Murray The Camel Humphreys, head of the Syndicate's labour racketeering department, Paul Ricca, later head of the Syndicate until imprisoned for tax evasion, and Louis Little New York Campagna, on charges of conspiracy to seize control of the Bar-tenders' Union and its treasury. This particular case collapsed because George B. McLane, business agent of the union, refused to testify when called as witness for the State. Furthermore, in 1951 Evans was accused by a Los Angeles police captain testifying before the Kefauver Senate crime investigation committee of being involved in a gambling ring; he made allegations of a plot by Chicago and Minneapolis gangsters to remove the Los Angeles mayor from office, so as to further their prosperity.

After that Evans had entered the cleaning business – and the laundry union racket. This had been facilitated by Glimco. The Industrial Garment Service had specialized in providing tunics, overalls and cleaning rags to filling stations and garages. Seven firms already in the field had not done too well subsequently. They estimated that between 1952 and 1954 they had lost 250 thousand dollars a year in business to Evans's company. They described it as 'an Evans laundry supported by Glimco muscle'. Interviewed at the time, Glimco said: 'It's just a friendly relationship. I help him but there's no muscle in it.'

In the company of Tony Accardo, Syndicate president (or The Man, in hood parlance, meaning the supreme commander), Sam Mooney Giancana (The Boss, or executive head), Lennie Patrick and Eugene Luffman, Glimco and Evans had been subpœnaed to testify before a special Cook County grand jury charged with investigating a wave of labour-racketeering bombings. Both had refused to do so. Despite this fairly public record of shady activities, officially Evans had had an unblemished character.

If I had required any reminder of the purpose of my temporary residence in Chicago, this would have supplied it – and the reminder that today the Chicago of the Capone era is not profoundly reformed. Actually, it was not urgently needed, for during that tropical mid-summer the reminders had been coming regularly and dramatically. Prior to this during my stay Joseph Bronge, a Melrose Park beer distributor had been gravely wounded by three gunmen in revenge for revealing to a Federal grand jury that he had been forced to employ Joseph Gagliano, a known Chicago hoodlum, as a salesman; John Miraglia, former associate of Paul Needle-Nose Labriola, a gangster who was poisoned, strangled and shot in 1954, was approached from behind in the Orange Lantern saloon on West Division and shot four times in the back by two masked men; on the same day Edward Kochanski, a Cicero strong-arm man, was found dead in an alley, his head riddled with bullets; Mario Melchiore described as a real estate dealer, was pulled from his car and killed by two gunmen on the West Side; the Chicago Master Barbers' Association were in the midst of a prolonged struggle to rid themselves of eleven self-appointed members of their board of directors, all of whom had gang connexions and police records, and who had drawn 250 thousand dollars from the Association in nine years – which may explain why I had to pay two dollars for a haircut in Chicago; the United States Attorney's office announced that evidence would be given to the Federal grand jury by B-girls employed in a Hurley, Wisconsin, honky-tonk strip, that they had been trained by Ralph Bottles Capone in 'mooching, dipping and jackrolling' bar customers; and five Chicago policemen were subpoenaed to testify before the Federal grand jury investigating narcotics traffic arising out of the rigged trial of a heroin pedlar.

Since I left, the pace does not seem to have slackened. A new vicering, under the supervision of James The Monk Allegretti, has been exposed by a sixteen-year-old Rush Street prostitute; William The Saint Skally, identified by the Senate Rackets Committee as the Syndicate's 'master counterfeiter', was found dead of bullet wounds in a River Forest school parking lot – and then came the shot-gun slaying of Roger The Terrible Touhy in December 1959, followed by the arrest of seventeen policemen and the subjecting of 130 more to lie-detector tests in the exposure of a hundred thousand dollar police burglary ring, a story which *Time* magazine in March 1960 began: 'Some of Chicago's 11,200 cops must be honest . . .' and which sparked the wisecrack that now in Chicago the children play Cops and Cops.

The death of Touhy filled thousands of column-inches in the world's press, and was missing from the Chicago newspapers for hardly a day during the two months after he and his ex-policeman bodyguard, Walter Miller, were cut down in a blast of pellets on the doorstep of Touhy's sister's West Side house. Roger Touhy – the fourth of her brothers to be shot to death by gangsters or police – was the most prominent survivor of the Prohibition wars, the basic reason for his survival being that he had spent the past twenty-five years in prison for the kidnapping of John Jake the Barber Factor, a Capone crony, in 1933. Touhy published his account of the episode last year, in a book entitled *The Stolen Years*, in which he declared: 'I was a rich, but honest bootlegger. I was a fall guy for the Chicago Capone mob. I was rotting in prison on the falsified testimony of a swindler and ex-convict, John Jake the Barber Factor.' In the 'twenties in partnership with Matt Kolb, Touhy had run the liquor business of North-West Cook County, an empire of suburban speakeasies and a slot-machine franchise, and bragged that he made a million dollars a year. He also made an enemy of Capone, and, after Kolb had been murdered by Capone hoods, Touhy received his ninety-nine year sentence on the kidnap charge. He was killed twenty-two days after his parole from Illinois Stateville Penitentiary. The general theory was that the Mafia had decided that Touhy would create trouble by attempting to regain gang-leadership and must die. Familiarly, in the tradition of Chicago crime over the past forty years, general theories were as near a solution as could be approached.

The exposure the following month of the police crime-ring caused the Chicago *Tribune* to publish a four-page survey of the present police-politics-crime tripartite treaty, and the theme word running throughout was 'clout' – an expression unknown outside Chicago, where it seems to have especial local significance and application, and meaning political influence. The headline over the investigation was 'MOB WIELDS CLOUT THROUGH POLITICIANS'. Another word that fell like a shadow across those four pages was Capone, for here, twenty-eight years after the end of his active dominance and twelve years after his death, was the same situation, the same machinery smoothly working, and some of the same men superintending it. 'The police-burglary scandal,' said the *Tribune*, 'was the wedge that opened for hundreds of thousands of Chicagoans a view of the shadow world that has existed for years right under their noses. In this shadow world clout is supreme. It may be money clout, political clout or gangster clout. It rules the police department through the Democratic party political machine. Politicians provide the fix and bagmen, members of the police department, collect the boodle for the politicians and the crooked police officers. Gambling, vice and violence thrive in such an atmosphere.' The article, by Wayne Thomas, said: 'Chicago is getting a shocking, first-hand glimpse of the kinky shadow-world everyone knows about but the existence of which practically no one admits . . . It is a world in which wrong is right – in which all incentive for honour, justice, suppression of crime, and even fundamental discipline has disappeared from broad divisions of the police department, the courts, the all-pervading Democratic political party machine that has a strangle-hold on Chicago . . . The breakdown of policing in certain Chicago areas has been so great that insurance underwriters refuse to insure merchandise on store shelves or packed away in even the best constructed storage sites. Chicago's desperate situation is epitomized by a joke told at bars and gatherings. A Chicago motorist was halted by a police squad on a boulevard late at night. As a policeman strode towards the citizen, the latter cranked down a window and asked: 'What's it to be – a ticket or a stickup?' A police captain told the *Tribune*: 'The regular Syndicate payoffs are going right along while the scandals are on Page One. The Syndicate is too big and too entrenched to be worried about a few stupid policemen who teamed up with a punk burglar. The Syndicate payoffs are big time, involve the whole city enforcement system, extend into the courts and state legislature, and perhaps higher. Everybody who is anybody wants to "forget the hysteria" over the burglar scandals – but don't, for heaven's sake, upset any apple carts involving the real payoff.'

Have times changed at all? No one with a sentimental attachment to the bootleg 'twenties need feel an unhappy outcast in Chicago today. Of course, the intervening years have thinned the numbers of those who survived the battles and the bullets of that extraordinary bloody carousel, when State Street rang all night with jazz and the rumble of beer-trucks, when the gangsters' cars toured the town like brigantines, when Society went down to the speakeasies and the mobsters up to Lake Shore Drive, when Big Bill Thompson and Al Capone had a city to sack, when it was difficult to distinguish an election from a guerrilla-attack, when machine-guns were erected on pavements and murder was done among the shopping crowds. What did happen to the men who were then the rich and the powerful, the robber barons and cocks-of-the-walk in those anarchic years?

Frank McErlane died of pneumonia in October 1932, more peacefully than Machine-Gun Jack McGurn, who himself fell before a burst of tommy-gun bullets while awaiting his turn in a Milwaukee Avenue bowling alley in February 1936. In April 1939 Johnny Torrio, after serving a prison sentence for tax evasion, suffered a heart attack while having his hair cut in a Brooklyn barber's and died: he was seventy-five and left 357 thousand dollars. In March 1943 Frank Nitti, Al Capone's cousin and successor as leader of the gang, died after being indicted by a New York grand jury conducting a nationwide racket investigation; one report stated that he was discovered shot in a ditch, but it was generally given out that he had committed suicide. In March 1944 the bullet-holed body of Sam Gervase was left behind a Division Street house, and nine days later his gambling associate, James De Angelo, was bumped off and stuffed into the luggage compartment of his car parked in North La Salle Street. In 1950 James M. Ragen, Snr, proprietor of the racing-news wire service that provided results for the Syndicate gambling ring was chopped down by bullets as he walked along the street.

In August 1954 Charles Cherry Nose Gioe, one of the Syndicate group found guilty in 1943 of having extorted more than a million dollars from the Hollywood film industry, was come upon shot to death in a parked car, and in the same month Frank Maritote (alias Diamond), aged sixty-one, who had been lately describing himself as a contractor, dropped mortally injured under a shot-gun barrage as he was opening his West Side garage. In June of the following year Louis Little New York Campagna was enjoying himself fishing in Florida, and he was seized by a fatal heart attack as he was landing a thirty-pound catch; he was fifty-seven. Others surprisingly overtaken by natural visitations were Phil D'Andrea, President of the Unione Siciliana, and Capone's financial secretary, Sam Golf Bag Hunt (so named after his arrest at the scene of an assault carrying a full-barrelled shot-gun in a golf club bag – an extension of the old violin case solution to the problem of transporting a sub-machine-gun about the streets). Hunt was a close business friend of Jack Greasy Thumb Guzik, who also died in his own bed in Chicago at the age of seventy in February 1956.

Two months previously another of Capone's financial organizers, Alex Louis Greenberg, was shot dead in a Chicago restaurant, and a few weeks before that, in November 1955, Willie the Squealer Bioff, a Capone labour racketeer who had been living quietly in Phoenix,

Arizona, where he was known as Bill Nelson, retired cattle broker, was blown to bits at the age of fifty-five when he pressed the self-starter on his car and it exploded under him. Capone's defeated enemy, Bugs Moran, died aged sixty-five of lung cancer in 1957 in a hospital ward of Leavenworth, Kansas, Federal penitentiary during the last of many prison terms.

Three ex-Capone executives whose lives ended naturally in bed were Bruno Roti, beer-runner in the old days and then leader of First Ward Democratic politics, who had reached seventy-seven when he died in 1957, Jim Emery (real name Vincenzo Ammeratto), one of Capone's friends and gunmen, who was given a traditional gangland funeral in March 1957 at Fort Lauderdale, Florida, and Claude Screwy Maddox (alias John Moore), Syndicate Cicero boss who died in June 1958. The following September Little Augie Pisano, aged sixty, union racketeer and gunman, was filled with bullets as he sat in his car, together with a thirty-two-year-old blonde, Mrs. Janice Drake, a one-time Miss New Jersey, in New York. Between 1955 and 1959 three more old Capone men, Nick Dean (alias Nick Circella), Frank Frigenti and Paul the Waiter Ricca were among the three hundred gangsters whom the Government have since 1945 denaturalized and deported to Italy as undesirables, who also included such powerful New York hoods as Lucky Luciano, Frank Costello, Ralph Liguori and Joe Adonis (self-exiled to beat a Federal perjury charge).

But mostly it is death, softly or roughly, that has removed these aging, rich roughnecks from the scene of their crimes and their gains, and, belatedly, they have gone as did Dion O'Banion, Hymie Weiss, Frank Capone, Big Jim Colosimo, John Scalise, the seven victims of the St. Valentine's Day Massacre, and the many hundreds of others who died under the guns they themselves had used or directed.

Others involved in that period and its events have also departed. Eliot Ness, the Prohibition agent leader of the Untouchables, who pulled the noose tight around Capone, succumbed to a heart attack in May 1957; he had quit security work and become president of a Pennsylvania paper company. In November 1959 Gustaf Aaron Youngquist, a member of the United States Supreme Court's Advisory Committee on Rules of Criminal Procedure, died in Minneapolis at the age of seventy-three – it was he who had been the leader of the investigation that had found the means of convicting Capone on tax grounds.

Big Bill Thompson died in Chicago on 19 March 1944 at the age of seventy-five, perhaps from chagrin at seeing America again embroiled in a European conflict in the company of perfidious Britain. There was an apposite postscript to his death. His salary during his three years of office as mayor had been 22,500 dollars a year, and it was announced that his estate would not exceed 187,500 dollars. However, on 1 April State Treasury officials visited his home and found a cache of strong boxes so tightly stuffed with banknotes and gold certificates that they avalanched to the floor as the lids were opened. The hoard amounted to 1,750,000 dollars. It was recalled in the press that Thompson had several times sponsored fund-raising drives for public assistance, and that on the occasion of one of these, for the relief of Mississippi flood victims in 1927, the State Attorney General made the hurtful allegation that only part of the collection had filtered through to relief. A court order directed Thompson to pay back ninety thousand dollars, which he did. But he did not, apparently, abandon his faith in charity.

On 1 April 1955 Prohibition's most raucous and acrimonious opponent died – Colonel Robert R. McCormick, editor and publisher of the Chicago *Tribune*, who attacked the anti-alcohol law with the same choleric fanaticism with which he attacked Britain, King George, Roosevelt, the New Deal, Communism, and all things that did not qualify for his exacting definition of 'One-hundred per cent Americanism'.

Today in Chicago there are, of course, many people who remember those fourteen bizarre years, but most who were then maturely in authority or actively involved are diminishing in numbers – the policemen are on pension, the crime reporters who covered the killings and chatted with Capone are retired or semi-retired. One of the most interesting, but hazily obscure, figures in this diffuse drama has already been gone nine years – Mrs. Theresa Maria Capone, who died at the age of eighty-five in Chicago in December 1952. There is no record of her ever having talked, to anyone who could have preserved her words, about her sons. Perhaps she could have explained much about them, about their talents and their turpitude; or perhaps she was, despite the bereavement of three of them, despite their records and their notoriety, proud of their success and fame as American citizens. She never said; perhaps she never understood much of what occurred outside that airless, enclosed Italian family circle.

The old familiar figures have mostly gone; the landscape remains much the same. Chicago today is a bigger, even more thickly populated city – a city undergoing the 'population explosion' described by Professor Hauser. The present figures are 3,700,000 for the city, 6,500,000 within the standard metropolitan area, and the opening of the St. Lawrence Seaway, connecting Chicago direct with the Atlantic, is expected to push this up to seven million in the next four years. The great proportion of the newcomers are Southerners, black and white, surging in to grab some of the bounding industrial prosperity that seems to cast a glittering aureole upon the city as you approach it by car along the great eight-lane freeways that soar airily across the complexes of cloverleaf junctions and flyovers, and swing you down on to the resplendently beautiful Lake Shore Drive. For mile upon mile the rainbow cars ooze with their big-engine casualness along the tree-shaded lake-front boulevards, on one side the sail-flecked blue glaze of Michigan, on the other the sparkling lean delicacy of glass and metal skyscraper apartment-houses and office blocks. But it is a thin rind of beauty. Penetrate a few blocks at any point and you come into the city's turbulent, seamy interior, a jungle of dark canyons and lunging, ugly, squalid streets which for long sections slide into some of the worst festering slums to be found anywhere, including Glasgow and the Middle East, a sleazy chaos that, in the words of a recent report, is 'decaying not structure by structure but by whole neighbourhoods and communities at a time'. It is also as racketty a town as it ever was – Rush Street and Clark Street and The Loop and Sixty-third Street and Halsted Street flaring and jangling through the early hours with restaurants, pizza parlours, night-clubs and jazz bars.

It is as racketty in the other sense. The guns today are more circumspect, although, as I have indicated, not entirely stilled. But, according to the last Chicago Crime Commission report, major offences are rising precipitously. In 1958 50,543 were recorded by the Police Department, an increase of more than six per cent over the previous year, and have been consistently rising for a decade. This figure included 305 murders, most of which, remarks Virgil W. Peterson, the operating director, are easy to solve. 'Unfortunately,' he continues, 'the same situation does not prevail with respect to gang killings, which are virtually never solved in Chicago.' There is a reiterative ring of familiarity throughout the entire document . . . Citizens unable to walk near their homes without placing their lives in jeopardy from petty robbers who prowl the neighbourhood . . . Hold-up victims ignoring police requests to view arrested suspects, others refusing to sign complaints after positively identifying the robbers . . . Too many 'miscarriages of justice' in the Criminal Court year after year . . . Slow moving and ineffective administration of justice hampering law enforcement . . . And, again, that name, as insistent as the bass note in a fugue, Capone – 'the old Capone mob', 'Capone syndicate hoodlums', 'the Capone group'. Senator Estes Kefauver's Committee ascertained that the Chicago crime-chieftains call themselves the Capone Syndicate 'out of respect' to their late leader.

In any event, it is improbable that the grasp that the old Capone system has on the life and the living of Chicago will slip; it is embedded, deep and matted as an oak's roots, and has had forty years of near immunity in which to take hold.

In one sense the Prohibition years were an interim period: they were the experimental stage of the evolving business gang. Today much of the gratuitous roughstuff and swagger has been expunged, and replaced by a discreet, outwardly conformist, standard of public behaviour. Men are still killed when it is more prudent to kill them, but the extravagant Wild West pistol-blazing and the pitched street-battles, the diamond belt-buckles and the jazz-band parties, the flashing bill-rolls and the personality-cult, have been veiled. Such reticent publicity-shirkers as Accardo, Giancana and Glimco – spectacled, dark-suited, straight-hatted – have the weighty, sombre sobriety of expensive undertakers. Probably none is richer than, or as rich as, Capone was at his time of high summer; although the clout the Syndicate operates and the intricate web of its political influence is palpably effective, probably none of the members, individually or as a group, has quite the galvanically direct power that Capone had in the day when he could kick a mayor down the steps of his town hall and scream orders at a judge over the telephone. The pattern has changed – and has become more frightening, for it has simultaneously spread and submerged; the Chicago gangster today, the quiet spider, is cleverer, more covert and less accessible, and therefore a more dangerous and virulent creature.

In America, theoretically to excise this canker, there are approximately forty thousand separate public law enforcement agencies at five levels of government, employing 200 thousand men and women, and costing the taxpayers one billion dollars annually. Within a fifty-mile radius of Chicago there are 350 municipal, county, and state police forces employing several thousand personnel.

In a lecture he gave only a year ago Virgil Peterson, of the Chicago Crime Commission, pointed to the gross duplication of effort and equipment, the confusion and the frequent conflict of authority created by this lunatic pattern that prevails throughout the nation. He quoted the words of Andrew D. White: 'With few exceptions, the city governments of the United States are the worst in Christendom – the most expensive, the most inefficient, and the most corrupt', and continued: 'Another factor contributing very materially to the crime problem in America is the development of a philosophy, both in the courts and legislatures, that assumes that it is more important to handcuff the police than to handcuff the criminal. There has emerged an extremely technical administration of criminal justice with highly restrictive rules of evidence which, as a practical matter, makes it virtually impossible in many situations to enforce the laws against the professional, strongly organized and united criminals.'

He concluded: 'A sneering, contemptuous, and arrogant underworld, composed of blackmailers, extortionists and murderers, has been able to control substantial segments of our economy. It is time the people of this country awaken to the dangers of this problem and mobilize the forces of good to destroy the forces of evil.'

So evil did not end with the repeal of Prohibition; good did not flood in with the gush of returning beer. The American gangster is more than a simple rogue, or even a simply identified psychotic. He is a fascinatingly intricate new creation, a Frankenstein monster composed of a hundred separate racial, economic and sociological factors never before assembled together, and now coagulated by the pressures of urban life in contemporary America. This living aberration has been produced by such inheritances, influences and infusions as the city slum, racial inferiorities, ambition, alien traditions, money-criteria, political immaturity, ideals of liberty, metropolitan attitudes, the motor-car and the fire-arm, confused and defective laws, official cynicism, ruthlessness and greed, and, let them not be omitted, daring and imagination. And all these elements first came together at a particularly propitious moment of time, in the person of Capone.

Which may explain the surpassingly odd product of those now far-off years of violence and plunder, which by comparison with later refinements of technique seem amateurish and boyishly bumptious – the apparent permanence of Al Capone in world history. I know of no other modern criminal who has insinuated himself into the standard reference books – a forty-nine line entry in *The New Universal Encyclopaedia*, twenty-three lines in *Chambers's Encyclopaedia*, even twenty-seven lines in the *Encyclopaedia Britannica* Year Book for 1947 and two separate mentions in the latest edition of the *Encyclopaedia Britannica* itself in the sections on Chicago and Cicero.

Yet more surprising, he continues to exert a strange fascination upon delinquents of other countries who were babies or unborn when he died. In 1948 a twenty-three-year-old Londoner was arrested in a Harrow Road shop after he had threatened a barber with a revolver, announcing that he was an American gangster and the brother of Al Capone. Last year (1959) a twenty-year-old Londoner was charged with threatening to kill a nurse with a loaded revolver – he told a doctor that sometimes he felt like Al Capone. In February of this year (1960) a twenty-three-year-old West Croydon ex-public schoolboy stole £500 from his Mayfair office and planned to throw the blame on his secretary by shooting her, dismembering her body and burying her in cement in a garage he had rented – in the name of 'Mr. Capone'. A woman named Olga Conti, arrested in Rome in March 1950 for swindling housewives by taking money for fur coats she neglected to deliver, stated – in mitigation? – that she was the mother of Al Capone. The legend has even leaped the iron curtain. In March 1950 three East Berlin teenagers held up eight policemen in one night and stole their guns. Accused of two murders, fifteen attempted murders and many robberies with violence, one of them, eighteen-year-old Werner Gladow, told the Soviet Sector Court that he had decided to become an American-style gangster after reading crime stories and seeing Hollywood films. Al Capone, he said, was his idol.

The claim that he did a spell in Sing-Sing and worked for Al Capone is today employed as a credential by a Cockney with a tattooed face and a fur collar who is one of the most popular Sunday performers at Speakers' Corner in London's Hyde Park.

In a more general sense the very name of Chicago continues to remain an evocative word for headline-writers everywhere. 'CHICAGO SHOOTING IN LONDON CAFE', 'CHICAGO-STYLE CAR SHOOTING', 'CHICAGO GUN-WAR IN SOHO' have all been recent headlines in British newspapers, and it has become an accepted comparison for judges and magistrates, in the tenor of Mr. Justice Donovan's remark in the Old Bailey after hearing a roughish case: 'It sounds like Chicago in the worst days of Prohibition rather than London in 1956.' Last year Independent Television presented a feature programme on Al Capone, a montage of old film; the paper-back of the Burrows-Ackerman production *Al Capone*, with Rod Steiger in the name part, is on the bookstalls.

Nor is this mainly a European fixation, a derivative of distant glamour. American CBS television last year showed the Desilu Playhouse production of *The Untouchables*, a dramatized version of the Ness squad's campaign against the Capone gang, which has since been sent out on the cinema circuits as *The Scarface Mob*.

Moreover, I was in Chicago when *Al Capone* opened there. In the previous day's issue of the Chicago *Tribune*, a display advertisement, portraying Capone with silver trilby, cigarette and scar, was set in five different positions on the entertainments page. Each had the same headline: 'TOMORROW "AL CAPONE" TAKES OVER THE', and beneath, respectively: 'SOUTH SIDE', 'WEST SIDE', 'NORTH SIDE', 'NORTH-WEST SIDE,' 'SUBURBS.'

The name Capone may still be a seller in Chicago, a redolence of ancient high jinks and thrills, but on a more realistic and sombre level his presence is still felt as an influence and a condition of American society. In December 1950 a Chicago *Tribune* editorial, headlined 'THE HOODLUM TERROR IN CHICAGO POLITICS', protested against political conspiracy and said: 'Capone is dead and his brothers are bums, but he lives as a cancer in Chicago politics. We have the "West Side bloc"; the "Italian bloc" . . . They vote Capone. They belong to the mob.'

Since Johnny Torrio in 1920 recognized Prohibition as the rock on which to found a new-style empire of business vice, almost one thousand gang murders have been committed in Chicago: seventeen of the killers were convicted. No important gangster has ever been imprisoned by the city or state legal authorities; the few that have been were put there as a result of Federal intervention.

The bootlegger was created by the cheating citizen, the gunman by the dissembling politician, the racketeer by the faint-hearted trader and businessman. Chicago, we must conclude, created its own reputation and also the ludicrously wicked record of those particular Prohibition years which seems likely to endure as one more garishly infamous than any other city has or will put up in competition. Nor does that reputation show signs of languishing from malnourishment. Chicago has not lost its hankering to 'have the best – even if it's the worst'.

Bibliography

Algren, Nelson, *Chicago: City On The Make*, Doubleday, 1951.

Allen, F. L., *Only Yesterday: An Informal History of the* 1920*s in America*, Penguin, 1931.

Asbury, Herbert, *The Underworld of Chicago*, Hale, 1942. *The Great Illusion: An Informal History of Prohibition*, Doubleday, 1950.

Burnett, W. R., *Little Caesar*, Cape, 1929.

Condon, Eddie, narration by Thomas Sugrue, *We Called It Music*, Peter Davies, 1948.

Dedmon, Emmett, *Fabulous Chicago*, Random House, 1933.

Gunther, John, *Inside U.S.A.*, Hamish Hamilton, 1947.

Hecht, Ben, *A Child of the Century*, Simon and Schuster, 1954.

Horan, James D., *The Mob's Man*, Hale, 1960.

Irey, Elmer L., with Slocum, William J., *The Tax Dodgers*, Greenberg, 1948.

Katcher, Leo, *The Big Bankroll: The Life and Times of Arnold Rothstein*, Gollancz, 1958.

Kefauver, Estes, *Crime In America*, Gollancz, 1952.

Kogan, Herman, and Wendt, Lloyd, *Chicago: A Pictorial History*, Dutton, 1958.

Landesco, John, *Organised Crime in Chicago: Part III of The Illinois Crime Survey*, Illinois Association for Criminal Justice, 1929.

Lerner, Max, *America As A Civilisation: Life and Thought in the United States Today*, Cape, 1958; *The Unfinished Country*, Weidenfeld & Nicolson, 1959.

Liebling, A. J., *Chicago: The Second City*, Knopf, 1952.

Lohman, Joseph D., *Juvenile Delinquency*, Cook County Sherriff's Office, 1957; *Law Enforcement and Delinquency Controls*, Cook County Sherriff's Office, 1958.

Lomax, Alan, *Mister Jelly Roll*, Cassell, 1952.

Maxwell, Gavin, *God Protect Me From My Friends*, Longmans, 1956; *The Ten Pains of Death*, Longmans, 1959.

Mead, Margaret, *The American Character*, (published in America as *And Keep Your Powder Dry*), Penguin, 1943.

Merz, Charles, *The Great American Band-Wagon: A Study of Exaggeration*, Star, 1928.

Mezzrow, Mezz, *Really The Blues*, Random House, 1946.

Ness, Eliot, with Fraley, Oscar, *The Untouchables*, Messner, 1957.

O'Connor, Richard, *Hell's Kitchen*, Redman, 1958.

Oliver, Paul, *Blues Fell This Morning*, Cassell, 1960.

Park, R. E., and Burgess, E. W., *The City*, University of Chicago, 1927.

Parkes, Henry Bamford, *The American People: Their Civilisation and Character*, Eyre & Spottiswoode, 1949.

Pasley, Fred. D., *Al Capone: The Biography of a Self-Made Man*, Faber, 1931.

Peterson, Virgil W., *Barbarians In Our Midst*, Little, Brown, 1952.

Ramsey, Jr., Frederic, and Smith, Charles Edward, *Jazzmen*, Sidgwick & Jackson, 1957.

Sann, Paul, *The Lawless Decade: A Pictorial History of a Great American Transition*, Arco, 1957.

Shapiro, Nat, and Hentoff, Nat, *Hear Me Talkin' To Ya*, Peter Davies, 1955.

Shaw, Artie, *The Trouble With Cinderella*, Jarrolds, 1955.

Smith, Alson J., *Chicago's Left Bank*, Regnery, 1953.

Sondern, Frederic, *Brotherhood of Evil: The Mafia*, Gollancz, 1959.

Steffens, Lincoln, *The Autobiography of Lincoln Steffens*, 1931; *Shame of the Cities*, 1904.

Sullivan, Edward D., *Look At Chicago*, Bles, 1930.

Tannenbaum, Frank, *Crime and the Community*, Ginn, 1938.

Thrasher, Frederic M., *The Gang*, University of Chicago, 1928.

Touhy, Roger, *The Stolen Years*, Pennington, 1959.

Turkus, Burton, B., and Feder, Sid, *Murder, Inc.*, Gollancz, 1952.

Whitehead, Don, *The FBI Story*, Muller, 1957.

Windle, Charles A., *The Case Against Prohibition*, Iconoclast, 1927.

Zorbaugh, Harvey W., *The Gold Coast and the Slum: A Sociological Study of Chicago's Near North Side*, University of Chicago, 1929.

Index

Index